D1569938

The Black Composer Speaks

edited by
David N. Baker, Lida M. Belt and Herman C. Hudson

A project of the Afro-American Arts Institute, Indiana University

The Scarecrow Press, Inc.
Metuchen, N.J. & London
1978

Library of Congress Cataloging in Publication Data
Main entry under title:

The Black composer speaks.

    Includes bibliographies, lists of the composers' works, and
index.
    1.   Composers--United States--Interviews.   2.   Afro-Amer-
ican composers--Interviews.   I.   Baker, David N. , 1931-   II.
Belt, Lida M.   III.   Hudson, Herman.   IV.   Indiana.   University.
Afro-American Arts Institute.
ML390.B64   780'.92'2 [B]   77-24146
ISBN 0-8108-1045-X

TABLE OF CONTENTS

FOREWORD

For too long a time black composers have been disregarded in our musical society. There are even notorious instances where an established composer who was black and widely performed had his blackness completely ignored.

This past treatment of black composers has been misleading in terms of the development of our musical culture. Furthermore, it has been damaging by limiting our knowledge regarding this society's musical heritage. We are therefore indebted to David Baker, Lida Belt, and Herman Hudson for their essential and informative work, The Black Composer Speaks. This book consists of interviews with fifteen contemporary black composers and gives us an insight into their personal backgrounds, their philosophies, their motivations, and their attitudes toward their work. Each composer reflects on his/her style and how it developed in a direct, personal manner not usually found in a compilation of this sort. The book also provides us with a listing of each composer's works so that anyone wishing to perform this music has easy access to the necessary information.

All of us are indeed grateful to the compilers for providing us with this significant publication, one which will help us expand our knowledge and understanding of the important role that black artists have played and are still playing in developing and expanding the musical consciousness of our society. The Black Composer Speaks is a book for everyone--regardless of race!

Robert H. Klotman
President, Music Educators National Conference
Chairman, Music Education Department
Indiana University

Thomas Jefferson Anderson, Jr. (courtesy of the composer)

CHAPTER I

THOMAS JEFFERSON ANDERSON, JR.

Thomas Jefferson Anderson was born August 17, 1928 in Coatesville, Pennsylvania. His educational background includes a B. M. (1950) from West Virginia State College, an M. M. E. (1951) from Pennsylvania State University, and a Ph. D. (1958) from the University of Iowa, in addition to study at the Cincinnati Conservatory of Music and the Aspen School of Music. His composition teachers included T. Scott Huston, Phillip Bezanson, and Darius Milhaud. Prior to his 1973 appointment to the chairmanship of the music department at Tufts University, he held positions at West Virginia State College, Langston University, Tennessee State University, and Morehouse College.

Dr. Anderson has received a number of honors and awards including MacDowell Colony Fellowships (1960-61, 1963, 1968), the Fromm Foundation Award (1964), and the Copely Foundation Award (1964). From 1969 to 1971 he served as composer-in-residence with the Atlanta Symphony Orchestra on a grant from the Rockefeller Foundation. Among the commissions he has received are those from Thor Johnson, Robert Shaw, Fisk University, West Virginia State University, the Symphony of the New World, and the National Endowment for the Arts.

Dr. Anderson has written works for a variety of vocal and instrumental combinations. Among his best-known compositions are the Chamber Symphony (recorded on CRI), Squares (recorded by the Baltimore Symphony Orchestra as part of the Black Composers Series produced by Columbia Records), and Variations on a Theme by M. B. Tolson (recorded on Nonesuch). His orchestration of Scott Joplin's opera Treemonisha brought him nationwide recognition. Dr. Anderson is also very active as a lecturer-consultant on black music and has participated in a number of conferences and projects in that capacity.

Part I: General Questions

1. Q: What persons, events, and works (of art, literature, etc.) have influenced you in general as well as in terms of your

1

musical activities?

A: I have been influenced by five teachers of composition: George Ceiga, T. Scott Huston, Philip Bezanson, Richard Hervig, and Darius Milhaud. Through the art work of Paul Shimon, Richard Hunt, Charles Young, Hyde Solomon, and Anne Truitt I have learned the value of projection on different levels. Conductors Guy Fraser Harrison, Thor Johnson, and Robert Shaw were most elucidating in personal conversations. The poetry of Robert Hayden, Pauline Hanson, M. B. Tolson, Pearl Lomax, and Milton Kessler has also influenced compositions.

2. Q: How would you define black music?

A: Any composition written by a black composer is black music. The qualitative measure into blackness obviously depends on the individual's experience and perception. [1]

3. Q: What features of your own music do you see as uniquely black (in terms of both musical and philosophical considerations)?

A: The measure of blackness in my music is at two levels. The first are those things which most listeners can easily identify as being associated with black life style--jazz cadences and progressions, spirituals, rhythmic patterns, color, textures, and forms. The second aspect deals with the subconscious. What part is black, white, or otherwise cannot be identified by me, nor is there any concern to segment or compartmentalize these forces.

4. Q: In what ways is your music a reflection of your personal philosophy (social, political, etc.)?

A: Music is an extension of the personality. Like all people, I foresee my life as one of constant fluctuation. The pendulum moves towards the esthetic in a work like Transitions, commissioned by the Fromm Foundation, and towards political statements in the composition In Memoriam Malcolm X, commissioned by the Symphony of the New World for Betty Allen.

5. Q: What do you see as the position or role of the black artist in contemporary society?

A: The role of the black artist, like that of any artist, is to expand the dimensions within the human experience, build new ways of communication, and express a sense of fidelity to his or her own personal traditions.

6. Q: Please discuss any problems you may have encountered in getting your works performed, published, and recorded. [2]

A: The black artist, like the black community, is colonized. I am personally convinced that the availability of records, performances, commissions, and publishers has little to do with musical worth. My friend M. B. Tolson used to refer to this contradiction as "the artistry of circumstance."

If you happen to be in the right place at the right time, something may develop. The "right times" are always dictated by forces beyond any single individual's control. Example: What years did William Grant Still receive most of his honorary degrees?[3] What was the political state of the black community then?

7. Q: What do you consider, at this point in your life, to be your most significant achievement(s) aside from your compositions?

   A: My life has been devoted to many concerns. I could list my composition students, involvement in social issues, educational attainment, professional achievements, and family life as possible considerations.

8. Q: What do you see as the responsibilities and obligations of the educational system (at all levels) to the study of black music?

   A: The obligation of all institutions is to teach truth. Black contributions have been literally ignored from 1619 in Jamestown to the current day. It now becomes incumbent on all of us to bridge this gap in our education. The form will depend on the commitment of both black and white scholars, philanthropy, universities and colleges, performing organizations, and book publishers.

9. Q: Do you feel that the people who write about your music (critics in particular) understand what you are doing? Exemplify and discuss.

   A: I have never been overly concerned about criticism. The artist must be his most severe critic, since he possesses the ideal standard in abstract. Darius Milhaud told me years ago to ignore what people wrote about my music. What he saw then and I saw later was the uniqueness of each individual.

10. Q: What advice would you give the aspiring young black composer?

    A: For the young struggling black composer, I would like to recommend three things. First, never stop believing in your own abilities as a creative artist. Secondly, analyze the compositions of others and your own works with a high degree of scrutiny. Finally, place little emphasis on the plaudits of the society. Your obligation is to the documentation of our experiences in this country. If you see your life in real terms and are prepared for cultural isolation, your music will become a significant part of the continuous documentation of our struggles within these walls of freedom.

Part II: Music Questions

1. Q: When you sit down to begin a new composition on your own

initiative or inspiration (as opposed to a commissioned work), what procedure or approach do you follow?

A: I have my own system of composing. The music is organized around basic patterns or note groupings which have the potential to exist in varying environments. These figures of two to eleven notes are used in combinations, conjunct or disjunct relationships, harmonic clusters, or any of a number of possibilities. The character of the work is therefore determined by my development of these primary sources. A doctoral dissertation on my music by Bruce Thompson was recently funded by Phi Mu Alpha Sinfonia Foundation. [4] This study, for Indiana University, will include detailed analysis of my techniques.

2. Q: When composing a commissioned work or a work written for a specific occasion or person, does your procedure or approach differ from the one you described in question 1? If so, in what way?

A: The procedure does not change. However, the way it is used can be different. If I am working on a composition such as Watermelon, which is based on a street cry and related materials, I begin to think pianistically. If the composition calls for a chamber ensemble, my ear begins to hear combinations of sound from the source material. Each instrument, either used as solo or in combination, develops musically its own tailor-made part.

3. Q: In general, with regard to your writing, what genre(s) do you prefer?[5]

A: I enjoy mixing styles. In my composition Swing Set, for clarinet and piano, one can see the references with a clear degree of contrast. This work is influenced by Webern, Schoenberg, Joplin, Bartok, and current trends. Listening to the piece, however, one would have to identify the style as Anderson.

4. Q: What do you consider your most significant composition? Please discuss.

A: My most significant composition to date is Horizon '76 for large orchestra and soprano. The work was commissioned by the National Endowment for the Arts and makes use of a text by Milton Kessler. The piece, which is approximately one hour in length, is unique in its treatment of time, structure, scoring, and use of material. The work is influenced by primitive cultures and therefore starts before the concert begins by having small solo groups playing in the audience as people come into the hall. A series of independent introductions are performed on stage as the leader strolls in to conduct the overture. The first section is called "A Song" and is built around the tuning note of the orchestra. The last part of the work is performed as the last piece on the program. It is titled "F Natural" and begins with a theme and variations. The theme is composed of fragmen-

tary sets and the variations exist in modified free time with
adherence to strict compositional techniques. This section
is followed by a series of explorations into the American experience, or should I say dream, with an outstanding text.
Aspirations, lynching, history, soul life style, death, and
other emotional feelings are examined. The last section is
a fantasia which recalls in abstract what has already taken
place. The work closes with groups of musicians leaving
the stage, like Haydn's Symphony No. 45 in F♯ Minor, and
the song " America" emerges from the texture by a solo
viola.

5. Q: Please comment on your treatment of the following musical
        elements and give examples from your compositions that
        illustrate the techniques you describe:

   A. Melody
       TJA: Melody may exist in both long or short lines.
             The use of leaps and adjacent relationships are
             common.

   B. Harmony
       TJA: Harmony grows out of my contrapuntal relation-
             ships. On occasions, as in the last section of
             my Variations on a Theme by M. B. Tolson, I
             have used the blues progression as a chaconne.

   C. Rhythm
       TJA: The music shows a preference for symmetrical
             rhythms with shifting accents.

   D. Form
       TJA: All forms are the outgrowth of my source ma-
             terial and tend towards single movement struc-
             tures. The internal sections, however, make
             use of traditional concepts.

   E. Improvisation
       TJA: In Chamber Symphony I wrote a section which
             sounded improvised yet was completely composed.
             Since that time I have tried to use this as a basic
             concept. In the chamber work Beyond Silence I
             made use of a musical shorthand for an impro-
             vised cadenza. My reaction was one of pleasure;
             however, I would like to have more control over
             these events in the future.

   F. Text (both choice and treatment)
       TJA: I have always chosen poets who were personal
             friends. The words dictate the music and my
             choice becomes one of mood. The music there-
             fore serves as a reinforcement to what has been
             said or is about to be stated.

G. Instrumentation or medium (both in terms of choice of
particular combinations as well as the way in which
they are treated compositionally)

TJA: Each work has a particular sound. The instrumentation or combination comes to me before I
write my source material.

6. Q: Have difficulties with performance practice (inflection, phrasing, etc.) been a significant problem in having your works
performed to your own satisfaction?

   A: I never consider performance problems a major barrier in
the writing of any work. My works range from Five Easy
Pieces to complex compositions like Block Songs, Intervals,
and Connections. It is the duty of the composer to write
music to the best of his or her ability. The performer
must meet this challenge. If a group cannot play a composition it should not be programmed. It is important for
all performers to work closely, if possible, with the composer and have available enough rehearsal time.

7. Q: What major works are currently in progress? Please describe and discuss.

   A: I am currently working on an operetta, The Shell Fairy.
The text is based on a story by Dr. Chester M. Pierce of
the Harvard University Medical School and the Graduate
School of Education. The adaptation and lyrics have been
written by Sara S. Beattie, an author of children's books.

8. Q: Given unlimited time and finances (and no restrictions whatsoever) what would you write?

   A: More works for large orchestra.

9. Q: If given the opportunity would you choose to devote yourself
to composition on a full-time basis? Why or why not?

   A: I enjoy teaching very much. My students stimulate me and
force me to grow as a composer. My only regret is that
time for composition is limited.

10. Q: How would you describe your compositional style?
    A: This question has already been answered. 6

11. Q: What have been the influences of other composers, styles,
and other types of music on your compositional style?
    A: This question has already been answered. 7

12. Q: Has your style changed across your career? If so, what
influenced these changes or developments?
    A: My style has remained rather constant in sound; however,
the internal procedure has changed from time to time.
The reason relates to the study of scores, hearing a performance or recording, talking to other composers, and
thinking up a different approach to the same problem.

13. Q: When you are listening to music for your own enjoyment, what are your preferences?

A: I have no preferences in listening to music. Jazz, avant garde, baroque, ethnic music, and several other styles are part of my continuous musical environment.

Notes to Chapter I

1. For additional remarks by Dr. Anderson on the problems of defining black music see Dominique-René de Lerma, Black Music in Our Culture, (Kent, Ohio: Kent State University Press, 1970), pp. 71-76. The material cited is a portion of panel discussion in which T. J. Anderson, Hale Smith, and Olly Wilson were the primary participants.

2. Dr. Anderson chose to address himself only to the general portion of question 6; he did not respond to 6A, 6B, and 6C.

3. A partial list of Dr. Still's honorary degrees can be found in Eileen Southern, The Music of Black Americans (New York: W. W. Norton and Company, Inc., 1971), p. 460.

4. Bruce Thompson, "Musical Style and Compositional Techniques in Selected Works of T. J. Anderson" (Ph.D. diss., Indiana University, in progress).

5. Dr. Anderson chose to address himself to style rather than genre in answering this question.

6. See Dr. Anderson's responses to II-1, II-3, and II-5.

7. See Dr. Anderson's responses to I-1 and II-3.

LIST OF COMPOSITIONS

AND NOW THE DOWNPOUR CEASES (1966)
See PERSONALS

ASSIMILATION (1964)
See FIVE ETUDES AND A FANCY

BALLONCHIO (1963)
See FIVE BAGATELLES FOR OBOE, VIOLIN, AND HARPSI-CHORD

BARCAROLLE (1963)
See FIVE BAGATELLES FOR OBOE, VIOLIN, AND HARPSI-CHORD

BEYOND SILENCE (1973)
Cantata for tenor, B♭ clarinet, trombone, viola, violoncello, and piano. Text by Pauline Hanson. App. 15 min. American Composers Alliance, 1973. First performance (1973) at the Busch-Reisinger Museum of Harvard University by the Boston Musica Viva, Richard Pittman, conductor; Scott Macallister, tenor.

BLOCK SONGS (1972)
Soprano and children's toys (chromatic pitch pipe, musical jack-in-the-box, and musical busy box). Text by Pearl Lomax. 12 min. Composers Facsimile Edition, 1972.

BLUES (1963)
See FIVE BAGATELLES FOR OBOE, VIOLIN, AND HARPSI-CHORD

BOEA (1963)
See FIVE BAGATELLES FOR OBOE, VIOLIN, AND HARPSI-CHORD

BURLETTA (1963)
See FIVE BAGATELLES FOR OBOE, VIOLIN, AND HARPSI-CHORD

CACCIA (1960)
See NEW DANCES

CACHUCHA (1960)
See NEW DANCES

CAN-CAN (1960)
See NEW DANCES

CANDOR (1965)
See FIVE PORTRAITURES OF TWO PEOPLE

CANVASS (1965)
See FIVE PORTRAITURES OF TWO PEOPLE

CAPRICIOUSNESS (1965)
See FIVE PORTRAITURES OF TWO PEOPLE

CHAMBER SYMPHONY (1968)
Orchestra. One movement. App. 14 min. Composers Facsimile Edition, 1969. Recorded by the Royal Philharmonic Orchestra, James Dixon, conductor (Composers Recordings Inc. CRI SD-258). Commissioned by Thor Johnson. First performance (1969) by the Nashville Little Symphony, Thor Johnson, conductor.

CLASSICAL SYMPHONY (1961)
Orchestra. Three movements. 14 min. Composers Facsimile

Edition, rental. Commissioned by the Oklahoma City Junior
Symphony. First performance (1961) by the Oklahoma City
Junior Symphony, T. Burns Westman, conductor.

COMPLEMENTS (1964)
    See FIVE ETUDES AND A FANCY

CONCORDANCE (1965)
    See FIVE PORTRAITURES OF TWO PEOPLE

CONNECTIONS: A FANTASY FOR STRING QUINTET (1966)
    App. 12 min. Composers Facsimile Edition, 1967. Dedicated
    to Darius Milhaud. First performance (1968) in Nashville, Tenn.
    by the Blair String Quartet assisted by Ovid Collins, viola.

CONTEMPLATION (1965)
    See FIVE PORTRAITURES OF TWO PEOPLE

COUNJAI (1960)
    See NEW DANCES

COUNTRY DANCE (1960)
    See NEW DANCES

DARKNESS BRINGS THE JUNGLE TO OUR ROOM (1966)
    See PERSONALS

DIALOGUE (1962)
    See SIX PIECES FOR CLARINET AND CHAMBER ORCHESTRA

DIVERSITIES (1964)
    See FIVE ETUDES AND A FANCY

ELEGY (1962)
    See SIX PIECES FOR CLARINET AND CHAMBER ORCHESTRA

EPILOGUE (1962)
    See SIX PIECES FOR CLARINET AND CHAMBER ORCHESTRA

F NATURAL (INTERLUDE, RITORNELLO AND FANTASIA) (1975)
    See HORIZON '76

FANCY (1964)
    See FIVE ETUDES AND A FANCY

FIVE BAGATELLES FOR OBOE, VIOLIN, AND HARPSICHORD (1963)
    Five movements: Boea; Barcarolle; Burletta; Blues; Ballonchio.
    $8\frac{1}{2}$ min. Composers Facsimile Edition, 1966. First perform-
    ance (1963) at the University of Oklahoma Composers Symposium.

FIVE EASY PIECES FOR VIOLIN, PIANO, AND JEWS HARP (1973)
    5 min. American Composers Alliance, 1973. Written for and
    first performed by the composer's children (1974) at the Win-
    chester Unitarian Church (Winchester, Mass.).

FIVE ETUDES AND A FANCY (1964)
Woodwind quintet. Six movements: Assimilation; Complements; Transference; Diversities; Recurrence; Fancy. App. 9 min. Composers Facsimile Edition, 1967. First performance (1964) at the Aspen School of Music, Harry Schulman, conductor.

FIVE PORTRAITURES OF TWO PEOPLE (1965)
Piano, four hands. Five movements: Canvass; Contemplation; Capriciousness; Concordance; Candor. 12 min. Composers Facsimile Edition, 1966. First performance (1968) at the First Unitarian Church (Nashville, Tenn.) Enid Katahn and Lucien Stark, pianists.

HORIZON '76 (1975)
Soprano and orchestra. Text by Milton Kessler. Two parts: (1) A Song (Serenades, Introductions and Overture) and (2) F Natural (Interlude, Ritornello and Fantasia). 50 min. American Composers Alliance, 1975. Commissioned by the National Endowment for the Arts for the Bicentennial of the United States.

IN MEMORIAM MALCOLM X (1974)
Soprano and orchestra. Text by Robert Hayden. 10 min. American Composers Alliance, 1974. Commissioned by the Symphony of the New World for Betty Allen. First performance (1974) at Lincoln Center by the Symphony of the New World, Leon Thompson, conductor; Betty Allen, soprano.

IN MEMORIAM ZACH WALKER (1968)
Band. App. $4\frac{1}{2}$ min. Composers Facsimile Edition, 1968. First performance (1969) by the Coatesville High School Band (Coatesville, Pa.), Donald Suter, conductor.

INTERVALS (1970-71)
Orchestra. Seven movements. 1 hour. Composers Facsimile Edition, 1972. Commissioned by Robert Shaw. Movements 2-6 are designed to be played during intermission; movements 1 and 7 may be performed separately under the title INTERVALS XIII.

INTERVALS XIII
See INTERVALS

INTRODUCTION AND ALLEGRO (1959)
Orchestra. 8 min. Composers Facsimile Edition, rental. First performance (1959) by the Oklahoma City Symphony Orchestra, Guy Fraser Harrison, conductor.

LET US DANCE BY METAL WATERS BURNED (1966)
See PERSONALS

LET US GO BACK INTO THE DUSK AGAIN (1966)
See PERSONALS

LIBERAMENTE (1962)
See SIX PIECES FOR CLARINET AND CHAMBER ORCHESTRA

A MOMENT WE PAUSE TO QUENCH OUR THIRST (1966)
See PERSONALS

NEW DANCES (1960)
Orchestra. Five movements: Caccia (Italy); Can-Can (France); Counjai (Africa); Cachucha (Spain); Country Dance (USA). 17 min. Composers Facsimile Edition, 1967. First performance (1960) by the Oklahoma City Symphony Orchestra, Guy Fraser Harrison, conductor.

ODE (1962)
See SIX PIECES FOR CLARINET AND CHAMBER ORCHESTRA

ONCE MORE, LISTENING TO THE WIND AND RAIN (1966)
See PERSONALS

PERSONALS (1966)
Cantata for narrator, mixed chorus, and brass ensemble. Text by Arna Bontemps. Six parts: Once more, listening to the wind and rain; Darkness brings the jungle to our room; And now the downpour ceases; Let us dance by metal waters burned; A moment we pause to quench our thirst; Let us go back into the dusk again. App. 15 min. Composers Facsimile Edition, 1967. Commissioned by Fisk University in celebration of its 100th anniversary. First performance (1966) at Fisk University. Gladys Forde, narrator; Fisk University Choir, Robert Jones, conductor; brass ensemble from the Nashville Symphony Orchestra.

PROLOGUE (1962)
See SIX PIECES FOR CLARINET AND CHAMBER ORCHESTRA

PYKNON OVERTURE (1958)
Orchestra. This work was a portion of the composer's Ph.D. thesis.

RECURRENCE (1964)
See FIVE ETUDES AND A FANCY

ROTATIONS (1967)
Band. App. 15 min. Composers Facsimile Edition, 1968.

THE SHELL FAIRY (in progress)
A fantasy play with music. Text based on a story by Chester M. Pierce; adaptation and lyrics by Sara S. Beattie.

SIX PIECES FOR CLARINET AND CHAMBER ORCHESTRA (1962)
Six movements: Prologue; Liberamente; Dialogue; Ode; Elegy; Epilogue. App. 13 min. Composers Facsimile Edition, 1966. First performance (1962) by the Oklahoma City Symphony Orchestra, Guy Fraser Harrison, conductor; Earl Thomas, clarinet.

A SONG (SERENADES, INTRODUCTIONS AND OVERTURE) (1975)
See HORIZON '76

SQUARES: AN ESSAY FOR ORCHESTRA (1965)
App. 10 min. Composers Facsimile Edition, 1966. Recorded
by the Baltimore Symphony Orchestra, Paul Freeman, conductor (Columbia M-33434: Vol. 8, Black Composers Series).
Commissioned by West Virginia State College in celebration of
its 75th anniversary. First performance (1966) at the Third
Annual Interamerican Festival of the Arts (Chickasha, Oklahoma)
by the Oklahoma City Symphony Orchestra, Guy Fraser Harrison,
conductor.

STRING QUARTET NO. 1 (1957)
This work was a portion of the composer's Ph. D. thesis.

SWING SET (1972)
Clarinet and piano. App. 12 min. Composers Facsimile Edition, 1972. Commissioned by Thomas Ayres. First performance (1973) at the University of Iowa (Iowa City). Thomas
Ayres, clarinet; Carol Lesniak, piano.

SYMPHONY IN THREE MOVEMENTS (1963)
Orchestra. Three movements. App. 15 min. Composers Fac-
simile Edition, 1966. Dedicated to the memory of John F. Ken-
nedy. First performance (1964) at the Festival of Twentieth-
Century Music at Oklahoma City University by the Oklahoma
City Symphony Orchestra, Guy Fraser Harrison, conductor.

THIS HOUSE (1971)
Male chorus with 4 chromatic pitch pipes. Text is based on
permutations of the word MOREHOUSE. App. $5\frac{1}{2}$ min. American Composers Editions, 1971. Dedicated to Wendall Whalum
and the Morehouse College Glee Club. First performance
(1972) at the MENC 23rd National Biennial Convention (Atlanta,
Ga.) by the Morehouse College Glee Club, Wendall Whalum, conductor.

TRANSFERENCE (1964)
See FIVE ETUDES AND A FANCY

TRANSITIONS: A FANTASY FOR TEN INSTRUMENTS (1971)
Flute, B♭ clarinet, bassoon, F horn, B♭ trumpet, trombone,
violin, viola, violoncello, and piano. App. $13\frac{1}{2}$ min. Composers Facsimile Edition, 1971. Commissioned by the Berkshire Music Center in cooperation with the Fromm Music Foundation. First performance (1971) at the Berkshire Music Center (Lenox, Mass.). Charles Darden, conductor.

TRIO CONCERTANTE (1960)
Clarinet, trumpet, trombone, and band. 12 min. American
Composers Alliance, rental.

VARIATIONS ON A THEME BY M. B. TOLSON (1969)
Cantata for soprano, alto saxophone, trumpet, trombone, piano,
violin, and violoncello. Text by M. B. Tolson. App. 16 min.
Composers Facsimile Edition, 1969. Recorded by Jan de Gae-
tani, soprano, and the Contemporary Chamber Ensemble, Arthur
Weisberg, conductor (Nonesuch 71303). First performance
(1970) in Atlanta. Bernadine Oliphint, soprano; T. J. Anderson, conductor.

WATERMELON (1971)
Piano. 6 min. Composers Facsimile Edition, 1971. First
performance (1972) at Indiana University (Bloomington). Hans
Boepple, piano.

BIBLIOGRAPHY

"Black Composers. " Newsweek, 15 April 1974.

Brooks, Tilford. "A Historical Study of Black Music and Selected
Twentieth Century Black Composers and Their Role in American Society. " Ed. D. dissertation, Washington University, 1972.

Claghorn, Charles E. Biographical Dictionary of American Music.
West Nyack, N. Y.: Parker Publishing Company, 1973.

De Lerma, Dominique-René, ed. Black Music in Our Culture: Curricular Ideas on the Subjects, Materials, and Problems. Kent,
Ohio: Kent State University Press, 1970.

_____. Reflections on Afro-American Music. Kent, Ohio: Kent
State University Press, 1973.

Hildreth, John. "The Keyboard Works of a Select Group of Black
Composers. " Ph. D. dissertation, Northwestern University, in
progress.

Hunt, Joseph. "Conversation with Thomas J. Anderson: Blacks and
the Classics. " The Black Perspective in Music 1 (Fall 1973):
156-165.

Roach, Hildred. Black American Music: Past and Present. Boston: Crescendo Publishing Company, 1973.

Southern, Eileen. "America's Black Composers of Classical Music. " Music Educators Journal 62 (November 1975): 46-59.

_____. The Music of Black Americans. New York: W. W. Nor-
ton, 1971.

Thompson, Bruce. "Musical Style and Compositional Techniques in

Selected Works of T. J. Anderson." Ph.D. dissertation, Indiana University, in progress.

_____. "T. J. Anderson: Composer." The Sinfonian Newsletter 24 (February 1975): 4+.

Trythall, Gilbert. "T. J. Anderson." BMI: The Many Worlds of Music, April 1969, p. 17.

Who's Who Among Black Americans, 1st ed. (1975-1976), s.v. "Anderson, Thomas J."

Yuhasz, Sister Marie Joy. "Black Composers and Their Piano Music, Part II." The American Music Teacher 19 (April/May 1970): 28+.

CHAPTER II

DAVID NATHANIEL BAKER, JR.

David Nathaniel Baker was born December 21, 1931 in Indianapolis, Indiana. His educational background includes B. M. E.
(1953) and M. M. E. (1954) degrees from Indiana University in addition to private study and consultation with George Russell, Thomas
Beversdorf, Bernard Heiden, Gunther Schuller, Juan Orrego-Salas,
John Lewis, John Eaton, and William Russo. Mr. Baker has been
a member of the faculty of Indiana University since 1966, and currently serves as chairman of the Jazz Studies department in the
School of Music. Prior to 1966, he held positions at Lincoln University (Mo.) and Indiana Central College in addition to teaching
privately and in the Indianapolis public school system. Recognized
nationally as one of the leading figures in jazz education, he has
also served as a lecturer-consultant-clinician for numerous colleges,
universities, and other institutions. He holds positions on a variety
of boards and commissions, and is currently chairman of both the
Jazz/Folk/Ethnic section of the Music Advisory Panel to the National Endowment for the Arts and the Jazz Advisory Panel to the John
F. Kennedy Center for the Performing Arts.

Mr. Baker's sizable compositional output covers a wide range
of genres and styles. In addition to his numerous works for jazz
ensemble, he has written compositions for orchestra, solo voice,
chorus, chamber ensemble, and piano. A considerable number of
his larger works involve a variety of combinations of vocal and instrumental ensembles and soloists; examples of compositions of this
type include Black America, Levels (nominated in 1973 for the Pulitzer Prize), Psalm 22, Le Chat Qui Péche (1974), and the seven concerti for solo instrumentalists and jazz ensemble. Among the artists
from whom he has received commissions are Janos Starker, Josef
Gingold, Harvey Phillips, Natalie Hinderas, James Pellerite, Bertram
Turetzky, Bill Brown, and Ruggiero Ricci.

In addition to his activities as a teacher and composer, Mr.
Baker maintains a full schedule of performing and writing. Although
forced by injuries to abandon the trombone at the height of a successful career, his performances as a cellist and bassist have won
him widespread recognition in both the jazz and classical idioms.
He is also a well-known and prolific author, with more than one
hundred books and articles on jazz and other areas of Afro-American music to his credit.

David N. Baker, Jr. (courtesy of the composer)

Part I: General Questions

1. Q: What persons, events, and works (of art, literature, etc.)
        have influenced you in general as well as in terms of your
        musical activities?
    A: Well, certainly I think you have to say family. Nobody es-
        capes that influence because that's the thing that shapes the
        way people are. If I were going to talk about people out-
        side of my family who have been influential in the way I
        think, particularly about music, I'd have to say all my
        music teachers, particularly those who were a part of what
        I was about when I was first getting started in music. Rus-
        sell Brown at Crispus Attucks was a very positive influence.
        So were LaVerne Newsome and Norman Merrifield, also at
        Attucks, and Jim Compton, who was my very first music
        teacher at P.S. 26. Of course, my composition teachers
        at Indiana University had a decided influence--Bernard
        Heiden, Thomas Beversdorf, Juan Orrego-Salas, and John
        Eaton. I suspect the prime influences have been George
        Russell and J. J. Johnson and really virtually everybody
        and everything I have come in contact with.
            As to books, works of art, etc. I think the Bible, the
        Rosicrucians, the writings of Gurdjieff[1] and Ouspensky, [2]
        the book <u>Living Time</u>, [3] the whole of black history--musical
        and otherwise--and then all of the legion of jazz players who
        weave a pervasive influence on everybody and everything
        that has to do with music--Charlie Parker, Dizzy Gillespie,
        John Coltrane, Sonny Rollins--and my immediate contacts,
        Wes Montgomery and Slide Hampton, and even some of my
        students--Freddie Hubbard and people like that.

2. Q: How would you define black music?
    A: There was a time when I think I might have been able to
        come up with what I thought was a working definition, but
        now I'd say it's the music of black people, embracing the
        total black experience; that's about as much as I could come
        up with. Certainly I could be more specific by talking
        about the things that have already been written about it, but
        I'll just allude to them by saying that I agree very much
        with Gunther Schuller[4] as he interprets A. M. Jones[5] in
        saying that black music is a music which is based on a
        constant conflict of rhythms. Black music is music which
        is about the business of being the sum total of all music with
        which it has come into contact.

3. Q: What features of your own music do you see as uniquely
        black (in terms of both musical and philosophical considera-
        tions)?
    A: It's very difficult to even answer that question. I've always
        felt that the strongest facet of my music, the thing that
        shows up in all my music, is a concern for rhythm--meter,
        time, elements that fall loosely under that purview. I would

say also polymeter, improvisation, a general lack of obsession with tradition--the fact that I don't adhere rigidly to any kind of tradition or even any genre or style because I have a total respect and love for all music--and the fact that I view music in a decidedly African way, as a total experience and not apart from other aspects of life. I think that in my music, particularly in the music which I've been writing in the last three or four years, I've moved more and more towards acceptance of my own total background. The use of inflection, ellipsis, greater latitude in all facets of the musical components with which I work-- these are things which I think define my music.

4. Q: In what ways is your music a reflection of your personal philosophy (social, political, etc.)?

   A: Well, I don't know how music could not be a reflection of your personal philosophy, so I think it's probably redundant for me to even try to answer that. The things that I'm about are the things which obviously have come forth in the music I write, particularly if I don't work to attenuate those things in the music--and I don't; I try not to let anything get between me and what I have to say. I use craft and all of those things as a means of expressing what it is I feel about life. I think the fact that I work with all available forms (irrespective of genre, origin, etc.) and the fact that many of my works have been devoted to, dedicated to, and are about black people says, I think, something about what I feel philosophically, politically, and socially about my music. For instance, I've written works to Dr. Martin Luther King, [6] one to Malcolm X, [7] another called Coltrane in Memoriam, another entitled A Tribute to Wes, another called Bird;[8] even when I haven't been so consciously about the business of writing to a specific person, I think that one can trace elements even in just specific movements of my works. I've felt that very often a particular movement or a particular work was inspired primarily by what I feel about my heroes. I think my choice of materials is a reflection of what my personal philosophy is, the fact that I draw very heavily on jazz components in my writing--improvisation, jazz scales, African rhythms, gospel music, R&B, the blues, inflection, and wide latitude regarding all musical components. I think all of this would probably fit under this question.

5. Q: What do you see as the position or role of the black artist in contemporary society?

   A: Well, I think it's essentially the role of any artist vis-à-vis his own ethnic background, and that is to somehow crystallize and project those things which are unique to his particular ethnic background to other people--to somehow or another take something very specific, like the kinds of things that form his life, and translate them into universal terms so that they then have some meaning to everybody.

I feel as a black artist that I do this in my own music; I
try to crystallize the black experience and maintain a link
with the past to affect a kind of continuum that reflects
where I come from, where I am, and where I'm going.

6. Q: Please discuss any problems you have encountered in getting
your works performed, published, and recorded.

A: I think that these kinds of problems would have to be the
same for any composer--black, white, green, or otherwise.
However, until recently, lack of access to performing groups
and media outside the jazz idiom would have been something
that would have been a special problem for the black composer. Another problem has been that aside from jazz
works, the works that blacks have written have not been
considered seriously as far as art music. Case in point:
several people came to me this summer saying that they
were doing papers comparing works of various contemporary
composers. When I asked where were the black composers,
the answer I got was that they were talking about traditional
works. It seems to me that this is a very big problem for
black composers because in order to be part of the tradition, or to have your works classified as traditional from
the standpoint of accessibility and performance, you have
to have them played; to have them played, they have to be
part of the tradition. It's a funny kind of circle that doesn't
allow you to move forward.

It is still extremely difficult to get your works published
or recorded. This is not perhaps as acute as it would have
been at another time, but it is still a preoccupation with
the past that makes it necessary for Columbia Records,
RCA Victor, Decca and all the other recording companies
to be more concerned with re-recordings of the Beethoven
Fifth, the Bruckner Second, and the Surprise Symphony
than to be concerned about the business of introducing and
acclimatizing people to new music. As far as publishers
go, by and large blacks do not own or control machinery,
so we operate at the largess of whites. I can remember
submitting works and having them turned back; sometimes,
certainly, it was motivated by a lack of concern with what
I had to say or what I did, but other times it's that black
composers are often just not taken that seriously. I think
it was Paul Freeman who pointed out that at this time last
year there weren't a dozen works by black composers listed
as available in the Schwann catalogue. [9] I think that is a
very very serious problem. Whites have the ability and
the machinery and the muscle to determine what is good,
what is marketable, and what is desirable. So if they decide that something by a black composer is not marketable,
not desirable, not good (for whatever reasons), consequently,
it's not published or recorded.

6A. Q: How much of your actual output has ever been performed?
Published? Recorded?

A: Everything I've ever written has been performed, with may-be a couple of notable exceptions. I've heard all my music, which has made it possible for me to progress. The main reason, of course, that I hear so much of my music is that much of it is in an idiom that can be performed immediately because I have access to a whole university of students to play my music. But as far as performances across the country and across the world go, not a whole lot of it has been performed, although still quite a bit. Almost nothing outside of jazz, however, has been published or recorded, with the exception of a whole spate of recordings that are now starting to come out: the cello sonata; the recording of my work Black America; the suite that I wrote for the Louisville orchestra, Le Chat Qui Pêche; my Sonata for Tuba and String Quartet with Harvey Phillips; and the Sonata for Piano and String Quintet with Helena Freire. Other than that, anything that has been recorded has been along the lines of jazz. As far as published works, not that much, even though I had quite a bit of stuff with down beat magazine. But they were not essentially music publishers, so consequently the music did not have much widespread accessibility. However, Associated Music has published two small orchestra pieces of mine[10] as well as Le Chat Qui Pêche, Kosbro, and also my cello concerto; it could well be that they might pick up a large portion of my cata-logue. Joseph Carley's company[11] has published all of my string things as well as some other things. All of my books and many of my jazz pieces have already been published through down beat and other firms; all of my books are pub-lished by down beat with the exception of Contemporary Tech-niques for the Trombone, which is published by Charles Colin.

6B. Q: Have you encountered difficulty in getting your works pro-grammed?

A: Well, I think that goes without saying. When you start talking about the fact that not much has been performed, then it automatically follows that there must be a problem in getting works programmed. I would say that it has been less acute in the last two years for a number of reasons. First of all, there has been some concern with displaying the works of blacks. There has also been some concern on the part of organizations like AAMOA[12] to make sure that these works get in front of people, so that now it is possible to go to these seminars once or twice a year and hear your works; in my case, I've had works performed at the last two seminars. Also, many of the orchestras are having to respond to the need to be contemporary, to be relevant. Consequently, many orchestras are asking for works that somehow or another reflect a more popular cul-ture. And in my case, because I feel very comfortable with music across the board--jazz, rock, pop, what have you--it means that all of a sudden my music is very much in demand.

6C. Q: Are there specific problems in getting a satisfactory per-
        formance? Exemplify and discuss.
    A: Well, I think that the problems exist for me as well as
        everybody else, blacks and non-blacks. One major problem
        is that symbols are totally inadequate in dealing with an
        oral/aural art, even though we find ways to make them
        work. But if you happen to be dealing with a music which
        reflects a more non-traditional approach, then you have
        more problems. It is very difficult many times when I
        want something that suggests a jazz inflection, or suggests
        something which is much closer to vocal music than to in-
        strumental music; then it is necessary for me to be about
        the business of using a lot of verbal explication or making
        a tape for people to listen to. Also, it seems that many
        people are unable to deal with the music of blacks on its
        own aesthetic terms; I think of my music specifically. If
        the music doesn't conform to what they believe the music
        should be, they are reluctant to deal with it. I find that
        this happens on a lot of levels. For instance, I once had
        a guy tell me that he didn't like to play my music because
        he thought it was totally undisciplined; what he meant by
        that was that it didn't conform to the established norms
        for what he felt jazz (or any other kind of music) should be.
            I think that another problem for most blacks is that many
        people do not take them seriously when they are working in
        an art music tradition, or working in areas outside of those
        prescribed by tradition. Very often when I write a piece of
        music and take it in to an orchestra, their first reaction is
        to try to play it and make it sound like it's a jazz piece.
        Or when kids come up to me after they play a piece like
        Kosbro (which shows virtually no jazz influence) and say,
        "Hey! We really like that new jazz piece!" Or the kind
        of thing that happens when various people play my music
        and insist on attaching programmatic titles that reflect jazz
        rather than what the music is about. All of these things
        mitigate against a satisfactory performance.
            I also find that I have to find a lot of different ways to
        say what I have to say to make a piece of music happen.
        For instance, in the piece that I wrote for the Louisville
        orchestra, [13] I purposely used 12/8 time and other things
        to write a kind of swing rather than tell somebody who is
        outside the culture how to swing, or how to play the music
        and make it happen. These people are steeped in the tradi-
        tion of Beethoven, Brahms, and Bach, so that if you talk
        to them about the style of that music, they know immediate-
        ly what to do and there's no problem. But they don't know
        what to do (and there's been no effort to teach them what
        to do) when they are dealing with the music of a black com-
        poser, particularly one who chooses to work with high ethnic
        content in his music. So it is necessary for me to indicate,
        through artificial means, what I want--to try and have them
        understand that way rather than to have them go through
        eight years of matriculation (as they had to do with other

music) to be able to assimilate the styles and approaches
which I and other black composers might be using. [14]

7. Q: What do you consider, at this point in your life, to be your
        most significant achievement(s) aside from your composi-
        tions?

    A: Well, I suspect if it's anything, it's having set up a sphere
        of influence vis-à-vis jazz music and vis-à-vis the moving
        forward of that music. I would have to say my books on
        improvisation, [15] my trombone book, [16] my teaching prowess,
        and my positions on various boards across the country and
        across the world, like the National Endowment for the Arts,
        the Board of Negro Music History, the State Department
        Cultural Committee, and the Rockefeller Recording Project.
        These kinds of things I consider very very significant achieve-
        ments because they are things that allow me to have a great
        deal of influence in perpetuating and promoting the things in
        which I believe and which I think many people--black and
        white--believe about what should be happening with music.
        Perhaps overriding all of that is my ability to reach stu-
        dents; I think the fact that I probably reach and influence as
        many students as any other teacher in the country working
        in my area is of significance.

8. Q: What do you see as the responsibilities and obligations of
        the educational system (at all levels) to the study of black
        music?

    A: First of all, I think the main thing that the educational
        system has more of an obligation to do than anything else
        is to accept all music without bias--to be able to put the
        music in a perspective and deal with it on its own terms
        (aesthetically, musically, socially, etc.) without trying to
        bias a student about what is good and what is bad--to pro-
        vide a broad spectrum of music and a broad spectrum of
        experiences out of which he can draw his own conclusions.
        I am not saying that there shouldn't be some guidance, but
        I think that the guidance has to be across the board; in
        other words, I don't think it is possible any longer to teach
        only the music that comes out of a tradition that started
        with Palestrina and runs up through Boulez. I think we
        have to start talking about other kinds of music and I think
        that the educational system has to be able to deal with this
        territory. To quote Edgar Z. Friedenberg: "If the univer-
        sity is to continue to stand astride the only legitimate high-
        way to advancement, it must quit demanding tolls in coins
        that only some travelers can acquire and calling this 'main-
        taining standards.'" I think that this is a very very real
        kind of consideration. It seems to me that universities and
        institutions of higher learning (as well as the entire educa-
        tional system) also have to be about ridding themselves of
        the syndrome of the Black History Week phenomenon, where
        they set aside one week that is devoted to ethnic groups
        instead of having it be part of the continuing concerns of

everybody involved in education. I think my views are well-
known enough that, if you want to go further, it might be
well to see them crystallized in a more concrete and com-
pact form in Black Music in Our Culture, [17] the article I
wrote for Black World, [18] the big article I wrote in Black
Communications, [19] and in many of the articles I've done
for down beat. [20] The last thing I'd say about this whole
thing--about what the educational system has as its obligations and responsibilities to all music, but particularly to
black music--is that it must help rid the system of Anglo-
Saxon ethnocentrism; it must get about the business of dealing with music on its own terms and not poisoning young
minds with a lot of things which were outmoded twenty years
ago and no less so now.

9. Q: Do you feel that the people who write about your music
(critics in particular) understand what you are doing? Exemplify and discuss.

A: Well, it's very difficult to say because that's taking it as
though there were a critic, a measuring stick--as though
they were all one person. I'd say that by and large the only
times I have real concerns are when people insist on measuring my works against standards which are not relevant.
For instance, to take a work like my tuba concerto (or any
of the concerti I have written which come out of the jazz
idiom even though they use classical compositional techniques) and then measure them only in terms of western art
music aesthetics is, to me, a complete misunderstanding of
what my music is about. By the same token, those people
who heap accolades on my music simply because it's a phenomenon that I am a black person and writing music in a
western art tradition don't understand it either. I don't
want anybody bending over backwards either way. I think
Hale Smith put it very very well in his credo "Here I
Stand";[21] he talks about the fact that the only time it is
relevant or important that I'm black or not is when I stand
up to take my bows, and when I do that, everybody will
know it anyway. Beyond that, measure my music and understand it according to what it has to say and what it has to
do. The fact is that you don't judge the music of Ravi
Shankar by the same standards that you do Heifitz playing
Paganini. I think that it means that critics have to be about
the business of being well-versed across the board--either
that or don't write about specific kinds of music. When I
write a piece of music that is stylistically and consistently
a piece of western art music, judge me by the same standards you judge Bach and Handel. But if I write a piece
which does not conform solely to either western art music
tradition or jazz (and that is most often the case), then my
work must be judged by a critic who understands both
aesthetics.

10. Q: What advice would you give to the aspiring young black
composer?

A: Be yourself. Write following your own mind, following your aesthetic and creative bent. Make as few concessions as possible to what people expect you to do. Underneath that, you have to study and know your craft; a person is decidedly crippled who's got all of the creative ability in the world and has no means by which to convey what he has to say. You have to be about the business of knowing and understanding music in its totality. You have to be a craftsman; you have to know how to use materials and this kind of thing. In broader terms, listen to everybody and everything; don't close the doors to any kind of music or any kind of life experience. Be aware of your history and your tradition, but don't be blind to what's going on contemporaneously or what might be lying ahead of you. And then, beyond that, I think you have to bug people to play your music.

Part II: Music Questions

1. Q: When you sit down to begin a new composition on your own initiative or inspiration (as opposed to a commissioned work), what procedure or approach do you follow?

   A: It would differ with every work, I'm certain, but there are general kinds of things that I consider. First of all, I think about the medium for which I will write. I think about the length of the work ahead of time. I think about what form (or forms) it should take. I think about structure, and what kinds of raw materials I'll use; I find that I'll examine a wealth of raw materials--set systems, rows, jazz and folk materials, etc.--before I ever even think about writing a piece of music. I also try to hear what that piece should sound like in my mind's ear before I ever start to write. If I am doing a concerto, obviously I learn whatever instrument it is that I'm going to write for. I think each piece brings with it its own set of imperatives and I never <u>never</u> enter the arena of composition with a whole lot of pre-set notions about what should happen. I look at what I've got to say and how long I intend to say it; then I go about the business of setting up a sort of unique procedure to go with that piece, a procedure which will probably be discarded at the end of that piece.

2. Q: When composing a commissioned work or a work written for a specific occasion or person, does your procedure or approach differ from the one you described in question one? If so, in what way?

   A: Only slightly. I find (and I learned this the hard way) that if I'm writing for a particular performer--particularly a concerto, or even a piece which involves a performer with whom I feel fairly acquainted--the first thing I do is work with the performer. I ask questions. I submit drafts of

the work to the performer. I have him make suggestions
and have him tell me what doesn't work. If the work is
for a particular instrument, I make a point of living with
that instrument before I start to write. I listen to and look
at as much music as possible in the genre for which I'm
writing. For instance, if I'm writing a trio (as I just
have for the Beaux Arts Trio), I'll probably spend a young
fortune on scores, tapes, and records to listen to as much
music as possible by other people who have written for that
medium. I also ask questions of everybody about everything that conceivably could happen within that piece. And
then I'm constantly re-examining, restructuring, and re-
appraising what it is that I'm trying to do with the piece,
so in a commissioned work the only thing different that
happens is my close alliance with whoever the work is for.
Now, with a work like the piece I wrote for the J. C.
Penney's commission,[22] that was a completely different
kind of thing in that I had to come up with a format--some-
thing that would adequately project the theme of the Bicentennial. But by and large the considerations are pre-com-
positional considerations.

3. Q: In general, with regard to your writing, what genre(s) do
       you prefer?
    A: Got no preference.

4. Q: What do you consider your most significant composition?
       Please discuss.
    A: There are two things that I have to say here. First of all,
       I think Black America is my magnum opus to date. I con-
       sider Black America my most significant work because it is
       a synthesis of all that I'm about, and because it chronicles
       one of the most significant events in my life and in the lives
       of most black people--the assassination of Dr. Martin Luther
       King.[23] Secondly, and more realistically perhaps, I con-
       sider my most significant and important work to be whatever
       work I'm currently working on.

5. Q: Please comment on your treatment of the following musical
       elements and give examples from your compositions that
       illustrate the techniques you describe.

    A. Melody
        DNB: Lyrical, romantic. I think in terms of long,
             flowing lines even though they are often conceived
             in terms of rows and set systems. I always
             think in terms of melody, and I think in terms
             of lyrical and flowing lines (whatever that means
             to a reader). As to what pieces typify that, I'd
             say the second movement of the cello sonata is
             an excellent example of how I feel about the way
             lines should move. Kosbro is another piece which

is full of melody. I would think that almost
everything that happens in every movement of
Le Chat Qui Pêche is typical of what I feel about
melody.

B. Harmony
    DNB: As to harmony, pretty much jazz-inflected. It is
          dodecaphonic very often. It changes according to the
          needs of the piece that I'm writing. It might be
          twelve-tone in which harmonies are incidental. It
          might be vertical. It might be bi-tonal or poly-tonal.
          As far as harmony goes, I'm an eclectic.

C. Rhythm
    DNB: It's the prime focus of my music. I think that I'm
          very much indebted to African music for the way I
          feel and the way I work with rhythm. I could never
          escape my debt to jazz. Also, on other levels, I
          think I have a strong debt to Charles Ives and prob-
          ably to Bartok as far as what I do with rhythm. I'm
          about the business very often of polymetric and multi-
          metric schemata. I'm also about the business (as I
          notice a lot of other composers are) of the use of
          rhythmic ostinato as a unifying factor in my pieces.
          I think any piece of mine will be typical, particularly
          the concerti and particularly the pieces which are
          dedicated to particular people like Charlie Parker;[24]
          the John Coltrane piece[25] is a splendid example of
          that. I think that the tuba concerto is probably the
          culmination of a lot of searching for new techniques
          and new ways of dealing with rhythm. I think the
          last movement of the Sonata for Piano and String
          Quintet is a splendid example of how I use metric
          modulation and other rhythmic procedures. But by
          and large, all my music will bear examination from
          the standpoint of what I do with rhythm.

D. Form
    DNB: Well, I use a lot of different things. I use all the
          available forms that come out of the tradition--sonata
          allegro and this kind of thing. I have a strong af-
          finity to ground bass type forms. I like theme and
          variations very much, and I write theme and varia-
          tions very frequently. I also use the ostinato forms
          --passacaglia and this kind of thing. I use all the
          jazz and pop forms--the blues, rhythm,[26] song forms,
          and everything else I can get my hands on. Most
          often, however (with the exception of perhaps a pas-
          sacaglia or a theme and variations), the form is
          post facto. I write a piece and then go back to see
          what the form was. I think all the things I talked
          about are immediately discernible in looking at my
          music. If I were talking about extended forms,

there's a sonata allegro form, like Kosbro. And yet
every one of the movements in Le Chat Qui Pêche is
a completely different thing; the first one is a song
form, the second one is a blues, the third one is
through-composed, the fourth one is a calypso (with
fugal interruptions and things like that), and the last
one is a bougaloo. It kind of runs the gamut. I
see all different kinds of forms, for instance, in the
cello sonata; the first movement is sonata allegro,
the last movement is sonata allegro, and the middle
movement is a ternary form. I don't really feel any
inclination to be boxed in as far as what form is,
but you can find a preponderance of ostinato and
bass-repetitive forms.

E. Improvisation
DNB: Rarely do I use improvisation in anything outside of
jazz. In my jazz works, obviously improvisation is
the essence of those works. Let's say this: any
time I have a work that involves a jazz band, improvisation is part of the music. However, outside
of a jazz or thirdstream context, I try to maintain
complete control over my product so I rarely use
aleatoric techniques within my traditional writing
(not to say that I won't sometimes do that because
it may turn out that I'll do it more frequently as I
get more and more comfortable with all of these
particular forms and techniques).

F. Text
DNB: By and large, in my works that have demanded text,
I've chosen either the Bible or texts by black writers.
That has to do more with the circumstances than anything else. I've chosen works by Mari Evans,
Langston Hughes, Sol Edwards, Carl Hines, and
Stanley Warren, but I also like to feel that I have an
affinity with all sensitive writers because I have
written things by William Blake and other writers
who are non-blacks. Maybe I should say something
about treatment; treatment varies with the circumstances. In an orchestral context, very often I use
text and things in the manner of Charles Ives, that
is, where you are not supposed to be able to understand
everything that is going on but you get some kind of a
composite, an overview just from looking at all of the
differing elements coming together. I very often
use sprechstimme and layers of words. I often write
using my own text. I try to remain faithful to the
speech patterns and yet add another dimension to the
poet's work. Any time I don't feel that I can bring
another dimension, another level of understanding to
a work, then I don't bother. If the work is totally
complete and can't stand to be treated from outside,

then I let it alone; that's usually the yardstick that I use before I write a piece.

G.   Instrumentation or medium
     DNB: Well, the medium is usually dictated by the circum-
           stances, but I have a real affinity for voices and
           strings.   I think if I were to choose what I'd like
           to write for, it would be strings and voices an in-
           ordinate amount of the time.   Of course, I also feel
           very very close to jazz band because that has been
           my principal medium of expression.   And, of course,
           orchestra.   I like to experiment with different colors
           and different sonar possibilities, so I imagine I will
           be moving eventually into electronic music and music
           that is produced in other ways.

6.   Q: Have difficulties with performance practice (inflection, phras-
           ing, etc.) been a significant problem in having your works
           performed to your own satisfaction?
     A: Well, stylistic problems exist with all kinds of music; it
           doesn't make any difference if you're talking about Bach or
           electronic music.   I try to get around that by doing a num-
           ber of different things, and one is to try to know the group
           that I'm writing for since most of the time I am writing on
           commission.   I try to write with a performer (or particular
           performers) in mind; sometimes that translates into just an
           ideal--what I would like it to be.   Then I try my best to
           communicate that to a performer, through the use not only
           of symbols but verbal explication and tapes of me playing
           my own works.   I find that by using tapes, records, sing-
           ing, and trying different kinds of notation, that it is possible
           very often to communicate things that would not normally be
           communicable through traditional means.

7.   Q: What major works are currently in progress?   Please de-
           scribe and discuss.
     A: Well, I just completed a cello concerto and a tuba concerto.
           I have a trio (for the Beaux Arts Trio) which is one move-
           ment shy of being finished. [27]   I have a piece for orchestra,
           trumpet, and jazz band in progress.   I just finished a piece
           today for a group called the Electric Stereopticon, which is
           J. B. Floyd and a trio with all the electronics and everything
           (plus I added a cello).   At present I'm working on the fol-
           lowing: (1) an opera based on the life of Malcolm X; (2)
           a piece for solo contrabass, tracing the history of the jazz
           bass (commissioned by Bertram Turetzky); (3) a new or-
           chestra piece (requested by Paul Freeman); (4) a set of
           variations for violin and piano (commissioned by Ruggiero
           Ricci);[28] (5) a concerto for two pianos and jazz orchestra
           (commissioned by Charles Webb and Wallace Hornibrook);
           (6) a sonata for flute and jazz instruments (electric piano,
           vibraphone, electric bass, and percussion) which was com-
           missioned by James Pellerite; and (7) a musical (in colla-
           boration with Mari Evans).

8. Q: Given unlimited time and finances (and no restrictions whatsoever), what would you write?

A: Just the things I'm presently writing. As far as I'm concerned, unlimited time and finances have absolutely no influence on what I do because knowing that you're never going to be rich, you go ahead and write what you want to write anyway. And I don't think I would do any more if I had more time because I believe I'm already maximizing my potential.

9. Q: If given the opportunity would you choose to devote yourself to composition on a full-time basis? Why or why not?

A: No. I need all of my activities--playing, writing, teaching, composing, etc.--because they all feed each other. If I were to give up any one of them, I'm sure that all the others would suffer commensurately.

10. Q: How would you describe your compositional style?

A: Eclectic, but essentially romantic.

11. Q: What have been the influences of other composers, styles, and other types of music on your compositional style?

A: I'm influenced by everybody and everything with which I come into contact. Specific influences would include Duke Ellington, George Russell, Gil Evans, Bartok, Ulysses Kay, Alben Berg, Charles Ives, Bird, Dizzy, J. J., and almost every other black composer with whom I've worked very much--Talib, Hale Smith, George Walker, T. J., Olly, Quincy--you name it. If I've come into contact with them, they've influenced me somehow or another.

12. Q: Has your style changed across your career? If so, what influenced these changes or developments?

A: Well, I'm sure that it has matured, and that in itself represents a change. I've expanded my thinking to embrace a broader spectrum of musics. The fact that I've had people play my music and play it very well has spurred me to write in every conceivable medium, for every conceivable combination of instruments, and in almost every conceivable style. So I would say that if there have been changes, they've been changes that have had more to do with expansion than substance.

13. Q: When you are listening to music for your own enjoyment, what are your preferences?

A: Everything! Everything from Buck Owens and Lightnin' Hopkins to Dizzy Gillespie, John Cage, and Xenakis--even Muzak!

Notes to Chapter II

1. Georges Ivanovitch Gurdjieff (1872-1949), Russian mystic and

philosopher. His magnum opus, All and Everything, is a three-part
work of which Harcourt, Brace and Company has published parts one
and two (New York: 1950). Two books which provide a particularly
good introduction to Gurdjieff's ideas are J. G. Bennett's works Is
There "Life" on Earth?: An Introduction to Gurdjieff (New York:
Stonehill, 1973) and Gurdjieff: Making a New World (New York:
Harper and Row, 1973).

2. Peter Demianovich Ouspensky (1878-1947), Russian philosopher
and author. His books The Fourth Way, Tertium Organum, and
A New Model of the Universe are considered among the most important philosophical works of the twentieth century. A former pupil
of Gurdjieff, Ouspensky wrote In Search of the Miraculous: Fragments of an Unknown Teaching (New York: Harcourt, Brace, 1949)
as a record of his eight-year study with the great philosopher.

3. Maurice Nicoll. Living Time and the Integration of the Life
(London: Stuart & Watkins, 1952).

4. Gunther Schuller. Early Jazz: Its Roots and Musical Development (New York: Oxford University Press, 1968), pp. 10-26.

5. A. M. Jones. Studies in African Music. 2 vols. (London:
Oxford University Press, 1959).

6. Mr. Baker is referring to his composition Black America.

7. Mr. Baker is referring to his composition Three for Malcolm.
In addition, the composer is currently collaborating with poet Mari
Evans on an opera based on the life of Malcolm X.

8. Other works of this type include Louis Armstrong in Memoriam
(1972) and a composition dedicated to the memory of Cannonball
Adderley on which Mr. Baker is working at the present time.

9. This interview took place on August 6, 1975.

10. Mr. Baker is referring to his composition Two Improvisations
for Orchestra.

11. Creative Jazz Composers, Inc.

12. The Afro-American Music Opportunities Association. This
organization, founded in 1969 by C. Edward Thomas, supports a
variety of projects and activities in the area of black music.

13. Mr. Baker is referring to his composition Le Chat Qui Pêche
(1974).

14. This is also relevant to I-8.

15. Jazz Improvisation, Techniques of Improvisation (4 vols.), and
Advanced Improvisation. See the bibliography for complete citations.

16. Contemporary Techniques for the Trombone. 2 vols. (New York: Charles Colin, 1974).

17. Dominique-René de Lerma, ed. Black Music in Our Culture (Kent, Ohio: Kent State University Press, 1970), pp. 12-22.

18. "The Battle for Legitimacy: 'Jazz' Versus Academia," Black World, November 1973, pp. 20-27.

19. "The Rhetorical Dimensions of Black Music: Past and Present," in Black Communication: Dimensions of Research and Instruction, ed. Jack L. Daniel (New York: Speech Communication Association, 1974), pp. 3-27.

20. See especially "Jazz: The Academy's Neglected Stepchild," down beat, 23 September 1965, pp. 29-32.

21. Hale Smith, "Here I Stand," in Readings in Black American Music, ed. Eileen Southern (New York: W. W. Norton, 1971), pp. 286-289.

22. Mr. Baker is referring to his composition The Soul of '76.

23. A lengthy and detailed description of Black America is given by Mr. Baker in Reflections on Afro-American Music (Dominique-René de Lerma, ed.), pp. 95-97.

24. Mr. Baker is referring to his compositions Bird and Blues for Bird.

25. Mr. Baker is referring to his composition Coltrane in Memoriam.

26. In this context Mr. Baker's use of the term rhythm refers to the form of George Gershwin's composition "I Got Rhythm."

27. This work was completed in early 1976 and appears in the list of compositions under the title Roots.

28. This work was completed in early 1976 and appears in the list of compositions under the title Ethnic Variations on a Theme of Paganini.

LIST OF COMPOSITIONS

ABYSS (1968)
Soprano and piano. Text by Carole Wright. Four movements: Perception; Observation; Introspection; Penetration. 12 min. First performance (1968) at Indiana University (Bloomington, Indiana). Carole Wright, soprano; Carl Fuerstner, piano.

ADUMBRATIO   (1971)
   Jazz ensemble. *   10 min.

ADUMBRATIO   (1971)
   Jazz nonet (trumpet, alto saxophone, tenor saxophone, trombone, baritone saxophone, guitar, piano, electric bass, and drums). 10 min.   Three Fifteen West Fifty-Third Street Corp.   (Dave Baker Jazz Rock Series), 1971.

AFRO-CUBAN SUITE   (1954)
   Band.   One movement.   15 min.

THE ALARM CLOCK   (1973)
   See THE BLACK EXPERIENCE (1973).

AL-KI-HOL   (1956)
   Jazz ensemble.   10 min.

ALL THE ENDS OF THE EARTH SHALL REMEMBER   (1966)
   See PSALM 22.

ALMOST   (1973)
   Jazz ensemble.   12 min.

ALMOST   (1973)
   For melody and chord symbols see Baker, Advanced Improvisation, p. 233.

AN ALMOST DEATH   (1975)
   See GIVE AND TAKE.

ANDY JACOBS'S CAMPAIGN SONG   (1972)
   Incidental music for a television show.   Commissioned by Andrew Jacobs, Jr. for use in his 1972 congressional campaign.

ANJISA   (1973)
   Jazz ensemble.   10 min.

ANJISA   (1973)
   For melody and chord symbols see Baker, Advanced Improvisation, p. 234.

ANY HUMAN TO ANOTHER   (1973)
   Chorus (SATB) and piano.   Text by Countee Cullen.   6 min.

APOCALYPSE   (1964)
   Jazz ensemble.   15 min.

*The designation "jazz ensemble" as used in David Baker's list of compositions refers specifically to an ensemble having the following instrumentation: five saxophones (two alto saxophones, two tenor saxophones, and baritone saxophone), five trumpets, three trombones, bass trombone, tuba, piano, bass, and drums.

APRIL B (1959)
Jazz ensemble. 10 min.

APRIL B (1959)
Jazz nonet (trumpet, alto saxophone, tenor saxophone, trombone,
baritone saxophone, guitar, piano, electric bass, and drums).
10 min.   Three Fifteen West Fifty-Third Street Corp.   (Dave
Baker Jazz Rock Series), 1970.

APRIL B (1959)
For melody and chord symbols see Baker, Arranging and Composing for the Small Ensemble: Jazz/R&B/Jazz-Rock, p. 46.

AU DEMAIN (1973)
Jazz ensemble. 15 min.

AUCON (1973)
Jazz ensemble. 10 min.

AUEV (1973)
Jazz ensemble. 11 min.

AUJOURD'HUI (1973)
Jazz ensemble. 9 min.

AULIL (1973)
Jazz ensemble. 12 min.

AULIL (1973)
Jazz septet (trumpet, alto saxophone, tenor saxophone, trombone,
piano, bass, and drums). 4-10 min. Studio PR, 1976.

AULIL (1973)
For melody and chord symbols see Baker, Advanced Improvisation, p. 234.

BAKER'S SHUFFLE (1970)
String orchestra. 4 min. Creative Jazz Composers, 1976.

BALLADE (1967)
F horn, alto saxophone, and violoncello. 7 min. Commissioned
by and dedicated to Peter Gordon. First performance (1967) at
Indiana University (Bloomington, Indiana). Peter Gordon, horn;
James Greene, alto saxophone; and Nella Hunkins, violoncello.

BASH (1972)
Jazz ensemble. 10 min.

THE BEATITUDES (1968)
Chorus (SATB), soloists, narrator, jazz ensemble, string or-
chestra, and dancers. Biblical text. 12 parts: Instrumental
Prelude; Vocal Introduction; Blessed Are the Poor in Spirit;
Blessed Are They That Mourn; Blessed Are the Meek; Blessed

Are They That Hunger; Blessed Are the Merciful; Blessed Are
the Clean in Heart; Blessed Are the Peacemakers; Blessed Are
They Who Suffer Persecution; Blessed Are Ye When Men Shall
Revile You; Instrumental Postlude.   1 hour.   Commissioned by
Christian Theological Seminary.

BEBOP REVISITED   (1974)
Jazz ensemble.   12 min.

BEBOP REVISITED   (1974)
For melody and chord symbols see Baker, Advanced Improvisation, p. 235.

LA BELLE FLEUR   (1964)
Jazz ensemble.   7 min.

BILY   (1974)
Jazz ensemble.   11 min.

BIRD (TO THE MEMORY OF CHARLIE PARKER)   (1970)
Jazz ensemble.   Four movements: The Blues; In Beauty; Bird's
Lady; Past-Present-Future.   35-50 min.   Dedicated to Charlie
Parker.

BLACK AMERICA: TO THE MEMORY OF MARTIN LUTHER KING,
JR.   (1968; has undergone several revisions)
Cantata for jazz ensemble, narrators, chorus (SATB), soloists,
and string orchestra.   Four movements: The Wretched of the
Earth (Machinations, Missionaries, Money, Marines); Kaleido-
scope; 125th Street; Martyrs: Malcolm, Medgar, Martin.   Texts
utilized include the following: Black Man: White World (Stanley
Warren); The Burying Ground (traditional); I Dream a World
(Langston Hughes); Sorrow Is the Only Faithful One (Pauli Murray);
Now That He Is Safely Dead (Carl Hines); Thou Dost Lay Me
in the Dust of Death (Biblical); If We Must Die (Claude McKay).
App. 45 min.   Recorded by University of Illinois Press for
later release; Indiana University Jazz Ensemble, David N. Baker,
conductor; Linda Anderson, Janice Albright, Bob Ingram, Pablo
Elvira, and Julie Smith, soloists; John Joyner and Solomon
Edwards, narrators.   Broadcast yearly on the anniversary of
Dr. King's death by Voice of America.   First performance (1968)
at Indiana University (Bloomington, Indiana).   Indiana University
Jazz Ensemble, David N. Baker, conductor; Linda Anderson,
Janice Albright, Beverly McElroy, and Robert Ingram, soloists;
David Arnold and Orlando Taylor, narrators.

BLACK ART   (1968)
See SONATA FOR PIANO.

BLACK CHILDREN   (1970)
See FIVE SONGS TO THE SURVIVAL OF BLACK CHILDREN.

THE BLACK EXPERIENCE (1968)
   Theme music for the television show "The Black Experience."
   See SON-MAR.

THE BLACK EXPERIENCE (1973)
   Tenor and piano. Text by Mari Evans. Seven parts: I Who
   Would Encompass Millions; The Insurgent; Status Symbol; A Good
   Assassination Should Be Quiet; The Rebel; The Alarm Clock;
   Early in the Morning. App. 15 min. Commissioned by and
   dedicated to Bill Brown.

THE BLACK FRONTIER (1971)
   Music for the television series "The Black Frontier" (NET).
   Four one-hour shows: The New Americans; The Cowherders;
   The Buffalo Soldiers; The Exodusters.

BLACK MAN, BLACK WOMAN (1969)
   Jazz ensemble. 15 min. Based on materials from I HEARD
   MY WOMAN CALL.

BLACK THURSDAY (1964)
   Jazz ensemble. 7 min.

BLACK THURSDAY (1964)
   Jazz nonet (trumpet, alto saxophone, tenor saxophone, trombone,
   baritone saxophone, guitar, piano, electric bass, and drums).
   7 min. Three Fifteen West Fifty-Third Street Corp. (Dave
   Baker Jazz Rock Series), 1970.

BLACK THURSDAY (1964)
   For melody and chord symbols see Baker, Arranging and Composing for the Small Ensemble: Jazz/R&B/Jazz-Rock, p. 52.

BLACK-EYED PEAS AND CORNBREAD (1970)
   String orchestra. 4 min. Creative Jazz Composers, 1976.

BLESSED ARE THE CLEAN IN HEART (1968)
   See THE BEATITUDES.

BLESSED ARE THE MEEK (1968)
   See THE BEATITUDES.

BLESSED ARE THE MERCIFUL (1968)
   See THE BEATITUDES.

BLESSED ARE THE PEACEMAKERS (1968)
   See THE BEATITUDES.

BLESSED ARE THE POOR IN SPIRIT (1968)
   See THE BEATITUDES.

BLESSED ARE THEY THAT HUNGER (1968)
   See THE BEATITUDES.

BLESSED ARE THEY THAT MOURN (1968)
See THE BEATITUDES.

BLESSED ARE THEY WHO SUFFER PERSECUTION (1968)
See THE BEATITUDES.

BLESSED ARE YE WHEN MEN SHALL REVILE YOU (1968)
See THE BEATITUDES.

BLUE STRINGS (1970)
String orchestra. 4 min. Creative Jazz Composers, 1976.

BLUES (1966)
String orchestra. 5 min. Creative Jazz Composers, 1976.
Adaptation of "Deliver My Soul" from PSALM 22.

BLUES FOR BIRD (1972)
Jazz ensemble. 25 min. Dedicated to Charlie Parker.

BLUES FOR BIRD (1972)
For melody and chord symbols see Baker, Advanced Improvisation, p. 236.

BLUES WALTZ (1976)
Violin, violoncello, and piano. See ROOTS.

BLUES WALTZ (NEE TERRIBLE T) (1970)
Piano. See FIVE SHORT PIECES FOR PIANO.

DE BOOGIE MAN (1973)
Jazz ensemble. 10 min.

BORDERLINE (1972)
See SONGS OF THE NIGHT.

BOSSA BELLE (1973)
Jazz ensemble. 10 min.

BOUGALOO (1971)
Jazz ensemble. 10 min.

THE BRANCH OF A GREEN TREE (1975)
See GIVE AND TAKE.

BROTHER (1973)
Jazz ensemble. 12 min.

BROTHER (1973)
For melody and chord symbols see Baker, Advanced Improvisation, p. 236.

BRUSHSTROKES (1966)
Jazz ensemble. Theme for the television show "Brushstrokes"
(WTTV; Indianapolis, Indiana). 2 min.

BUCK (1975)
Jazz ensemble. 7 min.

THE BUFFALO SOLDIERS (1971)
See THE BLACK FRONTIER.

BUS RIDE (1973)
Jazz ensemble. 15 min.

BUS RIDE (1973)
For melody and chord symbols see Baker, Advanced Improvisation, p. 237.

BUT I AM A WORM (1966)
See PSALM 22.

CALYPSO-NOVA NO. 1 (1970)
Jazz ensemble. 10 min.

CALYPSO-NOVA NO. 1 (1970)
Jazz nonet (trumpet, alto saxophone, tenor saxophone, trombone, baritone saxophone, guitar, piano, electric bass, and drums). 5 min. Three Fifteen West Fifty-Third Street Corp. (Dave Baker Jazz Rock Series), 1971.

CALYPSO-NOVA NO. 1 (1970)
String orchestra. 4 min. Creative Jazz Composers, 1976.

CALYPSO-NOVA NO. 2 (1971)
Jazz ensemble. 10 min.

CALYPSO-NOVA NO. 2 (1971)
String orchestra. 10 min. Creative Jazz Composers, 1976.

CALYPSO ROW (1976)
See ROOTS.

CANONIZATION II (1975)
See GIVE AND TAKE.

CATALYST (1966)
Jazz ensemble. 15 min.

CATHOLIC MASS FOR PEACE (1969)
Alternate title: VOTIVE MASS FOR PEACE. Chorus (SATB) and jazz ensemble. Five parts: Entrance Antiphon; Give Peace to Your People; Congregational Refrain; Great Amen; Recessional (Psalm 150). Commissioned by the National Catholic Music Educators Association. First performance (1969) in Cleveland, Ohio at the National Catholic Music Educators Association National Convention.

CATTIN' (1971)
Jazz ensemble. 15 min.

CFB (1972)
Jazz ensemble. 10 min.

CFB (1972)
For melody and chord symbols see Baker, Advanced Improvisation, p. 237.

CHANSON (1974)
See SIX POEMES NOIR POUR FLUTE ET PIANO.

CHARIOTS (1972)
Jazz ensemble. 9 min.

LE CHAT QUI PECHE (1969)
Jazz ensemble. 10 min. Recorded by the Indiana University
Jazz Ensemble, David N. Baker, conductor (Silver Crest
CBD-69-6B: 1969. 15th National Conference. College Band
Directors National Association.

LE CHAT QUI PECHE (1969)
Jazz nonet (trumpet, alto saxophone, tenor saxophone, trombone,
baritone saxophone, guitar, piano, electric bass, and drums).
10 min. Three Fifteen West Fifty-Third Street Corp. (Dave
Baker Jazz Rock Series), 1970.

LE CHAT QUI PECHE (1974)
Orchestra, soprano, and jazz quartet (alto/tenor saxophone,
piano, bass, and drums). Text by the composer. Five move-
ments: Soleil d' Altamira; L'Odeur du Blues; Sons Voiles;
Guadeloupe-Calypso; Le Miroir Noir. App. 28 min. Associated
Music, 1975. Recorded by the Louisville Symphony Orchestra,
Jorge Mester, conductor, with soloists Linda Anderson, Jamey
Aebersold, Dan Haerle, John Clayton, and Charlie Craig (First
Edition LS-751). Commissioned by and dedicated to the Louis-
ville Symphony Orchestra. First performance (1974) by the
Louisville Symphony Orchestra, Jorge Mester, conductor. Solo-
ists: Linda Anderson, soprano; Jamey Aebersold, alto/tenor
saxophone; Dan Haerle, piano; John Clayton, bass; Charlie
Craig, drums.

CHE (1969)
Jazz ensemble. 10 min. Dedicated to Ché Guevera.

CHECK IT OUT (1970)
Jazz ensemble. 10 min. Recorded by the Indiana University
Jazz Ensemble, David N. Baker, conductor (Canterbury Records,
no number; Jazz at Canterbury).

CHECK IT OUT (1970)
Jazz nonet (trumpet, alto saxophone, tenor saxophone, trombone,
baritone saxophone, guitar, piano, electric bass, and drums).
4 min. Three Fifteen West Fifty-Third Street Corp. (Dave
Baker Jazz Rock Series), 1971.

CINQUATRE (1964)
Jazz ensemble. 12 min.

CLEGRE (1973)
Jazz ensemble. 10 min.

COLTRANE (1968)
Piano. See SONATA FOR PIANO.

COLTRANE IN MEMORIAM (1967)
Jazz ensemble. Four movements: Lachrymose; Blues; Apocalypse; Lachrymose. 15-30 min. Dedicated to John Coltrane.

CONCERTO FOR BASS VIOL AND JAZZ BAND (1972)
Bass viol, jazz ensemble, string quartet, and solo violin. Four
movements. 35 min. Commissioned by and dedicated to Gary
Karr. First performance (1973) at Indiana University (Bloom-
ington, Indiana) by the Indiana University Jazz Ensemble, David
N. Baker, conductor; Gary Karr, bass viol.

CONCERTO FOR CELLO AND CHAMBER ORCHESTRA (1975)
Three movements. 15 min. Associated Music, 1975. Commissioned by and dedicated to Janos Starker. First performance
(1975) in Minneapolis, Minnesota by the St. Paul Chamber Orchestra, Dennis Russell Davies, conductor; Janos Starker,
violoncello.

CONCERTO FOR FLUTE AND JAZZ BAND (1971)
Flute/alto flute, jazz ensemble, and string quartet. Three
movements. 25 min. Commissioned by and dedicated to James
Pellerite. First performance (1971) at Indiana University
(Bloomington, Indiana) by the Indiana University Jazz Ensemble,
David N. Baker, conductor; James Pellerite, flute.

CONCERTO FOR TROMBONE, JAZZ BAND, AND CHAMBER
ORCHESTRA (1972)
Four movements. 35 min. Commissioned by and dedicated to
Thomas Beversdorf. First performance (1973) at Indiana University (Bloomington, Indiana) by the Indiana University Jazz Ensemble, David N. Baker, conductor; Thomas Beversdorf, trombone.

CONCERTO FOR TRUMPET, ORCHESTRA, AND JAZZ BAND (in
progress).
Commissioned by and dedicated to Dominic Spera.

CONCERTO FOR TUBA, JAZZ BAND, PERCUSSION, CHOIR, DAN-
CERS, SLIDES, AND TAPE RECORDERS (1975)
Text by the composer. Four movements. 40 min. Commissioned by and dedicated to Harvey Phillips. First performance
(1975) at Indiana University (Bloomington, Indiana) by the Indiana University Jazz Ensemble, David N. Baker, conductor;
John Howell, vocal conductor; Harvey Phillips, tuba.

CONCERTO FOR TWO PIANOS, JAZZ BAND, CHAMBER ORCHES-
TRA, AND PERCUSSION (1976)
Four movements. 35 min. Commissioned by and dedicated to
Charles Webb and Wallace Hornibrook. First performance to
take place in the fall of 1977 at Indiana University (Bloomington,
Indiana) by the Indiana University Jazz Ensemble, David N.
Baker, conductor; Charles Webb and Wallace Hornibrook, pianists.

CONCERTO FOR VIOLIN AND JAZZ BAND (1969)
Three movements. 25 min. Recorded for future release by
violinist James Getzoff; accompanied by an ensemble conducted
by Carmen Dragon (personnel includes Ray Brown, Shelley
Manne, Don Menza, Tommy Newsome, Bill Perkins, and Bud
Shank). Commissioned by and dedicated to Josef Gingold. First
performance (1969) at Indiana University (Bloomington, Indiana)
by the Indiana University Jazz Ensemble, David N. Baker, conductor; Josef Gingold, violin.

CONTRASTS (1976)
Violin, violoncello, and piano. Four movements: Passacaglia;
A Song; Episodes (CEI/CCP); Kaleidoscope. App. 32 min.
Commissioned by the Western Arts Trio. First performance
(1976) at the University of Wyoming (Laramie, Wyoming) by the
Western Arts Trio.

THE COWHERDERS (1971)
See THE BLACK FRONTIER.

CREATE IN ME A CLEAN HEART (1967)
See LUTHERAN MASS.

CUZIN' DUCKY (1973)
Jazz ensemble. 10 min.

CUZIN' LARRY--THE CHAMP (1973)
Jazz ensemble. 12 min.

CUZIN' LARRY--THE CHAMP (1973)
For melody and chord symbols see Baker, Advanced Improvisation, p. 238.

CUZIN' LEE (1973)
Jazz ensemble. 15 min.

CUZIN' LEE (1973)
For melody and chord symbols see Baker, Advanced Improvisation, pp. 238-239.

DABD (1973)
Jazz ensemble. 10 min.

DABD (1973)
For melody and chord symbols see Baker, Advanced Improvisa-

tion, p. 239.

DAKIAP (1973)
Jazz ensemble. 17 min.

DAVE'S WALTZ (1957)
Jazz ensemble. 6 min.

DE BOOGIE MAN (1973)
For a title beginning with the article DE, see the word directly
following it.

DELIVER MY SOUL (1966)
Chorus (SATB), narrators, jazz ensemble, string orchestra,
and dancers. See PSALM 22.

DELIVER MY SOUL (1968)
Violin and piano. 5 min. First performance (1968) at the
Indianapolis Museum of Art. David Collins, violin; John
Gates, piano. Adaptation of "Deliver My Soul" from PSALM
22.

DIGITS (1972)
Jazz ensemble. 9 min.

DO DE MI (1965)
Jazz ensemble. 10 min.

A DOLLAR SHORT AND A DAY LATE (1964)
Jazz ensemble. 10 min.

THE DREAM BOOGIE (1970)
See FIVE SONGS TO THE SURVIVAL OF BLACK CHILDREN.

THE DUDE (1962)
Jazz nonet (trumpet, alto saxophone, tenor saxophone, trombone,
baritone saxophone, guitar, piano, electric bass, and drums).
7 min. Three Fifteen West Fifty-Third Street Corp. (Dave
Baker Jazz Rock Series), 1970.

THE DUDE (1962)
Violoncello and piano. 7 min.

EARLY IN THE MORNING (1973)
See THE BLACK EXPERIENCE (1973)

ELECTRIC STERE-OPTICON (1975)
Violoncello and electronic instruments. 30 min. Commissioned
by and dedicated to J. B. Floyd.

END (1972)
See SONGS OF THE NIGHT.

EPISODES (CEI/CCP) (1976)
    See CONTRASTS.

EROS AND AGAPE (1969)
    Jazz ensemble. 10-15 min.

EROS AND AGAPE (1969)
    For melody see Baker, Arranging and Composing for the Small
    Ensemble: Jazz/R&B/Jazz-Rock, p. 55.

ETC. (1972)
    Jazz ensemble. 10 min.

ETC. (1972)
    For melody and chord symbols see Baker, Advanced Improvisa-
    tion, pp. 239-240.

ETHNIC VARIATIONS ON A THEME OF PAGANINI (1976)
    Violin and piano. Theme and nine variations. Based on Paga-
    nini's 24th caprice. App. 9 min. Recorded by Ruggerio Ricci
    for Vox (to be released in 1976). Commissioned by and dedicated
    to Ruggerio Ricci.

EVENING SONG (1970)
    Piano. See FIVE SHORT PIECES FOR PIANO. Also part of
    SONGS OF THE NIGHT.

EVENING SONG (1970)
    String orchestra. 4 min. Creative Jazz Composers, 1976.

AN EVENING THOUGHT (1974)
    Jazz ensemble. 10 min.

THE EXODUSTERS (1971)
    See THE BLACK FRONTIER.

FANTASY (1954)
    Soprano, brass ensemble, and harp. Text by Albert Cobine.
    5 min.

FANTASY FOR WOODWIND QUINTET (1969)
    5 min.

THE FELIX WALK (1973)
    Jazz ensemble. 15 min.

THE FELIX WALK (1973)
    For melody and chord symbols see Baker, Advanced Improvisa-
    tion, p. 240.

FIRST DAY OF SPRING (1969)
    Jazz ensemble. 10 min.

FIRST DAY OF SPRING (1969)
    String orchestra. 5 min. Creative Jazz Composers, 1976.

FIVE SETTINGS FOR SOPRANO AND PIANO (1969)
    If There Be Sorrow (text by Mari Evans); The Smile (text by
    William Blake); The Optimist (text by Kenneth Ferling); A Song
    (text by Paul Laurence Dunbar); Parades to Hell (text by Solo-
    mon Edwards). 12 min. Commissioned by and dedicated to
    Janice Albright. First performance (1969) at Indiana University
    (Bloomington, Indiana). Janice Albright, soprano; Douglas Mur-
    dock, piano.

FIVE SHORT PIECES FOR PIANO (1970)
    Reve; To Bird; Passacaglia; Evening Song; Blues Waltz (née
    Terrible T). 15 min.

FIVE SONGS TO THE SURVIVAL OF BLACK CHILDREN (1970)
    Chorus (SATB) Unaccompanied. Now That He Is Safely Dead
    (text by Carl Wendell Hines, Jr.); Religion (text by Conrad
    Kent Rivers); Black Children (text by Conrad Kent Rivers);
    The Dream Boogie (text by Langston Hughes); If We Must Die
    (text by Claude McKay). 17 min. Commissioned by and dedi-
    cated to the Fisk Jubilee Singers. First performance (1970)
    at Fisk University (Nashville, Tenn.) by the Fisk Jubilee Sing-
    ers, Richard Turner, conductor.

FOLKLIKE (1973)
    Jazz ensemble. 10 min.

FOLKLIKE (1973)
    Jazz septet (trumpet, alto saxophone, tenor saxophone, trombone,
    piano, bass, and drums). 4-10 min. Studio PR, 1976.

FOLKLIKE (1973)
    For melody and chord symbols see Baker, Advanced Improvisa-
    tion, p. 241.

FRAGMENTS (1972)
    See SONGS OF THE NIGHT.

THE FUNERAL IS ALL (1975)
    See GIVE AND TAKE.

FUUP BLUES (1973)
    Jazz ensemble. 10 min.

FUUP BLUES (1973)
    For melody and chord symbols see Baker, Advanced Improvisa-
    tion, pp. 241-242.

GEO RUS (1974)
    Jazz ensemble. 25 min. Dedicated to George Russell.

THE GEORGIA PEACH (1973)
Jazz ensemble.   12 min.

THE GEORGIA PEACH (1973)
For melody and chord symbols see Baker, Advanced Improvisation, pp. 242-243.

GETHSEMANE (1972)
See SONGS OF THE NIGHT.

THE GIFT (1975)
See GIVE AND TAKE.

GIVE AND TAKE (1975)
Soprano and chamber ensemble (flute/alto flute, oboe/English horn, viola, violoncello, and percussion).   Text by Terence Diggory.   Six movements: The Branch of a Green Tree; The Gift; The Funeral Is All; They Will Not Tell; An Almost Death; Canonization II.   15 min.   Commissioned by and dedicated to Edith Diggory.   First performance (1975) in Bloomington, Indiana.   Edith Diggory, soprano; David N. Baker, conductor.

GIVE PEACE TO YOUR PEOPLE (1969)
See CATHOLIC MASS FOR PEACE.

GOLGOTHA (1976)
Jazz ensemble.   10 min.   First performance (1976) at Indiana University (Bloomington, Indiana) by the Indiana University Jazz Ensemble, David N. Baker, conductor.

A GOOD ASSASSINATION SHOULD BE QUIET (1973)
See THE BLACK EXPERIENCE (1973).

GREEN MINUS YELLOW (1973)
Jazz ensemble.   15 min.

THE GRIP (1973)
For melody and chord symbols see Baker, Advanced Improvisation, p. 243.

GUADELOUPE-CALYPSO (1974)
Jazz ensemble.   See WALT'S BARBERSHOP.

GUADELOUPE-CALYPSO (1974)
Orchestra, soprano, and jazz quartet.   See LE CHAT QUI PECHE.

HARLEM PIPES (1973)
Jazz ensemble.   15 min.   Dedicated to Marian McPartland.

HARLEM PIPES (1973)
Orchestra and jazz trio.   See TWO IMPROVISATIONS FOR ORCHESTRA AND JAZZ COMBO.

HARLEM PIPES (1973)
    For melody and chord symbols see Baker, Advanced Improvisation, pp. 243-244.

HELLO WORLD (1959)
    Jazz ensemble. 6 min.

HERMAN'S THEME (1976)
    Jazz ensemble. 10-12 min. Dedicated to Herman Hudson.

HERMAN'S THEME (1976)
    Jazz septet (trumpet, alto saxophone, tenor saxophone, trombone, piano, bass, and drums). 4-10 min. Studio PR, 1976.

HHHCCC (1975)
    Jazz ensemble. 10 min.

HHHCCC (1975)
    Jazz septet (trumpet, alto saxophone, tenor saxophone, trombone, piano, bass, and drums). 4-10 min. Studio PR, 1976.

HONESTY (1960)
    Jazz ensemble. 12 min. Recorded by the Indiana University Jazz Ensemble, David N. Baker, conductor (Canterbury Records, no number: Jazz at Canterbury). Recordings of HONESTY arranged for smaller ensembles include those by the George Russell Sextet (Riverside RLP-9375: Ezz-thetics; Milestone M-47027: Outer Thoughts); by Jamey Aebersold (Isis I-608); and by Clark Terry (unreleased).

HONESTY (1960)
    Jazz nonet (trumpet, alto saxophone, tenor saxophone, trombone, baritone saxophone, guitar, piano, electric bass, and drums). 5 min. Three Fifteen West Fifty-Third Street Corp. (Dave Baker Jazz Rock Series), 1971.

HOY HOY (1973)
    Jazz ensemble. 12 min.

HOY HOY (1973)
    For melody and chord symbols see Baker, Advanced Improvisation, p. 244.

I AM POURED OUT LIKE WATER (1966)
    See PSALM 22.

I DREAM A WORLD (1973)
    Chorus (SATB) and piano. Text by Langston Hughes. 5 min.

I HEARD MY WOMAN CALL (1969)
    Incidental music for I Heard My Woman Call, a dramatic presentation adapted from Eldridge Cleaver's Soul on Ice. 1 hour. First performance (1969) in Bloomington, Indiana.

THE I. U. SWING MACHINE   (1968)
    Jazz ensemble.   7 min.   Recorded by the Indiana University
    Jazz Ensemble, David N. Baker, conductor (Silver Crest CBD-
    69-6A: 1969. 15th National Conference. College Band Direc-
    tors National Association).   Dedicated to the Indiana University
    Jazz Ensemble.

THE I. U. SWING MACHINE   (1968)
    For melody and chord symbols see Baker, Arranging and Com-
    posing for the Small Ensemble: Jazz/R&B/Jazz-Rock (pp. 49-
    50) and Jazz Improvisation (pp. 41-42).

I WHO WOULD ENCOMPASS MILLIONS   (1973)
    See THE BLACK EXPERIENCE (1973).

I WILL TELL OF THY NAME   (1966)
    Chorus (SATB), narrators, jazz ensemble, string orchestra,
    and dancers. See PSALM 22.

I WILL TELL OF THY NAME   (1966)
    Jazz ensemble. See PEACE, MY BROTHER.

IF THERE BE SORROW   (1969)
    See FIVE SETTINGS FOR SOPRANO AND PIANO.

IF WE MUST DIE   (1970)
    See FIVE SONGS TO THE SURVIVAL OF BLACK CHILDREN.

IMAGE   (1974)
    See SIX POEMES NOIR POUR FLUTE ET PIANO.

IMPROVISATION # 1 FOR UNACCOMPANIED VIOLIN   (1975)
    4 min.   Commissioned by and dedicated to Ruggiero Ricci.

IMPROVISATION # 2 FOR UNACCOMPANIED VIOLIN   (1975)
    5 min.   Commissioned by and dedicated to Ruggiero Ricci.

IN MEMORIAM: FREEDOM   (1971)
    See JAZZ SUITE FOR SEXTET IN MEMORY OF BOB THOMP-
    SON.

INFINITY   (1964)
    Jazz ensemble.   5 min.

THE INSURGENT   (1973)
    See THE BLACK EXPERIENCE (1973).

INTROSPECTION   (1968)
    See ABYSS.

J IS FOR LOVELINESS   (1962)
    Jazz ensemble.   3 min.   Arrangement for smaller ensemble
    recorded by Jamey Aebersold on Isis I-608.

J IS FOR LOVELINESS (1962)
    For melody and chord symbols see Baker, Arranging and
    Composing for the Small Ensemble: Jazz/R&B/Jazz-Rock,
    p. 51.

THE JAMAICAN STRUT (1970)
    String orchestra. 4 min. Creative Jazz Composers, 1976.

JAZZ MASS (1967)
    See LUTHERAN MASS. For the jazz mass (Roman Catholic)
    see CATHOLIC MASS FOR PEACE.

JAZZ SUITE FOR SEXTET IN MEMORY OF BOB THOMPSON (1971)
    Alternate title is IN MEMORIAM: FREEDOM. Trumpet, tenor
    saxophone, trombone, piano, bass, and drums. One movement.
    15 min.

JUST BEFORE SEPTEMBER (1968)
    Jazz ensemble. 5 min.

JUST BEFORE SEPTEMBER (1968)
    For melody and chord symbols see Baker, Arranging and
    Composing for the Small Ensemble: Jazz/R&B/Jazz-Rock,
    p. 45.

K.C.C. (1966)
    Jazz ensemble. 8 min.

KALEIDOSCOPE (1968)
    Jazz ensemble, narrators, chorus (SATB), soloists, and string
    orchestra. See BLACK AMERICA.

KALEIDOSCOPE (1976)
    Violin, violoncello, and piano. See CONTRASTS.

KENTUCKY OYSTERS (1958)
    Jazz ensemble. 8 min. Arrangement for smaller ensemble
    recorded by the George Russell Sextet (Riverside RLP-9341:
    Stratusphunk).

KENTUCKY OYSTERS (1958)
    Jazz nonet (trumpet, alto saxophone, tenor saxophone, trom-
    bone, baritone saxophone, guitar, piano, electric bass, and
    drums). 8 min. Three Fifteen West Fifty-Third Street Corp.
    (Dave Baker Jazz Rock Series), 1971.

KENTUCKY OYSTERS (1958)
    For melody and chord symbols see Baker, Arranging and Com-
    posing for the Small Ensemble: Jazz/R&B/Jazz-Rock (p. 53)
    and Jazz Improvisation, (p. 109).

KID STUFF (1972)
    See SONGS OF THE NIGHT.

KOSBRO (1973; revised in 1975)
>   Orchestra. App. 13 min. Associated Music, 1975. Commis-
>   sioned by and dedicated to Paul Freeman. First performance
>   (1974) by the Houston Symphony, Paul Freeman, conductor.

LACYPSO (1974)
>   Jazz ensemble. 10 min.

LE ROI (1957)
>   Jazz ensemble. 8 min. Recordings of LE ROI arranged for
>   smaller ensembles include those by Charles Tyler (ESP 1059:
>   Eastern Man Alone); by Philly Joe Jones and Elvin Jones (At-
>   lantic 1428: Together); and by the Hector Costita Sexteto (Fer-
>   mata FB-97: Impacto).

LE ROI (1957)
>   For melody and chord symbols see Baker, Arranging and Com-
>   posing for the Small Ensemble: Jazz/R&B/Jazz-Rock (p. 42)
>   and Jazz Improvisation (p. 43.)

LET'S GET IT ON (1970)
>   Jazz ensemble. 10 min.

LET'S GET IT ON (1970)
>   Jazz nonet (trumpet, alto saxophone, tenor saxophone, trombone,
>   baritone saxophone, guitar, piano, electric bass, and drums).
>   10 min. Three Fifteen West Fifty-Third Street Corp. (Dave
>   Baker Jazz Rock Series), 1971.

LEVELS: A CONCERTO FOR SOLO CONTRABASS, JAZZ BAND,
>   FLUTE QUARTET, HORN QUARTET, AND STRING QUARTET
>   (1973)
>   Three movements. 35 min. Commissioned by and dedicated to
>   Bertram Turetzky. First performance (1973) at the Claremont
>   Music Festival (Claremont, California). David N. Baker, con-
>   ductor; Bertram Turetzky, contrabass. This work was nominated
>   for the Pulitzer Prize in 1973.

LIGHT BLUE, DARK BLUE (1962)
>   Jazz ensemble. 10 min.

THE LITTLE PRINCESS (1959)
>   Jazz ensemble. 10 min.

THE LITTLE PRINCESS (1959)
>   For melody and chord symbols see Baker, Arranging and Com-
>   posing for the Small Ensemble: Jazz/R&B/Jazz-Rock, p. 47.

LITTLE PRINCESS WALTZ (1959)
>   String orchestra. $3\frac{1}{2}$ min. Creative Jazz Composers, 1976.

A LITTLE WALTZ (1973)
>   Jazz ensemble. 5 min.

THE LONE RANGER AND THE GREAT HORACE SILVER (1957)
Jazz ensemble. 7 min.

LOUIS ARMSTRONG IN MEMORIAM (1972)
Jazz ensemble. Seven movements: Introduction; Genesis;
Funeral March; The Creoles; 1928; Evolution; Louis/Life/Love.
40 min. Commissioned by Grand Valley State College. First
performance (1973) at Grand Valley State College by the Indiana
University Jazz Ensemble, David N. Baker, conductor.

LUMO (1973)
Jazz ensemble. 7 min.

LUNACY (1959)
Original title: STONE NUTS. Jazz ensemble. 7 min. Arrange-
ment for smaller ensemble recorded by the George Russell
Sextet (Decca DL-74183: The George Russell Sextet in Kansas
City.

LUNACY (1959)
Original title: STONE NUTS. Jazz nonet (trumpet, alto saxophone, tenor saxophone, trombone, baritone saxophone, guitar,
piano, electric bass, and drums). 7 min. Three Fifteen West
Fifty-Third Street Corp. (Dave Baker Jazz Rock Series), 1971.

LUTHERAN MASS (1967)
Chorus (SATB) and jazz septet. Text based on the liturgy of
the Lutheran Church. Ten parts: Prelude; Introit; Kyrie;
Gloria; Gradual; Credo; Sanctus; Agnus Dei; Nunc Dimittis;
Postlude. Also includes the offertory Create in Me a Clean
Heart (Biblical text). 45 min. Commissioned by the National
Lutheran Campus Ministry. First performance (1967) in Bloom-
ington, Indiana. David N. Baker, conductor.

LYDIAN APRIL (1959)
Jazz ensemble. 12 min.

MA 279 BOUGALOO (1970)
Jazz ensemble. 10 min.

MA 279 BOUGALOO (1970)
Jazz nonet (trumpet, alto saxophone, tenor saxophone, trombone,
baritone saxophone, guitar, piano, electric bass, and drums).
10 min. Three Fifteen West Fifty-Third Street Corp. (Dave
Baker Jazz Rock Series), 1971.

MABA TILA (1973)
Jazz ensemble. 12 min.

MABA TILA (1973)
Jazz septet (trumpet, alto saxophone, tenor saxophone,
trombone, piano, bass, and drums). 4-10 min. Studio
PR, 1976).

MABA TILA (1973)
For melody and chord symbols see Baker, Advanced Improvisation, pp. 244-245.

MAKE A JOYFUL NOISE (1963)
Jazz ensemble. 5 min.

MALCOLM (in progress)
Opera based on the life of Malcolm X. Libretto by Mari Evans.

M'AM (1953)
Jazz ensemble. 9 min.

MAMA TU (1973)
Jazz ensemble. 11 min.

MARTYRS: MALCOLM, MEDGER, MARTIN (1968)
See BLACK AMERICA.

MAUMA (1973)
Jazz ensemble. 15 min.

MAUMA (1973)
For melody and chord symbols see Baker, Advanced Improvisation, p. 245.

MEET THE ARTIST (1970)
Theme music for television show "Meet the Artist."

MEN SHALL TELL OF THE LORD (1966)
Chorus (SATB), narrators, jazz ensemble, string orchestra, and dancers. See PSALM 22.

MEN SHALL TELL OF THE LORD (1966)
Soprano and piano. Arrangement of "Men Shall Tell of the Lord" from PSALM 22.

MID-EVIL (1973)
Jazz ensemble. 5 min.

LE MIROIR NOIR (1974)
Jazz ensemble. 12-15 min.

LE MIROIR NOIR (1974)
Jazz septet (trumpet, alto saxophone, tenor saxophone, trombone, piano, bass, and drums). 4-10 min. Studio PR, 1976.

LE MIROIR NOIR (1974)
Orchestra, soprano, and jazz quartet. See LE CHAT QUI PECHE.

MOD WALTZ (1970)
String orchestra. 4 min. Creative Jazz Composers, 1976.

MODALITY, TONALITY, AND FREEDOM   (1962)
    Alto saxophone, 5 trumpets, 4 trombones, tuba, piano, bass,
    and drums. Three movements. 30 min. Commissioned by and
    dedicated to Jamey Aebersold.

MON   (1973)
    Jazz ensemble. 10 min. Same tune as "L'Odeur du Blues"
    (LE CHAT QUI PECHE).

MONKIN' AROUND   (1962)
    Jazz ensemble. 5 min. Dedicated to Thelonius Monk.

A MORNING THOUGHT   (1973)
    Jazz ensemble. 12 min.

MY GOD, MY GOD   (1966)
    See PSALM 22.

MY INDIANAPOLIS   (1969)
    See REFLECTIONS.

THE NEW AMERICANS   (1971)
    See THE BLACK FRONTIER.

NIGHT: 4 SONGS   (1972)
    See SONGS OF THE NIGHT.

NINA, EVER NEW   (1966)
    Jazz ensemble. 15 min.

NOCTURNE   (1974)
    See SIX POEMES NOIR POUR FLUTE ET PIANO.

NONE A PLACE ME BE   (1971)
    Jazz ensemble. 10 min.

NONE A PLACE ME BE   (1971)
    For melody and chord symbols see Baker, Advanced Improvisa-
    tion, p. 246.

NOW THAT HE IS SAFELY DEAD   (1970)
    Chorus (SATB) unaccompanied. See FIVE SONGS TO THE SUR-
    VIVAL OF BLACK CHILDREN.

NOW THAT HE IS SAFELY DEAD   (1972)
    Soprano and piano. See SONGS OF THE NIGHT.

OBSERVATION   (1968)
    See ABYSS

L'ODEUR DU BLUES   (1974)
    Jazz ensemble. See MON.

L'ODEUR DU BLUES   (1974)
Orchestra, soprano and jazz quartet.   See LE CHAT QUI PECHE.

OMNISCIENT   (1974)
See SIX POEMES NOIR POUR FLUTE ET PIANO.

ONE FOR J.S.   (1969)
Jazz ensemble.   7 min.

ONE FOR J.S.   (1969)
Jazz nonet (trumpet, alto saxophone, tenor saxophone, trombone,
baritone saxophone, guitar, piano, electric bass, and drums).
7 min.   Three Fifteen West Fifty-Third Street Corp.   (Dave
Baker Jazz Rock Series), 1970.

125th STREET   (1968)
Jazz ensemble, narrators, chorus (SATB), soloists, and string
orchestra.   See BLACK AMERICA.

125th STREET   (1969)
Jazz nonet (trumpet, alto saxophone, tenor saxophone, trombone,
baritone saxophone, guitar, piano, electric bass, and drums).
10 min.   Three Fifteen West Fifty-Third Street Corp.   (Dave
Baker Jazz Rock Series), 1970.   Dedicated to Dr. Martin Luther
King, Jr.   Adaptation of materials from BLACK AMERICA
(1968).

121 BANK   (1960)
Jazz ensemble.   10 min.   Dedicated to George Russell.   Arrangement for smaller ensemble recorded by the George Russell Sextet (Decca DL-79220:   The George Russell Sextet at the
Five Spot).

THE OPTIMIST   (1969)
See FIVE SETTINGS FOR SOPRANO AND PIANO.

PAGANINI VARIATIONS   (1967)
See ETHNIC VARIATIONS ON A THEME OF PAGANINI.

PAPILLON   (1974)
See SIX POEMES NOIR POUR FLUTE ET PIANO.

PARADES TO HELL   (1969)
See FIVE SETTINGS FOR SOPRANO AND PIANO.

PASSACAGLIA   (1970)
Piano.   See FIVE SHORT PIECES FOR PIANO.

PASSACAGLIA   (1976)
Violoncello, violoncello, and piano.   See CONTRASTS.

PASSION   (1956)
Original title: SANDRA.   Jazz ensemble.   5 min.

PASSION (1956)
For melody and chord symbols see Baker, Arranging and Composing for the Small Ensemble: Jazz/R&B/Jazz-Rock, p. 53.

PASSIONS (1966)
Brass quintet. 8 min. Published in Montreal as part of the Montreal Brass Quartet Series. Commissioned by the Montreal Brass Quintet.

PASTORALE (1959)
String quartet. 5 min. Fema Music Publications (Interlochen Series), 1975.

PEACE, MY BROTHER (1966)
Jazz ensemble. 7 min. Arrangement of "I Will Tell of Thy Name" from PSALM 22.

PENETRATION (1968)
See ABYSS.

PENICK (1970)
Jazz ensemble. 10 min. Recorded by the Indiana University Jazz Ensemble, David N. Baker, conductor (Canterbury Records, no number: Jazz at Canterbury).

PENICK (1970)
Jazz nonet (trumpet, alto saxophone, tenor saxophone, trombone, baritone saxophone, guitar, piano, electric bass, and drums). 10 min. Three Fifteen West Fifty-Third Street Corp. (Dave Baker Jazz Rock Series), 1971.

PERCEPTION (1968)
See ABYSS.

PIECE FOR VIOLONCELLO AND PIANO (1966)
10 min.

PO' NED (1956)
Jazz ensemble. 10 min.

POPPY FLOWER (1972)
See SONGS OF THE NIGHT.

PRAISE HIM (1966)
See PSALM 22.

PRELUDE (1967)
Jazz ensemble. 8 min.

PRELUDE (1967)
Jazz nonet (trumpet, alto saxophone, tenor saxophone, trombone, baritone saxophone, guitar, piano, electric bass, and drums). 8 min. Three Fifteen West Fifty-Third Street Corp. (Dave

Baker Jazz Rock Series), 1970. Also published in Baker,
Arranging and Composing for the Small Ensemble: Jazz/R&B/
Jazz-Rock, pp. 168-173.

THE PROFESSOR (1966)
Jazz ensemble. 10 min.

THE PROFESSOR (1966)
Jazz nonet (trumpet, alto saxophone, tenor saxophone, trombone,
baritone saxophone, guitar, piano, electric bass, and drums).
10 min. Three Fifteen West Fifty-Third Street Corp. (Dave
Baker Jazz Rock Series), 1971.

THE PROFESSOR (1966)
For melody and chord symbols see Baker, Arranging and Composing for the Small Ensemble: Jazz/R&B/Jazz-Rock, p. 54.

PROMISE AND PERFORMANCE (1974)
Music for a documentary drama. Text by Dr. Victor Amend.
One hour.

PSALM 22 (1966)
A modern jazz oratorio. Chorus (SATB), narrators, jazz en-
semble, string orchestra, and dancers. Biblical text. 18 parts:
Prelude; My God, My God; Yet Thou Art Holy; But I Am a
Worm; Narration; I Am Poured Out Like Water; Thou Dost Lay
Me in the Dust of Death; Narration; Deliver My Soul; Pastorale;
I Will Tell of Thy Name; Yea, to Him Shall All the Proud of the
Earth Bow Down; All the Ends of the Earth Shall Remember;
Narration; Praise Him; Praise Him; Men Shall Tell of the Lord;
Finale. One hour. Commissioned by and first performed (1966)
at Christian Theological Seminary (Indianapolis, Indiana).

PSALM 23 (1968)
Chorus (SATB) and organ. Biblical text. 12 min. Commissioned by the United Christian Missionaries. First performance
(1968) at Indiana University (Bloomington, Indiana) by the Cris-
pus Attucks High School Choir (Indianapolis, Indiana), Anderson
T. Dailey, conductor.

PSALM 150 (1969)
See CATHOLIC MASS FOR PEACE.

RAMU (1972)
Jazz ensemble. 10 min.

THE REBEL (1973)
See THE BLACK EXPERIENCE (1973).

REFLECTIONS (1969)
Alternate title: MY INDIANAPOLIS. Jazz ensemble and orchestra. 20 min. Commissioned by the Indianapolis Arts Council for the Indianapolis Summer Symphony. First performance
(1969) by the Indianapolis Summer Symphony.

RELIGION (1970)
Chorus (SATB) unaccompanied. See FIVE SONGS TO THE SURVIVAL OF BLACK CHILDREN.

RELIGION (1972)
Soprano and string quartet. See SONGS OF THE NIGHT.

REVE (1974)
Flute and piano. See SIX POEMES NOIR POUR FLUTE ET PIANO.

REVE (1970)
Piano. See FIVE SHORT PIECES FOR PIANO. Also part of SONGS OF THE NIGHT (1972).

REX (1973)
Jazz ensemble. 5 min.

ROLY POLY (1968)
Jazz ensemble. 15 min.

ROLY POLY (1968)
Jazz nonet (trumpet, alto saxophone, tenor saxophone, trombone, baritone saxophone, guitar, piano, electric bass, and drums). 15 min. Three Fifteen West Fifty-Third Street Corp. (Dave Baker Jazz Rock Series), 1970.

ROLY POLY (1968)
For melody and chord symbols see Baker, Jazz Improvisation, p. 44.

ROMANZA AND MARCH (1961)
3 trombones. 5 min.

ROOTS (1976)
Violin, violoncello, and piano. Five movements: Walpurgisnacht; Blues Waltz; Sorrow Song, Calypso Row; Finale. 25 min. Commissioned by and dedicated to the Beaux Arts Trio. First performance to take place December 4, 1976 at the Library of Congress by the Beaux Arts Trio.

A SALUTE TO BEETHOVEN (1970)
Piccolo, flute, oboe, clarinet, bassoon, horn, backstage flute choir, jazz ensemble, and pre-recorded tape. 15 min. Commissioned by Sidney Foster and dedicated to Ludwig van Beethoven. First performance (1970) at Indiana University (Bloomington, Indiana); David N. Baker and Don Moses, conductors.

SANDRA (1956)
See PASSION.

SANGRE NEGRO (1974)
Jazz ballet. Jazz ensemble, flute choir, and percussion ensemble. 15 min. Commissioned by Marina Svetlova.

Choreography by John Schenz and Stephen Rausch. First performance (1974) at Indiana University (Bloomington, Indiana).
David N. Baker, conductor.

SANGRE NEGRO (1974)
    Jazz ensemble. 20 min.

SANGRE NEGRO (1974)
    Orchestra and jazz trio. See TWO IMPROVISATIONS FOR
    ORCHESTRA AND JAZZ COMBO.

SATCH (1976)
    Jazz septet (trumpet, alto saxophone, tenor saxophone, trombone,
    piano, bass, and drums). 4-10 min. Studio PR, 1976.

THE SCREEMIN' MEEMIES (1958)
    Jazz ensemble. 5 min. Recorded by the Indiana University Jazz
    Ensemble, David N. Baker, conductor (Silver Crest CBD-69-6B:
    1969. 15th National Conference. College Band Directors Nation-
    al Association).

SET (1976)
    Jazz septet (trumpet, alto saxophone, tenor saxophone, trombone,
    piano, bass, and drums). 4-10 min. Studio PR, 1976.

THE SEVEN LEAGUE BOOTS (1970)
    Jazz nonet (trumpet, alto saxophone, tenor saxophone, trombone,
    baritone saxophone, guitar, piano, electric bass, and drums).
    10 min. Three Fifteen West Fifty-Third Street Corp. (Dave
    Baker Jazz Rock Series), 1971.

SHADOWS (1966)
    Jazz ensemble. 8 min.

SHIMA 13 (1973)
    Jazz ensemble. 15 min.

SHIMA 13 (1973)
    Jazz septet (trumpet, alto saxophone, tenor saxophone, trombone,
    piano, bass, and drums). 4-10 min. Studio PR, 1976.

SILVER CHALICE (1966)
    Jazz ensemble. 15 min. Recorded by the Indiana University
    Jazz Ensemble, David N. Baker, conductor (Silver Crest CBD-
    69-6A: 1969. 15th National Conference. College Band Direc-
    tors National Association.

SIMPLICITY (1973)
    Jazz ensemble. 5 min.

SIX POEMES NOIR POUR FLUTE ET PIANO (1974)
    Rêve; Papillon, Omniscient; Chanson; Image; Nocturne. 13 min.

SLOW GROOVE (1970)
    String orchestra. 4 min. Creative Jazz Composers, 1976.

THE SMILE (1969)
    See FIVE SETTINGS FOR SOPRANO AND PIANO.

SOFT SUMMER RAIN (1968)
    Jazz ensemble. 5 min. Recorded by the Indiana University
    Jazz Ensemble, David N. Baker, conductor (Silver Crest CBD-
    69-6B: 1969. 15th National Conference. College Band Direc-
    tors National Association). Also recorded in an arrangement
    for smaller ensemble by Jack Wilson (Blue Note BST-84328:
    Song for My Daughter).

SOFT SUMMER RAIN (1968)
    For melody and chord symbols see Baker, Arranging and Com-
    posing for the Small Ensemble: Jazz/R&B/Jazz-Rock, p. 50.

SOLEIL D'ALTAMIRA (1974)
    Jazz ensemble. App. 6 min.

SOLEIL D'ALTAMIRA (1974)
    Orchestra, soprano, and jazz quartet. See LE CHAT QUI
    PECHE.

SOMBER TIME (1970)
    String orchestra. 3 min. Creative Jazz Composers, 1976.

SON-MAR (1968)
    Jazz ensemble. 7 min. Recorded by the Indiana University
    Jazz Ensemble, David N. Baker, conductor (Silver Crest CBD-
    69-6A: 1969. 15th National Conference. College Band Direc-
    tors National Association). Used as theme music for the tele-
    vision show "The Black Experience" (WTTV; Indianapolis, Indi-
    ana).

SON-MAR (1968)
    Jazz nonet (trumpet, alto saxophone, tenor saxophone, trombone,
    baritone saxophone, guitar, piano, bass, and drums). 7 min.
    Three Fifteen West Fifty-Third Street Corp. (Dave Baker Jazz
    Rock Series), 1970.

SONATA FOR BRASS QUINTET AND PIANO (1970)
    Three movements. 15 min. First performance (1972) at In-
    diana University (Bloomington, Indiana). Helena P. Freire, pi-
    ano.

SONATA FOR PIANO (1968)
    Three movements: Black Art; A Song--After Paul Laurence Dun-
    bar; Coltrane. 25 min. Commissioned by and dedicated to
    Natalie Hinderas.

SONATA FOR PIANO AND STRING QUINTET (1971)
    Four movements. App. 38 min. AAMOA Press. Recorded

by Helena Freire, pianist (AAMOA NS-7401). Commissioned by and dedicated to Helena Freire. First performance (1972) at Indiana University (Bloomington, Indiana). Helena Freire, piano.

SONATA FOR TUBA AND STRING QUARTET (1971)
Four movements. App. 20 min. Recorded by Harvey Phillips, tuba, and the Composers String Quartet (Golden Crest CRS-4122). Commissioned by and dedicated to Harvey Phillips.

SONATA FOR TWO PIANOS (1971)
Four movements. 25 min. Commissioned by and dedicated to Ken and Frina Boldt.

SONATA FOR VIOLA AND PIANO (1966)
. Three movements. 15 min. Commissioned by Hugh Partridge.

SONATA FOR VIOLA, GUITAR, AND CONTRABASS (1973)
Four movements. 25 min. Commissioned by and dedicated to Hugh Partridge.

SONATA FOR VIOLIN AND CELLO (1974)
One movement. 7 min.

SONATA FOR VIOLIN AND PIANO (1967)
Alternate title: SONATA IN ONE MOVEMENT. 12 min. Commissioned by and dedicated to David Collins. First performance (1967) at the Indianapolis Museum of Art. David Collins, violin.

SONATA FOR VIOLONCELLO AND PIANO (1973)
Three movements. App. 19 min. Associated Music, 1975. Recorded by Janos Starker, violoncello, and Alain Planès, piano (Columbia M-33432: Vol. 6, Black Composers Series).

SONATA IN ONE MOVEMENT (1967)
See SONATA FOR VIOLIN AND PIANO.

A SONG (1969)
Soprano and piano. See FIVE SETTINGS FOR SOPRANO AND PIANO.

A SONG (1976)
Violin, violoncello, and piano. See CONTRASTS.

A SONG--AFTER PAUL LAURENCE DUNBAR (1968)
See SONATA FOR PIANO.

A SONG OF MANKIND (1970)
Chorus (SATB), orchestra, jazz ensemble, rock band, vocal soloists, lights, and sound effects. One hour. Commissioned by Faith for a City, Inc. for the Indiana Sesquicentennial. This work is a seven-part cantata, each part of which was written by a different composer; David Baker wrote one part of this work. First performance (1971) at the Indiana War Memorial (Indianapolis, Indiana).

SONGS OF THE NIGHT (1972)
Soprano, string quartet, and piano (Rêve and Evening Song are
for solo piano; all other parts of this work are for soprano and
string quartet). 12 parts: Rêve; Night: 4 Songs (text by Langston Hughes); Fragments (text by Langston Hughes); Kid Stuff
(text by Frank Horne); Poppy Flower (text by Langston Hughes);
Borderline (text by Langston Hughes); Where Have You Gone?
(text by Mari Evans); Gethsemane (text by Arna Bontemps);
Religion (text by Conrad Kent Rivers); Now That He Is Safely
Dead (text by Carl Wendell Hines, Jr.); End (text by Langston
Hughes); Evening Song. App. 14½ min. Commissioned by and
dedicated to Rita Sansone. First performance (1972) at Indiana
University (Bloomington, Indiana). Rita Sansone, soprano.

SONS VOILES (1974)
Orchestra, soprano, and jazz quartet. See LE CHAT QUI
PECHE.

SORROW SONG (1976)
See ROOTS.

SOUL OF A SUMMER'S DAY (1969)
Jazz ensemble. 15 min.

SOUL OF '76 (1975)
Jazz ensemble. 15 min. J. C. Penney, 1975. Commissioned
by J. C. Penney in commemoration of the Bicentennial of the
United States.

SOUL ON ICE (1969)
See I HEARD MY WOMAN CALL.

SOUL SIX (1969)
Jazz ensemble. 10 min. Based on materials from I HEARD
MY WOMAN CALL.

SOUL SIX (1969)
For melody and chord symbols see Baker, Advanced Improvisation, pp. 246-247.

SPEPAI (1972)
Jazz ensemble. 10 min.

SPLOOCH (1962)
Jazz ensemble. 10 min.

STATUS SYMBOL (1973)
See THE BLACK EXPERIENCE (1973)

STEREOPHRENIC (1959)
Jazz ensemble. 9 min. Arrangement for smaller ensemble
recorded by the George Russell Septet (Riverside RLP-9412:
The Stratus Seekers).

STICKIN' (1973)
Jazz ensemble. 20 min.

STICKIN' (1973)
For melody and chord symbols see Baker, Advanced Improvisation, p. 247.

STONE NUTS (1959)
See LUNACY.

STRING QUARTET NO. 1 (1962)
One movement. 9 min. Commissioned by and dedicated to the Meredian String Quartet.

SUITE FOR UNACCOMPANIED VIOLIN (1975)
Five movements. 25 min. Commissioned by and dedicated to Ruggiero Ricci.

SUITE FROM BLACK AMERICA (1970)
Jazz ensemble. 12 min. Based on materials from BLACK AMERICA (1968). Won down beat award as the best composition of the 1970 National Collegiate Jazz Festival.

SUITE (SWEET) LOUIS (A TRIBUTE TO LOUIS ARMSTRONG) (1971)
Percussion ensemble. One movement. 15 min. Commissioned by the American Conservatory Percussion Ensemble and dedicated to Bobby Tillis.

SUMMER 1945 (1968)
See A SUMMER'S DAY IN 1945.

A SUMMER'S DAY IN 1945 (1968)
Alternate title: SUMMER 1945. Jazz ensemble and pre-recorded tape. 30 min.

THE SUNSHINE BOOGALOO (1970)
String orchestra. 4 min. Creative Jazz Composers, 1976.

TERRIBLE T (1962)
Jazz ensemble. 15 min.

TERRIBLE T (1962)
Jazz nonet (trumpet, alto saxophone, tenor saxophone, trombone, baritone saxophone, guitar, piano, electric bass, and drums). 15 min. Three Fifteen West Fifty-Third Street Corp. (Dave Baker Jazz Rock Series), 1970.

TERRIBLE T (1962)
For melody and chord symbols see Baker, Arranging and Composing for the Small Ensemble: Jazz/R&B/Jazz-Rock, p. 52.

THAT'S THE WAY, LORD NELSON (1968)
Jazz ensemble. 15 min. Commissioned by and dedicated to

Jim Nelson. First performance (1968) at Indiana University
(Bloomington, Indiana) by the Indiana University Jazz Ensemble,
David N. Baker, conductor.

THAT'S THE WAY, LORD NELSON (1968)
    Trumpet, tenor saxophone, bass and percussion. 12 min. Com-
    missioned by and dedicated to Jim Nelson.

THEME AND VARIATIONS (1970)
    Woodwind quintet. Theme and four variations. 8 min.

THEY WILL NOT TELL (1975)
    See GIVE AND TAKE.

THING (1959)
    Jazz ensemble. 5 min.

THOU DOST LAY ME IN THE DUST OF DEATH (1966)
    Chorus (SATB) unaccompanied. 4 min. Associated Music,
    1975. Arrangement of "Thou Dost Lay Me In the Dust of
    Death" from PSALM 22.

THOU DOST LAY ME IN THE DUST OF DEATH (1966)
    Chorus (SATB) and string orchestra. See PSALM 22.

THREE FOR MALCOLM (1970)
    Jazz ensemble. 15 min. Dedicated to Malcolm X.

THREE JAZZ MOODS (1963)
    Brass ensemble. Three movements. 15 min. Commissioned
    by Howard Liva for the Purdue Brass Choir.

THREE VIGNETTES (1968)
    Jazz ensemble and four French horns. Three movements.
    8 min.

THREE VIGNETTES (1968)
    For melody and chord symbols see Baker, Arranging and Com-
    posing for the Small Ensemble: Jazz/R&B/Jazz-Rock, pp. 43-
    44.

TO BIRD (1970)
    Piano. See FIVE SHORT PIECES FOR PIANO.

THE TRIAL OF CAPTAIN HENRY FLIPPER (1972)
    Incidental music for the television show "The Trial of Captain
    Henry Flipper" (NET).

A TRIBUTE TO WES (1972)
    Jazz ensemble. 25 min. Dedicated to Wes Montgomery.
    First performance (1972) at Indiana University (Bloomington,
    Indiana) by the Indiana University Jazz Ensemble, David N.
    Baker, conductor.

TRIPLET BLUES (1970)
    String orchestra. 4 min. Creative Jazz Composers, 1976.

TUFFY (1973)
    Jazz ensemble. 10 min.

TWENTY-FIFTH AND MARTINDALE (1973)
    Jazz ensemble. 12 min.

TWENTY-FIFTH AND MARTINDALE (1973)
    Jazz septet (trumpet, alto saxophone, tenor saxophone, trombone,
    piano, bass, and drums). 4-10 min. Studio PR, 1976.

TWO FACES OF THE BLACK FRONTIER (1971)
    Jazz ensemble. 7-15 min. Recorded by the Indiana University
    Jazz Ensemble, David N. Baker, conductor (Canterbury Records,
    no number: Jazz at Canterbury). Based on materials from THE
    BLACK FRONTIER.

TWO IMPROVISATIONS FOR ORCHESTRA AND JAZZ COMBO (1974)
    Orchestra and jazz trio (piano, bass, and drums). Two move-
    ments: Harlem Pipes (8 min.); Sangre Negro (7-10 min.). As-
    sociated Music, 1975. First performance (1974) by the Louis-
    ville Symphony Orchestra, Jorge Mester, conductor. Dan
    Haerle, piano; Rufus Reid, bass; Jack Gilfoy, drums.

UNCLA (1973)
    Jazz ensemble. 10 min.

UNCLEE (1973)
    Jazz ensemble. 12 min.

VERISM (1959)
    Jazz ensemble. 8 min.

VIBRATIONS (1972)
    Jazz ensemble. 6 min.

VORTEX (1962)
    Jazz ensemble. 6 min.

VOTIVE MASS FOR PEACE (1969)
    See CATHOLIC MASS FOR PEACE.

W830007K (1975)
    Jazz ensemble. 10 min. First performance (1976) at Indiana
    University (Bloomington, Indiana) by the Indiana University Jazz
    Ensemble, David N. Baker, conductor.

W830007K (1975)
    Jazz septet (trumpet, alto saxophone, tenor saxophone, trombone,
    piano, bass, and drums). 4-10 min. Studio PR, 1976.

A WALK WITH A CHILD   (1968)
    Voice and guitar.   Text by Andrew Jacobs, Jr.   3 min.   Music
    for use in Andrew Jacobs's 1968 congressional campaign.

WALPURGISNACHT   (1975)
    Jazz ensemble.   17 min.

WALPURGISNACHT   (1976)
    Violin, violoncello, and piano.   See ROOTS.

WALT'S BARBERSHOP   (1974)
    Jazz ensemble.   10 min.   Same tune as "Guadeloupe-Calypso"
    (LE CHAT QUI PECHE).

THE WALTZ   (1957)
    Jazz ensemble.   6 min.

WAR GEWESEN   (1959)
    Jazz ensemble.   6 min.   Arrangement for smaller ensemble
    recorded by the George Russell Sextet (Decca DL-74183:   The
    George Russell Sextet in Kansas City).

WESTERN SONG   (1966)
    Jazz ensemble.   15 min.

WHEN?   (1972)
    Jazz ensemble.   7-8 min.

WHEN?   (1972)
    For melody and chord symbols see Baker, Advanced Improvisa-
    tion, p. 248.

WHERE HAVE YOU GONE?   (1972)
    See SONGS OF THE NIGHT.

WHEW!!   (1972)
    Jazz ensemble.   20 min.

WHEW!!   (1972)
    For melody and chord symbols see Baker, Advanced Improvisa-
    tion, p. 248.

A WIND IN SUMMER   (1971)
    Jazz ensemble.   14 min.   Recorded by Toots Thielemans
    (unreleased).

WOODWIND QUINTET FROM THE BLACK FRONTIER   (1971)
    5 min.   From the music for the television series "The Black
    Frontier."

THE WRETCHED OF THE EARTH   (1968)
    See BLACK AMERICA.

YEA, TO HIM SHALL ALL THE PROUD OF THE EARTH BOW
DOWN (1966)
See PSALM 22.

YET THOU ART HOLY (1966)
See PSALM 22.

------------------- (in progress).
Flute, electric piano, vibraphone, electric bass, and percussion.
12-15 min. Commissioned by and dedicated to James Pellerite.

BIBLIOGRAPHY

Part I: Works about the composer

"Baker ... Jazz and the Liturgy." Indiana Alumni Magazine, De-
cember-January, 1970/71.

Barman, Greg. "Dave Baker--Jazzman." WIUS TipSheet (WIUS
Radio/Indiana University Student Broadcast Association), no.
33 (1975), pp. 4-6.

Bourne, Michael. "Defining Black Music: An Interview with David
Baker." down beat, 18 September 1969.

Caswell, Austin B. "David Baker: A Wise and Powerful Voice."
down beat, 14 October 1971.

Claghorn, Charles E. Biographical Dictionary of American Music.
West Nyack, N.Y.: Parker Publishing Company, 1973.

"Dave Baker's Sonata for Tuba and String Quartet for Harvey Phillips." down beat, 7 October 1976.

"David Baker." Musart 21 (February-March 1969): 44.

De Lerma, Dominique-René, ed. Black Music in Our Culture:
Curricular Ideas on the Subjects, Materials, and Problems.
Kent, Ohio: Kent State University Press, 1970.

_____. Reflections on Afro-American Music. Kent, Ohio: Kent
State University Press, 1973.

De Michael, Don. "Vortex: The Dave Baker Story." down beat,
17 December 1964.

Devens, Jeff. "Hoosier in Profile: Dave Baker." The Indianapolis
Star, 7 March 1971, Sunday Magazine section, pp. 12-18.

Everett, Thomas. "Five Questions, Fifty Answers." The Composer
5 (Spring-Summer 1974): 71-79.

Feather, Leonard. The Encyclopedia of Jazz in the Sixties. New
York: Horizon Press, 1966.

_____. The New Edition of the Encyclopedia of Jazz. New York:
Horizon Press, 1960.

Herrema, Robert D. "Choral Music by Black Composers. " The
Choral Journal 10 (1970): 15-17.

"He's a Black Man. " A series of 60-second nationwide radio spots
on prominent blacks sponsored by Sears and produced by Laub-
hon Moran-Noyes, Inc. (circa 1969). One of these programs
was about David Baker.

Hildreth, John. "The Keyboard Works of a Select Group of Black
Composers. " Ph.D. dissertation, Northwestern University, in
progress.

Jones, Eve. "Jazz Goes Classical. " The Indianapolis Star, 18
August 1968, Sunday Magazine section, pp. 42-45.

Keating, Sister Marie Thomas. "Jazz--A Tanglewood Conversation."
Music Educators Journal 57 (March 1971): 55-56.

"The Professor Plays Jazz. " Ebony, May 1970.

Putney, Michael. "Jazz Thrives--and Expands--on the Campus, "
National Observer, 24 May 1971.

Roach, Hildred. Black American Music: Past and Present. Boston: Crescendo Publishing Company, 1973.

Schuller, Gunther. "Indiana Renaissance. " Jazz Review 2 (September 1959): 48-50.

Solothurnmann, Jurg. "The Diverse David Baker. " Jazz Forum 7
(1973): 46-50.

Southern, Eileen. The Music of Black Americans. New York:
W. W. Norton, 1971.

Who's Who Among Black Americans, 1st ed. (1975-76), s.v. "Baker,
David Nathaniel, Jr. "

Part II: Works by the composer

Baker, David N. Advanced Improvisation. Chicago: Maher Publications, 1974.

_____. Arranging and Composing for the Small Ensemble: Jazz/
R&B/Jazz-Rock. Chicago: Maher Publications, 1970.

Baker, David N. "The Battle for Legitimacy: 'Jazz' Versus Academia." Black World, November 1973, pp. 20-27.

_____. "Bill Harris." down beat, 9 January 1969.

_____. "Bobby Bryant's 'Good Morning Starshine' Solo." down beat, 2 October 1969.

_____. "Charlie Parker's 'Now's the Time' Solo." down beat, 11 November 1971.

_____. "Clark Terry's 'Feedin' the Bean.'" down beat, 16 April 1970.

_____. Contemporary Techniques for the Trombone. 2 vols. New York: Charles Colin, 1974.

_____. "Curtis Fuller." down beat, 20 February 1969.

_____. "Curtis Fuller's 'Bongo Bop' Solo." down beat, 18 January 1973.

_____. "Dizzy Gillespie's 'One Bass Hit.'" down beat, 19 February 1970.

_____. "Double Brass: J. J. Johnson and Freddy Hubbard." down beat, 4 February 1971.

_____. "Gary Bartz' 'Rise' Solo." down beat, 24 June 1971.

_____. "Herbie Mann's 'Memphis Underground' Solo." down beat, 10 December 1970.

_____. "How to Use Strings in Jazz: Part II." down beat, 25 April 1974. Same as "How to Use Strings in Jazz." Orchestra News 14. The "Part II" appearing in the title of this article is erroneous. It has been included in the citation because it appears in the title of the article as printed in down beat. "How to Use Strings in Jazz" was published in its entirety in the April 25, 1974 issue.

_____. "How to Use Strings in Jazz." Orchestra News 14 (September 1974): 11.

_____. "Hubert Laws' 'Gula Matari' Solo." down beat, 15 April 1971.

_____. "J. J. Johnson, Part Two." down beat, 31 October 1968.

_____. "J. J. Johnson: Trombone Giant." down beat, 22 August 1968.

_____. Jazz chapter. In The Black American Reference Book, edited by Mabel M. Smythe. Englewood Cliffs, N. J.: Prentice Hall, Inc., 1976.

_____. Jazz Improvisation: A Comprehensive Method of Study for All Players. Chicago: Maher Publications, 1969.

_____. A Jazz Improvisation Method for Stringed Instruments. Volume One: Violin and Viola. Chicago: down beat Music Workshop Publications, 1976.

_____. A Jazz Improvisation Method for Stringed Instruments. Volume Two: Cello and Bass Viol. Chicago: down beat Music Workshop Publications, 1976.

_____. Jazz Improvisation--The Weak Link. " The Instrumentalist 26 (November 1971): 21-24.

_____. Jazz Styles and Analysis: Trombone. Chicago: Maher Publications, 1973.

_____. "Jazz: The Academy's Neglected Stepchild. " down beat, 23 September 1965.

_____. "Jean-Luc Ponty. " down beat, 21 August 1969.

_____. "Jeremy Steig's 'Superbaby' Solo. " down beat, 14 May 1970.

_____. "John Coltrane's 'Giant Steps' Solo and Composition. " down beat, 22 July 1971.

_____. "Johnny Hodges' 'Passion Flower' Solo. " down beat, 20 August 1970.

_____. "Kid Ory. " down beat, 1 March 1973.

_____. "Lew Soloff's 'Lucretia's Reprise' Solo. " down beat, 17 September 1970.

_____. "Miles Davis' 'Petits Machins' Solo. " down beat, 25 December 1969.

_____. "Milt Jackson's 'Theme from the Anderson Tapes. '" down beat, 2 March 1972.

_____. A New Approach to Ear Training for the Jazz Musician. Studio PR, 1976.

_____. "A Periodization of Black Music History. " In Reflections on Afro-American Music, edited by Dominique-René de Lerma. Kent, Ohio: Kent State University Press, 1973.

Baker, David N. "Pharoah Sanders' Solo 'Sun in Aquarius; Part Two.'" down beat, 22 June 1972.

_____. Review of Black Composers Series (Columbia Records). down beat, 10 October 1974.

_____. Review of Charles Ives: The 100th Anniversary (Columbia Masterworks M4-32504). down beat, 16 January 1975, p. 32.

_____. Review of The Evolving Bass, by Rufus Reid. down beat, 27 March 1975.

_____. "The Rhetorical Dimensions of Black Music: Past and Present." In Black Communication: Dimensions of Research and Instruction, edited by Jack L. Daniel. New York: Speech Communication Association, 1974.

_____. "Richard Davis' 'Shiny Stockings' Solo." down beat, 23 December 1971.

_____. "Roswell Rudd's 'Wherever June Bugs Go.'" down beat, 3 February 1972.

_____. "Stan Getz' 'Con Alma' Solo." down beat, 24 December 1970.

_____. "The String Approach in Jazz." (Part I of a series). Orchestra News 9 (March 1970): 5-6. Same as "The String Player in Jazz, Part I." down beat.

_____. "The String Approach in Jazz." (Part II of a series). Orchestra News 9 (May 1970): 8-9. Same as "The String Player in Jazz, Part II." down beat.

_____. "The String Approach in Jazz." (Part III of a series). Orchestra News 9 (September 1970): 10-11. Same as "The String Player in Jazz, Part III." down beat.

_____. "The String Player in Jazz, Part I." down beat, 5 March 1970. Same as "The String Approach in Jazz." (Part I of a series). Orchestra News.

_____. "The String Player in Jazz, Part II." down beat, 30 April 1970. Same as "The String Approach in Jazz." (Part II of a series). Orchestra News.

_____. "The String Player in Jazz, Part III." down beat, 28 May 1970. Same as "The String Approach in Jazz." (Part III of a series). Orchestra News.

_____. Techniques of Improvisation. Volume 1: A Method for Developing Improvisational Technique (Based on the Lydian Chromatic Concept by George Russell). Rev. ed. Chicago: Maher Publications, 1971.

_____. Techniques of Improvisation. Volume 2: The II V$_7$ Progression. Rev. ed. Chicago: Maher Publications, 1971.

_____. Techniques of Improvisation. Volume 3: Turnbacks. Chicago: Maher Publications, 1971.

_____. Techniques of Improvisation. Volume 4: Cycles. Chicago: Maher Publications, 1971.

_____. "Ted Dunbar's 'There Is No Greater Love' Solo." down beat, 31 January 1974.

_____. "Thad Jones' 'H and T Blues' Solo." down beat, 1 February 1973.

_____. "Thad Jones' Solo on 'Oh! Karen O.'" down beat, 20 December 1973.

_____. "Two B. B. King Solos." down beat, 10 June 1971.

_____. "Two Classic Louis Armstrong Solos." down beat, 16 September 1971.

_____. "Two Electronic Solos: 1. Jean-Luc Ponty's 'Sunday Walk' 2. Monk Montgomery's 'Big Boy.'" down beat, 23 July 1970.

_____. "Urbie's 'Slats' transcribed and annotated by David Baker." down beat, 3 June 1976.

_____. "Vic Dickensen's 'Bourbon Street Parade' Solo." down beat, 17 August 1972.

_____. "Wes Montgomery's 'Naptown Blues' Solo." down beat, 14 September 1972.

_____; Brown, Marian Tally; Klotman, Phyllis Rauch; Klotman, Robert Howard; Walker, Roslyn Adele; and Williams, Jimmy L. The Humanities Through the Black Experience. Kendall/Hunt Publishing Company, 1976.

CHAPTER III

NOEL G. DA COSTA

Noel Da Costa was born December 24, 1929 in Lagos, Nigeria. His family moved to the West Indies when he was three, and then to New York City eight years later. Of his early educational experiences Mr. Da Costa states: "At the age of eleven, I began to study violin with Dr. Barnabas Istok, a Hungarian violinist. I studied with him until I was twenty years old. Studying the violin made me sensitive to a lyric quality in music, which would later influence my compositional ideas. During my secondary educational studies, I was fortunate to be in the classes of Countee Cullen, the distinguished black poet. Mr. Cullen encouraged me to realize the organization of words into poetic and musical statements."

Mr. Da Costa's educational background includes a B.A. in music (1952) from Queens College of the City University of New York and an M.A. in theory and composition (1956) from Columbia University. While at Columbia he received a Seidl Fellowship in composition and two years later was awarded a Fulbright Fellowship to study with Luigi Dallapiccola in Florence, Italy. After two and one-half years, he returned to the United States and joined the faculty of the Hampton Institute. Prior to assuming his current position as Associate Professor of Music at Rutgers University, Mr. Da Costa also taught at Queens College and Hunter College.

Mr. Da Costa's compositional output includes a number of dramatic works and works for children in addition to compositions for a wide variety of vocal and instrumental combinations. Many of his works reflect his involvement in and knowledge of African, West Indian, and Afro-American folk traditions. Among his best-known works are Two Pieces for Unaccompanied Cello, Blue Mix (written for bassist Ron Carter), Silver Blue and Three Short Pieces for Alto Flute (recorded on Eastern Recordings by Antoinette Handy), Five Verses with Vamps, and The Singing Tortoise (a theater piece for children based on a Haitian folk tale). In addition to his activities as a composer and educator, Mr. Da Costa is vice president of the Society of Black Composers and continues his performing career as a violinist.

Noel G. Da Costa (courtesy of the composer)

Part I: General Questions

1. Q: What persons, events, and works (of art, literature, etc.)
   have influenced you in general as well as in terms of your
   musical activities?

   A: In my education I've had instruction from many persons;
   therefore, it is a little difficult to pinpoint which ones influenced me the most. Collectively I've been influenced by
   all of them. Looking back, especially on my earlier education, I can think of two names: Countee Cullen, the Afro-
   American poet, and Robert Dixon. I met these two men
   as a junior high school student at PS 139 in Harlem. It was
   in the English class of Mr. Cullen that I had my first composition lessons, so to speak; as a poet he tried to instill
   in us an appreciation of the English language. We wrote a
   lot of poetry, and I learned to sense the quality and sound
   of words in various structures. I think his influence was
   very significant. On the other hand, Robert Dixon, a music

teacher at the same institution, encouraged us to sing spirituals even though some of the teachers (who had very middle-class attitudes) would say, "Can't he find other pieces from the repertoire to have you kids sing instead of always those spirituals?" But he knew what he was doing, because the spiritual is at the foundation of a very rich heritage in the Afro-American experience. The pieces we sang are a part of my memory bank; they made a very deep impression on me as a youngster when I was in school.

Later on, going through the college and university scene, I had many teachers who were quite good. I want particularly to name Otto Luening and Jack Beeson because I was in their seminars in composition at Columbia University. But studying with Luigi Dallapiccola in Florence, Italy was a major experience for me, primarily because I was able to pick up valuable compositional technique from him. He was a very disciplined human being who was extremely broad in many areas outside of his immediate field, so the contact with him was extremely fruitful.

After returning to the United States on completion of a Fulbright experience with Dallapiccola, I accepted a position at Hampton Institute, a black college at Hampton, Virginia. This opened my eyes to the very fascinating cultural and educational programs in many of these schools. I enjoyed hearing the spirituals once again and seeing black youth at work getting involved with education on their own terms. This was a very striking contrast with my European experience as a student and I enjoyed it immensely.

I think that also from my early experiences with Countee Cullen I grew to appreciate the poetry of Langston Hughes, Countee Cullen himself, Paul Laurence Dunbar, and Owen Dodson. I have set the poetry of all of these poets to music.

I should make the point that the places I've lived in my life have had an effect on me. The fact that I was born in Lagos, Nigeria of parents from Kingston, Jamaica and left Africa at the age of three means that the African experience is not a vivid one. But I do recall impressions of growing up in the West Indies because I lived there from the age of three until I was eleven. We lived on the islands of Jamaica, Barbados, Antigua, and Trinidad. I enjoyed hearing the inflection of the language, and on each island I could detect a difference. This intrigued me no end. Coming here at the age of eleven to Harlem, I heard a very beautiful language change--very rich, covering a wide range from the deep South to the West Indies. I think it made me sensitive to inflection, which was later to serve me in composition.

2. Q: How would you define black music?
   A: I feel that there is a category that covers certain musics played and invented by blacks in the New World. At the base of this is a rich musical vocabulary arrived at from

a distillation of the original African sources. In the United
States we have a thematic heritage coming out of field hollers, chants, and spirituals. There are also strong musical
traditions in the West Indies and other parts of the Caribbean
and Latin America. As a child, I heard interesting music
when we were living in Trinidad. A calypso band would
come and practice in our back yard in the evenings and I
heard a music invented spontaneously, led by a singer who
often improvised his lyrics on the spot. He had great facility with the language and used the technique of speech
going in and out of song, which meant that he could set just
about anything to music. I have observed this in America
as well, in the performances of black rhythm and blues
singers who sing fantastic combinations of words and make
them fit. I think it is a familiarity with language and inflection which is at the root of all of this.

In terms of defining black music, a few essentials are
necessary. I feel that the black performer is most essential in performing this music. This may sound like a contradiction because it can be said that if one notates something, anyone should be able to play it; however, I am
speaking of black music which is not notated. Musical
notation, as far as we know, is Western and is not at the
heart of the original idea behind black music in the New
World. Those of us who are involved with the notated experience have to realize that the notes which we put on
paper aren't enough, regardless of how close we come to
indicating what we want. We still need players and singers
with a certain heritage at their fingertips, performers who
can extend themselves beyond what is on the printed page,
even to the point of going well beyond what is normally
expected. We are trained in conservatories to play with a
certain tone and a "correct" technique, but a player who is
involved with expressing an idea may feel that all the training is inadequate. To fully express himself he must draw
on techniques which are not necessarily a part of the Western aesthetic. This ties in with my second point, which is
that there are certain inflections in black music. A piece
played by different individuals should not sound the same.
The quality of sound that one makes as a singer or the air
that is blown through a saxophone is very special; it can be
imitated, but I doubt if it can be duplicated. Those of us
who are formally trained and who think we are writing
black music might be fooled because we have all of this
academic background; at a certain point we have to leave
it behind and, if we are lucky, come up with an aesthetic
which is closer to our heritage.

3. Q: What features of your own music do you see as uniquely
        black (in terms of both musical and philosophical considera-
        tions)?
    A: I stay away from analyzing my own work; I leave that for
        others to do. But I have been conscious of one or two

things in my output. In a work called <u>Five Verses with</u> <u>Vamps</u>, I used the idea of the vamp as found in jazz and the end tag which is found in many jazz pieces as well as at the end of popular songs. I used these two concepts as structural devices, which are at the heart of this composition. The idea of repeating certain fragments and then moving on is a device which also works well in this piece. In another work, <u>Extempore Blue</u> for solo piano, I attempted a notated synthesis of blues style. I've heard this piece in concerts and the reaction indicates that it's successful. Whether these things are considered black depends on who is listening and what their point of reference is!

4. Q: In what ways is your music a reflection of your personal philosophy (social, political, etc.)?

   A: That's a tough one. I feel that what one writes as a composer should be in harmony with his social-political thinking. As a composer dealing in symbols, it is difficult to say in words what one feels. To say what I feel philosophically would take a major essay. I'd rather let who I am come through in my compositions, and maybe I'll write an extended essay later in life.

5. Q: What do you see as the position or role of the black artist in contemporary society?

   A: The role of the black artist in this culture is not fully recognized. It is as though he does not officially exist! Consider the major music journals. How often is a piece by a black composer analyzed and made available for critical evaluation? How often is his work published by a leading establishment company? It seems as if there are special enclaves and musical cliques in the white political musical structure. Black artists must try to get into a situation of power so that they can direct their words to people who are basically receptive!

   One comment I would like to make is that Eileen Southern's journal <u>The Black Perspective in Music</u> is a marvelous journal. Professor Southern gives the composers a regular listing of their new compositions, and also an opportunity to write analytic essays from <u>their</u> perspective.

6. Q: Please discuss any problems you may have encountered in getting your works performed, published, and recorded.

   A: Well, some of that I've included in my answer to question five. You can usually get a composition heard if it involves one or two people. If you have a larger ensemble--twelve or more performers--it's difficult unless you are at an institution where the performers will do it free of charge. I find that unaccompanied works and works for under four people can usually be heard.

   Concerning publication: I have a couple of pieces officially in print in the normal commercial outlets. This is just not adequate at all. I feel that we have to get involved in organizing companies ourselves, making this music available either in composer manuscript editions or, in the case of the shorter works, engraved editions. Having works published by a major company can be very frustrating because often the company will look through your entire compositional output and only pick up the one or two pieces which fit into their idea of what is marketable. We need to work around this and try to get organized. I have formed my own company--Atsoc Music[1]--and through this company I will have things available for anyone who is interested. At first it will be my own works; later I would like to include others if they want.

Recording presents some problems because of the expense involved. Without personal resources and financial assistance it is difficult to get pieces recorded.

6A. Q: How much of your actual output has ever been performed? Published? Recorded?

A: I have compositions that have never been heard; however, I would say that by and large most of my works have been heard at least once. There's an old saying that you can have a piece played once but then you have difficulty getting it heard the second time around; it's really the case, I think.

Only two compositions have been published.[2] I'm getting a lot of mail from people who have heard compositions of mine and are asking for copies, so I'm sending out a lot of music myself. Later on, hopefully, distribution can be handled by an outlet firm, with Atsoc doing the publishing only.

I have two works recorded, both by Antoinette Handy on Contemporary Black Images in Music for the Flute.[3] These two works are Silver-Blue and Three Short Pieces for Alto Flute. These are the only two available.

6B. Q: Have you encountered difficulty in getting your works programmed?

A: Yes, but not for any reason other than the fact that there are many composers around; the groups who play our music have to perform the works of a large number of composers, so some of us are not heard quite as often as one might like. It's very important to hear your works, and this is the reason that the Society of Black Composers is active. We are arranging (on a shoe-string) to give concerts and make ourselves known at large. Due to financial limitations we can only give concerts if invited. But I think that if we had the opportunity to give a series of concerts every year, it might lead to recordings of our works and serve as a rich source of new music by black composers.

Hearing each other's works is a vital thing. Although at the moment the Society of Black Composers has an undetermined head count, we have between ten and sixteen composers whose works we can schedule at any time. We have

the instrumentalists of the Symphony of the New World as
possible performers in anything we do, and we have a
group of sixteen instrumentalists who could be called at a
moment's notice to play our works. But to sponsor all of
this we need funds!

6C. Q: Are there specific problems in getting a satisfactory performance? Exemplify and discuss.

A: Yes. If you have a group and they are doing you a favor
by playing for a small amount, they are not available for
unlimited rehearsal. At times you must get the work re-
hearsed in one or two rehearsals, which is usually not
enough. There are other considerations. For example,
at a place like Indiana University, you have a built-in situation in that you can utilize the talented instrumentalists
who are right there as students. Here[4] you accept those
who are available or who are not involved in a major recording session that week; you might not always have your
first choice. In a city like this, performing new music is
done in between recording dates or the other activities the
players must be involved with to survive!

7. Q: What do you consider, at this point in your life, to be your
most significant achievement(s) aside from your compositions?

A: Actually, just to be in a good frame of mind in the
context of the difficult and contradictory society here in
America.

8. Q: What do you see as the responsibilities and obligations of
the educational system (at all levels) to the study of black
music?

A: Speaking as a person who is involved in education,[5] this is
certainly a neglected area. The musical foundation at most
American colleges and universities is based on the European
musical past. It means getting involved with music from
Gregorian chant on down, and every student supposedly gets
a thorough grounding in this whether that's his natural bent
or not. I feel that, especially in the great state universities, other options should be there; the opportunity should
be provided for the study of Oriental music, African music,
Afro-American music, and so on. I see some movement
in that direction at UCLA and a few other spots, but it's
not enough.

On the regular college music scene, I think an Afro-
American student should be able, for example, to study harmony in a situation where the musical examples would be
drawn not from European sources but from the music of
Duke Ellington and others. This would appeal not only to
black students, but also to white students--to all American
students who appreciate jazz and the music of the popular

culture. I think that making these additional courses available would be of great service in broadening the concept of music study in America.

Of course it really starts with conditioning on the elementary and secondary levels. Educators in those areas should try to restructure and give their students a varied approach to American music-making which would include the Afro-American experience. Some attempts are being made in certain black schools coming out of the individual initiative of the teachers, but youths of varied backgrounds should also share this experience.

9. Q: Do you feel that the people who write about your music (critics in particular) understand what you are doing? Exemplify and discuss.

    A: Some of them do, but on the whole the critic is essentially involved with his job and that job is to attend concerts. Quite often, for one reason or another, he would rather not be there. So he's actually doing the very routine job of attending the concert for those who could not attend (or who do not attend concerts) and reporting the event in such a way that they feel they've attended the concert because they read the next day that such-and-such happened, that so-and-so's piece was glorious or not so good, and that someone made a mistake.

    I feel that we need some significant music criticism, where the critic has time to study a score and make a very thorough discussion of the work in question. But I don't think we have much of that happening at the moment.

10. Q: What advice would you give to the aspiring young black composer?

    A: Even before he is in college he should have a grounding in Afro-American music. By that I mean he should use recordings and try to listen to as much music coming out of his own heritage as he can. He should hear the blues. He should hear King Oliver and Jelly Roll Morton. He should be aware of Duke Ellington and his contributions. He should be aware of the creative output of those fantastic black pianists who have revolutionized keyboard style--Earl Hines, Art Tatum, and others. Also, the notated music of Scott Joplin should be made available to him. After being saturated with this music, he will have a foundation from which to take what he can and arrive at his own creative world. If he attends college, it might be a good idea to study something else--literature, psychology, science, philosophy, aesthetics--to be as broad as possible. Sometimes a composition student can pick up the technical details from one or two teachers if they are the right people for him, and he can still maintain his individuality. If he must go through the sequence of courses in the regular academic sense, he should try to get as much as he can from the experience, but avoid getting lost in the European aesthetic.

Part II: Music Questions

1.   Q: When you sit down to begin a new composition on your own initiative or inspiration (as opposed to a commissioned work), what procedure or approach do you follow?

2.   Q: When composing a commissioned work or a work written for a specific occasion or person, does your procedure or approach differ from the one you described in question one? If so, in what way?

(Ed. note: Mr. Da Costa chose to answer questions one and two together.)

A: I think question one and question two are the same. If it's a commissioned work, it's a work that I have been asked about beforehand and one which might possibly coincide with what I wanted to do anyway. I find that the idea of getting involved with a work on one's own initiative happens whether the work is commissioned or not.

If, however, I am writing for a specific individual, I take that person's technique into account. When I wrote a piece for Ronald Lipscomb, a cellist friend of mine, I had the sound of his tone in my head. I had heard him many times and was familiar with his technical equipment, and this helped me structure a piece for him. I enjoy working like that. I would write a song cycle for a singer named Barbara Grant in the same way; I know her range and of her exceptional musicality, and it gives me additional possibilities. So when working with individuals, I take their background (and mine) and what they do on their instruments in the positive sense and just write a piece for them, which can then be performed later by other people.

Q: After you determine what the parameters are, how do you write? Do you start with melodic sketches, rhythmic materials, form? What kind of procedure do you follow?

A: It varies from composition to composition. We are getting into a difficult area, that is, how one works. A piece comes in many, many ways. It depends on the medium. Usually I make a sketch of some kind. At times I might not know how I can go ahead, but eventually things start happening and out of these notes I can make some sense. Usually when I have a text, though, the melody comes easier. I'm able to hear lines from words and inflection. Maybe that's why I've written a lot of pieces which include the voice.

For every piece I might have a different approach. This would mean that I would have to analyze how I work, and I'd rather not do that right now.

3. Q: In general, with regard to your writing, what genre(s) do you prefer?

   A: I enjoy writing pieces which include the human voice. I also enjoy writing abstract pieces for small combinations of instruments. However, of late I'm getting into a need for larger ensembles, and it could be that I will be doing works for larger instrumental groups in the near future.

4. Q: What do you consider your most significant composition? Please discuss.

   A: Actually, the one I'm working on now; whatever you're working on at the present is always the most important in the creative sense. But I did like some of the discoveries I made in writing a piece called Jes' Grew Variations, a work for solo violin. It's a homage to Buddy Bolden, the early New Orleans trumpet player. In this piece I get involved with feeling and with looking back for a quasi-improvisational style. The first section I call "Chant," and in it the solo instrument is doing just that, in a very free way. The second movement is a theme and variation idea in which the tune "I Thought I Heard Buddy Bolden Say" is played and elaborated upon. The third part is a very fast, outgoing, rhythmic movement. I feel that the sounds I captured in this piece are right and are quite different from other things I had done before. The piece was the result of my involvement with early New Orleans musical styles; it's an example of how one can get back into one's own heritage, in a sense. After all of my exposure to the music of the West, a conflict arose and I found myself asking questions like "Who are you really?" (I am speaking here about what comes out compositionally which, due to certain influences, is in conflict with one's "true" voice.) I think that especially composers who have worked through universities have to face questions like that.

      Composition cannot be taught; one can guide a student in certain ways, but the student actually teaches himself. However, the influence of the teacher is great. In certain universities and conservatories, all the students write a certain way; if you deviate, you're either not understood or you're considered not representative of that school. A composer must take stock of himself, re-evaluate, and attempt to come up with a significant statement of his own. I think that every artist passes through a time when his influences show; hopefully, he moves out of this and his own true statement then emerges. Jes' Grew is important because it represents this in my own development.

5. Q: Please comment on your treatment of the following musical elements and give examples from your compositions that illustrate the techniques you describe:
      A. Melody
      B. Harmony
      C. Rhythm

D. Form
E. Improvisation
F. Text (both choice and treatment)
G. Instrumentation or medium (both in terms of choice of particular combinations as well as how you treat them compositionally)

NDC: I consider this a technical question that would best be answered if I mailed in some information after reflecting upon it.

(Ed. note: Mr. Da Costa, in a letter responding to our request for his answer to this question, wrote: "I have had second thoughts about question #5 concerning technical points, and would prefer not to submit an answer. It is a very complex question and I do not have the time now to justly answer it." Mr. Da Costa's decision not to answer this question is in keeping with the option extended to all of the composers allowing them the freedom to choose not to answer any of the questions they did not wish to discuss.)

6. Q: Have difficulties with performance practice (inflection, phrasing, etc.) been a significant problem in having your works performed to your own satisfaction?

A: I am quite concerned about inflection and phrasing. Those musicians who can extend themselves beyond what is normally accepted (and into what might even be called ugly playing at times) are the people I enjoy having play and sing my works. I learn a great deal from the performers themselves; I, too, am active in playing and conducting my own works.

All I can say about this is that there is a musical inflection that I'm hearing. It is a part of my notation, but notation can only go so far. Certain instrumentalists understand this; they take the notes I put on paper and make them work. [6]

Q: Do you feel constricted by the limitations of conventional notation when it comes to getting the kind of inflection and phrasing you want?

A: I think so. Occasionally I can find ways of indicating what I want by inventing notation. I have done a little of that in a piece of mine for organ called Spiritual Set. The first part involves held notes, and I had to find a way of notating what I had in mind. With each piece we find ways of notating customary techniques like the fall-off or the slur into a note, but in addition to that I think we need to have a way to indicate types of intonations where a player might be asked to play flat, come up, sink back into flatness at a certain point, and come up again. This is a relatively new area. We have to invent ways of notating what we hear as accurately as we can; the players must take it from there.

7. Q: What major works are currently in progress? Please describe and discuss.

A: I'm doing a work for symphony orchestra, chorus, and two soloists--a soprano and a soprano saxophonist doubling on tenor saxophone. This is a large-scale work and was commissioned by the New York State Council on the Arts in conjunction with the Symphony of the New World. The working title is A Ceremony of Spirituals, and I've gone back to the Afro-American spiritual for the thematic basis of the composition. It will be a three-movement work.

The second large-scale piece I have in mind will be done with the poet and playwright Owen Dodson. It is a dance opera based on The Confession Stone, a cycle of meditations from Biblical sources written in folksy human terms. We see it as a two-dimensional work, with dance and song (and speech) going on at the same time. This is why we call it a dance opera. I also have a song cycle based on The Confession Stone. This is an earlier work and stands as an individual piece, but I'm hoping to extract thematic material from it.

At times, if I need a break, I will get involved with shorter pieces for unaccompanied instrument or for two or three instruments. I have a lot of friends and they often ask me for pieces for concerts or recitals. I enjoy doing this, so quite often I will stop a large-scale work to give it a rest, and do a shorter work before returning to the larger work.

8. Q: Given unlimited time and finances (and no restrictions whatsoever), what would you write?

A: A few years ago I had a faculty research leave, which meant that I was essentially free to compose. It was a wonderful feeling knowing that my time was my own. It would be nice if once every couple of years I had a semester free; I think that would possibly be healthier than having all the time free, even though I can see the advantages of having all your time free when you're really involved with a new work and you want to spend an extended period of time on it.

If I really had the time free, I would know what to do with it, but I know it's not possible because composers are a luxury in America. We are really not needed and yet we are needed desperately because, in a sense, we are voices of the culture. So I don't see the possibility of these conditions being offered; however, if they were offered, I would definitely know what I would do.

9. Q: If given the opportunity, would you choose to devote yourself to composition on a full-time basis? Why or why not?

A: Yes, if composition meant being free to explore the music of other composers as well as music of the past, and being active in playing and conducting while one was composing. I think that these activities fertilize my compositional activities. I would, however, keep the majority of my time for composition.

10. Q: How would you describe your compositional style?
    A: It's a synthesis of all my musical influences thus far, and I'm still growing! As long as I live I'll be doing that, using my cultural roots as a point of contact.

11. Q: What have been the influences of other composers, styles, and other types of music on your compositional style?
    A: I think especially of Luigi Dallapiccola. He was Italy's most important composer in the sense that he had a very elegant style. Everything about his melodic invention was Italian. He was a reflection of his own culture even though he incorporated the discipline of Schoenberg and Webern into his compositional method; one saw through all of that a strong lyricism that was his cultural heritage. The big thing that I got from him, without discussing it with him, was that one's own culture should shine through all the other influences.

    I watched Dallapiccola at work in his home. He was a very disciplined man. He had a job teaching piano at the Cherubini Conservatory, but in a sense he was just there as an adjunct maestro because he insisted on spending his time the way he chose. This meant doing a number of things--keeping his mornings free; living near the sea from June until September and composing intensively; returning and being involved as a pianist playing his own works and the works of other composers. Getting a glimpse of a person like this, who turned down fabulous offers all through his life to be free to do as he chose, was a great stimulation. There was also the thoroughness with which he approached living and the discipline of being a learned man, memorizing the Greek philosophers, Dante, Proust, and so on.

    Q: Were there any other styles or types of music, especially in relation to your African and West Indian experiences, that were influential in terms of developing your own style?
    A: My African "heritage" is of interest! My folks, who were originally from Jamaica, West Indies, went as social missionaries to Lagos, Nigeria, and I was born there. When we left, I was only three years old, so for me the African experience is whatever I can remember up to age three in addition to my thoughts of Africa later in life, coupled with a natural identification with Africa. However, my heritage is more West Indian-American because of the fact that I lived in the West Indies until I was eleven. I should actually say that it is West Indian-Harlem American because I grew up in Harlem and that's a fascinating cultural experience in itself.

    A piece of mine called In The Circle is an example of a piece which is somewhat influenced by West Indian music.

After visiting Haiti a few winters ago, I wrote In The Circle, which is based on a Haitian idea and is scored for
four electric guitars and a couple of drums.

12. Q: Has your style changed across your career? If so, what
     influenced these changes or developments?
    A: I think my style has changed in an organic sense. I've
     kept the concept of contrapuntal movement because moving
     your material in lines gives you another option besides
     moving in blocks of sound. I think that I'm less abstract
     these days than I was immediately after working with Dal-
     lapiccola. I've left the abstract style and the non-tonal
     concepts; I now have tonal references once again.
        You pass through a whole set of ideas concerning com-
     positional style in search of your true voice. You explore
     a number of different possibilities and these considerations
     in turn are influential in the development of your style.

13. Q: When you are listening to music for your own enjoyment,
     what are your preferences?
    A: Duke Ellington, Sarah Vaughn, the blues (the classic women
     singers as well as the early bluesmen from Mississippi and
     other areas)--I can listen to a very wide range. Strangely
     enough, when I think of listening for enjoyment, it's not
     Western music that I listen to; it's the blues, Fletcher Hen-
     derson, Duke Ellington, early Louis Armstrong, and so
     forth. I also listen to what a lot of the experimental jazz-
     men are doing. John Coltrane's intensity is extremely mov-
     ing, and his discoveries with large architecture and sound
     background show how one can search out and discover. On
     Meditations he gets involved with the simple song "Bless
     This House O Lord We Pray" and out comes a major com-
     position ("The Father and the Son and the Holy Ghost") in
     which he uses the intervals of this song, particularly the
     third, to produce a very moving composition. "Bless This
     House" is not an Afro-American song, but the way in which
     it is played converts it into an Afro-American piece. In ad-
     dition to Afro-American music, I enjoy listening to African
     music and Caribbean music, especially high life and calypso.

Notes to Chapter III

1. Correspondence should be addressed to Atsoc Music, P.O. Box
270, Radio City Station, New York, New York 10019.

2. Five Verses with Vamps was published in 1975 by King's Crown
Music Press (Galaxy Music Corporation). Tambourines was published
in 1970 by United Church Press.

3. Eastern ERS-513.

4. Mr. Da Costa is referring to New York City.

5. Mr. Da Costa is currently Associate Professor of Music at Rutgers University.

6. Mr. Da Costa also discusses these considerations in his response to I-2.

LIST OF COMPOSITIONS

AFFIRMATION (1974)
See SPIRITUAL SET FOR ORGAN.

AS I PICKED IT UP (1964)
See FOUR HAIKU SETTINGS.

BABU'S JUJU (1974)
Theater piece for children. Soprano, children's chorus, and percussion (3 players). Libretto by George Bass. 30 min. Atsoc Music. First performance (1974) in the Flint, Michigan school system.

BE NEAR TO US (1966)
See TWO PRAYERS OF KIERKEGAARD.

BEYOND THE YEARS (1974)
Soprano and organ. Text by Paul Laurence Dunbar. 14 min. Atsoc Music. First performance (1974) at St. Stephen's Lutheran Church (Wilmington, Del.). Barbara Grant, soprano; Lorna McDaniel, organ.

BLUE MIX: A COMPOSITION IN THE FORM OF A CHART (1970)
Solo contrabass/Fender bass and violoncello, contrabass, and percussion (1 player). App. 17 min. Atsoc Music. Written for and dedicated to Ron Carter.

THE BLUE MOUNTAINS (1962)
Mezzo-soprano, flute, oboe, clarinet, bass clarinet, F horn, trumpet, viola, violoncello, contrabass, and percussion. See IN THE LANDSCAPE OF SPRING.

THE BLUE MOUNTAINS (1962)
Soprano, flute, clarinet, percussion, and piano. See IN THE LANDSCAPE OF SPRING.

BLUE TUNE (1971)
See TWO PIECES FOR PIANO.

A CEREMONY OF SPIRITUALS (in progress)
Soprano, soprano/tenor saxophone, orchestra, and chorus. Commissioned by the New York State Arts Council in conjunction with the Symphony of the New World.

CHIELO (1971)
    Organ. 7 min. Atsoc Music. First performance (1973) at the
United Church on the Green (New Haven, Conn.). Lorna
McDaniel, organ.

CHIME TONES (1973)
    F horn, vibraphone, and chimes. 8 min. Atsoc Music. First
performance (1973) at the University of Nebraska School of Music. Clarence Cooper, French horn.

CLAVE TUNE (1971)
    See TWO PIECES FOR PIANO.

THE COCKTAIL SIP (1958)
    Opera in one act. Soprano, mezzo-soprano, contralto, tenor,
baritone, bass-baritone, and chorus. Libretto by Townsend
Brewster. 40 min. Atsoc Music.

THE CONFESSION STONE (1969)
    Soprano, trio (SSA), and instrumental ensemble (flute, oboe,
clarinet, bassoon, F horn, trumpet, viola, violoncello, contrabass, and piano). Text by Owen Dodson. 20 min. Atsoc Music. First performance (1969) in New York City; Society of
Black Composers.

THE CONFESSION STONE (in progress)
    Dance opera. Text by Owen Dodson.

COUNTERPOINT (1970)
    Double chorus, solo quintet (SSATB), and organ (or two pianos).
Text by Owen Dodson. App. 9 min. Atsoc Music. First per-
formance (1973) at the Kennedy Center by the Hampton Institute
Choir, Roland Carter, conductor.

DUSTBOWL (circa 1956)
    See TWO SONGS.

EAGERLY LIKE A WOMAN RUNNING TO HER LOVER (1964)
    See FOUR GLIMPSES OF NIGHT.

EPIGRAMS (1965)
    Solo viola and flute, clarinet, bass clarinet, bassoon, vibraphone,
and piano. 10 min. Atsoc Music.

EXTEMPORE BLUE (1972)
    Piano. 7 min. Atsoc Music. First performance (1974) at
Carnegie Hall. Wanda Maximilian, piano.

FANFARE RHYTHMS (1970)
    Four trumpets (or trumpet choir) and percussion. 6 min. At-
soc Music.

THE FIRST FIREFLY (1964)
    See FOUR HAIKU SETTINGS.

FIVE EPITAPHS (1956)
Soprano and string quartet. Text by Countee Cullen. For a Poet; For My Grandmother; For Paul Laurence Dunbar; For a Lady I Know; If You Should Go. 12 min. Atsoc Music. First performance (circa 1956) at Queens College (Flushing, N.Y.). Charlotte Holloman, soprano.

FIVE/SEVEN (1969)
Chorus (SSA) and organ. Text is a vocalise. 3 min. Atsoc Music.

FIVE VERSES WITH VAMPS (1968)
Violoncello and piano. 5 movements. 9 min. Kings Crown Music Press (Galaxy Music), 1976. First performance (1970) at Alice Tully Hall. Evalyn Steinbock, violoncello.

FLEEING THE HUNTER (1964)
See FOUR HAIKU SETTINGS.

FOR A LADY I KNOW (1956)
See FIVE EPITAPHS.

FOR A POET (1956)
See FIVE EPITAPHS.

FOR MY GRANDMOTHER (1956)
See FIVE EPITAPHS.

FOR PAUL LAURENCE DUNBAR (1956)
See FIVE EPITAPHS.

FOUR GLIMPSES OF NIGHT (1964)
Baritone, flute, clarinet, bass clarinet, tenor saxophone, trumpet, piano, and percussion (1 player). Text by Frank Marshall Davis. Eagerly Like a Woman Running to Her Lover; Night Is a Curious Child; Peddling from Door to Door; Night's Brittle Song. 10 min. Atsoc Music. First performance (1965) at the Donnell Library Composers' Showcase (New York City). Arthur Thompson, baritone.

FOUR HAIKU SETTINGS (1964)
Soprano and piano. The First Firefly (text by Issa); As I Picked It Up (text by Taigi); Fleeing the Hunter (text by Ryota); Suddenly You Light (text by Chine-jo). 8 min. Atsoc Music. First performance (1972) at the University of Kansas (Lawrence). Mary House, soprano; Jill Schmelzer, piano.

FOUR PRELUDES FOR TROMBONE AND PIANO (1973)
App. 8 min. Atsoc Music. Commissioned by and dedicated to Robert Gillespie. First performance (1973) at the Juilliard School of Music. Robert Gillespie, trombone.

FUN HOUSE (1968)
Incidental music for George Bass's play Fun House. Soloists,

chorus, and instrumental ensemble. 1 hour 30 min. Atsoc
Music.

GABRIEL'S TUNE FOR THE LAST JUDGMENT (1970)
Solo trumpet. 15 min. Atsoc Music.

HOW MANY MILES TO BABYLON (1955)
See I SEE THE MOON.

I HAVE A DREAM (1971)
Chorus (SATB) and organ. Text by Dr. Martin Luther King,
Jr. 4 min. Atsoc Music. First performance (1973) in Provi-
dence, R. I. by the Black Chorus of Brown University.

I SEE THE MOON (1955)
Children's chorus (two parts) and piano. Texts based on English
nursery rhymes. Three movements: I See the Moon; The Moon,
It Shines as Bright as Day; How Many Miles to Babylon. 8 min.
Atsoc Music.

IF YOU SHOULD GO (1956)
See FIVE EPITAPHS.

I'M SO GLAD TROUBLE DON'T LAST ALWAY (1963)
Chorus (SAATBB) unaccompanied. Arrangement of spiritual.
4 min. Atsoc Music. Dedicated to and first performed (1966)
by the Hampton Institute Choir, Roland Carter, conductor, at
the Golden Auditorium of Queens College.

IN SPACE (1972)
Solo contrabass. 12 min. Atsoc Music. First performance
(1973) at the Space for Innovative Development in New York City.
Ron Carter, contrabass.

IN THE CIRCLE (1970)
4 electric guitars, Fender bass, and percussion (1 player). 12
min. Atsoc Music. The composer describes this work as an
interpolation on a Haitian folk tale.

IN THE LANDSCAPE OF SPRING (1962)
Mezzo-soprano, flute, oboe, clarinet, bass clarinet, F horn,
trumpet, viola, violoncello, contrabass, and percussion. Text
based on three Zenrin poems. Three movements with interludes
after movements one and two: In the Landscape of Spring; Sitting Quietly, Doing Nothing; The Blue Mountains. 10 min. Atsoc Music. First performance (1964) at the University of Illinois
by the David Garvey Ensemble.

IN THE LANDSCAPE OF SPRING (1962)
Soprano, flute, clarinet, percussion, and piano. Text based on
three Zenrin poems. Three movements with interludes after
movements one and two: In the Landscape of Spring; Sitting
Quietly, Doing Nothing; The Blue Mountains. 10 min. Atsoc

Music. First performance (1965), ASCAP Composers' Showcase.
Georgia Davis, mezzo-soprano; Coleridge-Taylor Perkinson,
piano.

INTERLUDE (1956)
See SOUNDPIECE FOR WOODWIND QUINTET.

INVOCATION (1974)
See SPIRITUAL SET FOR ORGAN.

IT'S TIME TO SLEEP (1972)
See TWO SONGS FOR JULIE-JU.

JES' GREW # 1: CHANT VARIATIONS FOR VIOLIN (1973)
Violin and electric piano. 12 min. Atsoc Music. First per-
formance (1973) at the Gallery of Music in Our Time in New
York City. Max Pollikoff, violin; Paul Griffin, electric piano.

JUMP (1956)
See SOUNDPIECE FOR WOODWIND QUINTET.

THE KNEE-HIGH MAN (1973)
Theater piece for children. Two soloists (boy soprano and boy
alto), narrator, children's chorus, flute, piano, and percussion
(1 player). Text based on an Afro-American folk tale adapted
by George Bass. 30 min. Atsoc Music. First performance
(1973) at the Manhattan Country School in New York City.

THE LAST JUDGMENT (1970)
Chorus (SSA), speaker, piano, and percussion (1 player). Text
by James Weldon Johnson. 15 min. Atsoc Music.

LET DOWN THE BARS O DEATH (1957)
Chorus (SSATB) unaccompanied. Text by Emily Dickinson. 3
min. Atsoc Music. First performance (1962) by the Hampton
Institute Choir, Henry N. Switten, conductor.

LITTLE LAMB (1952)
Chorus (SATB) unaccompanied. Text adapted by the composer
from William Blake's poem "The Lamb." 4 min. Atsoc Music.
First performance (1952) at Queens College (Flushing, New York)
by the Queens College Choir, Noel Da Costa, conductor.

MAGNOLIA BLUE (1975)
Violin and piano. 10 min. Atsoc Music.

MARYTON (HYMN TUNE VARIATIONS) (1955)
Organ. 6 min. Atsoc Music.

THE MOON, IT SHINES AS BRIGHT AS DAY (1955)
See I SEE THE MOON.

MY PEOPLE (1974)
Mezzo-soprano and piano. Text by Langston Hughes. 5 min.

Atsoc Music.

NIGHT IS A CURIOUS CHILD   (1964)
See FOUR GLIMPSES OF NIGHT.

NIGHT'S BRITTLE SONG   (1964)
See FOUR GLIMPSES OF NIGHT.

NOVEMBER SONG   (1974)
Concert scene for soprano, violin, saxophone, and piano (with improvisation).   Text by Gwendolyn Brooks.   7-15 min.   Atsoc Music.

O GOD OF LIGHT AND LOVE   (1971)
Chorus (SATB) and organ.   Text by George Bass.   3 min. Atsoc Music.   Written for and first performed at the wedding of George and Ramona Bass (January 1972) by the Brown University Student Choir.

OCCURRENCE FOR SIX   (1965)
Flute, clarinet, bass clarinet, tenor saxophone, trumpet, and contrabass.   11 min.   Atsoc Music.

OH GRANT THAT WE MAY HEAR   (1966)
See TWO PRAYERS OF KIERKEGAARD.

PASSAGES   (1969)
Solo trumpet.   9 min.   Atsoc Music.

PEDDLING FROM DOOR TO DOOR   (1964)
See FOUR GLIMPSES OF NIGHT.

PRAISE   (1974)
See SPIRITUAL SET FOR ORGAN.

PRAYER OF STEEL   (1975)
Baritone and piano.   Text by Carl Sandburg.   4 min.   Atsoc Music.   First performance (1963) in a recital given at the Abyssinian Baptist Church (New York City).   Eugene Brice, baritone; Jonathan Brice, piano.

PREPARE ME ONE BODY   (1960)
Soprano or tenor, chorus (SATB), and organ.   Spiritual in the form of an anthem.   5 min.   Atsoc Music.

PSALM TUNE VARIATIONS   (1959)
Brass quintet.   Theme and five variations.   8 min.   Atsoc Music.

QUIETLY ... VAMP IT AND TAG IT   (1971)
Orchestra.   An educational piece in the form of a chart (especially for a younger audience).   8 min.   Atsoc Music.

RIFF TIME (1972)
Violin, violoncello, piano, and percussion (5 players). Written especially for a younger audience, who will participate in the percussion parts. 10-15 min. Atsoc Music.

RISE UP SHEPHERD (circa 1956)
Chorus (SATB) unaccompanied. Arrangement of spiritual. 3 min. Atsoc Music. First performance (1956) by the Queens College Choir, John Castellini, conductor.

'ROUND ABOUT THE MOUNTAIN (1974)
See SPIRITUAL SET FOR ORGAN.

SILVER BLUE (1964)
Solo flute. 6 min. Atsoc Music. Recorded by D. Antoinette Handy (Eastern ERS-513: Contemporary Black Images in Music for the Flute).

THE SINGING TORTOISE (1971)
Theater piece for children. Soprano, baritone, narrator, children's chorus, flute, piano, and percussion (1 player). Text based on a Haitian folk tale adapted by Martin J. Hamer. 30 min. Atsoc Music. First performance (1973) at the Manhattan Country School in New York City.

SITTING QUIETLY, DOING NOTHING (1962)
Mezzo-soprano, flute, oboe, clarinet, bass clarinet, F horn, trumpet, viola, violoncello, contrabass, and percussion. See IN THE LANDSCAPE OF SPRING.

SITTING QUIETLY, DOING NOTHING (1962)
Soprano, flute, clarinet, percussion, and piano. See IN THE LANDSCAPE OF SPRING.

SLEEP (circa 1956)
See TWO SONGS.

SONG (1956)
See SOUNDPIECE FOR WOODWIND QUINTET.

SOUNDPIECE FOR WOODWIND QUINTET (1956)
Three movements: Song; Interlude; Jump. 13 min. Atsoc Music.

SPACES (1966)
Trumpet and contrabass. 12 min. Atsoc Music.

SPIRITUAL--'ROUND ABOUT THE MOUNTAIN (1974)
See SPIRITUAL SET FOR ORGAN.

SPIRITUAL SET FOR ORGAN (1974)
Four movements: Invocation; Affirmation; Spiritual--'Round

About the Mountain; Praise. 12 min. Atsoc Music. First
performance (1974) in Wilmington, Delaware. Lorna McDaniel,
organ.

STATEMENT AND RESPONSES (1966)
Flute, oboe, bass clarinet, trumpet, trombone, tuba, viola,
violoncello, and contrabass. 15 min. Atsoc Music.

"STILL MUSIC" NO. 1 (1965)
Two violins. 10 min. Atsoc Music.

STREET CALLS (1970)
Solo trombone. 9 min. Atsoc Music.

SUCH A PRETTY BLACK GIRL IS MY JULIE-JU (1972)
See TWO SONGS FOR JULIE-JU.

SUDDENLY YOU LIGHT (1964)
See FOUR HAIKU SETTINGS.

TAMBOURINES (1970)
Children's chorus, piano, and Fender bass. Text by Langston
Hughes. 5 min. United Church Press, 1970.

THREE SHORT PIECES FOR ALTO FLUTE (1968)
Solo alto flute. 7 min. Atsoc Music. Recorded by D. Antoi-
nette Handy (Eastern ERS-513: Contemporary Black Images in
Music for the Flute).

... THROUGH THE VALLEY ... (1969)
Chorus (SATB) unaccompanied. Based on the spiritual "We
Shall Walk Through the Valley." Text is a vocalise on the
syllable AH. 4½ min. Atsoc Music. First performance (1972)
by the Harlem Chorale.

TIME ... ON AND ON (1971)
Violin, tenor saxophone, and pre-recorded electronic sounds.
40 min. Atsoc Music.

A TRIO FOR THE LIVING (1966)
Incidental music for George Bass's play A Trio for the Living.
Soloists, chorus, and organ. 1½ hours. Atsoc Music.

TRIPTICH FOR ORGAN: PRELUDE, PROCESSIONAL, POSTLUDE
(1973)
10 min. Atosc Music. First performance (1972) as part of the
Fairleigh Dickinson Concerts at the New York Cultural Center.
Eugene Hancock, organ.

TWO PIECES FOR PIANO (1971)
Clave Tune; Blue Tune. 5 min. Atsoc Music.

TWO PIECES FOR UNACCOMPANIED CELLO (1973)
Based on Ewe chant rhythms. 1 min. Atsoc Music. First

performance (1973) at Alice Tully Hall.   Ronald Lipscomb,
violoncello.

TWO PRAYERS OF KIERKEGAARD (1966)
Children's chorus (SA) and organ.   Text by Sören Kierkegaard.
Be Near to Us; Oh Grant That We May Hear.   5 min.   Atsoc
Music.

TWO SHAKER SONGS (1964)
Chorus (SATB) unaccompanied.   Harmonization of original
Shaker melodies.   Text from The Lord's Prayer.   One move-
ment.   5 min.   Atsoc Music.

TWO SONGS (circa 1956)
Soprano and piano.   Text by Langston Hughes.   Sleep; Dustbowl.
6 min.   Atsoc Music.

TWO SONGS FOR JULIE-JU (1972)
Soprano and piano.   Text by George Bass.   Such a Pretty Black
Girl Is My Julie-Ju; It's Time to Sleep.   7 min.   Atsoc Music.
First performance (1974) at Carnegie Hall.   Betty Lane, soprano;
Wayne Saunders, piano.

VOCALISE (1972)
Unaccompanied soprano voice.   Text is the syllable AH.   6 min.
Atsoc Music.

WE ARE CLIMBING JACOB'S LADDER (1962)
Chorus (SSATTB) unaccompanied.   Arrangement of spiritual.
App. $3\frac{1}{2}$ min.   Atsoc Music.

WE SHALL WALK THROUGH THE VALLEY (1969)
See THROUGH THE VALLEY.

BIBLIOGRAPHY

Claghorn, Charles E.   Biographical Dictionary of American Music.
West Nyack, N.Y.:   Parker Publishing Company, 1973.

Roach, Hildred.   Black American Music: Past and Present.   Boston: Crescendo Publishing Company, 1973.

Southern, Eileen.   "America's Black Composers of Classical Music."   Music Educators Journal 62 (November 1975): 46-59.

_____.   The Music of Black Americans.   New York: W. W.
Norton, 1971.

CHAPTER IV

TALIB RASUL HAKIM

Talib Rasul Hakim (formerly Stephen A. Chambers) was born February 8, 1940 in Asheville, North Carolina. His educational background includes study at the Manhattan School of Music, New York City College of Music, and the New School for Social Research in addition to private instruction and consultation with Robert Starer, William Sydeman, Hall Overton, David Reck, Morton Feldman, Chou Wen-Chung, Charles Whittenberg, and Ornette Coleman. Formerly a member of the faculty of Pace College, Mr. Hakim currently holds positions at Nassau Community College and Adelphi University.

Mr. Hakim has been the recipient of a number of honors and awards including the ASCAP Composer's Award (1967-1973) and fellowships to the Bennington Composers Conference (1964-1969). He has received grants from the National Endowment for the Arts and the Creative Artist Public Service Program and commissions from the Brooklyn Chamber Orchestra and the University of Wisconsin at River Falls. Natalie Hinderas, the Symphony of the New World, the Atlanta Symphony Orchestra, the New York Chamber Players, the Dallas Symphony Orchestra, the Houston Symphony Orchestra, the Washington D. C. Youth Orchestra, and the Oakland Youth Orchestra are among the artists and ensembles to have performed his compositions. Among his best-known works are Shapes (recorded by the Oakland Youth Orchestra), Sound-Gone (recorded by pianist Natalie Hinderas), and Visions of Ishwara (recorded by the Baltimore Symphony as part of the Black Composers Series produced by Columbia Records).

A co-founder and past president of the Society of Black Composers, Mr. Hakim is active as a lecturer-panelist on black music and has participated in programs and symposia at a number of educational institutions. He is also a poet; his first book of poems, Forms on #3, was published in 1968 by Afro-Arts, Inc.

Part I: General Questions

1. Q: What persons, events, and works (of art, literature, etc.) have influenced you in general as well as in terms of your musical activities?

93

Talib Rasul Hakim (courtesy of the composer)

A: My mother was the first person to get the ball rolling, so
    to speak. She started the whole thing. That was because
    her first husband had been a musician of sorts and it
    seemed to her that I, among the other children, would be
    the first to get into music. Later on there was a family
    musical orientation in that my brothers and sisters were
    all involved in music as a result of the initial thrust from
    my mother. And then as I moved on, there were a few
    junior high and high school music teachers who were very
    influential in keeping that creative impulse alive. I was
    introduced to European classical music when I was in high
    school. After I graduated from high school, I came to
    New York and at the Manhattan School of Music I was intro-
    duced to a number of European classical composers who
    started or have continued to help me develop toward a mu-
    sical sense; I'm speaking of composers such as Beethoven,
    Mozart, Brahms, and Debussy. In terms of other people
    influencing me later on, Margaret Bonds (who is now de-
    ceased) was the first living touchable black composer to
    help me tune into a sense of spirituality about music. In
    the early sixties, during my initial stay in New York, I
    met Ornette Coleman. He was a great influence. After
    that I met Eric Dolphy, who is now deceased. He was also

a great influence. Hale Smith was and is a very close
friend; he helps me a great deal in terms of developing
concepts about things other than music. The music of
Miles Davis and the late John Coltrane had a lot to do with
my musical concepts. My readings in Eastern religions,
philosophy, and astrology have had a great deal to do with
my development. These are the things--the persons, events,
and works of art, literature, etc. --that have had a great
deal of influence in my direction in terms of being a musician.

2. Q: How would you define black music?
   A: This should probably have been the first question. Anyhow,
   as I define it, it is a music reflecting the multi-dimensional aspect of the black experience within the black diaspora.
   It is also a concept functioning as a viable social-political
   vehicle for those black composer-musicians who openly acknowledge their role as image-makers, educators and/or
   teachers, and priests (which we will get into later on). [1]
   It is also a music utilizing certain basic components in a
   stylistic manner primarily peculiar to non-European western
   cultures.

3. Q: What features of your own music do you see as uniquely
   black (in terms of both musical and philosophical considerations)?
   A: In terms of features there are two aspects of the music that
   I write that I think reflect an essential awareness of blackness. First, my music is percussive; it is repetitious and
   it tends sometimes to be incantatory. It is also very rhythmic, sometimes overtly and other times not. There is an
   inner pulse that permeates most of my work and this inner
   pulse reflects my awareness of the same kind of inner pulse
   that is predominant in most non-European forms of music.
   Especially is this so when one talks in terms of percussiveness and certain textures. Generally the textures of most
   non-European music tend to be heavy, at least when we talk
   about the African concept of rhythmic nuances. This is very
   important to understand when one talks about those qualities
   inherent in black music. If there are a great deal of multi-
   rhythmic aspects in my music then naturally my textures
   will be heavy. There is a sense of percussiveness. I use
   a great deal of percussive-like sounds; even when I'm using
   brass or so-called non-percussive instruments, I use these
   instruments in a percussive manner. This gets to the second aspect which is very important, in that conceptually I
   approach music in a manner similar to the music-makers
   of most non-European cultures--it is functional; it is part
   and parcel of a social-political awareness of a people or a
   culture of which I am a part. The music is qualitative
   rather than quantitative.

4. Q: In what ways is your music a reflection of your personal
   philosophy (social, political, etc.)?

A: I answer: it is hoped that whenever the music is performed, both performer and listener will experience some degree of inner stirring, that they will experience some philosophical, religious, political, emotional, intellectual experience. Whatever they may. When I sit down to write music, all I'm thinking of is trying to recreate those images in sound that I experience during my daily growth period. To accomplish this I apply intellectual skill and artistic craftsmanship. Both performer and listener will have to experience whatever they can experience.

5. Q: What do you see as the position or role of the black artist in contemporary society?

A: Because of the multi-dimensional aspect of the black experience, I believe that the black creative artist should be thoroughly in tune with that and should determine for himself the tools he wishes to use and the manner in which he uses them. His function primarily should be the utilization of his art form as an instrument of communication, not only in raising the level of social-political awareness and consciousness of the people but also in rejuvenating and revitalizing the inner essence of their spirituality. We should try to come to the realization that the process of creativity is a religious act. It is an act affirming life rather than negating life. So, acknowledging that act as a religious act, it seems to me that it is imperative that the primary function of the black creative artist should be to revitalize and rejuvenate that inner spirituality. If people just deal with the entertainment aspect of art, they are not fulfilling their overall mission; they are refusing (or are unwilling or unable) to deal with that inner spirituality. How can they not say that they are involved in a religious act? The process of composing is on one side a very technical, very highly skilled intellectual process; on the other side, the composer uses this intellectual process as a kind of vehicle to release and share this inner spirituality. We're talking about the black creative artist acknowledging the dynamics of what it means to create. If one acknowledges that, then one has to acknowledge such an act as a religious act. The inner creative impulse is inherent in all people. What makes artists different from non-artists is the fact that we have acknowledged that and have done something about it in terms of manifesting it in various concrete forms. And where does this creative impulse come from? It comes from the higher force, the Divine Intelligence; such an acknowledgment is in itself religious. Therefore, aside from an art form being an instrument of communication, continuously raising the level of social-political consciousness and awareness, it should also be rejuvenating and revitalizing this inner spirituality.

6. Q: Please discuss any problems you may have encountered in getting your works performed, published, and recorded.

A: O.K. What I did with number six was to start from the bottom and work up, 'cause that's the way it hit me.

6C. Q: Are there specific problems in getting a satisfactory performance? Exemplify and discuss.

A: My difficulty has had to do with the fact that a few white professional ensembles and orchestras are either unable or unwilling to muster up enough respect, sensitivity, and awareness to properly execute the subtle nuances inherent in most of my works. The manner in which I write compels me to verbalize directions if they are not terribly clear. As Cecil Taylor always says, notes are only a guide; you can play the notes but there are some other things that you cannot put down on paper. It is this something that, if I am present, I try to convey to the performers. If the performers are terribly into being virtuosos on their instruments and into a cultural aesthetic that is predominantly white, the difficulty arises when the performers and I approach the same thing--music--and I'm coming at it from a different perspective, a different viewpoint. That gets in the way with some people.

6B. Q: Have you encountered difficulty in getting your works programmed?

A: I don't have difficulty getting works programmed, primarily because I haven't pushed to get works programmed. I'm not into pushing. I'm aware of opportunities for performances and I am made aware of opportunities by people who are doing performances, and I'll either take advantage of these opportunities or I'll just leave it alone. I don't foresee myself trying to push to get works programmed.

6A. Q: How much of your actual output has ever been performed? Published? Recorded?

A: I've had quite a few performances, but strangely enough, out of New York. I've been writing and living here in New York for the past ten years or more, but I've had more performances outside of New York in those ten years than I have had in New York, primarily because the situation in New York is a closed, selective, competitive one and I prefer not to devote my energies to trying to do anything about that. That will come.

I have had a few performances in New York. As a matter of fact, my first important piece was performed here ten years ago as part of the Music in Our Time series. [2] The first opportunity I had to have an entire program dedicated to my works was in 1973 when I was the guest artist-in-residence at the University of Wisconsin at River Falls.

In terms of published works, I have just signed a contract with Bote und Bock, a West German firm. G. Schirmer/ AMP are their American representatives.

Recordings. There are two out, both on the Desto label. Sound-Gone was recorded by Natalie Hinderas and Shapes was recorded by the Oakland Youth Orchestra. <u>Placements</u>, a piece for five percussion and piano, will be coming out on Desto sometime in the spring of 1976. The Baltimore Symphony recorded <u>Visions of Ishwara</u> for Columbia's Black Composers Series, and that has now been released.

7. Q: What do you consider, at this point in your life, to be your most significant achievement(s) aside from your compositions?

A: It is this: a realization of the importance of my continuous development toward spiritual enlightenment. That is the most significant achievement to date and I'm still developing that.

8. Q: What do you see as the responsibilities and obligations of the educational system (at all levels) to the study of black music?

A: We talk about responsibilities--I've listed them: (1) to realize their own inadequacies in properly recording and documenting all aspects of black American music, (2) to bring to light the truth in regard to the significant and lasting contributions of black composer-musicians to the overall activity of music-making, and (3) to provide opportunities for the research, study, presentation, and perpetuation of all forms of black American music.

9. Q: Do you feel that the people who write about your music (critics in particular) understand what you are doing? Exemplify and discuss.

A: The whole concept of critiquing is foreign to the traditional non-European way of life. In most traditional non-European societies you do not have anyone sitting on the side critiquing a performance because the act of creativity is a collective act and all of the inhabitants of that particular culture or society are participants in the creative process. So the whole concept of critiquing is foreign except to the western mind because that is the way of the western mind.

Usually the cultural standards that most critics use to analyze or describe a work of art or music (and we are talking now specifically about black music) are antithetical to standards used by the involved artists. What the critic is doing is using concepts that are not germane to the standards used by the particular creative artist in question.

What I find is that the lay listener's response is usually more unique, exciting, and interesting. My concern for critics has to do with listening to the <u>people</u>; <u>they</u> are the critics. I like to know what they have to say. Professional critics use other standards that are not necessarily germane to me. What's really significant to me is the people themselves and what they have to say about it. That's what I want to hear--what the <u>people</u> have to say.

10. Q: What advice would you give to the aspiring young black composer?

A: The first thing is to study: study scores, study life, study
people, study yourself. Black composers--young aspiring
black composers--study and learn. Learn to listen: listen
to music and listen to the truth. Learn to love. Read:
read about things, read papers, read a great deal and decide for yourself. Stay in tune with current events both
musical and otherwise. The important thing is, don't over-
aspire to be successful; don't over-aspire to be successful,
especially in the commercial sense in terms of dollars and
cents. Be concerned with having sense with an "s" and
not cents with a "c."

Part II: Music Questions

1. Q: When you sit down to begin a new composition on your own
initiative or inspiration (as opposed to a commissioned
work), what procedure or approach do you follow?

    A: Composing, to me, is a communicative art. In my own
way, I am informing both the listener and the participants
or performers that I am in fact engaged in a ritualistic
celebration of praise and worship to the Divine Creator for
bestowing upon me the ability to ignite the inner spark of
creativity. The first and foremost area of concern for me
when I sit down to write is to be absolutely certain that the
materials I've chosen and the manner in which I choose to
make use of them result in touching and moving the inner
spirit of both performer and audience. That's my primary
concern. If, in addition to that, my blackness causes the
political nature of the work to emerge, so be that also.
But be that as it may, it will be there no matter what. I
don't worry about that because I know that if the first thing
is taken care of, then the second thing will be intact.

2. Q: When composing a commissioned work or a work written
for a specific occasion or person, does your procedure or
approach differ from the one you just described in question
one? If so, in what way?

    A: It's not too different. The concerns I described in the
answer to question one are there regardless of whether I'm
commissioned to do the work or not. Now, in terms of
differences, I would say that some things depend on the performance level of the ensemble. For instance, I have just
finished a piece for the Washington, D.C. Youth Orchestra
which premiered at the Kennedy Center June 7, 1975.[3] I
had to make a few adjustments for their level of performance, but that only happened when I went to rehearsal and
saw that they had a little difficulty with the work. So I
proceeded to make a few minor adjustments that did not
take away from the essence of the music. But other than
that, I write as I write.

3. Q: In general, with regard to your writing, what genre(s) do
you prefer?

A: In terms of genre, whatever my inner ear directs me to do--anything from solos, duets, trios, quartets, and chamber music to orchestra. It does not matter. What I hear will direct me to the particular medium.

4. Q: What do you consider your most significant composition? Please discuss.

A: I'll start off by saying that the Duo was first because of what I said previously.[4] Then Sound-Gone was extremely important because I started to use certain materials in a particular way that I felt was saying what I wanted to say in terms of my religious-philosophical concepts. Sound-Gone started a trend of using certain materials like clusters, multi-rhythmic things, and voices in a particular way. Then there's Sound-Images, written in 1969 for orchestra and female chorus. This piece incorporated a great deal of percussion and voices, and I was continuing to manifest a spiritual attunement with this piece. Visions of Ishwara, which has just been recorded by the Baltimore Symphony, was a kind of culmination of instrumental pieces reflecting an inner spirituality. Tone Prayers started in another direction with voices. This piece was commissioned by the choral ensemble at the University of Wisconsin when I was there in 1973; it was written for mixed chorus (SATB), piano, and percussion. Tone Prayers was the first piece that I did for mixed chorus and it was sort of an extension of the previous instrumental pieces that dealt with a kind of subdued inner spirituality. Tone Prayers comes out that way because the text is original and specifically talks about the Divine Creator.

5. Q: Please comment on your treatment of the following musical elements and give examples from your compositions that illustrate the techniques you describe.

A. Melody
TH: First of all, I'm not a melodic composer. I am what I would consider a motivic and intervallic composer in that I utilize certain brief melodic-intervallic motifs that are heard repeatedly. I think in terms of various intervallic relationships rather than harmonic relationships as such.

B. Harmony
TH: My harmonies tend to be not harmony but clusters of sound--sound clusters--and once in a while one may hear parallel fourths and fifths, but even that has to do with being a part of the melodic content which most times is very simple and very repetitive. But I don't work from a melodic standpoint; I work simply from a sound-movement approach in that I'm concerned with the movement of sound and I use certain rhythmic concepts.

C. Rhythm
   TH: The essence of my music is primarily rhythmic.
   This is the element that is the essence of music
   and it is this element that I'm working with and
   have been working with. Sometimes the rhythmic
   content is overt; other times it is not as overt.
   The piece that the D. C. Youth Orchestra performed is very rhythmic. [5] As a matter of fact,
   I had to use two conductors because it is a multi-
   rhythmic piece. So the rhythmic aspect is the
   most important aspect of my music and I think
   in terms of rhythm more than anything else.
   Short motivic and intervallic materials are used
   simply because they're natural ingredients of
   utilizing rhythm.

D. Form
   TH: My form is free in that I have no set form. The
   overall sound approach motivates my form which,
   for the most part, is free.

E. Improvisation
   TH: I use very little improvisation and that which I
   do use is directed improvisation. I utilize a
   process of fixed composition rather than continuous
   composition. I don't write jazz because jazz is a
   kind of continuous composition. Fixed composition
   is primarily notated, so I am a fixed composer in
   that I utilize fixed notation with little or no improvisation. The improvisation that I do utilize in my
   fixed compositional approach is given a fixity in
   terms of duration, in terms of dynamics, in terms
   of tempo. The pitches are arbitrary; I don't give
   any pitch directions. I simply give duration, dynamics, and tempo or movement.

F. Text
   TH: The text is usually original. The only text other
   than my own that I did use was for a piece entitled Tone Poem; the text was taken from Langston Hughes' poem "The Negro Speaks of Rivers."
   In terms of treatment of text, the rhythm of the
   vowel sounds attracts my attention and I simply
   try to recapture them musically. I try to color
   the instrumental aspects of the music just the
   same as the color given by the vowel sounds of
   the words. It's a juxtaposition of colors--vocal
   colors and instrumental colors. The text and the
   music are totally interrelated.

G. Instrumentation or medium
   TH: It has to do with color. When I want specific
   colors I use specific sounds. At this point and

for a few years now I have been involved in percussive sounds and I utilize these percussive
sounds in a way that will reflect whatever I choose
to do. What I am saying is that I don't have any
special kind of technique to capture a particular
sound or color or fix; I don't treat them in a particular way.

6. Q: Have difficulties with performance practice (inflection, phrasing, etc.) been a significant problem in having your works
performed to your own satisfaction?

A: It depends upon the performing organization. The difficulty
I have simply has to do with the attitude of performers. I
believe that the proper attitude is a prerequisite for a successful performance and that anything a composer asks of a
performer can be done if the performer has the proper attitude about the whole concept of music-making. If he is not
involved in a job, or money, or time; if he is thoroughly involved in the religious aspect of creativity and music-making;
if his attitude is proper, then there will be no difficulty
whatsoever.

7. Q: What major works are currently in progress? Please describe and discuss.

A: I'm in the process of writing a piece for orchestra entitled
Concepts. I started it in December 1974 and I'm still working on it. I'm thinking in terms of another percussion
work using four or five percussionists, dancers, a female
chorus or a mixed chorus, and a narrator. That concept
of a piece has been in my head for quite some time and I
am still working it out.

8. Q: Given unlimited time and finances (and no restrictions whatsoever), what would you write?

9. Q: If given the opportunity would you choose to devote yourself
to composition on a full-time basis? Why or why not?

(Ed. note: Mr. Hakim chose to answer these two questions
together.)

A: I would further develop my whole compositional approach.
That is what I would do if given the time and finances, and
that goes on into the next question about opportunity. If
time and money afford one the opportunity then writing music
would be what I would do.

  If I had the time and the money (and that's what makes
the opportunity), I would definitely devote all my time to
writing music, which would be in effect continuing to develop my whole compositional approach.

10. Q: How would you describe your compositional style?

A: My style is one of motivic, intervallic, fixed, free-form
composition.

11. Q: What have been the influences of other composers, styles,
and other types of music on your compositional style?

A: Other than the people I have mentioned, there is no one that has really influenced me. I've heard music that I have been very interested in for a long time; the music of Morton Feldman has always interested me--very much so. But I'm not really influenced by any person and no other person's style influences me. No other types of music influence me.

12. Q: Has your style changed across your career? If so, what influenced these changes or developments?

A: In terms of change, I mentioned that I've been using a kind of percussive approach and also utilizing voices.[6] My works have become heavy in terms of texture, creating a multi-rhythmic thing. Overall sound continuums are quite prominent also. I'm involved in developing more subtleties, which may seem like a contrast because I'm talking about a percussive approach; I believe that a percussive approach can be used subtlely.

I've been using a lot of multi-rhythmic elements and sound continuums--blocks of sound moving. As a matter of fact, in Concepts I'm working with a sound continuum wherein I use the entire orchestra. I want to get this full sound and I want to have this sound moving--moving, moving, and continuously moving in different directions and at different time spans. That in itself will give me heavy texture. You know, I think I'm not even working deliberately toward heavy textures because that will be automatic if I do what I'm doing. The sound movement is what I'm involved in. Sound-Gone, the piano piece I did in 1967, used the inside of the piano. It's not a unique technique; it's just that I used it in a particular way that satisfied my artistic credo and awakened me to the possibilities of using that same kind of approach with other instrumentations. That sound block, that sound continuum, the layers of sound juxtaposing themselves--that's the piece that started it out. And it went from there to Sound-Images and then to Visions of Ishwara. These pieces reflect my religious-philosophical aspect and where I'm going.

13. Q: When you are listening to music for your own enjoyment, what are your preferences?

A: When I'm not writing music and I'm listening for my own enjoyment, I listen to Cecil Taylor, Ornette Coleman, Miles Davis, John Coltrane, and I listen to some of the good rhythmic R&B tunes.

Notes to Chapter IV

1. See Mr. Hakim's response to I-5.

2. Mr. Hakim is referring to his composition Duo (1963) for flute and clarinet.

3. Mr. Hakim is referring to his composition Re/currences.

4. See Mr. Hakim's response to I-6A.

5. Re/currences.

6. See Mr. Hakim's responses to the following questions: I-3, II-4, and II-5G.

LIST OF COMPOSITIONS

CONCEPTS (in progress)
Orchestra.

CONTOURS (1966)
Oboe, bassoon, horn, trumpet, violoncello, and contrabass.
8 min. First performance (1967) at Town Hall as part of Max
Pollikoff's "Music in Our Time" series.

CURRENTS (1967)
String quartet. 10 min.

DUO (1963)
Flute and clarinet. 12 min. Galaxy Music, 1965. First performance (1964) at the Bennington Composers Conference (Bennington, Vt.).

ELEMENTS (1967)
Flute/alto flute, clarinet/bass clarinet, violin/viola, violoncello, piano, and glass and bamboo wind and hand chimes. 8 min. 12 sec. First performance (1969) on "Inside Bedford-Stuyvesant," WNEW-TV, New York City.

ENCOUNTER (1965)
Flute, oboe, clarinet, bassoon, horn, trumpet, and trombone.
10 min.

FOUR (1965)
Clarinet, trumpet, trombone, and piano. 7 min. First performance (1968) at the University of North Carolina (Chapel Hill) by the New Music Ensemble of the University of North Carolina.

INNER-SECTIONS (1967)
Flute, clarinet, trombone, piano, and percussion. 10 min.

MOMENTS (1966)
E♭ alto saxophone, bassoon, and horn. 12 min.

MUTATIONS (1964)
Bass clarinet, horn, trumpet, viola, and violoncello. 7 min.

NUMBERS (in progress)
Soprano, percussion, and contrabass.

ODE TO SILENCE (1964)
Soprano and piano. Text by the composer. 8 min.

PEACE-MOBILE (1964)
Woodwind quintet. 10 min.

A PIANO PIECE (1965)
Piano. 12 min.

PLACEMENTS (1970)
5 percussion instruments and piano. 13 min. Bote & Bock
(Associated Music) 1975. Recorded for future release on Folkways by pianist Stanley Cowell and percussionists Warren Smith,
Omar Clay, Joe Chambers, Barbara Burton, and Wilson Morman.

PORTRAITS (1965)
Alto flute, bass clarinet, 3 percussion, and piano. 12 min.

QUOTE-UNQUOTE (1967)
Bass-baritone, oboe, trumpet, and 2 percussion. Text by the
composer. 12 min.

RE/CURRENCES (1974)
Orchestra. 13 min. First performance (1975) at the Kennedy
Center by the Washington, D.C. Youth Orchestra, Lyn McLain,
conductor.

REFLECTIONS ON THE 5TH RAY (1972)
Narrator and chamber orchestra. Text by Theresa Schoenacher.
12 min. Commissioned by the Brooklyn Chamber Orchestra.
First performance (1972) by the Brooklyn Chamber Orchestra,
Stephen Gunzenhauser, conductor.

ROOTS AND OTHER THINGS (1967)
Flute/alto flute, oboe/English horn, clarinet/bass clarinet,
trumpet, horn, trombone, viola, violoncello, and contrabass.
10 min. First performance (1968) in Boston by the Society of
Black Composers.

SET-THREE (1970)
Soprano, violoncello, and piano. Text by the composer. 8
min. First performance (1970) at the Summer Convocation on
the Arts (Saratoga Springs, N.Y.).

SHAPES (1965)
Chamber orchestra. 10 min. Recorded by the Oakland Youth
Orchestra, Robert Hughes, conductor (Desto DC-7107: The
Black Composer in America). First performance (1970) by
the Oakland Youth Chamber Orchestra, Robert Hughes, con-
ductor.

SKETCHES (in progress)
Brass quintet.

SKETCHY BLUE-BOP (1973)
Concert jazz band. 14 min. Commissioned by the University
of Wisconsin (River Falls). First performance (1973) at the
University of Wisconsin (River Falls).

SIX PLAYERS AND A VOICE (1964)
Soprano, clarinet, trumpet, violoncello, 2 percussion, and
piano. Text by the composer. 10 min. First performance
(1969) at the New York City YMHA/YWHA as part of Max Pollikoff's "Music in Our Time" series.

SONG-SHORT (1967)
Soprano, alto flute, English horn, bass clarinet, horn, and
trombone. Text by the composer. 8 min.

SOUND-GONE (1967)
Piano. 12 min. Recorded by Natalie Hinderas (Desto DC-7102/
7103: Natalie Hinderas Plays Music By Black Composers).
First performance (1970) at Temple University. Natalie Hinderas, piano.

SOUND-IMAGES (1969)
Brass (2 trumpets, 2 flugelhorns, 4 horns, 3 trombones, tuba),
3 percussion, strings, and female chorus. Text by the composer. 10 min. First performance (1969) in New York City
by the Society of Black Composers.

THREE PLAY SHORT FIVE (1965)
Bass clarinet, percussion, and contrabass. 8 min. First performance (1966) as part of Max Pollikoff's "Music in Our Time"
series.

TIMELESSNESS (1970)
Flugelhorn, horn, trombone, tuba, 2 percussion, contrabass,
and piano. 15 min.

TITLES (1965)
Flute, oboe, clarinet, and bassoon. 10 min.

TONE-POEM (1969)
Soprano, percussion, contrabass, and piano. Text by Langston
Hughes. 9 min. First performance (1969) at Bowdoin College.

TONE-PRAYERS (1973)
Chorus (SATB) with percussion and piano. Text by the com-
poser. 10 min. Commissioned by the University of Wisconsin
(River Falls). First performance (1973) at the University of
Wisconsin (River Falls).

URANIAN-PROJECTIONS (1970)
Soprano, percussion, and piano. Text by the composer. 10 min.

VISIONS OF ISHWARA   (1970)
   Orchestra.   8 min. 55 sec.   Recorded by the Baltimore Symphony Orchestra, Paul Freeman, conductor (Columbia M-33434:
   Vol. 8, Black Composers Series).   First performance (1971)
   at Philharmonic Hall by the Symphony of the New World, Benjamin Steinberg, conductor.

BIBLIOGRAPHY

Part I: Works about the composer

Brooks, Tilford. "A Historical Study of Black Music and Selected
   Twentieth Century Black Composers and Their Role in American
   Society." Ed. D. dissertation, Washington University, 1972.

Claghorn, Charles E. Biographical Dictionary of American Music.
   West Nyack, N. Y.: Parker Publishing Company, 1973.

DeLerma, Dominique-René, ed. Black Music in Our Culture: Cur-
   ricular Ideas on the Subjects, Materials, and Problems. Kent,
   Ohio: Kent State University Press, 1970. (See index under
   CHAMBERS, Stephen A.)

Roach, Hildred. Black American Music: Past and Present. Boston: Crescendo Publishing Company, 1973. (See index under
   CHAMBERS, Stephen A.)

Southern, Eileen. "America's Black Composers of Classical Music." Music Educators Journal 62 (November 1975): 46-59.

_____. The Music of Black Americans. New York: W. W.
   Norton, 1971. (See index under CHAMBERS, Stephen A.)

Who's Who in the East. 14th ed. (1974-1975), s. v. "Chambers,
   Stephen Alexander. "

Who's Who in the East. 15th ed. (1975-1976), s. v. "Hakim, Talib
   Rasul. "

Part II: Works by the composer

Hakim, Talib Rasul. Forms on #3. New York: Afro-Arts, Inc.,
   1968.

CHAPTER V

HERBERT JEFFREY HANCOCK

Herbie Hancock was born April 12, 1940 in Chicago, Illinois. He began studying piano when he was seven years old, and at the age of eleven performed Mozart's Concerto in D Major with the Chicago Symphony Orchestra. During high school, while continuing to study classical music, he was introduced to jazz and began to learn improvisation by transcribing and playing the solos of such artists as Oscar Peterson and George Shearing.

In 1956 Mr. Hancock entered Grinnell College to study engineering, but his activities as a composer, arranger, and bandleader caused him to eventually change his major to composition. The lack of one sociology course kept him from receiving his diploma after four years; he was later awarded an honorary Doctor of Fine Arts degree by Grinnell in 1972.

Mr. Hancock's activities as a performer and recording artist are well-known and widely acclaimed. He has been associated with many outstanding musicians during his career, including Miles Davis, Donald Byrd, Sonny Rollins, Freddie Hubbard, Wayne Shorter, Wes Montgomery, Quincy Jones, and Stevie Wonder. He has also led a number of groups of his own, producing such award-winning albums as Mwandishi (named by Time as one of the ten best recordings of 1971) and Head Hunters (recognized as the largest selling album of its kind in the history of the record business). Mr. Hancock has received numerous other honors, including seven Grammy nominations, down beat's Reader's Poll award as Jazzman of the Year (1974), and Ebony's Black Music Poll awards in the Innovative Artist and Best Combo categories; in addition, he has been named Top Instrumentalist by Cashbox and Top Male Jazz Artist by Record World.

Among Mr. Hancock's best-known compositions are Maiden Voyage; Watermelon Man; Chameleon; Cantaloupe Island; Palm Grease; Butterfly; Blind Man, Blind Man; and his scores for the motion pictures Blow-Up and Death Wish.

Herbie Hancock (courtesy of Adams' Dad Management Company)

Part I: General Questions

1. Q: What persons, events, and works (of art, literature, etc.)
        have influenced you in general as well as in terms of your
        compositional activities?
    A: There haven't been too many people in art that have influ-
        enced my musical activities.   For literature, I would say
        books on so-called occult philosophy.   (When we Westerners
        use the word occult, half the time we're talking about some-
        thing Eastern; anything that is non-Western is "occult.")   I
        used to read a lot of those books to try to find the answers
        I needed to explain what the controlling factor in the creation

and expression of music is when it really works. And I
couldn't find any real answers. I just got more questions.
I got results that I really wanted and needed when I started
chanting.

Q: I know that the practice of Nichiren Shoshu Buddhism has
   been an important influence on you in terms of both your
   personal development and your musical development. What are
   some of the different ways that you feel it has affected you?
A: First of all, through the practice of this religion I have
   come to some conclusions about values. Part of my understanding of what is valuable has changed since I've been
   doing this practice. One example is the idea that the value
   of anything is determined by its positive effect on the lives
   of other human beings. I realized that if I played music
   and it didn't have any effect other than getting me off, I
   was ego tripping. It was like a masturbation of the mind.

Q: Are the practices and beliefs of this sect different from
   those of traditional Buddhism?
A: Nichiren Shoshu Buddhism is definitely not traditional Buddhism. It's completely different. There may be some aspects of it that are the same or related, but as far as the
   practice is concerned and the depth of what it proposes to
   be involved with, it's completely different from traditional
   Buddhism.

Q: How did you get involved in Nichiren Shoshu Buddhism?
A: Well, in the summer of 1972 I was working with my band
   in Seattle and I found out that Buster Williams, who was
   my bass player at that time, had just started into some
   kind of philosophy. I didn't know what it was and I didn't
   ask him anything about it, but I could see that he seemed
   to be a little more agreeable. Now he used to be the type
   of guy that had to have things his own way; that's the way
   he was. But I noticed that he seemed to be a little more
   willing to do things. I thought, "Well, that's nice" but I
   wasn't really interested. I had no idea what it was and I
   was pretty satisfied with the way things were going, so I
   didn't ask him about it.
       We had a ten-week engagement in Seattle. One Thursday
   the whole band hung out all night having a good time and
   just enjoying Seattle. We only got two hours of sleep. The
   next night was Friday night, the busiest night in the week
   in the club, and none of us felt like playing. You could
   feel in the atmosphere that the people were eager to hear
   the music, but we were all so tired that none of us felt like
   playing. I decided to call a different opening tune, one with
   an introduction by someone other than myself because I
   didn't want to have the responsibility for setting the pace for
   the entire evening. I called Toys, which starts with a bass
   solo. Now everybody was tired, including Buster. Buster
   started to play the introduction, which I normally let him
   play for about three minutes, and what he was playing was

so fantastic and so unbelievable that I let him play for
about twenty-five minutes. It was unlike anything I had
ever heard before, far above what I thought his potential
was in its projection of feeling and musicality. And I had
known him for ten years! When you know someone musically for ten years, you know their best nights and you know
beyond that how far they can go. This was way above that.
I couldn't believe it. I couldn't believe he was actually
creating that music. I saw him doing things that were
physically impossible. I wish I had videotaped it because
you wouldn't have believed the things he was doing. Just
phenomenal things! And the audience was completely mes-
merized by what he was doing. Then I felt an energy wel-
ling up inside me that was completely wiping away my tired-
ness. He really inspired me and he inspired the whole
band. We wound up playing a fantastic set of music that
sounded like magic. People came up to us afterwards with
tears in their eyes thanking us for that experience.

I grabbed Buster in his dressing room and I said, "Man,
I know you are into some kind of philosophy and whatever
it is, if it can make you play the bass like that, I've got
to know what it is. I've got to check it out for myself."
And he told me that he had been chanting for two weeks to
explain the thing to me and to have me be receptive. He
had wanted to tell me about it, but he wanted me to be receptive. And it happened in exactly the right way--through
the music. That was further proof to him that it worked.
I asked him, "What is this chanting?" and he told me that
the basic part is saying Nam Myoho Renge Kyo over and
over again, saying each syllable evenly. It sounded so far
removed from anything I could accept that it sounded to me
like something somebody might have made up. It just
sounded ridiculous. I couldn't believe that him saying Nam
Myoho Renge Kyo could actually make him play the bass
like that. Then he told me that I didn't have to believe in
it, that it would work whether I believed in it or not.
That's what really blew my mind! So I said to myself,
"If that's true, then this must be a fact rather than a be-
lief. It must be a fact like any other fact we experience,
like the fact that fire will burn you or that the law of
gravity is a fact." And I have found out since then that it
is a law. That's why it works whether you believe in it
or not. It's a basic law of nature.

Q: How much time do you spend doing this every day?
A: I chant for at least an hour a day. A half hour in the
morning and a half hour in the evening are the best times
to do it. Sometimes I chant when I'm driving or walking
down the street, but it has to be done out loud so that the
sound is created internally and manifested externally. This
is not just a spiritual philosophy. It is a life philosophy.
Your life is not just your spirit; it's also your physical
body, which includes your health. It's also the material
world that you live in because you are a product of your

environment   So this practice affects you spiritually, physically, and materially.

The way you use this practice is to chant for the things that you want, for the things that you think will make you happy, whether they are small desires or big desires.   Desire is the basic motivating factor in the human being, and your desires are clues to your present life condition.   The reason I suspect this is because my desires have changed over the years; they've changed because I've grown.   Fifteen years ago, my life condition was at a certain level and my desires reflected that level (or were maybe a little above that level because many of the desires cannot be attained at the time you want them and require you to grow).   But I have learned a lot since then and my desires have changed because my life condition has changed.   I never asked any of the Buddhists about this, but I have a feeling that it is true.   That is why when you chant for the things you want, the universe responds to the sound Nam Myoho Renge Kyo because it is the sound of the life force of all phenomena in the universe.   When you chant for what you want, the universe perks up its ears and immediately starts reacting to that sound.   And things happen to you! Things start to happen that put you into a position to get the things that you want.   When you chant, your daily life is affected by it.   You might wind up getting all the things that you want, but in the process, your life has to grow.   What happens is that the conditions necessary for you to start realizing what you need to realize and to start doing the things that need to be done in order to get what you want begin to be present.   Meaningful experiences happen more often, and you are able to grow faster.   What might normally take five years of growth might happen in one year or in five months.

I'm always surprised when this works.   I'm always surprized when I see myself growing and changing.   And it happens so naturally.   It sounds crazy, but it really works! It's a fact that sound has power.   We know that music has power and can influence people.   We say that music soothes the savage beast, we have music therapy, and we know about the psychological effects music has on people.   The sound of the music has enormous power.   With chanting, it's the human being saying the chant that is the power.   As you see it working, you will eventually realize for yourself that it is really the chanting that's work and not luck or coincidence or whatever.   Then your faith will start to grow.

This has affected my whole life.   Here's how I used to feel. I used to feel that music was my god.   I had already come to certain conclusions about the fact that life is eternal and continuous, and that my life did not begin with Herbie Hancock's birth and would not end with Herbie Hancock's death. I had also come to the conclusion that God did not create the universe, and that the universe has always been and always will be.   Buddhism doesn't advocate disbelieving or believing in anything; it just says to believe in yourself. Whatever else you want to believe in is up to you.   Through

this practice, you will find out what is true and what is
false, but you will find it out from yourself. As you start
to change, you start to realize more about yourself. As
experiences happen that allow your life to grow faster, you
grow and you are able to understand more. You actually
start to get a vantage point that allows you to see more of
what's happening around you and puts you into a better position to make decisions about things. There is a wisdom
that develops. You develop a confidence and a stability not
based on a dependence on conditions outside of yourself.

I found out that my music is a reflection of my life condition. My music gets better as I grow more. It gets
deeper and the projection of emotion is better. I realize
now that my music depends first on the growth of my life,
and that it's not the other way around. My life doesn't depend on the growth of my music, but my music will not
grow if my life doesn't grow. You can't get better from
the essence of the music. The essence is not in anything
technical--notes, chords, or any of that. It's in feelings
and in the projection of powerful, dynamic, and inspirational
feelings. No matter how hard and long you practice, you're
not going to get that. That only comes from your life and
what life condition you're in. This practice of Buddhism
works on my life. As it works on my life, the music gets
better and starts to take on a character that is more representative of me. The music that I'm playing now is actually more representative of me than what I had been playing before. The part that I have included now is that part
that is common between my life and the lives of other peo-
ple--the musical expression of common feelings.

Most people deal with the basic, earthy things as opposed
to the cosmic, and people dig funky music! I like funky
music and I've liked it for many years, but I never included
it in my music. Sometimes I included it, but always in disguise. To disguise it took the essence of the funk away
from it, though, and so the very thing I liked best about it
was lost. Now I'm doing it straight funk and it's opened up
a whole new thing for me. I've come to find out that the
rules and the criteria for appreciating funky music are different from the kind of jazz I had been playing before. It's
hard for jazz musicians to dig funky music and consider it
valuable because they are using their set of values. Funky
music has its own set of values, established by the people
who create the music and the people who listen to it. I'm
finding out what that is and I dig it. So do a lot of other
people. I'm not losing any of what I had before; I'm getting
it in a better or more valuable perspective because I can
see the effect in terms of the people who are buying the
records. I see that so many more people really like it and
a lot of people who liked my music before like this more.
So I'm starting to really accomplish the things that I consider valuable through the chanting.

Q: Are there other influences you'd like to discuss in the context of this question?

A: They're mostly musicians. Igor Stravinsky influenced me in terms of orchestral sounds and colors as well as in terms of composition. Bartok has influenced me compositionally and so has Penderecki, although I've only been listening to him in recent years. Messiaen has influenced me from a rhythmic standpoint, and I have the book that he wrote on his theory of rhythm.[1] Miles Davis influenced me in my playing and also in the concept of the development of music by the whole band rather than just by myself. If anybody brings a composition in to Miles, he breaks it down to a skeletal form in such a way that each person in the group can start putting the pieces back together. You still have the essence of the original composition, but you create a new composition on that essence. Each person forms his own part on the skeleton and consequently feels more a part of the music. He feels that rather than playing someone else's music, he's part of the creation of the composition itself. I try to do that in my band because I like that idea.

Let me name some more people. John Coltrane has influenced me. McCoy Tyner and Keith Jarrett have influenced my playing. Another person who has influenced me compositionally is Robert Farnon. Do you know who he is? He arranges mood music, and he's the best. He can take a standard like Laura and put some changes in there that you would not believe! The Hi-Los were another influence on me harmonically. Actually I shouldn't say the Hi-Los, I should say Clare Fischer because it was really his arrangements for the Hi-Los that were a major influence on my voicings. Gil Evans was an influence, too, for orchestrating and sound, and when I say Gil, that also includes Miles because Miles was such a big influence on Gil orchestrally. The album Miles Ahead was also a big influence on me.

There have been some other things. Daphnis et Chloé by Ravel was a big influence. Some of the music of Debussy has also influenced me. Tony Williams has been a big influence on me rhythmically. Sly Stone (and his band and his music), James Brown, Rufus, Stevie Wonder--all of them have influenced me. Also, the music I've heard by Ravi Shankar, Ali Akbar Khan, and other Indian musicians has influenced me. That's a pretty good cross-section of influences!

2. Q: How would you define black music?

A: I'll try to come as close as I can, but black music is really undefinable. Maybe I can talk about some of its aspects, though. I would say that it is music that is, in effect, the experiences of black people in this country. The music I know as black music is music that came from this country from the experiences of black Americans. The music is really the sound of the music of humanity, but it came through black people because of the kinds of experiences we have had. The reason it has been such a big influence on the world is because everybody can find a piece of them-

selves in the music--in the rhythm, in the emotion, in the
subtle nuances in the music. This is why when people ask
me if I think that white people have the capacity to play
soulful music, I tell them yes. Maybe the music that we
call black music could not have originated with white people
because of the difference in the experiences that they've
had, but certainly once they've been exposed to the music,
white people can definitely create the music because they're
aware of it. It's like recognizing a part of themselves.

As far as content is concerned, I would say that the
emphasis seems not to be as much on technical precision
as it is in European music. In many cases, that takes a
back seat to the expression of emotion in the music. The
rhythm has a warmth that doesn't seem to be prevalent in
Western European music. There's a flexibility. Everything
isn't played down the middle of the beat. There is a sub-
division within the pulse; certain things are played on the
back part of the beat and certain things are played on the
front part. In jazz, and maybe in all black music, there
is an element of improvisation which requires a certain
amount of moment to moment teamwork and is more detailed
as far as the rhythmic elements are concerned than Western
European music. Most of the harmonies that I've come into
contact with in Afro-American music seem to come from
what I know to be Western European music. Concerning
melody, we all know about the notes that are called blue
notes and the notes that bend and all of that stuff. I think
that comes from Africa. I've heard that some of the scales
are tempered a little different in Africa, and I think this is
a carry-over from that. In vocal music there is a lot of
ornamentation on notes, like the way Aretha Franklin sings.
I don't know where that comes from, but I assume it comes
from the African roots. Middle Eastern music and Asian
music have a lot of ornamentation, but it seems like European music doesn't have much at all.

3. Q: What features of your own music do you see as uniquely
        black (in terms of both musical and philosophical considera-
        tions)? I think you described that partially in your answer
        to question two. 2
    A: Right, although there is a lot of Western European influence
        in my music. That's what Afro-Americans are; we're more
        Western European than we are African, even though the Af-
        rican influence peeks through in the music and in other
        ways. In the music I used to do (and what I have in mind
        here is the way I played on albums like Maiden Voyage,
        Speak Like a Child, and The Prisoner), many of the black
        elements I have described were present in a subtle way. I
        know that subtle is a comparative term, so I would say that
        compared to out-and-out soul music, many of the black ele-
        ments in the music I used to play were more subtle or more
        sophisticated. But now my music has changed and I have
        both the out-and-out funk-soul thing and the more sophisti-
        cated subtle thing. I can go in and out of each one and

have different combinations of the two, sometimes simultaneously and sometimes separately.

Q: Where did the real breakthrough come for you?
A: In Head Hunters. My musical thing has always been pretty varied. I have gone through a lot of different stages, but the change I made with Head Hunters was radically different from any of the changes I had made before. That was because of the chanting and the realization that I told you about. [3]

4. Q: In what ways is your music a reflection of your personal philosophy (social, political, etc.)?
A: We've talked about that already. [4]

5. Q: What do you see as the position or role of the black artist in contemporary society?
A: Are we talking about the influence of the product as well as the role of the artist? Let's talk about the whole thing, not just the person. Black music has been a major influence on the world from the standpoint of jazz and improvisation and from the standpoint of popular music, rock & roll, rhythm & blues, and soul music. It has been a major influence on other music, but the major influence has been on people themselves because they really like it. Consequently, people all over the world are exposed to it a lot. It's a leader in the whole musical scene except for the fact that it doesn't have much influence on contemporary classical music. However, there is an improvisatory character to contemporary classical music that conceptually, I think, relates to jazz. It doesn't sound like jazz, it doesn't sound soulful, and it doesn't sound black; but it sounds improvised. We know that Bach improvised and that even before Bach, people improvised. But I don't think that their concept of improvisation was an influence on contemporary Western European music. I think that the influence came from the improvisation of jazz people. That has also influenced the theater and the ballet. Now the thing is that there are very few people in the world who realize this consciously. Black artists are not really being recognized as the source of something which has been so momentous in the world since the turn of the century.

6. Q: Please discuss any problems you may have encountered in getting your works performed, published, and recorded.
A: I have my own publishing company, [5] so I don't have trouble getting stuff published. When I did my first album, the record company tried to insist that I put my tunes in their company; however, Donald Byrd had already showed me how to establish my own publishing company before I got the contract, so I was able to tell the record company that my tunes were already published. They said okay, and it was a good thing they did because at that time I had written Watermelon Man and they would have published it and made a mint! As it was, I made a mint!! (laughter)

I haven't had any problems getting my works performed, and I haven't had any problems getting them recorded.

6A. Q: How much of your actual output has ever been performed? Published? Recorded?

A: I would say about 95%. Everything has been published, but not all of it has been printed. So far, only Watermelon Man has been printed, but I just made a deal with the Hansen Company and they are going to print up just about all of my things. I made a list of the things that I felt might be the best ones to be printed. I would say that 95% of what I've written has been recorded.

6B. Q: Have you encountered difficulty in getting your works programmed?

A: No, but when you say programmed, do you also mean programmed on the radio?

Q: The question was originally written to get at the problems of having works programmed by various artists and ensembles for performance purposes; however, in your case, I think that extending its scope to deal with the problems of getting air play is very relevant.

A: The problem I have is that my tunes are always too long to get much air play (and when the music was pretty far out and long, it was even more difficult to get it played!). Radio is a business, and when they feel that the music is not going to hold on to a certain number of listeners, they're going to be reluctant to play it. I don't think it's a conspiracy against me or my music or anything like that. It's just a matter of economics.

6C. Q: Are there specific problems in getting a satisfactory performance? Exemplify and discuss.

A: I haven't had any because I play with the best musicians that there are. I'm not talking about just my band. Before I had my own band, I was with Miles Davis for five years and you can't get people any better than Miles Davis, Wayne Shorter, Ron Carter, and Tony Williams!

7. Q: What do you consider, at this point in your life, to be your most significant achievement(s) aside from your compositions?

A: I had a beautiful experience performing one evening in November of 1970 at the London House in Chicago. I had a sextet at that time, and I think that that particular performance was the first real collective high I had ever experienced. It was even more than anything I had experienced with Miles. It was really uncanny the communication that went on. It almost sounded like perfect music. And there was no thought involved. It was like my fingers were playing themselves. And everybody else was playing the same way! It was just so perfect, so mean!! There was that experience, and then there was also the one in Seattle that I told you about that was fantastic. [6]

I think of Head Hunters as an achievement just because
800,000 people liked it enough to buy the record. I've been
told that Head Hunters is the largest selling jazz record
ever and that the only one that even comes close is Take
Five by Dave Brubeck. Head Hunters still sells a couple
thousand records every five days. That's 10,000 records
a week, right? I used to sell 40,000 records for the life
of an album, but Head Hunters, which is two years old
sells 40,000 a month! That's a lot of records!!

There are certain other significant achievements relating
to my own self-development, but those are very personal
things that are happening as a result of the chanting.

8. Q: What do you see as the responsibilities and obligations of
       the educational system (at all levels) to the study of black
       music?

    A: Well, they are starting to address the subject now. There
       are schools that have courses on black music or jazz or
       ethnomusicology, and now a number of colleges and univer-
       sities are starting to do that. Considering my answer to
       question number five, which was about the influence of
       black music in contemporary society, I think that the re-
       sponsibilities and obligations of the educational system
       should be on a parallel with the importance of the music.

       Now, in looking at the specifics, that is, performance,
       history and literature courses, and so on, all of those
       things should be included. Not just the history of black
       music, but performance. The violin is not an instrument
       that's been prevalent in black music or jazz, so consequent-
       ly there aren't many string players who can really play.
       There are only a handful who can play black music the way
       brass players, woodwind players, and rhythm players can
       play it. There needs to be somebody teaching the technique
       of how to perform that kind of music. I think it would open
       other doors in classical music, and it would certainly open up
       the use of string instruments in jazz. But as it is, there are
       just certain things you can't write for string players because
       they're not going to play them the way the brass players can
       play them. So performance is very important just to expand
       the horizons of a lot of the classical players.

9. Q: Do you feel that the people who write about your music
       (critics in particular) understand what you are doing? Ex-
       emplify and discuss.

    A: Most of them don't, and that's really too bad. They might
       be eloquent writers, but as far as their own lives are con-
       cerned, I think they're a little too narrow-minded. They
       might be more open-minded than the average person in some
       cases but too narrow-minded to be critics. In other words,
       they have too much power in their hands for their scope.
       Sometimes they are too personal without explanation in their
       criticism. They'll say that this was bad or that this was
       good without saying that this is what they think and that
       their experience only includes this or that. They won't

qualify their statements enough to give the people a better understanding of the actual situation. They kind of set themselves up as tin gods.

Of course, I'm not saying that all of them are like that, but most of the ones I've run across have been like that. And that's not to say that they aren't nice people either. Many of them are very nice people. Some of my best friends are music critics! (laughter) Leonard Feather hates what I am doing now. (I don't think he liked what I did before too much, but compared to what I'm doing now, he loves that!) He hates what I'm doing now, but on a personal level I still consider him my friend. I realize that his scope just does not include the kinds of things that I am doing. The only thing I object to is the fact that he uses his value system to judge this kind of music and that's not fair. He doesn't like funky music so he shouldn't criticize it. He should say that he is not qualified to criticize it because he's not; any person involved with funky music knows that.

10. Q: What advice would you give to the aspiring young black composer?

A: Well, the first thing that I would say is start chanting Nam Myoho Renge Kyo. Get your life together; the development of your life is the foundation behind the development of your music. Second, be careful not to take what is told to you or what you read as fact. A lot of times musicians can get stifled by rules that they read in textbooks or by the things that their teachers tell them. As long as you remember that rules are just guidelines, that will help you find out what it is that you're trying to produce at any given moment in the music, or will help you get what you want into the music. Be careful about getting stifled. Third, listen to as many different kinds of music as you can. Try to find out as much as you can not only about the specific area you're dealing with, but about all aspects of music. For example, if you're a performer, find out about composing, about orchestrating, about other instruments, about recording, and about the business. I've found out that the more I know about the various aspects of the music business, the more it helps me do the different things that I do.

Part II: Music Questions

1. Q: When you sit down to begin a new composition on your own initiative or inspiration (as opposed to a commissioned work), what procedure or approach do you follow?

A: The very first thing I do is decide what it is that I'm trying to do and who the music is going to be for--for myself, for the musicians, for young people, or whatever. In my case, once I have an idea of what I want to do and who will most likely like it (and if I can be as honest as I can, that's going to be people 35 and under, a category which I'm almost out of myself. You notice I didn't say under 35!), I usually start with a bass line. Then, if the piece is going to be a pattern-type piece, I try to think about what kind of rhythmic pattern can be going on.

Now, I start with the bass line. I try to think about the bass not only as a melodic instrument but also as a rhythmic instrument in conjunction with the drums, and I try to put the two of them together in a way that makes some kind of sense according to my taste. This business of taste is a hard thing to speak about. It's my taste, but my taste coming from what standpoint? My taste as a musician or my taste as a human being? I use my taste as a human being rather than my taste as a musician to decide what's right and what's wrong in the music because my taste as a musician might be too esoteric. I used to have a hard time trying to hear music just as a person. I could only hear it in terms of the kinds of things that make musicians happy. I've gotten away from that, and now I try to listen in terms of what the non-musician (or educated non-musician) might hear. Then I try to figure out where it gets boring, where it needs to change, and what kind of changes should be made. Should there be rhythmic changes, changes in density, harmony colors? Once I do that, that pretty much takes care of the basic part of the composition with the exception of the melody. Then I have to deal with questions like where should there be melody? Should it go all the way through or should it only be in certain parts (and in what parts)? Should it be played strictly or can it be played in a skeletal way so that the person who's playing it will have more freedom to create his own part? I've got to make those kinds of decisions. There has got to be enough structure for the listener to be able to relate to it, so how far should I go? That's always the big question.

Once I'm done, I face the most difficult part and that is figuring out the title. It took me three months to find the title Maiden Voyage. I asked everybody I saw what the music sounded like. Finally, one of my sister's friends came over and, after listening to the tapes of the session and specifically that tune, he said, "It sounds like the sea or something," and I said, "Yes, that's right," and he said, "Maiden voyage." As soon as I heard it, I knew that was it. I chanted for the title Head Hunters. I was looking for a title that had something to do with the body (because it's a funky kind of music), something to do with the head (because there is something for the listener who will absorb the music intellectually), something primitive (because it appeals to man's basic emotional nature), and something sexual (because that's part of man, too). And the day I had to have the title, Head Hunters came. As I was chanting, I was writing down different things and BANG! It hit me and I knew that that was it. When I told my manager and record producer what the title was, he fell all up against the wall. He couldn't believe it because it fulfilled all the things I wanted. The heads of the people represent the

intellectual thing; it's primitive, because headhunters are
primitive people; it's the body because the head is part of
the body; and it's sexual, too. Really, choosing the titles
is the hardest part. I can do a whole movie score--40
pieces of music--in a couple of weeks, but it takes me
three months to find a title.

2. Q: When composing a commissioned work or a work written
for a specific occasion or person, does your procedure or
approach differ from the one you described in question one?
If so, in what way?

A: When I was talking about procedure before, I was talking
about starting out with a bass line. If I'm doing a movie
score, there might not even be a bass in it. It might just
require some melody on a solo instrument, so my approach
might be a little different and my considerations are going
to be different. I have to start with an understanding of
what my responsibilities are every step of the way with a
film. I have to satisfy the requirements of the director for
different parts of the film. There are times when I might
differ in opinion from the director, but I have to convince
him that my way of thinking will fulfill what he ultimately
desires more so than maybe what he has in mind. Now I'm
not talking about technical musical ideas like what chords
to use or something like that; I'm talking about what is supposed to happen conceptually during a certain scene. Those
kinds of things I might argue about. There are important
considerations. Should I underscore? Is what's happening
visually strong enough already to carry the scene and do I
just need to kind of put a cushion underneath so that what's
there will show its greatest strength? Or is what's happening visually a little too weak to carry the scene and should
the music be much stronger to fulfill the requirements? I
discuss these things with the director to begin with. I have
not done that many films, so I haven't had any real problems
with directors as yet. By the time we have a full discussion, we come to general agreements about most everything.
  Although Death Wish was my third film, it was the first
time I had to do the full scope of what film writers do.
With Blow-Up, I didn't have to catch any cues; I just had to
stay out of the way of what was happening visually. In the
next film, The Spook Who Sat by the Door, I didn't have the
information that I needed from the director before I wrote
the music in order to do all the stuff score writers are supposed to do, so Death Wish was the first time I had to do
the whole thing. There were many things I didn't know how
to do, so I bought Earle Hagen's book[7] and spent two weeks
studying it. I only had four weeks to write the music, so
I really wrote and recorded it in just two weeks!
  I have one more comment about number two, and that is
that I actually enjoy having limitations because they're like
guideposts. They're pre-set. I make a game out of it.
In a way, it makes things easier. You're not just flying
blind. You don't have to use your taste to determine what

should be nailed down where, because that's already a given. Take a film, for example. You already know how long it's got to be, you know what things have to be caught in the music and where they're supposed to go, and you can start by being very specific. In a way, that makes it easier for me. The other part of it is the idea of trying to make it all interesting and make it really sound musical. That's fun for me.

3. Q: In general, with regard to your writing, what genre(s) do you prefer?
   A: I like all the things I've done so far. I like working in TV and films, and I like records, too.

   Q: Is there anything you haven't done that you would like to do?
   A: Yes. I would like to do a symphonic work. I would also like someday to do a musical, although I don't think I'm ready to do a musical yet. I want to get into writing lyrics because I've never done that. One of these days, I'd also like to write a book.

4. Q: What do you consider your most significant composition? Please discuss.
   A: My most significant composition? Significant to whom? To me or to the people? Head Hunters was significant to me because it showed growth in my life and it worked. It was a very successful album, not from the money standpoint, but because so many people liked that album and are still buying it. Some people are on their second and third copies! I'm always knocked out when people tell me things like that about the album.
   I think that the best single composition I ever wrote was Maiden Voyage. You know, it's funny. I've heard some compositions since then that, to me, either sound like they were influenced by Maiden Voyage or were composed with the same kind of idea in mind. One example is What's Goin' On by Marvin Gaye, both in terms of the rhythmic thing as well as the way the chords move. You start with a 7th chord with the 11th on the bottom--a 7th chord with the suspended 4th--and then that chord moves up a minor third. That happens in What's Goin' On. My purpose in writing Maiden Voyage was to write a tune that had even eighth notes but didn't have the same kind of rock & roll back beat that I had been hearing around that time. Maiden Voyage has even eighth notes, but it's got a different kind of rhythm. It doesn't have any cadences; it just keeps moving around in a circle.
   I think Watermelon Man was a good composition, too. I analyzed it one time and it makes sense from beginning to end. It's a simple composition, but it makes sense.

5. Q: Please comment on your treatment of the following musical elements and give examples from your compositions that illustrate the techniques you describe.

A. Melody

HH: I think that most of my melodies sound like they are singable. I try to make them like that because I don't want people to get bored. I figure that if people can't remember them, they must be boring. A good example of melody for me is Maiden Voyage.

B. Harmony

HH: I use a lot of harmonies with fourths and fifths.

C. Rhythm

HH: Right now I'm into funky rhythms. Rhythm is so magnetic! There's an interesting kind of bass line I did on Palm Grease which is long, but is actually two bars of 5/4. One thing that I hate to do is to point a finger at the rhythms or the changing meters that I use. I try to make everything sound non-mathematical, non-computerized. It's not human to expose it that way. The bass line on Ostinato, which is on the album Mwandishi, is in 15/8, but it sounds very natural, and most people can't figure it out. If you listen to Palm Grease and listen to the bass part, listen to the drum part, and listen to the rhythm in the accompanying piano part, you'll hear an interplay of rhythms that's kind of interesting. It was really structured in a certain way to fit like pieces in a puzzle, but it flows.

Q: How much of that is preconceived and how much of it happens just because the performers are who they are?

A: Well, conceptually there is a lot there before we start to play, but the only thing you can play is an example of the conception; you can't play the conception. There is freedom to work within the conception and to keep changing things a lot. Now, we've talked a little about complex rhythms. Maiden Voyage is an example of the use of a simple rhythm.

D. Form

HH: My forms are basically simple right now because I'm not trying to concentrate on form. I just let the forms be pretty much the way they have been and concentrate more on other aspects such as rhythm. But in the past, I've used all kinds of forms. I've gone through the thing of trying to get away from the accepted forms and rhythms and harmonies, and I've got a lot of different kinds of music.

E. Improvisation

HH: I try to make things sound like they flow rather than sounding like I'm connecting up different chords. I try to make things sound more human and let things overlap when I'm improvising.

Q: How important is improvisation in terms of what you do compositionally?

A: I always leave 67½%. (laughter) I leave a lot of room for improvisation in the music that I write. I like to function off the philosophy that the musicians themselves should have a large input into a composition. If somebody brings me a fully composed piece for my band and unless it is really fantastic, I usually try to break it down. I try to figure out what its conception was from moment to moment and then restructure it so that the musicians themselves can really help determine how parts of it are supposed to be played. So improvisation is very important.

F. Text

HH: I haven't used text in an original composition. I haven't done any oratorios or large works like that involving extensive texts. Eventually I would like to do something like that, but that's not uppermost in my mind right now.

G. Instrumentation or medium

HH: The combination I liked the most was the one I used on Speak Like a Child, which was fluegelhorn, alto flute, and bass trombone. I also like mixing horns with different kinds of mutes and woodwinds. I have done some of that in my film scoring. I like mellow colors but I also like more strident colors as a contrast. I'm saying that, as opposed to a person who likes the really stark colors that have mellow things in contrast, my focus will be on the mellow things. That's just my own personal taste; I tend to gravitate toward that. I also like the use of effects--electronic and otherwise--in my compositions. The idea is to get away from depending on just notes to create music.

6. Q: Have difficulties with performance practice (inflection, phrasing, etc.) been a significant problem in having your works performed to your own satisfaction?

A: No, not at all.

7. Q: What major works are currently in progress? Please describe and discuss.

A: I'm working on a new album of my own and I'm producing two other albums. I didn't write any of the music for the

ones I am producing; there is just the one album of my own
that I'm working on as far as my own compositions are concerned. The compositions are really composed by everybody
in the band. The things we play may get written down later,
but they're not written out beforehand. We sit down and
somebody comes up with a bass line (or I might have one)
and maybe I might have one little thing written out--a melody or chords or something--and we just work on it together
from there. That's been happening now for about two or
three years.

8. Q: Given unlimited time and finances (and no restrictions what-
       soever), what would you write?
   A: I'd like to write something orchestral. I'd like to write
       something that is symphonic and funky and has a lot in it.
       It would be sort of a summary of the experiences I've had.

9. Q: If given the opportunity, would you choose to devote yourself
       to composition on a full-time basis? Why or why not?
   A: I wouldn't choose. I'd wait until the choice was made by
       the circumstances. If I came to a crossroads and had to
       choose, I'd chant and come up with an answer. But right
       now, I couldn't tell you what that would be.

10. Q: How would you describe your compositional style?
    A: You know, it would be easier for somebody else to answer
        that question than it would be for me to answer it. I'm
        too close to it. If I have to give you an answer, then I'll
        come up with something. Other people are the ones who
        are interested in figuring out what my style is; I don't care
        what my style is. When I get ready to write, I'm not
        thinking "I want to write this in Herbie Hancock style."
        Somebody else might want to figure out what my style is,
        but I don't care to. I'll try to give you an answer, though.
           Some of the things that I've already mentioned seem to
        be prevalent. [8] I can tell you that, just personally, I re-
        spond to melody, and I respond to that softness in ballads,
        and I respond to funky rhythms. Those are things that I
        can relate to right away and I might gravitate toward those
        things first. But what I do with them will vary. I'm one
        of those musicians who is really involved with a lot of dif-
        ferent styles. I take pride in being able to play on all
        kinds of different records and do them right. To try to
        do justice to all those different things is a challenge to me
        and keeps me from getting bored.

11. Q: What have been the influences of other composers, styles,
        and other types of music on your compositional style?
    A: Didn't I answer that before? I know I mentioned Stravinsky
        and a number of others. [9]

12. Q: Has your style changed across your career? If so, what
        influenced these changes or developments?
    A: I answered that already, but I don't know if I talked about

the changes that took place when I was going from albums like The Prisoner and Maiden Voyage to Mwandishi. When I left Miles, I started performing the music that I had been recording on my own, which included Maiden Voyage, Speak Like a Child, and those things. But then I started getting into the electric piano and devices a lot more, and I changed my band. I got Eddie Henderson, Julian Priester, and Billy Hart. (That was my second band. The first band had Johnny Cole, Garnett Brown, and Tootie Heath, and I went from Clifford Jordan to Joe Henderson.) The second band was a little further out. They were more into listening to people like Trane and Cecil Taylor, and were more interested in experimenting. I started getting into the idea of trying to use as little intellect as possible and try to somehow create the music based on reactions and intuition. That's when the music started getting out there and we did Mwandishi. We would usually have a framework because, if there is no framework and you depend entirely on intuition, you get to the point where you're blank and you have nothing to fall back on. All nights are not going to be great nights. Some nights we start out playing Ostinato and never even get to the tune. But then there are other times when nothing happens and we have to really lean heavily on the skeletal structure that we have. The keynote for that change is the focus on intuition, which is a lot to bite off!

Q: How does this relate to what you're doing with your current group?

A: The difference is that the band I've been discussing focused on intuition as opposed to using the structure. We purposely tried to avoid the simplest, easiest, or most obvious solution. In my present group we don't avoid anything. We do whatever is going to happen if we feel that we can maintain a relationship with the people who are listening to the music.

13. Q: When you are listening to music for your own enjoyment, what are your preferences?

A: I like modern jazz (and sometimes very avant-garde jazz), and I like contemporary classical music, impressionistic classical music, and electronic music. I think I mentioned before that I like Stravinsky and Bartok. All of the people that I talked about as having influenced me are among those I listen to for enjoyment. [10] These days I like listening to really funky music. I really dig listening to Rufus, and the different kinds of funky rhythms that happen in Sly Stone's music kill me! I don't listen to James Brown as much as I did a couple of years ago. I found that the approach Sly Stone uses is something that is more interesting to me.

Notes to Chapter V

1. Olivier Messiaen, The Technique of My Musical Language,

trans. John Satterfield. 2 vols. (Paris: Alphonse Leduc, 1956). The section dealing specifically with rhythm appears on pages 14-30 of volume one.

2. See especially the portion of Mr. Hancock's response to I-2 appearing in paragraph two.

3. See especially the portion of Mr. Hancock's response to I-1 appearing on pages 110-113.

4. See especially the portion of Mr. Hancock's response to I-1 appearing on pages 111-112.

5. The name of Mr. Hancock's company is Hancock Music.

6. See especially the portion of Mr. Hancock's response to I-1 appearing on pages 110-111.

7. Earle H. Hagen, Scoring for Films: A Complete Text (n. p.: E.D.J. Music, 1971). Distributed by Criterion Music Corporation (150 West 55th Street, New York, New York 10019).

8. See Mr. Hancock's responses to the following: I-2, I-3, II-1, and II-5.

9. See especially the portion of Mr. Hancock's response to I-1 appearing on page 114.

10. See especially the portion of Mr. Hancock's response to I-1 appearing on page 114.

LIST OF COMPOSITIONS

ACTUAL PROOF
   Jazz ensemble. Hancock Music. Recorded by Herbie Hancock (Columbia PC-32965: Thrust; Columbia single 3-10094: Actual Proof).

THE ALLEY
   See DEATH WISH.

ALONE AND I
   Jazz ensemble. Hancock Music. Recorded by Herbie Hancock (Blue Note BST-84109: Takin' Off).

AM I DOING THE RIGHT THING?
   See THE SPOOK WHO SAT BY THE DOOR.

AND WHAT IF I DON'T
   Jazz ensemble. Hancock Music. Recorded by Herbie Hancock (Blue Note BST-84126: My Point of View; Blue Note BN-LA399-

H2: Herbie Hancock).

ARE IN BEE
See THE SPOOK WHO SAT BY THE DOOR.

THE BED
See BLOW-UP.

BIRDHOUSE
Jazz ensemble. Selma Music. Recorded by the Pepper Adams-
Donald Byrd Quintet (Warwick W-2041: Out of This World).

BLIND MAN, BLIND MAN
Jazz ensemble. Hancock Music. Recorded by Herbie Hancock
(Blue Note BST-84126: My Point of View; Blue Note BST-89907;
The Best of Herbie Hancock; Blue Note BN-LA399-H2: Herbie
Hancock), by Donald Byrd (Verve V6-8609: Up with Donald
Byrd), by Clark Terry and Bobby Brookmeyer (Mainstream 320:
Clark Terry and Bobby Brookmeyer) and by Kai Winding (Quality
[Canada] V6-8661).

BLOW-UP
Film score. Metro-Goldwyn-Mayer. Sound track recorded on
MGM E-4447: The Original Sound Track Album of Blow-Up;
selections are as follows: The Bed, Blow-Up (Main Title),
Verushka (Part 1), Verushka (Part 2), The Naked Camera,
Bring Down the Birds, Jane's Theme, Stroll On (not written
by Herbie Hancock), The Thief, The Kiss, Curiosity, Thomas
Studies Photos, End Title Blow-Up.

BLUES FOR AN I.O.U.
See THE SPOOK WHO SAT BY THE DOOR.

BLUESVILLE
Co-written by A. Davis and Joe Josea. Modern Music.

BRING DOWN THE BIRDS
See BLOW-UP.

BUBBLES
Jazz ensemble. Co-written by Melvin M. Ragin. Co-published
by Hancock Music and Wahwatson Music. Recorded by Herbie
Hancock (Columbia PC-33812: Man-Child).

BUTTERFLY
Jazz ensemble. Co-written by Bennie Maupin. Hancock Music.
Recorded by Herbie Hancock (Columbia PC-32965: Thrust) and
by Henry Mancini (RCA Victor APDI-1025: Symphonic Soul).

CANTALOUPE ISLAND
Jazz ensemble. Hancock Music. Recorded by Herbie Hancock
(Blue Note BST-84175: Empyrean Isles; Blue Note BN-LA399-
H2: Herbie Hancock; Columbia PC-34280; Secrets), by Donald
Byrd (Verve V6-8609: Up With Donald Byrd), by Jean-Luc

Ponty (Blue Note BN-LA632-H2: Cantaloupe Island), by Nat Adderley (Atlantic 1460), by Hugh Masakela (MGM 4372), and by
El Chicano (MCA 548: Viva Tirado; Kapp 3632).

CHAMELEON
Jazz ensemble. Co-written by Harvey Mason, Bennie Maupin,
and Paul Jackson. Hancock Music. Recorded by Herbie Hancock (Columbia KC-32731: Head Hunters), by Maynard Fergu-
son (Columbia KC-33007: Chameleon), by Louis Bellson (Pablo
2310755: Louis Bellson/Explosion; RCA 755), and by Buddy
Rich (Pickwick 3301).

CIA
See THE SPOOK WHO SAT BY THE DOOR.

COBRA THEME
See THE SPOOK WHO SAT BY THE DOOR.

COBRA TRAINING
See THE SPOOK WHO SAT BY THE DOOR.

CROSSINGS (1974)
Jazz ensemble. Hancock Music. Recorded by Herbie Hancock
(Warner Brothers single WB-2807: Crossings).

CURIOSITY
See BLOW-UP.

DEATH WISH
Film score. Paramount. Sound track recorded on Columbia
PC-33199: Death Wish; selections are as follows: Death Wish
(Main Title), Joanna's Theme, Do a Thing, Paint Her Mouth,
Rich Country, Suite Revenge (A. Striking Back, B. Riverside
Park, C. The Alley, D. Last Stop, E. 8th Avenue Station),
Ochoa Knose, Party People, Fill Your Hands.

DO A THING
See DEATH WISH.

DOIN' IT
Jazz ensemble. Co-written by Melvin Ragin and R. Parker, Jr.
Co-published by Hancock Music and Wahwatson Music. Recorded
by Herbie Hancock (Columbia PC-34280: Secrets).

DOLPHIN DANCE
Jazz ensemble. Hancock Music. Recorded by Herbie Hancock
(Blue Note BST-84195: Maiden Voyage) and by Ahmad Jamal
(Impulse AS-9217: Freeflight; Impulse AS-9260: Reevaluations:
The Impulse Years).

DRIFTIN'
Jazz ensemble. Hancock Music. Recorded by Herbie Hancock
(Blue Note BST-84109: Takin' Off; Blue Note BN-LA399-H2:
Herbie Hancock).

THE EGG
    Jazz ensemble. Hancock Music. Recorded by Herbie Hancock
    (Blue Note BST-84175: Empyrean Isles).

8TH AVENUE STATION
    See DEATH WISH.

EMPTY POCKETS
    Jazz ensemble. Hancock Music. Recorded by Herbie Hancock
    (Blue Note BST-84109: Takin' Off; Blue Note BN-LA399-H2:
    Herbie Hancock).

END TITLE BLOW-UP
    See BLOW-UP.

THE EYE OF THE HURRICANE
    Jazz ensemble. Hancock Music. Recorded by Herbie Hancock
    (Blue Note BST-84195: Maiden Voyage).

FAT ALBERT ROTUNDA (1973)
    Jazz ensemble. Hancock Music. Recorded by Herbie Hancock
    (Warner Brothers WS-1834: Fat Albert Rotunda).

FAT MAMA
    Jazz ensemble. Hancock Music. Recorded by Herbie Hancock
    (Warner Brothers WS-1834: Fat Albert Rotunda) and by Woody
    Herman (Fantasy 9416: The Raven Speaks; Fantasy single 695:
    Fat Mama).

FILL YOUR HANDS
    See DEATH WISH.

FIREWATER
    Jazz ensemble. Hancock Music. Recorded by Herbie Hancock
    (Blue Note BST-84321: The Prisoner).

FREEMAN & JOY
    See THE SPOOK WHO SAT BY THE DOOR.

GENTLE THOUGHTS
    Jazz ensemble. Co-written by Melvin Ragin. Co-published by
    Hancock Music and Wahwatson Music. Recorded by Herbie
    Hancock (Columbia PC-34280: Secrets).

GOODBYE TO CHILDHOOD
    Jazz ensemble. Hancock Music. Recorded by Herbie Hancock
    (Blue Note BST-84279: Speak Like a Child; Blue Note BST-
    89907: The Best of Herbie Hancock); Blue Note BN-LA399-H2:
    Herbie Hancock).

HANG UP YOUR HANG UPS
    Jazz ensemble. Co-written by Melvin M. Ragin and Paul Jack-
    son. Hancock Music. Recorded by Herbie Hancock (Columbia

PC-33812: Man-Child; Columbia single 3-10239: Hang Up Your Hang Ups).

HE WHO LIVES IN FEAR
Jazz ensemble. Hancock Music. Recorded by Herbie Hancock (Blue Note BST-84321: The Prisoner; Blue Note BST-89907: The Best of Herbie Hancock).

HEARTBEAT
Jazz ensemble. Co-written by Melvin M. Ragin and Paul Jackson. Hancock Music. Recorded by Herbie Hancock (Columbia PC-33812: Man-Child).

HEY HO
Jazz ensemble. Hancock Music. Recorded by Herbie Mann (Atlantic 1483).

HIDDEN SHADOWS (1974)
Jazz ensemble. Hancock Music. Recorded by Herbie Hancock (Columbia KC-32212: Sextant).

HORNETS
Jazz ensemble. Hancock Music. Recorded by Herbie Hancock (Columbia KC-32212: Sextant) and by Herbie Hancock and the CTI All-Stars (CTI 6049: In Concert, vol. 2).

I HAVE A DREAM
Jazz ensemble. Hancock Music. Recorded by Herbie Hancock (Blue Note BST-84321: The Prisoner; Blue Note BST-89907: The Best of Herbie Hancock).

I LIKE THE WAY YOU SMELL
Unart Music.

I LOVE NEW YORK
Co-written by Claire Lynne Francis. Hancock Music.

JACK RABBIT
Jazz ensemble. Hancock Music. Recorded by Herbie Hancock (Blue Note BST-84147: Inventions and Dimensions; Blue Note BN-LA152-F: Succotash).

JANE'S THEME
See BLOW-UP.

JESSICA
Jazz ensemble. Hancock Music. Recorded by Herbie Hancock (Warner Brothers WS-1834: Fat Albert Rotunda).

JOANNA'S THEME
See DEATH WISH.

A JUMP AHEAD
Jazz ensemble. Hancock Music. Recorded by Herbie Hancock

(Blue Note BST-84147: <u>Inventions and Dimensions</u>; Blue Note BN-LA152-F: <u>Succotash</u>).

KING COBRA
Jazz ensemble. Hancock Music. Recorded by Herbie Hancock (Blue Note BST-84126: <u>My Point of View</u>; Blue Note BST-89907: <u>The Best of Herbie Hancock</u>).

THE KISS
See BLOW-UP.

LAST STOP
See DEATH WISH.

LI'L BROTHER
Jazz ensemble. Hancock Music. Recorded by Herbie Hancock (Warner Brothers WS-1834: <u>Fat Albert Rotunda</u>; Warner Brothers 2WS-2807: <u>Treasure Chest</u>).

LITTLE ONE
Jazz ensemble. Hancock Music. Recorded by Herbie Hancock (Blue Note BST-84195: <u>Maiden Voyage</u>) and by Miles Davis (Columbia PC-9150: <u>E. S. P.</u>).

MADNESS (1972)
Jazz ensemble. Hancock Music. Recorded by Miles Davis (Columbia CS-9594: <u>Nefertiti</u>).

MAIDEN VOYAGE
Jazz ensemble. Hancock Music. Recorded by Herbie Hancock (Blue Note BST-84195: <u>Maiden Voyage</u>; Blue Note BST-89907: <u>The Best of Herbie Hancock</u>; Blue Note BN-LA399-H2: <u>Herbie Hancock</u>); by Bobby Hutcherson (Blue Note BST-84231: <u>Happenings</u>); by Ramsey Lewis (Cadet 811: <u>Maiden Voyage</u>; Cadet 839: <u>The Best of Ramsey Lewis</u>); by Blood, Sweat, and Tears (Columbia 31780: <u>New Blood</u>); by Brian Auger (RCA Victor CPL-2-1230: <u>Live Oblivion, Vol. 2</u>); and by Denny Zeitlin (CBS 9548).

THE MAZE
Jazz ensemble. Co-written by John Scott. Hancock Music. Recorded by Herbie Hancock (Blue Note BST-84109: <u>Takin' Off</u>).

MIMOSA
Jazz ensemble. Hancock Music. Recorded by Herbie Hancock (Blue Note BST-84147: <u>Inventions and Dimensions</u>; Blue Note BN-LA152-F: <u>Succotash</u>).

THE NAKED CAMERA
See BLOW-UP.

NEW CONCERTO
Duchess Music.

OCHOA KNOSE
See DEATH WISH.

OH! OH! HERE HE COMES
Jazz ensemble. Hancock Music. Recorded by Herbie Hancock
(Warner Brothers WS-1834: Fat Albert Rotunda).

OLD FRIENDS
See THE SPOOK WHO SAT BY THE DOOR.

OLILOQUI VALLEY
Jazz ensemble. Hancock Music. Recorded by Herbie Hancock
(Blue Note BST-84175: Empyrean Isles; Blue Note BST-89907:
The Best of Herbie Hancock).

ONE FINGER SNAP
Jazz ensemble. Hancock Music. Recorded by Herbie Hancock
(Blue Note BST-84175: Empyrean Isles).

OSTINATO (SUITE FOR ANGELA)
Jazz ensemble. Hancock Music. Recorded by Herbie Hancock
(Warner Brothers WS-1898: Mwandishi; Warner Brothers 2WS-
2807: Treasure Chest).

PAINT HER MOUTH
See DEATH WISH.

PALM GREASE
Jazz ensemble. Hancock Music. Recorded by Herbie Hancock
(Columbia PC-32965: Thrust; Columbia single 3-10050: Palm
Grease).

PARTY PEOPLE
See DEATH WISH.

PEOPLE MUSIC
Jass ensemble. Co-written by Melvin Ragin and Paul Jackson.
Co-published by Hancock Music and Wahwatson Music. Recorded
by Herbie Hancock (Columbia PC-34280: Secrets).

PIPES
See THE SPOOK WHO SAT BY THE DOOR.

THE PLEASURE IS MINE
Jazz ensemble. Hancock Music. Recorded by Herbie Hancock
(Blue Note BST-84126: My Point of View).

PRETTY WILLIE
See THE SPOOK WHO SAT BY THE DOOR.

THE PRISONER
Jazz ensemble. Hancock Music. Recorded by Herbie Hancock
(Blue Note BST-84321: The Prisoner; Blue Note BN-LA399-H2:
Herbie Hancock).

PROMISE OF THE SUN
Jazz ensemble. Hancock Music. Recorded by Herbie Hancock (Blue Note BST-84321: The Prisoner).

RAIN DANCE
Jazz ensemble. Hancock Music. Recorded by Herbie Hancock (Columbia KC-32212: Sextant).

REQUIEM
Jazz ensemble. Hancock Music. Recorded by Donald Byrd (Blue Note BST-84101: Royal Flush).

RICH COUNTRY
See DEATH WISH.

RIOT
Jazz ensemble. Hancock Music. Recorded by Herbie Hancock (Blue Note BST-84279: Speak Like a Child; Blue Note BST-89907: The Best of Herbie Hancock) and by Miles Davis (Columbia CS-9594: Nefertiti).

RIVERSIDE PARK
See DEATH WISH.

SLEEPING GIANT (1972)
Jazz ensemble. Hancock Music. Recorded by Herbie Hancock (Warner Brothers WB-3038: Crossings; Warner Brothers 2WS-2807: Treasure Chest).

SLY
Jazz ensemble. Hancock Music. Recorded by Herbie Hancock (Columbia KC-32731: Head Hunters).

THE SORCERER
Jazz ensemble. Hancock Music. Recorded by Herbie Hancock (Blue Note BST-84279: Speak Like a Child) and by Miles Davis (Columbia CS-9532: Sorcerer).

SPANK-A-LEE
Jazz ensemble. Co-written by Paul Jackson and Mike Clarke. Hancock Music. Recorded by Herbie Hancock (Columbia PC-32965: Thrust).

SPEAK LIKE A CHILD
Jazz ensemble. Hancock Music. Recorded by Herbie Hancock (Blue Note BST-84279: Speak Like a Child; Blue Note BN-LA 399-H2: Herbie Hancock).

SPIDER
Jazz ensemble. Co-written by Melvin Ragin and Paul Jackon. Co-published by Hancock Music and Wahwatson Music. Recorded by Herbie Hancock (Columbia PC-34280: Secrets).

THE SPOOK WHO SAT BY THE DOOR
Film score. United Artists. Sound track recorded on Columbia
KC-32944: The Spook Who Sat by the Door; selections are as
follows: Main Theme, CIA, Are in Bee, Am I Doing the Right
Thing?, Cobra Theme, Blues for an I.O.U., Cobra Training,
Freeman & Joy, Pretty Willie, Old Friends, Pipes.

STEPPIN' IN IT
Jazz ensemble. Hancock Music. Recorded by Herbie Hancock
(Columbia PC-33812: Man-Child).

STRIKING BACK
See DEATH WISH.

SUCCOTASH
Jazz ensemble. Hancock Music. Recorded by Herbie Hancock
(Blue Note BST-84147: Inventions and Dimensions; Blue Note
BST-89907: The Best of Herbie Hancock; Blue Note BN-LA152-
F: Succotash).

SUITE FOR ANGELA
See OSTINATO.

SUITE REVENGE
See DEATH WISH.

SUN TOUCH
Jazz ensemble. Hancock Music. Recorded by Herbie Hancock
(Columbia PC-33812: Man-Child; Columbia single 3-10239:
Sun Touch).

SURVIVAL OF THE FITTEST
Jazz ensemble. Hancock Music. Recorded by Herbie Hancock
(Blue Note BST-84195: Maiden Voyage).

SWAMP RAT
Jazz ensemble. Co-written by Melvin Ragin and Paul Jackson.
Co-published by Hancock Music and Back Door Music. Recorded
by Herbie Hancock (Columbia PC-34280: Secrets).

TELL ME A BEDTIME STORY
Jazz ensemble. Hancock Music. Recorded by Herbie Hancock
(Warner Brothers WS-1834: Fat Albert Rotunda; Warner Broth-
ers 2WS-2807: Treasure Chest) and by Dr. Music (GRT of
Canada 1005).

TERRY
Co-written by Jerry Heyward, Robert Leak, James MacCawthall,
and David Cox. Starflower Productions Inc.

THE THIEF
See BLOW-UP.

THOMAS STUDIES PHOTOS
See BLOW-UP.

THREE BAGS FULL
Jazz ensemble. Hancock Music. Recorded by Herbie Hancock
(Blue Note BST-84109: Takin' Off; Blue Note BN-LA399-H2:
Herbie Hancock).

TOO MANY NIGHTS IN NEW YORK CITY
Co-published by Huffman Publishing and Unart Music.

TOYS
Jazz ensemble. Hancock Music. Recorded by Herbie Hancock
(Blue Note BST-84279: Speak Like a Child; Blue Note BN-
LA399-H2: Herbie Hancock).

THE TRAITOR
Jazz ensemble. Co-written by Melvin M. Ragin, Louis E.
Johnson, and Wayne Shorter. Hancock Music. Recorded by
Herbie Hancock (Columbia PC-33812: Man-Child).

TRIANGLE
Jazz ensemble. Hancock Music. Recorded by Herbie Hancock
(Blue Note BST-84147: Inventions and Dimensions; Blue Note
BN-LA399-H2: Herbie Hancock; Blue Note BN-LA152-F: Succo-
tash).

A TRIBUTE TO SOMEONE
Jazz ensemble. Hancock Music. Recorded by Herbie Hancock
(Blue Note BST-84126: My Point of View).

VEIN MELTER
Jazz ensemble. Hancock Music. Recorded by Herbie Hancock
(Columbia KC-32731: Head Hunters).

VERUSHKA
See BLOW-UP.

WATERMELON MAN
Jazz ensemble. Lyric written by Gloria Lynne. Hancock Mu-
sic. Recorded by Herbie Hancock (Blue Note BST-84109: Takin'
Off; Blue Note BST-89907: The Best of Herbie Hancock; Colum-
bia KC-32731: Head Hunters), by Nat Adderley (Prestige 10090:
Double Exposure), by Mongo Santamaria (Columbia CS-1060:
Mongo Santamaria's Greatest Hits; Columbia single 3-33087;
Trip TOP-60-3: Super Oldies of the 60s, vol. 3), by Trini
Lopez (NOLC 1637), by King Curtis (Capitol 3293), by the
Gerald Wilson Orchestra (United Artists 20099), by Gloria
Lynne (Mercury single), by Xavier Cugat (Polydor 60793), by
Harold Alexander (Flying Dutchman 10148), by Enoch Light
(Command 979: Impelling Dances of Our Times), by Buddy Guy
(Ampex 79323), by Fred Wesley and the JBs (People single
617), by Herbie Mann (CBS 7073), by Ray Bryant (Chess/Janus

50052), and by Woody Herman (Fantasy 9416: The Raven Speaks; Trip 5570: Encore: Woody Herman, 1963).

WIGGLE-WAGGLE
Jazz ensemble. Hancock Music. Recorded by Herbie Hancock (Warner Brothers WS-1834: Fat Albert Rotunda; Warner Brothers 2WS-2807: Treasure Chest).

YOU KNOW WHAT TO DO
Co-written by Billy Towne. Pine Knob Music

YOU'LL KNOW WHEN YOU GET THERE
Jazz ensemble. Hancock Music. Recorded by Herbie Hancock (Warner Brothers WS-1898: Mwandishi; Warner Brothers 2WS-2807: Treasure Chest).

BIBLIOGRAPHY

Anderson, Monroe. "Herbie Hancock, the Country's Leading Jazz Pianist, Sees Jazz Coming Back in a Big Way." The National Observer, 5 July 1971, p. 18.

Comas, B. "The Jazz Rap of Herbie Hancock." Soul, 10 May 1971.

Cuscuna, Michael. "Herbie Hancock's Declaration of Independence." down beat, 1 May 1969.

"88 Divided by 4: Herbie Hancock, Roger Kellaway, Joe Sample, Toshiko." down beat, 26 October 1972. This is part one of a roundtable discussion conducted by Harvey Siders.

"88 Divided by 4." down beat, 9 November 1972. This is part two of the roundtable discussion with Herbie Hancock, Roger Kellaway, Joe Sample, and Toshiko Akiyoshi conducted by Harvey Siders.

Feather, Leonard. The Encyclopedia of Jazz in the Sixties. New York: Horizon Press, 1966.

Freedland, Nat. "Herbie Hancock; A Crossover Artist Who Feels None the Worse for the Trip." Billboard, 29 June 1974, p. 40.

"Hancock Looks at Jazz." BMI: The Many Worlds of Music, December 1971, p. 5.

Heckman, Don. "Herbie Hancock." down beat, 21 October 1965.

"Improvising on the Beat." Time, 8 July 1974, pp. 37-38.

Jagajivan. "Musing with Mwandishi." down beat. 24 May 1973.

Johnson, Brooks. "Herbie Hancock: Into His Own Thing." down beat, 21 January 1971.

Koral, Burt. "Herbie Hancock: Continued Growth." International Musician 66 (April 1968): 11+.

Palmer, Bob. "Jazz/Rock '74: The Plain Funky Truth." Rolling Stone, 1 August 1974, pp. 16-17.

Priestley, Brian. "Herbie Hancock's 'Firewater' Solo Transcribed and Annotated by Brian Priestley." down beat, 26 November 1970.

"Study." The New Yorker, 12 June 1971, p. 29.

Tiegel, Eliot. "The Synthesizer: Improvising Requires Special Care Claims Herbie Hancock." Billboard, 8 February 1975, p. 28+.

Townley, Ray. "Hancock Plugs In." down beat, 24 October 1974.

Who's Who Among Black Americans, 1st ed. (1975-76), s.v. "Hancock, Herbert Jeffrey."

Who's Who in America. 38th ed. (1974-75), s.v. "Hancock, Herbert Jeffrey."

Who's Who in the East. 14th ed. (1974-75), s.v. "Hancock, Herbert Jeffrey."

CHAPTER VI

ULYSSES SIMPSON KAY

Ulysses Simpson Kay was born January 1, 1917 in Tucson, Arizona. His educational background includes a B. M. (1938) from the University of Arizona and an M. M. in composition (1940) from the Eastman School of Music, where he studied with Howard Hanson and Bernard Rogers. He was subsequently awarded scholarships which enabled him to study with Paul Hindemith at the Berkshire Music Center in 1941 and during the following academic year at Yale University. Later he also studied with Otto Luening at Columbia University.

From 1953 to 1968 Dr. Kay served as a consultant on concert music for Broadcast Music Inc. During this period he was also involved in a number of official travel missions, the most notable being the 1965 State Department Cultural Exchange Mission which sent American composers to the Soviet Union for the first time. Prior to his 1968 appointment as Professor of Music at the Herbert H. Lehman College of the City University of New York, Dr. Kay held faculty positions at Boston College and the University of California at Los Angeles.

Dr. Kay has received numerous honors and awards including a Ditson Fellowship, a Rosenwald Fellowship, a Fulbright Scholarship, and a Guggenheim Fellowship. He was twice awarded the prestigious Prix de Rome, and has been given honorary doctorates by Lincoln University (Pa.), Bucknell University (Pa.), the University of Arizona, and Illinois Wesleyan University. He has been the recipient of commissions from such organizations as the Koussevitsky Foundation, the National Symphony, Opera South, the Louisville Orchestra, the Atlanta Symphony, the American Choral Directors Association, the Juilliard School of Music, and the Harlem School of the Arts.

Dr. Kay's sizable compositional output includes works for orchestra, chamber ensemble, piano, chorus, voice and piano, and various solo instruments with piano or in combination with other instrumental ensembles. He has also written operas, a ballet, and scores for a number of television and film productions. Among his best-known works are Markings (recorded by the London Symphony Orchestra), Of New Horizons (winner of the 1946 American Broadcasting Company Award), Three Pieces After Blake, Brass Quartet

Ulysses S. Kay (courtesy of the composer)

(recorded by members of the American Brass Quintet), <u>Fantasy</u>
<u>Variations</u> (recorded by the Oslo Philharmonic Orchestra), <u>Choral</u>
<u>Triptych</u> (recorded by the King's Chapel Choir of Boston), <u>Umbrian</u>
<u>Scene</u> (recorded by the Louisville Orchestra), and his score for the
film <u>The Quiet One</u>.

Part I: General Questions

1. Q: What persons, events, and works (of art, literature, etc.)
      have influenced you in general as well as in terms of your
      musical activities?
   A: The influences are my uncle King Oliver, William Grant
      Still, and one teacher--Bernard Rogers.

2. Q: How would you define black music?
   A: Music written or conceived by blacks.

3. Q: What features of your own music do you see as uniquely
      black (in terms of both musical and philosophical considera-
      tions)?
   A: I have nothing especially other than its expressive content.

4. Q: In what ways is your music a reflection of your personal
      philosophy (social, political, etc.)?
   A: I have nothing to say other than it's a reflection of me.

5. Q: What do you see as the position or role of the black artist
      in contemporary society?
   A: To communicate his visions through his talent.

6. Q: Please discuss any problems you may have encountered in
      getting your works performed, published, and recorded.
   A: No special problems other than economic ones. This applies
      mainly to recordings.

6A. Q: How much of your actual output has ever been performed?
       published? recorded?
    A: Performance, I'd say 98%. Published, about 65%. Recorded,
       about 18%.

6B. Q: Have you encountered difficulty in getting your works pro-
       grammed?
    A: No more difficulty than most living composers.

6C. Q: Are there specific problems in getting a satisfactory per-
       formance? Exemplify and discuss.
    A: Depending on how difficult the work is, and the amount of
       rehearsal time; those are the only problems I run up against.

7. Q: What do you consider, at this point in your life, to be
      your most significant achievement(s) aside from your
      compositions?

A: I would say my travel experiences, relating to people, and teaching.

8. Q: What do you see as the responsibilities and obligations of the educational system (at all levels) to the study of black music?

    A: The answer would be to make the extensive works and influences of blacks known and to give blacks credit for the same.

9. Q: Do you feel that the people who write about your music (critics in particular) understand what you are doing? Exemplify and discuss.

    A: I would say that a few of these people who write about music know--or seem to understand and know--what they are doing, but I would say there are very few because it seems most critics are poorly prepared to deal with contemporary music in general. I think there are a few good ones: you might cite Tom Willis in Chicago and Donald Henahan in New York.

10. Q: What advice would you give to the aspiring young black composer?

    A: My advice would be for the composer to learn more and work to express a personal vision. By advising a composer to learn more I am referring basically to the craft, but I feel there is a great deal to learn about performance in terms of relating to musicians and performers (for instance, the percussion section) that they don't teach in school. I have been writing a long time, but not being a player, it's a very special world. A composer has to constantly study, try out, and think about these possibilities to improve his work--to learn more through study and personal growth.

Part II: Music Questions

1. Q: When you sit down to begin a new composition on your own initiative or inspiration (as opposed to a commissioned work), what procedure or approach do you follow?

    A: I start with a musical idea which might be a theme, a motif, or a progression, and I work from there trying to bring the idea to its fullest fruition.

2. Q: When composing a commissioned work or a work written for a specific occasion or person, does your procedure or approach differ from the one you described in question 1? If so, in what way?

    A: I would say not especially; it doesn't differ especially except that the procedure is conditioned by the group that commissioned the piece. If I'm writing for a certain set of circumstances, that does, in some way, determine characteristics of the piece--how difficult it is, how long it is, etc. Other than that, I work pretty much the same way.

3. Q: In general, with regard to your writing, what genre(s) do you prefer?
   A: I really prefer the symphony orchestra and the chorus, separately and together. I have written several cantatas, but I think separately is what I prefer.

4. Q: What do you consider your most significant composition? Please discuss.
   A: I would say Markings. I feel it is significant because it is big in scope as well as in expression, and I feel it's quite personal in terms of how it's worked out.

5. Q: Please comment on your treatment of the following musical elements and give examples from your compositions that illustrate the techniques you describe.[1]

   A. Melody
      UK: The adagio from my Serenade for Orchestra.

   B. Harmony
      UK: Markings. The very opening has a striking harmonic configuration. The usage in general is not functional tonal harmony but basically the piece is tonal.

   C. Rhythm
      UK: This would be in a lot of my pieces, but specifically I would cite the scherzo from the Serenade for Orchestra.

   D. Form
      UK: Markings again.

   E. Improvisation
      UK: There's none worth mentioning. I have a few little passages that are free in some of the chamber orchestra pieces, but they're so brief--like only a bar and a half. They sort of noodle on five or six notes while there's a fermata, so it's not really improvisation in the sense that you usually think of it.

   F. Text
      UK: Text would be Three Pieces After Blake, which is for soprano and orchestra. As far as choice of texts is concerned, I just wrote the Blake piece for myself--it wasn't commissioned. But usually if I have to write a choral piece or a vocal piece for someone, I'll read a lot; I'll just get an anthology of poetry or, if going through an

anthology I run across several poets who sort of
interest me, I'll get their collected works and
scan the poems. Usually, unless I have a lead
of the sort that somebody says that such-and-such
by Carlos Williams or Langston Hughes or whoever is a marvelous poem, I don't specifically
look for a particular poem. Occasionally I'll have a
lead--like a sort of patriotic piece for the Bicentennial or a choral piece for the Presbyterians or
something--but in general I just read. Ordinarily,
especially in an anthology, I'll read two or three
lines and if the poetry doesn't grip me, then forget it. Poetry is a special medium, and to compose I need a special kind of poetry; if I don't
have some kind of reaction within three or four
lines, then I'm convinced that the poem isn't for
me. I could read the other twenty lines or ten
pages; I've tried it many times, to be fair to the
author or to the poetry, but inevitably I've very
seldom found this intuitive reaction to be wrong.
If it grips me immediately, I can pursue it.
Once I've chosen the text, I really work melodically. Usually I choose a text in a context of two
or three poems that are going to make a piece.
I very seldom write one little psalm or song.
Even my cantatas--one of which is 25 minutes
long, another which is 30 minutes long--consist of
several movements which are four to six minutes
in length. I usually carry the text around with
me in the sense of practically memorizing it; I
kind of live with it. Then it sort of germinates
and thematic ideas come to me. But I never just
sit down and figure out that rhythmically the piece
is going to be

ta   da   ta   da   ta   da   ta   da

In fact, I've tried to study prosody and I can't
keep it on my mind. Every time it comes up I
have to look up the meters all over again.

G.   <u>Instrumentation or medium</u>
     UK: I would say <u>Markings</u>; there is something new in
         the scherzo section which I never did before.
         There is a use of percussion--the whole percussion
         choir--and what I call klangfarben melodie. It's
         sort of like the Schoenberg except it really doesn't
         stay on those two or three chords the way he has
         it in <u>Five Pieces for Orchestra</u>. Instead, the
         chord sort of radiates all around the orchestra.
         You'd have to look at the score to know what I
         mean. [2] It'll be in low muted strings and then a

little shift over to perhaps medium to moderately soft woodwinds to muted brass. At one point there is a four- or five-part string bass harmonic way up in the treble clef. So the concept stems from klangfarbenmelodie, except the chord shifts constantly. The chord is sustained, but I mean the color and the component notes of this changing chord shift constantly and it's there to hold together the movement of the percussion. The thematic thing is really in the percussion. It's not melodic; there is no xylophone or tune.

One other use of instrumentation that is, I feel, somewhat distinctive is in Markings, rehearsal number 38 to measure two of rehearsal number 41. The point of usage here is a kind of color melody that goes on in certain of the woodwinds. The thematic thing is in the woodwinds. It's also cued in one solo viola. That cue is only to give a little stability and sort of continuity to the melodic line. In fact, it would be better if it weren't played because if the woodwinds do it right you don't need the viola to do it. It's a very static sort of melody; it doesn't move around that much because the movement is really in the muted strings doing 32nd notes against it. This is not exactly a chorale prelude technique, but it stems from that. There are some doublings since this is a big orchestra piece and was originally written to be played outdoors. Even with the doublings each instrument only plays one note, so that perhaps stems from Webern somewhat except that his is much more pointilistic and brief and this is sostenuto. In fact, the marking is andante sostenuto. So melodically, I guess, it's closer to a chorale prelude technique than a Webern technique, but the fact that this melody is going on with accompanying moving texture in the strings is a little unusual and makes a good effect.

6. Q: Have difficulties with performance practice (inflection, phrasing, etc.) been a significant problem in having your works performed to your own satisfaction?

A: No. I write very easy music (laughter)--that was sort of tongue-in-cheek. Walter Hendl just did a piece of mine with the Juilliard orchestra and he said, "My God! That's so hard!" And it was simply a little triplet, a quarter note triplet within a 5/8 bar. It wasn't hard on the page, but it was very hard to get twenty-five strings to do it in good ensemble, so I was really kidding when I said I write very easy music. Basically, I don't think it's that hard. So for number six, I'll just say no, I write very easy music and we can let our readers chew that over!

7. Q: What major works are currently in progress? Please describe and discuss.

    A: I am doing a piece tentatively titled The Western Paradise. That's the title we're using, but it may be changed so that's why I said tentative. It's for female narrator and orchestra and was commissioned by the National Symphony for the Bicentennial. I read myself silly and couldn't find anything, so I finally had to get a writer to do a text for me. Basically it's the American Revolution as seen from the British point of view.

8. Q: Given unlimited time and finances (and no restrictions whatsoever) what would you write?

    A: The answer is an opera.

9. Q: If given the opportunity would you choose to devote yourself to composition on a full-time basis? Why or why not?

    A: Yes, I'd do it full-time, because I feel composing is the most challenging and fulfilling activity for me.

10. Q: How would you describe your compositional style?

    A: I'd describe it as traditional in terms of materials and attitudes toward them, but personal in expression.

11. Q: What have been the influences of other composers, styles, and other types of music on your compositional style?

    A: Inevitably there are influences, but I can't specify.

12. Q: Has your style changed across your career? If so, what influenced these changes or developments?

    A: I feel it has evolved to become more chromatic, more free in form and process, and this has happened in order to express newer ideas that have come to me. I think it has been a long-term proposition. Have you seen the article Slonimsky did on me in the ACA Bulletin?[3] He mentions chromatic things in some madrigals I did a long time ago --back in 1953 or 1954--and since then I have written things that are not chromatic at all, but then the chromatic does come back in, in the Serenade, in Markings, and in other things. So I would think this development is a long-term thing rather than taking place in specific periods in my career.

13. Q: When you are listening to music for your own enjoyment, what are your preferences?

    A: I would say opera and chamber music. I don't listen to music that much because there's no time, really, to sit down and listen to records. Occasionally, if I'm doing things around the studio like busywork or copying or something, I'll have the radio on. But I very seldom take the time to listen for my own enjoyment. There's no time to do that. In teaching I hear some things, but that's didactic rather than just enjoyment. But opera and chamber music --those are the things I like.

Notes to Chapter VI

1. Dr. Kay stated that he did not feel he should try to comment on treatment of the musical elements listed, but would cite examples from his compositions.

2. The section to which Dr. Kay refers is rehearsal number 28 to rehearsal number 31.

3. Nicholas Slonimsky, "Ulysses Kay," ACA Bulletin 7 (Fall 1957): 3-11.

LIST OF COMPOSITIONS

ADMIRAL BYRD (1960)
    Television. Score for the episode "Admiral Byrd" from the television series The Twentieth Century. CBS television network.

ALLELUIA (1962)
    Chorus (SATB) and piano or organ. See CHORAL TRIPTYCH.

ALLELUIA (1962)
    Chorus (SATB) and string orchestra. See CHORAL TRIPTYCH.

AMERICAN DANCES (1954)
    See SIX DANCES FOR STRING ORCHESTRA.

AMPLE MAKE THIS BED (1964)
    See EMILY DICKINSON SET.

ANCIENT SAGA (1947)
    Piano and string orchestra. 8 min. Revision of an earlier work entitled THE ROPE.

ANSWER TO A CHILD'S QUESTION (1966)
    See THE BIRDS.

ARIETTA (1957)
    See SERENADE NO. 2.

ARIOSO (1948)
    See CONCERTO FOR ORCHESTRA.

AS JOSEPH WAS A-WALKING (1943)
    Chorus (SATB) unaccompanied. Anonymous text. 3 min.

ASYMETRIC (1948)
    See PORTRAIT SUITE.

AULOS (1967)
Solo flute, 2 horns, string orchestra, and percussion. 14 min.
Commissioned by and dedicated to John Solum. First perform-
ance (1971) at Indiana University (Bloomington, Indiana) by the
Indiana University Chamber Orchestra, Wolfgang Vacano, con-
ductor; John Solum, flute.

AULOS (1967)
Flute and piano; reduction made by the composer. 14 min.

THE BIRDS (1966)
Chorus (SA) and piano; third song is for chorus (SSA) and piano. Five songs: The Great Black Crow (text by P. J. Bailey);
The Skylark (text by J. Hogg); The Peacock (text by W. Cow-
per); The Throstle (text by Alfred Lord Tennyson); Answer to
a Child's Question (text by S. C. Taylor). 14 min. Duchess
Music/MCA, 1969. Commissioned by Burton A. Cleaves for
the Simmons College Glee Club. First performance (1967) in
Boston by the Simmons College Glee Club.

BLACK RIDERS (1967)
See STEPHEN CRANE SET.

BLEEKER STREET SUITE (1968)
Piano sketch for elementary orchestra with recorders, etc.
Four movements: Entrata; Lullaby; Novellette; Ostinato. 7
min.

BLOSSOMING (1948)
See PORTRAIT SUITE.

THE BOOR (1955)
Opera. Libretto from Anton Chekov; translated by Vladimir
Ussachevsky and adapted by the composer. Three characters:
soprano, tenor, and bass. One act. 40 min. Commissioned
by the Koussevitsky Foundation of the Library of Congress and
dedicated to the memory of Serge and Natalie Koussevitsky.
First performance (1968) at the University of Kentucky (Lexing-
ton, Ky.).

BRASS QUARTET (1950)
Three movements: Fantasia; Arioso; Toccata. 10 min. Peer/
Southern Music, 1958. Recorded by the American Brass Quin-
tet (Folkways FM-3651: Music for Brass Quintet). First per-
formance (1952) at the Brooklyn Museum by the Third Street
Music School Quartet.

BRIEF ELEGY (1946)
Oboe and string orchestra. 5 min. First performance (1948)
in Washington, D.C. by the National Gallery Orchestra, Richard
Bales, conductor.

BRIEF ELEGY (1946)
Oboe and piano; reduction made by the composer. 5 min.

Duchess/Leeds Music (Leeds Solo series), 1964.

BURLESCA (1950)
   See PARTITA IN A.

THE CAPITOLINE VENUS (1969)
   Opera. Libretto by Judith Dvorak after Mark Twain. One act.
   45 min. Commissioned by the Quincy Society of Fine Arts.
   First performance (1971) at the Krannert Center for the Per-
   forming Arts, University of Illinois (Champaign-Urbana) by the
   University of Illinois Opera Group, Richard Aslanian, conductor;
   David Barron, director; Laura Zirner, designer.

CARNIVAL (1965)
   See CONCERT SKETCHES.

CHILDREN'S HOUR (1953)
   See TRIUMVIRATE.

CHORAL TRIPTYCH (1962)
   Chorus (SATB) and piano or organ; reduction made by the com-
   poser. Three songs: Give Ear to My Words; How Long Wilt
   Thou Forget Me, O Lord?; Alleluia. Biblical text. 13 min.
   Associated Music, 1967 (each published separately). Commis-
   sioned by Daniel Pinkham under a Ford Foundation Grant.

CHORAL TRIPTYCH (1962)
   Chorus (SATB) and string orchestra. Three songs: Give Ear
   to My Words; How Long Wilt Thou Forget Me, O Lord?; Alleluia. Biblical text. 13 min. Associated Music, 1967. Recorded by the King's Chapel Choir of Boston and the Cambridge
   Festival Strings, Daniel Pinkham, conductor (Cambridge Records
   CRM-416: Four Contemporary Choral Works). Commissioned
   by Daniel Pinkham under a Ford Foundation Grant. First performance (1963) in New York City at the Museum of Modern
   Art by the King's Chapel Choir of Boston, Daniel Pinkham, conductor.

CHRISTMAS CAROL (1943)
   Chorus (SSA) unaccompanied. Text by Sara Teasdale. 3 min.
   Peer/Southern Music, 1957.

COME AWAY, COME AWAY DEATH (1943)
   Chorus (TTB) unaccompanied. Text by William Shakespeare.
   3 min. Peer/Southern Music, 1954.

CONCERT SKETCHES (1965)
   Band. Six parts: Prologue; Parade; Promenade; Carnival;
   Holiday; Epilogue. 10 min. Written for the Ostwald Band
   Composition Award competition sponsored by the American Band-
   master's Association; this work was a semi-finalist.

CONCERTO FOR ORCHESTRA (1948)
   Three movements: Toccata; Arioso; Passacaglia. 18 min.

First performance (1953) in Venice, Italy by the Teatro La Fenice Orchestra, Jonel Perlea, conductor.

CONTEMPLATION (1952)
High voice and orchestra. See THREE PIECES AFTER BLAKE.

CONTEMPLATION (1962)
High voice, violin, violoncello, and piano. See TRIPTYCH ON TEXTS OF BLAKE.

A COVENANT FOR OUR TIME (1969)
See ONCE THERE WAS A MAN.

CRISIS (1948)
See THE QUIET ONE SUITE.

DANSE CALINDA SUITE (1947)
Alternate title: SUITE FROM THE BALLET "DANSE CALINDA." Orchestra. 14 min. First performance (1947) by the National Orchestra Association, Leon Barzin, conductor.

ECHO (1950)
See PARTITA IN A.

EIGHT INVENTIONS
See FOUR INVENTIONS.

ELYSIUM (1975)
See SOUTHERN HARMONY.

ELYSIUM IS AS FAR (1964)
See EMILY DICKINSON SET.

EMILY DICKINSON SET (1964)
Chorus (SSA) and piano. Text by Emily Dickinson. Three songs: Elysium Is as Far; Indian Summer; Ample Make This Bed. 6 min. Duchess Music (Leeds Masterwork Choral series, 1965). Commissioned by Burton A. Cleaves. Dedicated to the Simmons College Glee Club, Burton A. Cleaves, conductor. First performance (1965) in Boston by the Simmons College Glee Club, Burton A. Cleaves, conductor.

ENTRATA (1968)
See BLEEKER STREET SUITE.

THE EPICURE (1959)
Chorus (SATB) and piano. Text by Abraham Cowley. 4 min. Duchess Music/MCA. Arrangement of "The Epicure" from PHOEBUS, ARISE.

THE EPICURE (1959)
Soprano, bass, chorus (SATB), and orchestra. See PHOEBUS, ARISE.

EPIGRAMS AND HYMN   (1975)
    Anthem for chorus (SATB) and organ.   Text by John Greenleaf
    Whittier, the Reverend John Murray, and Samuel Longfellow.
    6 min.   Pembroke/Carl Fischer.   Commissioned by Princeton
    Theological Seminary, Bryn Mawr Presbyterian Church, and the
    Brick Presbyterian Church for the Bicentennial.   First perform-
    ance (1976) by the Brick Presbyterian Church Choir, T. Charles
    Lee, conductor.

EPILOGUE   (1948)
    See PORTRAIT SUITE.

EPILOGUE   (1957)
    See SERENADE NO. 2.

EPILOGUE   (1959)
    See PHOEBUS, ARISE.

EPILOGUE   (1965)
    See CONCERT SKETCHES.

ESSAY ON DEATH   (1964)
    Television film about John F. Kennedy.   A Leo Hurwitz Produc-
    tion for WNET (New York City).

EVEN SONG   (1950)
    See FUGITIVE SONGS.

F.D.R.:   FROM THIRD TERM TO PEARL HARBOR   (1958)
    Television.   Score for the episode "F.D.R.:   From Third Term
    to Pearl Harbor" from the television series The Twentieth Cen-
    tury.   CBS television network.

FACETS   (1971)
    Piano and woodwind quintet.   11 min.   Commissioned by the
    Eastman School of Music for its 50th anniversary and dedicated
    to Walter Hendl.   First performance (1971) at the Eastman
    School of Music by the Eastman School of Music Faculty En-
    semble "Musica Nova," Walter Hendl, conductor.

THE FALL OF CHINA   (1959)
    Television.   Score for the episode "The Fall of China" from
    the television series The Twentieth Century.   CBS television
    network.

FANFARE   (1945)
    See SUITE FOR ORCHESTRA.

FANFARE   (1950)
    See SHORT SUITE.

FANFARE FOR THREE TRUMPETS   (1974)
    See HERALDS II.

FANTASY (1957)
See SERENADE NO. 2.

FANTASY VARIATIONS (1963)
Orchestra. Introduction, theme, and 13 variations. 15 min.
Duchess Music/MCA, 1966; parts on rental. Recorded by the
Oslo Philharmonic Orchestra, Arthur Bennett Lipkin, conductor
(Composers Recordings Inc. CRI SD-209). Commissioned by
and first performed (1963) by the Portland (Maine) Symphony,
Arthur Bennett Lipkin, conductor.

FIFES AND DRUMS (1975)
See SOUTHERN HARMONY.

FINALE (1950)
See SHORT SUITE.

FIRST NOCTURNE (1973)
Piano. 6 min. MCA/Belwin Mills, 1973. Commissioned
by Mrs. Eric Stein. Dedicated to and first performed (1973)
by James Dick.

FIVE PORTRAITS (1972)
Violin and piano. 17 min. Commissioned by the McKim Fund
of the Library of Congress. First performance (1974) at the
Library of Congress. Ruggerio Ricci, violin; Leon Pommers,
piano.

FLOWERS IN THE VALLEY (1961)
Chorus (SATB) unaccompanied. Anonymous text. 5 min. C.
F. Peters (under the sponsorship of Sigma Alpha Iota in the
American Music Awards series), 1962. Dedicated to Sigma
Alpha Iota. First performance (1962) by the Illinois Wesleyan
University Choir, Lloyd Pfautsch, conductor.

FOREVER FREE (1962)
Alternate title: A LINCOLN CHRONICLE. Band. Three movements: Prelude; Toccata; Proclamation. Associated Music,
1975. Commissioned by Broadcast Music Inc. for a program at
the Lincoln Memorial commemorating the 100th anniversary of
the issuance of the Emancipation Proclamation. First performance (1962) at the Lincoln Memorial by the U.S. Marine Band,
Captain Dale Harpham, conductor.

FOUR HYMN-ANTHEMS (1965)
Chorus (SATB) and organ. God, the Lord (text by John Keble
paraphrased from the Psalms of David); Lo, the Earth (text by
Longfellow); Love Divine (text by Charles Wesley); O Come
Emmanuel (text is Veni, Veni Emmanuel). 10 min. Duchess
Music/MCA, 1965 (each published separately).

FOUR INVENTIONS (1946)
Piano. 5 min. Duchess Music/MCA, 1964. First perform-

ance (1947) at Town Hall. Lucy Brown, piano. This work is a revision of an earlier work entitled EIGHT INVENTIONS.

FOUR SILHOUETTES (1972)
Concert band. App. 3½ min. Duchess Music/MCA, 1973. First performance (1973) by the Lehman College Band, J. Dellicarri, conductor.

FUGITIVE SONGS (1950)
Medium voice and piano. Eight songs: Song Is Old (text by Hermann Hagedorn); That Day You Came (text by Lizette Reese); When the Wind Is Low (text by Cale Young Rice); Even Song (text by Ridgely Torrence); The Fugitives (text by Florence Wilkerson); The Mystic (text by Wittner Bynner); Sentence (text by Wittner Bynner); When I Am Dead (text by Elsa Barker). 18 min. First performance (1958) at Town Hall. Eugene Brice, baritone; Jonathan Brice, piano.

THE FUGITIVES (1950)
See FUGITIVE SONGS.

GALOP (1954)
See SIX DANCES FOR STRING ORCHESTRA.

GIVE EAR TO MY WORDS (1962)
Chorus (SATB) and piano or organ. See CHORAL TRIPTYCH.

GIVE EAR TO MY WORDS (1962)
Chorus (SATB) and string orchestra. See CHORAL TRIPTYCH.

GOD, THE LORD (1965)
See FOUR HYMN-ANTHEMS.

GOING HOME (1962)
Film score. United Nations Film Department production. Commissioned by and dedicated to Peter Hollander.

GRACE TO YOU, AND PEACE (1955)
Chorus (SATB) and organ. Biblical text adapted by Theodore Melnechuk. 5 min. H. W. Gray, 1957. First performance (1956) in Bethlehem, Pa. at the festival service for the 100th anniversary of the Moravian Church. This work won the Moravian Anthem Contest in 1956.

THE GREAT BLACK CROW (1966)
See THE BIRDS.

GUITARRA (1973)
Guitar. Three movements: Prelude; Arioso; Finale. 12 min. Commissioned by and dedicated to Wilbur P. Cotton.

HAD I A HEART (1971)
See TRIPLE SET.

HARLEM CHILDREN'S SUITE (1973)
Elementary orchestra. Three movements: Prelude, Aria; Finale. 9 min. Commissioned by the Harlem School of the Arts. Dedicated to Dorothy Maynor.

THE HELL-BOUND TRAIN (1970)
See PARABLES.

HERALDS (1968)
Brass octet (4 trumpets, 4 trombones). 1 min. First performance (1968) in New York City at the International Music Congress. Dedicated to Oliver Daniel.

HERALDS II (1974)
Alternate title: FANFARE FOR THREE TRUMPETS. 1 min. Written for the Graduate Center of the City University of New York. First performance (1974) by the Brooklyn College Brass Ensemble.

HOLIDAY (1965)
See CONCERT SKETCHES.

HOW LONG WILT THOU FORGET ME, O LORD? (1962)
Chorus (SATB) and piano or organ. See CHORAL TRIPTYCH.

HOW LONG WILT THOU FORGET ME, O LORD? (1962)
Chorus (SATB) and string orchestra. See CHORAL TRIPTYCH.

HOW STANDS THE GLASS AROUND? (1954)
Chorus (SSATB) unaccompanied. Text by James Wolfe. 3 min. 10 sec. Associated Music, 1956. Recorded by the Randolph Singers, David Randolph, conductor (Composers Recordings Inc. CRI-102: Lament for April 15 and Other Modern Madrigals). Commissioned by and dedicated to the Randolph Singers, David Randolph, conductor. Originally part of a work entitled TWO MADRIGALS.

HYMN-ANTHEM ON THE TUNE "HANOVER" (1959)
Alternate title: O WORSHIP THE KING. Chorus (SATB) and organ or piano. Text by Sir Robert Grant. 4 min. C. F. Peters, 1960.

INDIAN SUMMER (1964)
See EMILY DICKINSON SET.

INSCRIPTIONS FROM WHITMAN (1963)
Chorus (SATB) and orchestra. Text by Walt Whitman. Two movements. 25 min. Commissioned by the Tercentenary Commission of the State of New Jersey and the New Jersey Symphony for the New Jersey Tercentenary. First performance (1964) by the Women's Chorus of Douglass College, the New Jersey Oratorio Society Male Chorus of Atlantic City, and the New Jersey Symphony Orchestra, Kenneth Schermerhorn, conductor.

INTERLUDE   (1948)
   See THE QUIET ONE SUITE.

INTERLUDE   (1950)
   Concert band.   See SHORT SUITE.

INTERLUDE   (1950)
   Violin and piano.   See PARTITA IN A.

JOYS AND FEARS   (1948)
   See THE QUIET ONE SUITE.

JUBILEE   (1974-1976)
   Opera.   Libretto by Donald Door, based on the novel by Mar-
   garet Walker.   Thirteen principals, double chorus, and orches-
   tra.   Three acts.   App. 2 hours.   Commissioned by Opera
   South.   First performance to take place November 20, 1976 in
   Jackson, Mississippi by Opera South.

THE JUGGLER OF OUR LADY   (1956)
   Opera.   Libretto by Alexander King.   One act.   50 min.   First
   performance (1962) at Xavier University (New Orleans, La.).

THE LAND   (1962)
   Television.   Score for an NBC news documentary featuring
   Chet Huntley.

LAND OF BEGINNINGS   (1975)
   See SOUTHERN HARMONY.

LIKE AS A FATHER   (1955)
   See A NEW SONG.

A LINCOLN CHRONICLE   (1962)
   See FOREVER FREE.

A LINCOLN LETTER   (1953)
   Chorus (SATB) and bass soloist.   Text attributed to Abraham
   Lincoln. $4\frac{1}{2}$ min.   C. F. Peters, 1958.   Dedicated to Carl
   Haverlin.   First performance (1953) in Lincoln, Illinois by the
   College Choir of Lincoln College, William Tagg, conductor;
   Bruce Foote, bass.

THE LION, THE GRIFFIN, AND THE KANGAROO   (1951)
   Film score.   Hollander-Tait Productions, Inc.   Commissioned
   by Peter Hollander.

THE LITTLE ELF-MAN   (1966)
   See TWO SONGS FOR CHILDREN.

LITTLE TUNE   (1957)
   See TEN SHORT ESSAYS.

LO, THE EARTH (1965)
    See FOUR HYMN-ANTHEMS.

LOVE DIVINE (1965)
    See FOUR HYMN-ANTHEMS.

LULLABY (1968)
    See BLEEKER STREET SUITE.

LULLY, LULLAY (1954)
    See A WREATH FOR WAITS.

LYRIC (1950)
    See SHORT SUITE.

MAD SONG (1952)
    High voice and orchestra. See THREE PIECES AFTER BLAKE.

MAD SONG (1962)
    High voice, violin, violoncello, and piano. See TRIPTYCH ON
    TEXTS OF BLAKE.

MADRIGAL (1965)
    See TWO DUNBAR LYRICS.

MAKE BELIEVE (1957)
    See TEN SHORT ESSAYS.

MARCH (1950)
    See SHORT SUITE.

MARCH SONG (1957)
    See TEN SHORT ESSAYS.

MARKINGS (1966)
    Orchestra. 21 min. Duchess Music/MCA, 1968; parts on
    rental. Recorded by the London Symphony Orchestra, Paul
    Freeman, conductor (Columbia M-32783: Vol. 3, Black Com-
    posers Series). Commissioned by the Meadow Brook Festival,
    Oakland University (Rochester, Minn.). Written in memory of
    Dag Hammerskjold and dedicated to Oliver Daniel. First per-
    formance (1966) at the Meadow Brook Festival, Oakland Univer-
    sity (Rochester, Minn.) by the Detroit Symphony, Sixten Ehrling,
    conductor.

MUSIC (1953)
    See TRIUMVIRATE.

THE MYSTIC (1950)
    See FUGITIVE SONGS.

MYSTIC SHADOW (1967)
    See STEPHEN CRANE SET.

A NEW SONG   (1955)
Alternate title: THREE PSALMS FOR CHORUS.   Chorus (SATB)
unaccompanied.   Sing Unto the Lord; Like As A Father; O
Praise the Lord.   Biblical texts. C. F. Peters, 1961 (each published separately).   Commissioned by the Illinois Wesleyan University College Choir, Lloyd Pfautsch, conductor.   First performance (1956) at the Illinois Wesleyan University Annual Symposium on Contemporary American Music by the Illinois Wesleyan Collegiate Choir, Lloyd Pfautsch, conductor.

NEW YORK, CITY OF MAGIC   (1958)
Film score.   Commissioned by and produced by WNET (New
York City).   First showing (1961) in New York City at the
Museum of Modern Art.

NIGHT MARCH   (1953)
See TRIUMVIRATE.

NO!   (1959)
See PHOEBUS, ARISE.

NOEL   (1954)
See A WREATH FOR WAITS.

NOSOTROS   (1962)
Film score.   United Nations Film Department production.   Commissioned by and dedicated to Peter Hollander.

NOVELLETTE   (1968)
See BLEEKER STREET SUITE.

O COME EMMANUEL   (1965)
See FOUR HYMN-ANTHEMS.

O PRAISE THE LORD   (1955)
See A NEW SONG.

O WORSHIP THE KING   (1959)
See HYMN-ANTHEM ON THE TUNE "HANOVER."

ODE: TO THE CUCKOO   (1971)
See TRIPLE SET.

OF NEW HORIZONS   (1944)
Orchestra.   8 min. C. F. Peters, 1961; parts on rental.   Recorded for University of Arizona Records.   Commissioned by
Thor Johnson.   First performance (1944) in New York City by
the New York Philharmonic-Symphony Orchestra, Thor Johnson,
conductor.   This work won the American Broadcasting Company
Award in 1946.

THE OLD ARMCHAIR   (1970)
See PARABLES.

OLD LAMENT (1957)
    See TEN SHORT ESSAYS.

OLDEN TUNE: FINALE (1945)
    See SUITE FOR ORCHESTRA.

ONCE THERE WAS A MAN (1969)
    Alternate title: A COVENANT FOR OUR TIME. Narrator,
    chorus (SATB), and orchestra. Text by Randal Caudill. 17 min.
    Commissioned by the 1969 Worchester (Mass.) Music Festival.
    First performance (1969) in Detroit, Michigan by the Detroit
    Symphony, Sixten Ehrling, conductor; William Warfield, narra-
    tor.

ORGAN SUITE NO. 1 (1958)
    Three movements. 7 min. Commissioned by Marilyn Mason.
    First performance (1958) in New York City at St. Paul's Chapel.
    Marilyn Mason, organ.

OSTINATO (1968)
    See BLEEKER STREET SUITE.

PARABLES (1970)
    Chorus (SATB) and chamber orchestra. Two songs: The Old
    Armchair; The Hell-Bound Train. Anonymous texts. 12 min.
    Duchess Music/MCA, 1970; parts on rental. Commissioned by
    the American Choral Directors Association. First performance
    (1971) in Kansas City (Mo.) at the First Annual Convention of
    the American Choral Directors Association by the Kansas State
    University Concert Chorale, Rod Walker, conductor, and the
    Kansas State University Chamber Orchestra, Paul Roby, con-
    ductor.

PARADE (1965)
    See CONCERT SKETCHES.

PARTITA IN A (1950)
    Violin and piano. Four movements: Prelude; Burlesca; Inter-
    lude; Echo. 15 min. First performance (1952) at the Ameri-
    can Academy in Rome.

PASSACAGLIA (1948)
    See CONCERTO FOR ORCHESTRA.

THE PEACOCK (1966)
    See THE BIRDS.

PENTAGRAPH (1972)
    Chorus (treble voices) and piano. Five movements. 17 min.

PHOEBUS, ARISE (1959)
    Soprano, bass, chorus (SATB), and orchestra. Seven parts:
    Prelude (text by the composer); No! (text by Thomas Hood);

Tears, Flow No More (text by Lord Herbert of Cherbury);
Phoebus, Arise (text by William Drummond); Song (text by
Thomas Middleton and William Rowley); The Epicure (text by
Abraham Cowley); Epilogue (text by the composer). 30 min.
Commissioned by the International Music Council of New York
City. First performance (1959) at Town Hall by the Interracial
Fellowship Chorus and Orchestra, Harold Aks, conductor.

PIETA (1950)
English horn and string orchestra. 7 min. First performance
(1958) at Town Hall as part of the 19th Annual Festival of American Music. Knickerbocker Chamber Orchestra, Herman New-
man, conductor; Doris Goltzer, English horn.

PLAYING, PLAYING (1957)
See TEN SHORT ESSAYS.

POLKA (1954)
See SIX DANCES FOR STRING ORCHESTRA.

PORTRAIT SUITE (1948)
Orchestra. Five parts: Prologue; Asymetric; Reclining Figure;
Blossoming; Epilogue. 18 min. First performance (1964) in
Erie, Pa. by the Erie Philharmonic, James Sample, conductor.
This work won the 1948 award for the best composition by a
native Arizonan.

PRELUDE (1943; revised in 1975)
Solo flute. 1½ min. Pembroke/Carl Fischer, 1976. Recorded
by D. Antoinette Handy (Eastern ERS-513: Contemporary Black
Images in Music for the Flute).

PRELUDE (1950)
See PARTITA IN A.

PRELUDE (1957)
See SERENADE NO. 2.

PRELUDE (1959)
See PHOEBUS, ARISE.

PRELUDE (1962)
See FOREVER FREE.

PRESIDENTIAL SUITE (1965)
Orchestra. 12 min. Commissioned by the Greater Boston
Youth Symphony. First performance (1965) in Boston's Symphony
Hall by the Greater Boston Youth Symphony, Ulysses Kay, con-
ductor.

PROCLAMATION (1962)
See FOREVER FREE.

PROLOGUE (1948)
See PORTRAIT SUITE.

PROLOGUE (1965)
See CONCERT SKETCHES.

PROMENADE (1954)
See SIX DANCES FOR ORCHESTRA.

PROMENADE (1965)
See CONCERT SKETCHES.

THE QUIET ONE (1948)
Film score. A Film Documents, Inc. production.

THE QUIET ONE SUITE (1948)
Alternate title: SUITE FROM THE QUIET ONE. Orchestra.
Four movements: Joys and Fears; Street Wanderings; Interlude;
Crisis. First performance (1948) by the New York Little Sym-
phony, Ulysses Kay, conductor.

QUINTET CONCERTO (1974)
Solo brass quintet and orchestra. Solo brass quintet consists
of 2 trumpets, F horn, and 2 trombones; alternate part for
tuba is available. Three movements. 17 min. Commissioned
by the Juilliard School of Music. First performance (1974) at
the Juilliard School of Music. Walter Hendl, conductor.

RECLINING FIGURE (1948)
See PORTRAIT SUITE.

REVERIE AND RONDO (1964)
Alternate title: TWO PIECES FOR ORCHESTRA. 7 min. First
performance (1968) in Flint, Michigan by the Flint Symphony
Orchestra, William Byrd, conductor.

THE ROPE (1946)
Solo dancer and piano. 12 min. Commissioned by Eleanore
Goff. First performance (1947) in New York City. This work
was subsequently revised into ANCIENT SAGA.

ROUND DANCE (1954)
See SIX DANCES FOR ORCHESTRA.

SCHERZI MUSICALI (1968)
Chamber orchestra. 17 min. Duchess Music/MCA, 1971;
parts on rental. Commissioned by the Chamber Music Society
of Detroit for its 25th anniversary. First performance (1969)
in Detroit by the Princeton Chamber Orchestra and the Interlochen Arts Woodwind Quintet, Nicholas Harsanyi, conductor.

SCHERZO (1945)
See SUITE FOR ORCHESTRA.

SCHOTTISCHE (1954)
See SIX DANCES FOR STRING ORCHESTRA.

SECOND NOCTURNE (1973)
Piano. 5 min.

SENTENCE (1950)
See FUGITIVE SONGS.

SERENADE FOR ORCHESTRA (1954)
Four movements. Associated Music, 1955. Recorded by the
Louisville Orchestra, Robert Whitney, conductor (First Edition
Records LOU-545-8). Commissioned by the Louisville Phil-
harmonic Society. First performance (1954) by the Louisville
Orchestra, Robert Whitney, conductor.

SERENADE NO. 2 (1957)
Four F horns. Five movements: Prelude; Arietta; Toccata;
Fantasy; Epilogue. 12 min. Duchess Music/Leeds Music
(Leeds Music for Winds series), 1964. First performance at
the University of Illinois (Champaign-Urbana). Thomas Holden,
Kathryn Dieterich, Jan Bach, and Richard Ely, horns.

THE SHAPE OF THINGS (1960)
Television. Score for the NBC news program "World Wide 60."

A SHORT OVERTURE (1946)
Orchestra. App. 7 min. Duchess Music/MCA, 1973; parts
on rental. Recorded by the Oakland Youth Orchestra, Robert
Hughes, conductor (Desto DC-7101: The Black Composer in
America). First performance (1947) in New York City by the
New York City Symphony, Leonard Bernstein, conductor. This
work won the Third Annual George Gershwin Memorial Contest
in 1947.

SHORT SUITE (1950)
Concert band. Five movements: Fanfare; March; Interlude;
Lyric; Finale. 7 min. Associated Music, 1957. First per-
formance (1951) at Baylor University by the Baylor University
Golden Wave Band, Donald I. Moore, conductor.

SINFONIA IN E (1950)
Orchestra. Four movements. 20 min. Pembroke/Carl Fischer. Recorded by the Oslo Philharmonic Orchestra, George
Barati, conductor (Composers Recordings Inc. CRI-139). First
performance (1951) by the Eastman-Rochester Symphony Orchestra, Howard Hanson, conductor.

SING UNTO THE LORD (1955)
See A NEW SONG.

SIX DANCES FOR STRING ORCHESTRA (1954)
Alternate title: AMERICAN DANCES. Schottische; Waltz;

Round Dance; Polka; Promenade; Galop. 18-19 min. Duchess
Music (Leeds Contemporary Classics for Strings series), 1965.
Entire work recorded by the Westphalian Symphony Orchestra,
Paul Freeman, conductor (Turnabout 34546). Round Dance and
Polka recorded by the New Symphony Orchestra of London,
Salvador Camarata, conductor (Composers Recordings Inc.
CRI-119). First performance conducted by Alfred Antonini (CBS
radio, "String Serenade").

THE SKYLARK (1966)
See THE BIRDS.

SLUMBER SONG (1957)
See TEN SHORT ESSAYS.

SO GAY (1957)
See TEN SHORT ESSAYS.

SOLEMN PRELUDE (1949)
Band. 5 min. Associated Music. Commissioned by the Baylor
University Band, Donald I. Moore, conductor. First performance
(1950) at Baylor University by the Baylor University Golden
Wave Band, Donald I. Moore, conductor.

SONG (1959)
See PHOEBUS, ARISE.

SONG IS OLD (1950)
See FUGITIVE SONGS.

SONG OF JEREMIAH (1945)
Baritone, chorus (SATB), and orchestra. Biblical text. 19 min.
First performance (1954) by the Fisk University Choir, Harry
von Bergen, conductor.

SONG OF JEREMIAH (1945)
Baritone, chorus (SSA), and organ. Biblical text. 19 min.

SOUTHERN HARMONY (1975)
Orchestra. Based on themes and motives from William Walker's "The Southern Harmony" of 1835. Four movements: Prelude: Land of Beginnings; Fifes and Drums; Variants; Elysium.
21 min. Pembroke/Carl Fischer, 1976. Commissioned by the
Southeastern Regional Metropolitan Orchestra Managers Association. First performance (1976) by the North Carolina Symphony
Orchestra, John Gosling, conductor.

A SPIRIT (1967)
See STEPHEN CRANE SET.

SPRITE'S DANCE (1957)
See TEN SHORT ESSAYS.

A STARRY NIGHT   (1965)
    See TWO DUNBAR LYRICS.

STEPHEN CRANE SET   (1967)
    Chorus (SATB) and instrumental ensemble (flute, oboe, English
    horn, clarinet, bass clarinet, bassoon, 2 F horns, 2 trumpets,
    tenor trombone, bass trombone, and percussion).   Four parts:
    Black Riders; Mystic Shadow; A Spirit; War Is Kind.   Text by
    Stephen Crane.   App. 16 min.   Duchess Music/MCA, 1972;
    parts on rental.   Commissioned by the Chicago Musical College
    of Roosevelt University in honor of its 100th anniversary.   First
    performance (1968) at the Chicago Musical College.   David S.
    Larson, conductor.

STREET WANDERINGS   (1948)
    See THE QUIET ONE SUITE.

STRING QUARTET NO. 1   (1949)
    Withdrawn by the composer.

STRING QUARTET NO. 2   (1956)
    Four movements.   18 min.   First performance (1959) at the
    University of Illinois (Champaign-Urbana) by the Walden String
    Quartet.

STRING QUARTET NO. 3   (1961)
    Three movements.   15 min.   Commissioned by the University
    of Michigan.   Dedicated to and first performed (1962) by the
    Stanley Quartet.

SUBMARINE!   (1959)
    Television.   Score for the episode "Submarine!" from the tele-
    vision series The Twentieth Century.   CBS television network.

SUITE FOR FLUTE AND OBOE   (1943)
    Four movements: Prelude; Air; Minuet; Gigue.   5 min.
    Duchess Music/MCA, 1964.   First performance (1947) in New
    York City on a Composer's Forum concert.

SUITE FOR ORCHESTRA   (1945)
    Four movements: Fanfare; Three-four; Scherzo; Olden Tune:
    Finale.   17 min.   Associated Music, 1948.   First performance
    (1950) at Town Hall by the American Youth Orchestra, Dean
    Dixon, conductor.

SUITE FOR STRINGS   (1947)
    String orchestra.   Three movements.   14 min.   C. F. Peters,
    1961.   First performance (1949) in Baltimore, Maryland by the
    Baltimore Chamber Orchestra, Ulysses Kay, conductor.

SUITE FROM THE BALLET "DANSE CALINDA"   (1947)
    See DANSE CALINDA SUITE.

SUITE FROM THE QUIET ONE   (1948)
See THE QUIET ONE SUITE.

SUITE IN B   (1943)
Oboe and piano.   Three movements: Prelude; Recitative and
Air; Dance.   First performance (1949) at the American Aca-
demy in Rome.

SYMPHONY   (1967)
Orchestra.   Four movements.   25 min.   Commissioned by the
Illinois Sesquicentennial Commission.   First performance (1968)
by the Chicago Symphony Orchestra, Jean Martinon, conductor.

TEARS, FLOW NO MORE   (1959)
Chorus (SSA) and piano.   Text by Lord Herbert of Cherbury.
4 min.   Duchess Music/MCA.   Arrangement of "Tears, Flow
No More" from PHOEBUS, ARISE.

TEARS, FLOW NO MORE   (1959)
Soprano, bass, chorus (SATB), and orchestra.   See PHOEBUS,
ARISE.

TEN PIECES FOR CHILDREN   (1957)
See TEN SHORT ESSAYS.

TEN SHORT ESSAYS   (1957)
Alternate title: TEN PIECES FOR CHILDREN.   Piano.   So
Gay; Tender Thought; Sprite's Dance; Little Tune; Old Lament;
Make Believe; Two Voices; Playing, Playing; Slumber Song;
March Song.   7 min.   Duchess Music/MCA, 1965.

TENDER THOUGHT   (1957)
See TEN SHORT ESSAYS.

THAT DAY YOU CAME   (1950)
See FUGITIVE SONGS.

THEATER SET   (1968)
Orchestra.   Three movements: Overture; Ballad--Chase Music;
Finale.   App. 15 min.   Duchess Music/MCA, 1971.   Commis-
sioned by the Junior League of Atlanta for Robert Shaw and the
Atlanta Symphony Orchestra.   Dedicated to Robert Shaw.   First
performance (1968) by the Atlanta Symphony Orchestra, Robert
Shaw, conductor.

A THING OF BEAUTY   (1966)
Film score.   A Trafco production.   Commissioned by and dedicated to Fisk University.

THREE FANFARES FOR FOUR TRUMPETS   (1942)
4 min.   Duchess Music/Leeds Music, 1964.   First performance (1947) in New York City on a Composer's Forum concert.

THREE-FOUR (1945)
   See SUITE FOR ORCHESTRA.

THE THREE MUSKETEERS (1960)
   Television. A Talent Associates, Ltd. production. Commissioned by David Susskind.

THREE PIECES AFTER BLAKE (1952)
   High voice and orchestra. To the Evening Star; Mad Song;
   Contemplation. Text by William Blake. 14 min. First performance (1955). Shirley Emmons, soprano; David Broekman, conductor.

THREE PSALMS FOR CHORUS (1955)
   See A NEW SONG.

THE THROSTLE (1966)
   See THE BIRDS.

TO LIGHT THAT SHINES (1962)
   Chorus (SAB) and organ. Text by Samuel Johnson. 5 min.
   Duchess Music, 1964. Commissioned by the New York Society
   for Ethical Culture. First performance (1962) in New York City.

TO THE EVENING STAR (1952)
   High voice and orchestra. See THREE PIECES AFTER BLAKE.

TO THE EVENING STAR (1962)
   High voice, violin, violoncello, and piano. See TRIPTYCH ON
   TEXTS OF BLAKE.

A TOAST (1971)
   See TRIPLE SET.

TOCCATA (1948)
   See CONCERTO FOR ORCHESTRA.

TOCCATA (1957)
   See SERENADE NO. 2.

TOCCATA (1962)
   See FOREVER FREE.

TRIGON (1961)
   Wind orchestra. Three movements: Prelude; Canticle; Toccata. 12 min. C. F. Peters. Commissioned by the American
   Wind Symphony. First performance (1961) in Pittsburgh, Pa.
   by the American Wind Symphony, Robert A. Boudreau, conductor.

TRIPLE SET (1971)
   Chorus (TTBB) unaccompanied. Three parts: Ode: To the
   Cuckoo (text by Michael Bruce); Had I a Heart (text by R. B.
   Sheridan); A Toast (text by R. B. Sheridan). 9 min. MCA/
   Belwin Mills, 1972.

TRIPTYCH ON TEXTS OF BLAKE (1962)
High voice, violin, violoncello, and piano. Reduction by the composer of THREE PIECES AFTER BLAKE. To the Evening Star; Mad Song; Contemplation. 14 min. Pembroke/Carl Fischer. Commissioned by Kermit Moore. First performance (1963) at Winston-Salem Teachers College (Winston-Salem, North Carolina) by the Clarmoor Quartet.

TRIUMVIRATE (1953)
Chorus (TTBB) unaccompanied. Three parts: Music (text by Ralph Waldo Emerson); Children's Hour (text by Henry Wadsworth Longfellow); Night March (text by Herman Melville). 12 min. Peer/Southern Music, 1954. Commissioned by Leonard dePaur for the dePaur Infantry Chorus. First performance (1954) at Hunter College by the dePaur Infantry Chorus, Leonard dePaur, conductor.

TWO DUNBAR LYRICS (1965)
Chorus (SATB) unaccompanied. A Starry Night; Madrigal. Text by Paul Laurence Dunbar. 5 min. Duchess Music/MCA (Masterwork Choral series), 1966. Commissioned for the 75th anniversary of West Virginia State College. First performed there (1965).

TWO MADRIGALS (1954)
See HOW STANDS THE GLASS AROUND? and WHAT'S IN A NAME?

TWO MEDITATIONS (1950)
Organ. 5 min. H. W. Gray (Contemporary Organ series, #27), 1951. First performance (1952) at Fisk University. Arthur Croley, organ.

TWO PIECES FOR ORCHESTRA (1964)
See REVERIE AND RONDO.

TWO SHORT PIECES (1957)
Piano, 4 hands. 5 min. Franco Columbo.

TWO SONGS FOR CHILDREN (1966)
Voice and piano. Where the Boats Go (text by Robert Louis Stevenson); The Little Elf-Man (text by John Kendrick Bangs). 3 min. Published separately: Where the Boats Go is published by Canyon Press (Juilliard Project Collection), 1970; The Little Elf-Man is published by Duchess Music. Commissioned by the Juilliard School of Music and written for the Juilliard Repertory Project.

TWO VOICES (1957)
See TEN SHORT ESSAYS.

UMBRIAN SCENE (1963)
Orchestra. 12 min. Duchess Music/MCA, 1965; parts on rental. Recorded by the Louisville Orchestra, Robert Whitney,

conductor (First Edition Records LOU-651). Commissioned by
Edward B. Benjamin. First performance (1964) by the New
Orleans Philharmonic, Werner Torkanowsky, conductor.

VARIANTS (1975)
See SOUTHERN HARMONY.

VISIONS (1974)
Piano. App. 1 min. 15 sec. The Black Perspective in Music
3 (May 1975): 222-223. Dedicated to William Grant Still.

WALTZ (1954)
See SIX DANCES FOR STRING ORCHESTRA.

WAR IS KIND (1967)
See STEPHEN CRANE SET.

WELCOME YULE (1954)
See A WREATH FOR WAITS.

THE WESTERN PARADISE (1976)
Narrator and orchestra. Text by Donald Dorr. Five movements.
16 min. Commissioned by the National Symphony for the Bicentennial. First performance to take place October 12, 1976 in
Washington, D.C. by the National Symphony, Antal Dorati, conductor.

WHAT'S IN A NAME? (1954)
Chorus (SSATB) unaccompanied. Text by Helen F. More. 4
min. Leeds Music (Leeds Masterworks series), 1956; Duchess
Music/MCA. Recorded by the Randolph Singers, David Randolph, conductor (Composers Recordings Inc. CRI-102: Lament
for April 15 and Other Modern American Madrigals). Dedicated
to and first performed (1955) by the Randolph Singers, David
Randolph, conductor. Originally part of a work entitled TWO
MADRIGALS.

WHEN I AM DEAD (1950)
See FUGITIVE SONGS.

WHEN THE WIND IS LOW (1950)
See FUGITIVE SONGS.

WHERE THE BOATS GO (1966)
See TWO SONGS FOR CHILDREN.

WORLD WIDE 60 (1960)
See THE SHAPE OF THINGS.

A WREATH FOR WAITS (1954)
Chorus (SATB) unaccompanied. Three parts: Noel; Lully
Lullay; Welcome Yule. Anonymous text. 7 min. Associated
Music, 1956 (each published separately). Commissioned by

and dedicated to the Cornell University A Cappella Chorus, Robert Hull, conductor. First performance (1954) in Ann Arbor, Michigan.

BIBLIOGRAPHY

Part I: Works about the composer

Baker, Theodore. Baker's Biographical Dictionary of Musicians. 5th ed. (1958) completely revised by Nicholas Slonimsky, s.v. "Kay, Ulysses Simpson."

_____. Baker's Biographical Dictionary of Musicians. 1965 Supplement to the 5th edition by Nicholas Slonimsky, s.v. "Kay, Ulysses."

_____. Baker's Biographical Dictionary of Musicians. 1971 Supplement to the 5th edition by Nicholas Slonimsky, s.v. "Kay, Ulysses Simpson."

"Black Composers." Newsweek, 15 April 1974.

Brooks, Tilford. "A Historical Study of Black Music and Selected Twentieth Century Black Composers and Their Role in American Society." Ed.D. disssertation, Washington University, 1972.

Chapin, Louis. "Ulysses Kay." BMI: The Many Worlds of Music, February 1970.

Claghorn, Charles E. Biographical Dictionary of American Music. West Nyack, N.Y.: Parker Publishing Company, 1973.

Composers of the Americas. Washington, D.C.: Pan American Union. Vol. 7, 1961, pp. 34-45.

Daniel, Oliver. "The New Festival." ACA Bulletin 5, no. 1 (1955): 3-9+.

Dower, Catherine. "Ulysses Kay: Distinguished American Composer." Musart 24 (January/February 1972): 9-10+.

Edmunds, John, and Boezlner, Gordon. Some Twentieth Century American Composers: A Selective Bibliography. New York: The New York Public Library, 1959 and 1960. 2 vols.

Encyclopaedia Britannica (Micropaedia), 15th ed. (1974), s.v. "Kay, Ulysses Simpson."

Grove's Dictionary of Music and Musicians, 5th ed. (1954), s.v. "Kay, Ulysses," by Peggy Glanville-Hicks.

Hadley, Richard Thomas. "The Published Choral Music of Ulysses Kay--1943 to 1968." Ph. D. dissertation, University of Iowa, 1972.

Harris, Carl G. "A Study of the Characteristic Stylistic Trends Found in the Choral Works of a Selected Group of Afro-American Composers and Arrangers." D. M. A. dissertation, University of Missouri-Kansas City, 1972.

_____. "Three Schools of Black Choral Composers and Arrangers 1900-1970." The Choral Journal 14 (April 1974): 11-18.

Hayes, Laurence Melton. "The Music of Ulysses Kay, 1939-1963." Ph. D. dissertation, University of Wisconsin, 1971.

The International Who Is Who In Music. 5th ed. (1951), s. v. "Kay, Ulysses (Simpson)."

Kyle, Marguerite Kelly. "AmerAllegro." Pan Pipes 42 (December 1949): 108.

_____. "AmerAllegro." Pan Pipes 45 (January 1953): 57.

_____. "AmerAllegro." Pan Pipes 46 (January 1954): 47.

_____. "AmerAllegro." Pan Pipes 47 (January 1955): 51-52.

_____. "AmerAllegro." Pan Pipes 48 (January 1956): 56.

_____. "AmerAllegro." Pan Pipes 49 (January 1957): 55.

_____. "AmerAllegro." Pan Pipes 50 (January 1958): 59.

_____. "AmerAllegro." Pan Pipes 51 (January 1959): 70.

_____. "AmerAllegro." Pan Pipes 52 (January 1960): 56.

_____. "AmerAllegro." Pan Pipes 53 (January 1961): 61-62.

_____. "AmerAllegro." Pan Pipes 54 (January 1962): 57.

_____. "AmerAllegro." Pan Pipes 55 (January 1963): 56.

_____. "AmerAllegro." Pan Pipes 56 (January 1964): 64.

_____. "AmerAllegro." Pan Pipes 57 (January 1965): 66.

_____. "AmerAllegro." Pan Pipes 59 (January 1967): 82.

_____. "AmerAllegro." Pan Pipes 60 (January 1968): 78-79.

_____. "AmerAllegro." Pan Pipes 62 (January 1970): 68.

_____. "AmerAllegro." Pan Pipes 63 (January 1971): 65.

_____. "AmerAllegro." Pan Pipes 64 (January 1972): 63.

_____. "AmerAllegro." Pan Pipes 65 (January 1973): 59.

_____. "AmerAllegro." Pan Pipes 66 (January 1974): 59.

_____. "AmerAllegro." Pan Pipes 67 (January 1975): 60.

_____. "AmerAllegro." Pan Pipes 68 (January 1976): 57.

"The Odyssey of Ulysses." down beat, 2 October 1958.

"Return of Ulysses." Negro History Bulletin 17 (May 1954): 181. This is a reprint of the Time article.

"Return of Ulysses." Time, 8 March 1954, p. 71.

Roach, Hildred. Black American Music: Past and Present. Boston: Crescendo Publishing Company, 1973.

Slonimsky, Nicholas. "Ulysses Kay." ACA Bulletin 7 (Fall 1957): 3-11.

Southern, Eileen. "America's Black Composers of Classical Music." Music Educators Journal 62 (November 1975): 46-59.

_____. The Music of Black Americans. New York: W. W. Norton, 1971.

Thompson, Oscar. The International Cyclopedia of Music and Musicians. 9th ed. (1964) edited by Robert Sabin, s.v. "Kay, Ulysses Simpson."

"The Ulysses Kay 'Markings.'" Pan Pipes 63 (March 1971): 5.

Who's Who Among Black Americans, 1st ed. (1975-76), s.v. "Kay, Ulysses."

Who's Who in America. 38th ed. (1974-75), s.v. "Kay, Ulysses."

Who's Who in Music and Musicians' International Directory. 5th ed. (1969), s.v. "Kay, Ulysses."

"Writer Kay Named Professor of Music at Hunter College." Billboard, 8 June 1968, p. 40.

Wyatt, Lucius Reynolds. "The Mid-Twentieth Century Orchestral Variation, 1953-1963; An Analysis and Comparison of Selected Works by Major Composers." Ph.D. dissertation, University of Rochester, Eastman School of Music, 1974.

Yuhasz, Sister Marie Joy. "Black Composers and Their Piano Music, Part I." <u>The American Music Teacher</u> 19 (February/March 1970): 24+.

Part II: Works by the composer

Kay, Ulysses S. "Thirty Days in Musical Russia: A Diary of My Day-to-Day Impressions of Soviet Conductors, Orchestras, and Featured Works." <u>Hi Fi Review</u>, February 1959.

_____. "Where Is Music Going?" <u>Music Journal</u> 20 (January 1962): 48+.

Undine S. Moore (courtesy of the composer)

CHAPTER VII

UNDINE SMITH MOORE

Undine Smith Moore was born August 25, 1905 in Jarratt,
Virginia. She received her undergraduate degree with highest honors
from Fisk University and was awarded the first scholarship to the
Juilliard School of Music given to a Fisk graduate. Dr. Moore
continued her education with studies at the Juilliard School of Music,
the Eastman School of Music, the Manhattan School of Music, and
Columbia University, from which she received the Master of Arts
degree and a Professional Diploma in Music. She has been awarded
the honorary Doctor of Music degree by both Virginia State College
(1972) and Indiana University (1976).

In 1927 Dr. Moore was appointed to the faculty of Virginia
State College where, during her forty-five years in the music department, she taught such outstanding musicians as Billy Taylor,
Camilla Williams, and Leon Thompson. Since her retirement from
Virginia State in 1972, she has continued to be active as a teacher,
composer, lecturer, and consultant. She has taught on a part-time
basis at Virginia Union University and periodically serves as a visiting professor at the Colleges of St. Benedict and St. John and at
Carlton College. She also travels extensively, lecturing at colleges
and universities as well as participating in seminars, conferences,
and workshops.

Dr. Moore's compositional output includes a large number of
choral works, many of which are her well-known arrangements of
spirituals. She has also written works for solo voice, chamber ensemble, and various solo instruments. Among her best-known compositions are Afro-American Suite (recorded by the Trio Pro Viva);
Lord, We Give Thanks To Thee (commissioned by Fisk University
and recorded by a number of ensembles, including the Fisk Jubilee
Singers and the Virginia State College Choir); The Lamb (recorded
by the Virginia State College Choir and by the St. Stephens Church
Choir); and Daniel, Daniel Servant of the Lord (recorded by several
ensembles, including the Virginia State College Choir, the Fisk
Jubilee Singers, and the Oberlin College Choir).

173

Part I: General Questions

1. Q: What persons, events, and works (of art, literature, etc.) have influenced you in general as well as in terms of your musical activities?

   A: Persons
   My parents, James William Smith and Hardie Turnbull Smith, through their love, their wisdom, and their aspirations; my mother especially for her taste and love of reading, which made me as a child always afraid of being caught somewhere without a book.

   My sister and brother, Eunice Smith Byus and Clarence William Smith, who treated me, the youngest, as a special gift.

   My teachers: Lillian Allen Darden, a graduate of Fisk, who gave me excellent instruction and made occasions to give me all the experience in music she could manage; Alice M. Grass, pianist and organist, graduate of Oberlin, my teacher at Fisk who demanded perfection whether she always got it or not; Howard Murphy, who taught me theory and composition at Columbia and remained my adviser and friend throughout his life; Lillian Emette Cashin, teacher of comparative literature at Fisk.

   And, of great significance, James Arthur Moore, my husband, a scholar who received his doctorate in the early years and was secure enough to permit me a freedom denied many wives of my generation.

   Mary Moore Easter, my daughter, whose self, along with her varied talents, has been my pride and joy.

   Events
   My first appearance as accompanist for the Peabody High School when I was a fifth grader brought upstairs for high school commencement practice.

   My years at Fisk, where I heard great artist performers for the first time.

   My participation in the Mozart Society there, where the great large choral works were sung and the unaccompanied spiritual, directed by John Work, Sr., was an unbroken tradition.

   The years of my own playing when I was considered a real pianist. My scholarship at Fisk from Juilliard and my graduation at the top of my class.

   My visit to West Africa, where special performances were arranged for the two of us (Altona Johns and me) at the Daniel Sorrano Theatre through the arrangements of Ambassador Rudolph Aggrey. Our visit to the slave trading centers on the island of Gorée in Senegal and El Mina in Ghana. The performance and lecture we gave at the Nigerian embassy and the long hours observing the life of the "ordinary" people removed from the great urban centers, especially in Ghana and Abidjan.

   The gala concert of my works sponsored at Town Hall

by my students Leon Thompson, Billy Taylor, Camilla Williams, and Philip Medley. Receiving a citation from Mayor Lindsay and having the Doctor of Music degree conferred. I should include a somewhat similar gala concert and reception in my honor by the Beaux-Twenty Club, a group of seventy-six men in Petersburg. Very first-class performers did full justice to my music and I received, among other gifts, a proclamation and citation from the mayor of Petersburg.

My association with the Afro-American Arts Institute at Indiana University, which is a particularly strong motivating force in my life. The position of Chairman of the Honorary Advisory Committee and my contacts with the students and staff of this great university and its music school have opened a new world for me.

Art

There is such richness and variety in art that it is hard to make a choice. The sculpture, the masks, the jewelry, the instruments of Africa (I have seen every major exhibit in this country as well as others in Paris and West Africa itself); Dr. John Bigger's Celebration March, in which strong black African women seem to walk with such determination they will step off the canvas; Van Gogh's Self-Portrait, the essence of human pain and a reminder of my brother's personal tragedy; Monet's Water Lilies at the Jeu de Paume where I had not previously conceived of an entire pavilion of water lilies; all the varieties of the dance.

Literature

I have read all my life, and have never stopped buying books since the time as a child when I spent my dime on Saturday for a novel I exchanged with my best friend while we also worked through a set of Dickens. In college I read the English familiar essay and shortly after college, the poets of the Harlem Renaissance, particularly Langston Hughes. In what must have been an unusually delayed adolescence filled with "sturm und drang," I literally made it from day to day by reading the Stoic philosophers, especially Epictetus.

During all these times I also read (as I now do) the Bible, some philosophy, some anthropology, some psychology, some social science, and some fiction. I continue the above with less interest generally in fiction and much greater interest in biography. A few names out of many follow (these are samples and I suspect there is some tendency to emphasize choices of more recent years): The Narrative of Frederick Douglass[1]; The Negro American; A Documentary History by Benjamin Quarles[2]; Blaming the Victim by William Ryan[3]; Ralph Ellison; Toni Morrison; Paul Tillich; but above all, now, the poets Alice Walker, Anne Sexton, Margaret Walker, Gwendolyn Brooks, Yeats, and older poets I have loved for years.

2. Q: How would you define black music?

A: This is a difficult task for several reasons. In the first place, philosophers and aestheticians have wrestled with the definition of art (which music is) through the ages without reaching consensus. In the second place, one of the unique values of music is that it is essentially a non-representational and therefore utterly non-verbal art; hence the obvious difficulty of a verbal definition. Next, even the definition of the term "black man," though commonly accepted as understood and useful, is not a designation based on reason.

There are other vexing questions related to the phrase "black music," questions which do not occur with the same urgency when the terms "black idiom," "black musical style," or "music of the black man" are used instead. (Of course, even here there are certain reciprocal influences between the music of Afro-Americans and American whites which are normal in any such creative circumstances.) But, if the phrase "black music" is defined solely in terms of music containing significant elements derived from Africa, yet reflecting in an important way the presence of two cultures after the meeting of slaves from Africa with European and American traditions, then one will ask such questions as these: Is Dvorak's New World Symphony black music? Is Milhaud's Creation of the World black music? Or Ravel's Piano Concerto in G or Stravinsky's Ragtime for Thirteen Instruments? Are these black music though written by white men? On the other hand, is Olly Wilson's prize winner, Cetus (to cite only one example), "white" music though written by a black man?

I think the use of the term "black music" is somehow related to the large, if not entirely complete, body of the composer's expression. If he has, so to speak, "dabbled" in the black style in the necessarily superficial way of one for whom black culture is not a true part of his life experience, then these pieces of these white men are peripheral to their musical expression, which should be characterized, in general, by the vision of life expressed in the principal body of their work. This is not as impractical as it may seem. My experience with quite unsophisticated black students, ignorant enough of music history to be quite irreverent when certain names are mentioned, is that they found the specifically mentioned works of Milhaud, Ravel, and Stravinsky merely amusing--laughable attempts to imitate the students' own language.

It must be borne in mind, however, that blacks have many musics and some of them relate in an extremely universal way to the human condition. Dvorak's New World Symphony seems to me to fall into this category and, as such, is more honestly referred to by this universality than by either term, black or white, though of course the influence of the black idiom should not be ignored.

More important than this, however, in dealing with the basic vexing problems I have first posed, is the difference in the positions of black men and white men in relation to the music produced by the meeting of two cultures: African and American. White composers, being a part of the dominant culture, do not know or participate in the culture of the black man. With a highly institutionalized racism, they have not shared the common memories, sufferings, aspirations, modes of dress and speech, styles of life characteristic of those they have educated to feel inferior. To speak more simply, white men do not know the quality of black life.

On the other hand, on whatever status level, black people are aware of the qualities of the life of white people. As gardeners, cooks, nurses of white children, bar workers, street cleaners, garbagemen, prisoners, hotel bellhops, seamstresses, persons in the courts, in the educational world, and in the business world, black people know all their lives the inner workings of white life. Besides, since every dominant culture seeks to preserve its own values, the entire educational system of America, by design, inducts every black into American culture with its European heritage. Furthermore, the black man, though of African descent, is an American and is entitled to whatever is available to any other American. It must always be remembered, I repeat, that he is not merely an American, but an American with very special memories, sufferings, and aspirations.

The point is that the black composer has a more genuine and extensive participation in both cultures (his own and that of whites) while whites have real participation only in their own culture. To sum up, a black man writing in a "white" style is thus not writing out of the periphery of an experience which he knows only superficially. His blackness does not limit his choices; it amplifies them.

While I consider these reflections important and necessary, I have still not given a definition of the term "black music." With all these limitations and preliminaries, I believe the term is best used in its broad and generally understood sense. As John Storm Roberts says in Black Music of Two Worlds, "The concept of black music is an imprecise and changing one. To be more precise is to be too precise."4 While I often prefer to avoid problems by referring to "black musical style," or "the black idiom," or "music of the black man," I will say, if forced, that I use the term black music to describe music created mainly by people who call themselves black, and whose compositions in their large or complete body show a frequent, if not preponderant, use of significant elements derived from the Afro-American heritage.

I am confirmed in the validity of using this broad, rather loose definition by common usage in the other arts which seem not to make an issue of highly precise definition. For example, what is French literature? Italian literature? English literature? Southern literature? American literature? Spanish art? Similar types of situations which we have considered above as vexing variations in defining black music seem not, at present, to be the object of the same concern in these other arts. There are occasional individual cultural crossings-over; all sorts of unpredictable exceptions may occur in these arts. For example, El Greco (The Greek) was the embodiment of Spanish art, while Joseph Conrad, born and reared a Pole, is a master of English prose. All sorts of other type exceptions occur which seem not at present to be the object of the anxious concern in the language discussing these arts as in the term black music.

Allowing for all such imprecisions and exceptions, black music is, in its simplest and broadest terms, simply music written by a black man.

3. Q: What features of your own music do you see as uniquely black (in terms of both musical and philosophical considerations)?

A: Musically: Its rhythms; its choice of scale structures; its use of call and response; its general use of contrapuntal devices since, as expressed elsewhere, the black musics of my early experiences were emphatically not homophonic; the choice of timbres; melody as influenced by rhythms, timbres, scalar structure. When the harmony is non-tertian, it is apt to use the 4ths and 5ths so often sung by black people in the churches of my youth; the deliberate use of striking climax with almost unrestrained fullness.

Philosophically: In retrospect, it seems I have often been concerned with aspiration, the emotional intensity associated with the life of black people as expressed in the various rites of the church and black life in general--the capacity and desire for abundant, full expression as one might anticipate or expect from an oppressed people determined to survive.

4. Q: In what ways is your music a reflection of your personal philosophy (social, political, etc.)?

A: As I have just said, any remarks I make related to philosophy in my music are made on reflection in retrospect. Usually I have not been trying consciously to express a philosophy. In the process of composition, my mind is musically oriented, though of course personal philosophies are involved in a non-conscious way since, as I have said elsewhere, whatever is created is created out of the whole self.

I might add, my social and political philosophy emerge from the feeling that all liberation is connected, i.e. that as long as any segment of the society is oppressed--not free--then the whole society must suffer. I believe that racism is the chief curse of American society and that there are few problems in American life upon which it does not impinge. The evil effects of racism are as injurious, at least spiritually, to whites as to blacks. I believe that blacks endure a three-fold tragedy in their lives: (a) the problem of the human condition, (b) the racism of whites expressed toward them, and (c) the sufferings of blacks from the attacks of other blacks, rendered less humanistic to their own people by the cruelties they have endured in the culture in which they have been reared.

5. Q: What do you see as the position or role of the black artist in contemporary society?

A: His Role

The primary function of any artist in any period is to convey as honestly and sincerely as he can his personal vision of life. Since the artist belongs to the most sensitive segment of any society, a black composer in contemporary America, aware of his own plight and that of his people, could scarcely avoid some expression reflective of these conditions.

Without positing a social purpose as a requirement for art, he really cannot escape expressing his heritage somewhere in the body of his work. This expression, in the works of a really gifted artist, is a powerful agent for social change. The fury of Picasso's Guernica as a social agent as well as a work of art comes to mind. The refusal of Pablo Casals to play though courted by dictators focused the attention of the world on their misdeeds. In like fashion, T. J. Anderson and those who formed the black caucus of the MENC[5] have realized the power of artists to effect social change. Natalie Hinderas, lecturing on black music and playing superbly the works of a variety of black composers, is an agent for social change. Marian Anderson, by the power of her art, forced the city of Richmond, capital of the Confederacy, to reverse its stand on segregation in the Mosque, its concert hall; and Marian Anderson by her art, as is well-known, finally opened the doors of Constitution Hall to black artists when her rejection had been dramatized. Paul Robeson's career cannot fail to have changed the channels of social philosophy however disastrously his career may have been affected. Every artist need not approach social change in the same way. For Andre Watts, the sheer perfection of his playing is an agent of social change. (The conversation among whites in the lobby of the Mosque in Richmond at the intermission of his concert with the Richmond Symphony demonstrated this influence for anyone who listened.) Billy Taylor, appearing daily on the David Frost Show and in the New Orchestra Hall in Minneapolis, was and is an agent of social change. Leon Thompson, using his influence at the New York Philharmonic, is an agent of social change. I have just returned from the 36th session of the State of Virginia Music Camp where, of four guest conductors, John Motley (Director of Music, New York City Public Schools) was the only black, the first

black director. About 800 young people--less than 50
black--responded to his humanity and his superb skill in a
way that was touching and inspiring. To give almost a
thousand adolescents this deep experience cannot fail to
effect social change.

While we have emphasized the fact that the black artist
can scarcely avoid some reflection of his heritage in the
full body of his work, it is also clear that, like everyone
else, he lives in a jet age and, at a given time, these
aspects of contemporary life may certainly challenge his attention as they may interest any other artist.

His Position
    The artist is not highly valued in American society and,
of this group, the black artist is at the bottom. He will
have less time to write, to create. He will find greater
difficulty getting his work printed, recorded, performed.
He will be omitted from so-called serious texts or books
and lists of music. He will get comparatively little money,
which means that while his position may be very slowly
improving, in general his lot is not very different from that
of other blacks in any comparative scale. If he dies early,
others who imitate his works or use them exactly will often
reap the fame and fortune denied him and his descendants.

6. Q: Please discuss any problems you may have encountered in
        getting your works performed, published, and recorded.
    A: Problems
        I do not wish to be pretentious about my works. With-
out giving a history of my life, I may point out that one of
the most evil effects of racism in my time was the limits
it placed upon the aspirations of blacks, so that though I
have been "making up" and creating music all my life, in
my childhood or even in college I would not have thought of
calling myself a composer or aspiring to be one. I had no
early contact with anyone who had ever published anything--
no contact with anyone who knew how to go about getting
anything published. Worse still, I would, by my position
as a black child, have automatically assumed that this was
not intended for me even if I had heard it discussed.
        At college and graduate school I was considered to excel
in theory and composition, but I drifted later into being
what I could call a composer in my own language, by writing music to meet the demands of the situations in which I
worked--all sorts of pieces for rural Chesterfield school
children, pieces for church services, pieces for piano students and organ students. For a high school with a total
enrollment of 80 pupils (rural) I edited the Gilbert and
Sullivan operettas for performance, one each year. The
editing was technically well-done--practical and successful
in presentation. I did not have the thought that I was
"editing," nor would the thought of suggesting publication
of these editions to any company have occurred to me.

Later, I saw published such editions. I cannot logically blame the publishers for not publishing works which were never submitted, but I can blame a society which educated (?) me to feel my "otherness," that left me ignorant of that which was accessible to those of the dominant group with similar talent.

Long before the present practice of teaching theory through the practice of the composers, I wrote a book--A Recorded Supplement to Studies in Traditional Harmony. The explanations were all there, a wide range of musical examples meticulously copied. Dr. Howard Murphy, head of theory at Manhattan and at Columbia, read it and wrote me that he considered it a very superior piece of work and only wished it were available for individual use. I had learned by this time the names of some publishers to whom I submitted the work. It was always rejected, though in a few years the market was flooded with such works. Nevertheless, I have almost worn it out in my own teaching.

I conceived the idea of integrating examples from the works of black composers into the scores used in the study of literature and history. I prepared sample chapters and spent a week talking to publishers in New York. They felt the idea not feasible.

The existence of my published works, of course, acknowledges a more positive factor which I shall mention later.

Recordings
Robert Fountain and the Oberlin College Choir, Virginia State College, Virginia Union, Fisk University, and some state festival groups have recorded choral works in the noncommercial type series for which I am grateful. I should also mention Contemporary Black Images in Music for the Flute (Eastern ERS-513), which includes my Afro-American Suite for cello, flute, and piano.

6A. Q: How much of your actual output has ever been performed? Published? Recorded?

6B. Q: Have you encountered difficulty in getting your works programmed?

(Ed. note: Dr. Moore chose to answer questions 6A and 6B together.)

A: In summary, only a small percentage of what I have written has been published or recorded. I am grateful that those works which are published were accepted by the first publisher to whom they were sent. I feel less optimistic about my chances for publication of the Afro-American Suite, the cantata for male chorus, [6] the Choral Prayers in Folk Style, and the Three Pieces for Flute and Piano, though I have no difficulty whatsoever in getting them performed. Music publishing is a business, and there are many factors involved other than race. [7] What makes me really happy is the fact that I get so many requests for performance scores and

that a tremendous number of people have asked me to write
for their performance groups and many have asked for
pieces for solo performance. Often these are persons of
national reputation and significance.

Perhaps the most interesting piece I ever wrote for
piano I never even copied. It is short, but quite difficult.
Who would have published it? And, if published, who would
have played it?[8]

6C. Q: Are there specific problems in getting a satisfactory performance? Exemplify and discuss.

A: When I consider the way in which the works of acknowledged
master composers are "mangled" in performance every day,
and when I think of the tremendous amount of music available to performers, I feel I should express gratitude to
those who have chosen to perform what I have written.   I
have in my life had only three performances (where I was
present), at times I considered unusually significant in my
life and career, when I was embarrassed by the quality of
the performances because I thought they misrepresented completely what I had conceived and written.

Some Problems in Getting a Satisfactory Performance
Sometimes, apparently, voices of suitable range and
color are not available.   My setting of Langston Hughes's
"Mother To Son" falls into that category for all the voices
and especially for the alto soloist.   This is true, though
the vocal demands are no greater than one finds frequently
in the standard concert literature.   Perhaps the same point
might be made with reference to "Let Us Make Man in Our
Image" on a text from Milton's Paradise Lost.   Also, some
choral directors, planning a concert program where they
cover a wide range of "standard" literature, tend frequently
to choose my less difficult works.   (I'm still grateful!)   I
suppose they reason that if their rehearsal time is limited,
why not spend the major portion of that time on Bach instead of Undine Moore?   It is for this reason that, some
years ago, I never attempted to have published a four-voice
vocal fugue on a text by St. Augustine ("Thou hast made
us for thyself, and our hearts are restless 'til they repose
in thee.")   It is a demanding fugue and I think the reasoning
just mentioned would have operated against it.   Of course,
by now the fugue is less frequently written than formerly,
and some musicians question its relevance in the twentieth
century.

If I had continued to be a choir director, many of these
problems would have been solved or handled in a different
way.   In a sense, music is not too hard for the performers
if it is not too hard for the director.   A surprising number
of musicians (?) restrict themselves to works they have
sung under somebody else; they can deal with certain rhythmic and pitch problems and problems of phrasing, design,
and organization by "rote," so to speak, instead of having

to unravel anything for themselves. When the composer directs his own composition in performance, the concept of the piece can be made clear, and even if it is difficult, others will approach it more easily as a work they might conduct themselves.

(Alas! If works seem difficult, and easier pieces are frequently chosen, publishers will let the harder works go out of print. My publishers won't return a copyright then or under any circumstances.)

7. Q: What do you consider, at this point in your life, to be your most significant achievement(s) aside from your compositions?

A: 1. Teaching

Teaching has been a tremendously important activity in my life. A number of my students hold eminent positions. The NASM[9] referred to my theory classes as "alert pupils taught by a stimulating and inspiring teacher." I had the pleasure of teaching the following students among many others who seem to hold in very high regard what went on in our classrooms; each had some courses with me for each of four years, five times a week for the first two years. A partial list: Billy Taylor; Dr. Leon Thompson of the New York Philharmonic; Jewel Taylor Thompson, theory teacher at Hunter College, who did as her master's thesis at Eastman an analysis of the works of three black composers, of which I was one; Camilla Williams, who was the first black woman to sing opera with a major opera company in the United States and the first to sing a non-Negro role (she made her debut with the New York City Opera Company in Butterfly rather than Aida); Phillip Medley, a popular songwriter ("A Million to One," "The Twist") and owner of Starflower Publishing Company; Dr. Howell Jones, head of the Department of Music at Virginia State College; Dr. Chelsea Tipton, head of the Department of Music at Hampton Institute; Dr. T. Marshall Jones, head of the Department of Music at Albany State College; Clyde Walker, baritone, of the St. Paul Opera Company; Dr. Egbert Bacon, teacher of piano at Alabama State; Robert Alexander, choir director at Wilberforce College; Ruth Dabney Alexander, formerly a voice teacher at Antioch College; Robert Fryson, arranger, organizer, and soloist with the Voices Supreme (three times named the best male vocal gospel group); John Taylor, teacher of instrumental music in Hampton, Virginia; William Terry, pianist, interim Vice-President of Virginia State College; Ronald Cheatham, a 1975 honors graduate of Yale; James Pettis, pianist and recipient of the NANM[10] Young Pianists award following his New York debut in 1974; Herbert Richardson, Director of Music Education for the city of Perth Amboy, New Jersey; Michael Gordon (and numerous music teachers in New York whose work led Mayor Lindsay to give me a citation), who is now on the faculty of the School of Music at Indiana University; Barbara

Ratliff, violist, who has been practicing law since her
graduation from Yale; Marie Goodman, actress and singer;
Harry E. Savage, organizer of the Monroe Chorus, choral
consultant and director of the Armstrong Choir; Joseph
Bonner, jazz pianist with Freddie Hubbard; the late Arthur
Bouldin, distinguished choral conductor and lecturer; George
Ross, bassoonist and current faculty member of the School
of Music at Indiana University; Dr. Harry A. Johnson, international authority on audio-visual learning resources;
William Crump, specialist on the adolescent voice and head
of Fine Arts at Phoebus High School (Phoebus, Va.); Dr.
William Ryder of Southern University (junior and senior years
only); Dr. Kenneth Keeling of Lincoln University (junior and
senior years only); and Lois Williams, pianist and faculty
member at Northwestern University.

There are many students who have no national standing
whose work I respect as highly, for they are raising the
level of appreciation and musical understanding in small
communities. (Of course, all these students had many
other teachers.) I cannot say why they seem to value me
in a special way. Some I know were grateful because their
preparation in theory was sound enough to prevent their assignment to remedial or non-credit courses on the graduate
level. Besides, my association was long-continued and they
knew I expected much from them. I was pleased this week-
end when one of these students said, "You were loving and
kind, but firm."

2. Establishment of the Black Music Center at Virginia
   State College
   Perhaps, next to teaching, this is the most significant
activity of my career. The Center, with Altona Johns and
myself as co-directors, was established under three grants
from the National Endowment for the Humanities, three
from the Southern Educational Foundation, and Title III.
The Center was designed to disseminate information and appreciation for the contributions of the black man to the music
of the United States and the world. It included the establishment of a three-hour course for graduate or undergraduate credit. During the first two years, twenty-seven seminars including or emphasizing performance of black works
were held. Three institutes were held and in all our activities it was our purpose to focus attention not only on the
so-called "serious" works of black composers, but also on
those which represent the genius of the lowly, oppressed
black man. The seminars took cognizance of the fact that
the arts of black people are not historically separated. The
series of seminars, primarily focused on black music, included some experience with black literature, the arts,
dance, etc.

The seminars invited the participation of persons rep-
resenting varied aspects of American life. They were
eagerly attended by persons of many different races and

and cultures. Any idea of social status having value in the participation was considered false and unworthy. Performers and lecturers of the highest caliber were secured.

The largest presentation involved the hiring of the Richmond Symphony Orchestra with Dr. Leon Thompson as conductor of three concerts of works by black composers, one at Virginia State, one at Hampton, and a third in the city of Richmond. A concert piece was commissioned by the Center for these concerts. Hale Smith wrote the music, which was performed by Jewel Thompson. [11] Audiences hung from the rafters.

The books, recordings, audiotapes, videotapes, scores, the Johns-Moore series of Black Music Films, the collection of African instruments, etc. were housed in the college library upon our retirement. According to the commitment of the college to the foundations, they were to be made available on loan to all interested groups. The plan was not carried out fully to our satisfaction, but functions under an efficient librarian as part of Interlibrary Loan service.

Unfortunately, many otherwise well-educated black administrators have had little experience with the arts and are singularly lacking in appreciation of their own Afro-American heritage. The vitality of the Center still endures, nevertheless, in the large enrollments in the course The Black Man In American Music. This elective course, with a current enrollment of 129 students at Virginia State College, is pleasant to contemplate as it continues under the leadership of Dr. Carl Harris, a young man extremely competent in this field.

Finally, I would like to add that Herbert McArthur of the National Endowment for the Humanities said of our final report, "... You certainly accomplished a great deal with your grant, and you have every reason to be proud. The collection of materials which you sent speaks eloquently of your hard work and your imaginative approaches."

3. The Courses in Music and Art at Virginia State College
I was one of the organizers, after long study, of the first course designed for integrated study of the arts. I was a team teacher in this course and coordinator of all sections for several years. It was extremely rewarding and I learned as much as the students, since as a musician I had concentrated little on painting, sculpture, and architecture, though I had read in the various literary genres somewhat widely and had participated in dance studies through my daughter's classes.

8. Q: What do you see as the responsibilities and obligations of the educational system (at all levels) to the study of black music?

A: I believe that black music is a necessary study for blacks and whites in all stages of the curriculum. Tributes to the contribution of black musicians to the quality of American life have been common since Colonial days. The writings of Thomas Jefferson, Benjamin Franklin, Fanny Kemble, and others are too well-known to need citing. Blacks are everywhere in America and have been since the beginning. But tributes have had little effect on curricula. In 1975 even the most racist writers on music have begun to acknowledge (in print even) the unique contribution of blacks to the music of the world. But it is only a grudging beginning.

A music which has vitality enough to be heard everywhere in the world should be treated as worthy of national pride. To rear generations of youngsters who do not know this part of the American heritage is to rear a people ignorant of one of their country's past and present glories. While the study of black music is often valued for affective reasons, e.g., increasing the respect of blacks for themselves and the respect of others for them, I think the primary reason is also cognitive. This music exists as a fact and, properly taught in its historical perspective, it will reveal the true nature of American culture. It is the nature of art that it, better than anything else, communicates the essence of a nation's culture and history.

In a practical sense, this means (among other things) really making performance opportunities available to all at an early age. In Minnesota, in May 1975, I had two striking experiences which revealed some challenging deficiencies. The new Orchestra Hall was crowded for the performance of orchestral works by black composers. The Minnesota Orchestra (one black) performed with zest. Good! During the same week I attended rehearsals and a performance of the justly celebrated Minnesota Youth Orchestra. Open to everyone by audition, the elementary school orchestra had one black child. This organization is not racist in its acceptance of performers and the presence of one black child playing the cello means that black people need to give more thought to what is happening to black children in the fundamental early years. If we continue to concentrate on the top, we may end up paraphrasing Ralph Ellison, that the only thing standing in the way of more string players in the orchestra is not color alone.

Finally, I believe that, ideally, black music should be taught as a part of music study where it is relevant and appropriate. For a while it may be necessary to compensate for the neglect of the past by separate courses. But, particularly in the music enjoyed by the young, the black idiom is already integrated into the general American music sound. Neither blacks nor whites recognize the black elements and for the sake of truth, they should be taught what strands have dominated the music they love.

9. Q: Do you feel that the people who write about your music (critics in particular) understand what you are doing? Exemplify and discuss.

A: This question should be answered in the context of my
response to question number six, which discusses the way
I entered into publication. I was happy about the way my
<u>Afro-American Suite</u> was reviewed in the Bloomington
<u>Courier-Journal</u> after a performance at Indiana University.
The choral journals have dealt understandingly and kindly
with certain other works.[12] For reasons already discussed,
my most difficult works have not been reviewed.

10. Q: What advice would you give to the aspiring young black
composer?

A: The young black composer should listen to all the varieties
of music possible. He should perform. He should master
as thoroughly as possible the details of music as a craft;
he should develop his musicianship to the fullest. He
should let his life and his senses be stimulated by other
arts: painting, sculpture, dance, literature, drama, architecture. He should know some poetry, history, philosophy.
He should value the opportunity to direct or perform in
amateur groups which may include all races. He should
initiate them if possible. Besides rendering a service, he
will find through this practice the limitations, the advantages,
the unique possibilities, and the problems of various voices
and instruments.

Above all, he should remain close to his people, shar-
ing their thoughts, feelings, and anxieties. These are a
part of the roots which nourish and strengthen him. He
should be aware of the possibilities for social change which
may result from his art. He should remember that it is
the <u>whole</u> person who creates.

Part II: Music Questions

1. Q: When you sit down to begin a new composition on your own
initiative or inspiration (as opposed to a commissioned
work), what procedure or approach do you follow?

A: When I begin a new composition, it is often after a period
of "germination" which may be long or short; I do not try
to hurry the initial idea. It comes to me spontaneously
and whatever <u>it is</u> suggests what the general working-out
will be. From this point I am involved in choosing what
seems effective to me in terms of unity, variety, balance,
dominance, style, form, etc.--all technical considerations
which I hope are internalized in me.

Some situations have arisen where I <u>had</u> to have some
songs immediately. For example, Marie Goodman, a
contralto of unusually beautiful timbre in her low voice,
consented to substitute for a very high soprano who found
she could not attend or perform at a concert in my honor.
I felt that Marie deserved something which had been especially designed for the quality of her voice and her temperament. I went to sleep on that thought and when I awakened,

a line from Georgia Douglas Johnson's poem, "I Want to Die While You Love Me" sang itself to me with the full accompaniment to the line. I went to the piano in my night-gown and finished the song in the next two hours. The poem is highly romantic and the musical treatment echoes it. The piece was very well received.

2. Q: When composing a commissioned work or a work written for a specific occasion or person, does your procedure or approach differ from the one you described in question one? If so, in what way?

A: As is apparent, there is little difference in my real procedure here. I think about the commissioned assignment and then I let it alone until it is ready. I have read so much poetry, etc. that I have the feeling, if a text is involved, that the words have chosen me out of the past instead of my having searched for them. The details of the commission will naturally determine such matters as length, sometimes mood (as for a festive occasion), and medium (whether for mixed voices, male voices, for alto or soprano flute, etc.).

3. Q: In general, with regard to your writing, what genre(s) do you prefer?

A: I prefer most writing for unaccompanied mixed chorus. Since I have expressed a preference for choral composition and since I have heard certain well-established composers express some disdain for this genre, I would like to quote a passage from what I consider to be a classic work of scholarly dimensions, The Technique of Choral Composition by Archibald T. Davidson, James Edward Ditson Professor of Music, Harvard University: "... to be known as a symphonist is the ambition of probably 90 per cent of the musicians who commit their ideas to music paper. They look askance at the suggestion that a grasp of the refinements of choral technique presupposes much more than a review of the work of those who are recognized masters in this field, and they assume that compared with the complex resources of the modern orchestra, the limited physique of the chorus makes it unnecessary for one possessing the staple details of the composer's technique to know much more about voices than the limits of their range. There is, however, a choral technique as expert and as subtle as that for the orchestra, and the management of it in its more skillful manifestations demands even greater ingenuity than is required in instrumentation. How true this is will appear from a comparative survey of choral with orchestral resource."13

There follows a profitable discussion of differences in resources in three areas (range, dynamic, and color) too long to be quoted here. However, Davidson continues: "... From all this it is clear that the choral composer

must to the best of his ability make virtues of his limitations; he must ferret out every legitimate means of impres-
siveness. "14

   And finally, I quote: "... If the discipline which has
been set forth seems unduly arduous, implying something
idealistic rather than practical, it should be pointed out
that more than one composer has missed total greatness
only because he was deficient in choral craftsmanship. Ad-
mittedly the way is not short, nor is it easy; and he who
pursues it with patience and persistence to the end may,
after all, win no more than a conscientious workman's
reward; for the success of his music will, in the end, be
judged by the power of his eloquence and by his gifts as a
creative artist. "15

4. Q: What do you consider your most significant composition?
        Please discuss.
    A: It is hard to be objective about one's own compositions.
        Each is different and is valued for its own sake as are dif-
        ferent children in a large family. I think the third move-
        ment of my trio Afro-American Suite for alto flute, cello,
        and piano is the best of the four pieces in the suite. I
        think that Mother to Son (Langston Hughes) for alto solo
        with mixed chorus is fine in its use of vocal tone color and
        in the general writing. I think the term "arrangement" is
        not a proper designation for Daniel, Daniel Servant of the
        Lord; if anyone saw the meager fragment from which it
        grew, I think it would rightly be considered an example of
        theme and variations. I am happy because I could use all
        the contrapuntal skill I possess in Lord, We Give Thanks
        to Thee, which was commissioned to celebrate the 100th
        anniversary of the going-out of the Jubilee Singers of Fisk
        University. The fugue is completely black in its subject;
        the rhythms of the piece all are black and the climaxes
        call for the zest and intensity characteristic of blacks.
        The Christmas cantata for male voices with narrator, piano,
        organ, flute, percussion, and brass quartet is a good and
        practical work. 16

5. Q: Please comment on your treatment of the following musical
        elements and give examples from your compositions that
        illustrate the techniques you describe:
        A. Melody
        B. Harmony
        C. Rhythm
        D. Form
        E. Improvisation
        F. Text
        G. Instrumentation or medium (both in terms of choice of
            particular combinations as well as how you treat them
            compositionally.)
    A: See my response to question three, part I.

6. Q: Have difficulties with performance practice (inflection, phrasing, etc.) been a significant problem in having your works performed to your own satisfaction?

   A: See my response to question 6C, part I.

7. Q: What major works are currently in progress? Please describe and discuss.

   A: (a) Like everyone else able to hold a pen, I have been asked to do a large work on Martin Luther King. The piece is in what I call a period of "germination." I have a vague idea that it will be called something like Scenes from the Life of a Hero (or Scenes from the Life of a Martyr). I think perhaps the text will come from a variety of sources. Maybe I will write some of it myself. Unless I have a great change of mind, the text will definitely not be Martin's famous "I Have a Dream" speech. Perhaps there will be a large chorus, a speaking or singing narrator, orchestral accompaniment (or at least an ensemble from the orchestra), and possibly some use of electronic sources if I can master the technique. The duration of the work would be between 30 and 40 minutes. It would not strive for consistency of style, but it would be, I hope, at each point stylistically expressive of the particular part of the "life" being described.

   (b) I have not yet asked the permission of the author to use the text, but I am well on the way in an attempt to make a setting of Margaret Walker's For My People. [17] This is a choral work in which I hear the orchestra with voices, but I would try to write so that its essential structure could be expressed with piano only, since one should be practical in performance terms for various groups. As everyone knows, the poem is extremely comprehensive in its grasp of the life of blacks and the attempt to set it to music is challenging.

   Whether these are "major" works I leave to the judgment of the readers or listeners.

8. Q: Given unlimited time and finances (and no restrictions whatsoever), what would you write?

   A: I wish this question had been asked me ten years ago. I would like even at this point to be able to explore the possibilities of other than conventional sound sources. I would wish to write music of good quality, interesting and fresh, yet within the performance possibilities of the thousands of performers and groups for whom there must be a continuing repertoire. The masses of amateur choirs, school groups, church groups, etc. deserve a less banal repertoire of choices. To satisfy this need would, in my opinion, be an entirely worthwhile project. Was it Fauré who told his famous students at the Paris Conservatory, "Don't try to write a masterpiece every day."!

9. Q: If given the opportunity, would you choose to devote yourself

to composition on a full-time basis? Why or why not?

A: Trying to teach what I can about the great art of music, to stimulate students to realize what potentialities they have (which they often do not realize) and what opportunities are now open to them is extremely satisfying to me. I experience teaching itself as an art, and I have found it to have a valuable reciprocal relation to the art of composition. As long as I am able, I would like to do both. It would be fine to have a life so ordered that other everyday responsibilities did not impinge so heavily on my time. I am a widow of restricted means living in a fairly large house which must be managed in some way. The simple availability of a part-time typist or office assistant and a cleaning assistant would almost seem ideal as ways of making composing more possible.

This question was surely written for men. Their wives assume those dreary responsibilities which make it possible for them to compose. Even the many male composers who do not marry in order to avoid these responsibilities often have some kind of liaison with a woman who relieves them of the matters.

10. Q: How would you describe your compositional style?

A: It is tonal, generally, with some quite specific exceptions. The first and third of Three Pieces for Flute (or Clarinet) and Piano are twelve-tone. The basically tonal pieces have, sometimes, strongly modal references. The tonality is often free, so that I write without a key signature. There are many examples where the clichés of the cadence are avoided. There are numerous instances of the use of twentieth-century techniques. I believe it, with a few exceptions, to be largely dominated by the black idiom. There is somewhat frequent use of recitative-like styles and almost always strong contrapuntal influence for reasons cited above. (Besides, I teach counterpoint.)

11. Q: What have been the influences of other composers, styles, and other types of music on your compositional style?

A: Except for black influences, it is hard to say, except Bach.

12. Q: Has your style changed across your career? If so, what influenced these changes or developments?

A: As a student at Fisk and Columbia, I wrote Godowski-sounding pieces for the piano. Other works somehow seemed to follow lines that must have been suggested by the teacher's taste. Example: A large cantata for women's voices at Fisk, Sir Olaf and the Erl King's Daughter. I don't know whether my teacher, Sara Leight, was Scandinavian or not. She gave me the poem.

It takes some maturity for many people to realize that what is extremely familiar in one's life may be the subject of creative expression, much in the way that young writers of fiction or poetry often pass through periods of writing

192 / The Black Composer Speaks

about strange, exotic, or far-away themes before they
realize that their daily life is the secure source, what they
really know and really feel. After my master's degree at
Columbia, I seemed to realize how deeply touched I was by
the fragments of spirituals sung by my mother and father
around the house--how much the spirituals sung at Fisk were
a part of me. I began writing down the melodic fragments
sung by my family from Southside, Virginia. I was struck
by the fact that many of these melodies were not often heard.
At the time I recorded the fragments, I had no specific purpose for further use. There may have been some vague
but certainly undefined idea of some later use--not consciously though.

13. Q: When you are listening to music for your own enjoyment,
what are your preferences?

A: There is far too much music of different styles and periods
in the world for me to make a meaningful list. One day--
one hour, the choice is one thing; another, another. I enjoy the whole range of what is available. Without any favorites, I might list the following (for range of styles only):
Gregorian chant, madrigals, the incomparable Aretha Franklin, Fauré, Bartok, William Grant Still, Dawson, Stravinsky
(especially the Symphony of Psalms), Mozart, Vivaldi, John
Coltrane, Brahms, Harry Partch, George Walker, Gladys
Knight and the Pips, The Spinners, Beethoven. I think that
J. S. Bach is the one absolutely indispensable composer.

Notes to Chapter VII

1. Frederick Douglass, Narrative of the Life of Frederick Douglass,
ed. Benjamin Quarles (Cambridge, Mass.: Belknap Press, 1960).

2. Leslie H. Fishel and Benjamin Quarles, The Negro American;
a Documentary History (Glenview, Ill.: Scott, Foresman, 1967).

3. William Ryan, Blaming the Victim (New York: Pantheon Books,
1971).

4. John Storm Roberts, Black Music of Two Worlds (New York:
Praeger Publishers, 1972), vii. The underlining appearing in the
quoted material was done by Dr. Moore.

5. Music Educators National Conference

6. Dr. Moore is referring to her composition Glory to God.

7. Dr. Moore discussed this matter further, stating: "I believe
the most pressing need of black composers is a publishing house by
which their music can be made available to performers. Many
established publishers seem to treat blacks on a token quota system.
They think in terms of a commitment to one black composer at a
time."

8.   When asked to which of her compositions for piano she was referring, Mrs. Moore replied: "The piece has no title. If I were to christen it now, I might call it Warrior." She continued her discussion of the work by describing it as follows: "By the standards of 1975, I am usually stylistically addicted to mild dissonance, but this piece is sharply dissonant and much more irregular rhythmically. It is a piece which reflects a particular hostility and frustration I felt in a personal situation of some difficulty."

9.   National Association of Schools of Music

10.   National Association of Negro Musicians

11.   The title of Hale Smith's composition is Concert Music for Piano and Orchestra. The first performance was given February 24, 1972 in Richmond, Virginia. Dr. Leon Thompson conducted the Richmond Symphony Orchestra; Jewel Thompson was the piano soloist.

12.   For examples of recent reviews see the following issues of The Choral Journal: December 1973, p. 34 (Lord, We Give Thanks to Thee); March 1974, p. 27 (Lord, We Give Thanks to Thee); December 1974, p. 33 (Striving after God); March 1975, p. 30 (Fare You Well).

13.   Archibald T. Davison. The Technique of Choral Composition (Cambridge, Mass.: Harvard University Press, 1945), pp. 9-10. The underlining appearing in the material quoted from this source (notes 14-15) was done by Dr. Moore.

14.   Ibid., pp. 10-11.

15.   Ibid., pp. 14-15.

16.   Dr. Moore is referring to her composition Glory to God.

17.   Arna Bontemps, ed. American Negro Poetry (New York: Hill and Wang, 1963), pp. 128-130.

LIST OF COMPOSITIONS

AFRO-AMERICAN SUITE   (1969)
 Flute/alto flute, violoncello, and piano. Four movements: Andante (Nobody Knows the Trouble I See, Lord); Allegro molto e marcato (I Heard the Preaching of the Elder); Adagio ma appassionato (Who Is That Yonder?); Allegro molto e marcato (Shout All Over God's Heaven). App. 11½ min. Recorded by the Trio Pro Viva (D. Antoinette Handy, flute; Ronald Lipscomb, violoncello; and Gladys Perry Norris, piano) on Eastern ERS-513 (Contemporary Black Images in Music for the Flute). Com-

missioned by and first performed (1969) by the Trio Pro Viva
at District of Columbia Teachers College (Washington, D.C.)

ALLELUIA (1975)
Chorus (SATB) with optional organ accompaniment. Text is the
word "Alleluia." App. 2 min. 10 sec. First performance (1976)
by the choirs of St. Stephens Episcopal Church (Petersburg,
Va.), Clarence Whiteman, conductor.

ARISE, MY LOVE, MY FAIR ONE (1975)
See SCENES FROM THE LIFE OF A MARTYR (Excerpts).

BENEDICTION (1974)
Chorus (SATB) unaccompanied. Text by Donald Jeffrey Hayes.
App. 3 min. First performance (1975) at Commencement Ex-
ercises, Virginia State College (Petersburg, Va.). Virginia
State College Choir, Carl Harris, conductor.

THE BLIND MAN STOOD ON THE WAY AND CRIED (1932)
Chorus (SATB) unaccompanied. Arrangement of spiritual.
App. 2 min.

BOUND FOR CANAAN'S LAND (1960)
Chorus (SATB) unaccompanied. Arrangement of spiritual. App.
2 min. M. Witmark, 1960. Recorded by the Virginia State
College Choir, Carl Harris, conductor (Richsound 4112N10:
The Undine Smith Moore Song Book). First performance (1960)
at the Virginia State Music Festival, Virginia State College
(Petersburg, Va.) by the Armstrong High School Choir (Rich-
mond, Va.), Harry E. Savage, conductor.

CHORAL PRAYERS IN FOLK STYLE (1974)
Chorus (SATB) unaccompanied. Seven parts, but can be used
as separate pieces: Lord Have Mercy (app. 2 min.); Glory to
God in the Highest (app. 1 min.); I Believe This Is Jesus (ar-
rangement of spiritual, app. 1 min. 40 sec.); O Holy Lord (ar-
rangement of spiritual, app. 2 min. 50 sec.); Come Along in
Jesus' Name (arrangement of spiritual, app. 30 sec.); O That
Bleeding Lamb (arrangement of spiritual, 2 min.); We Shall
Walk Through the Valley in Peace (arrangement of spiritual,
app. 3 min.). App. 13 min. 25 sec.

A CHRISTMAS ALLELUIA (1970)
Chorus (SSA) unaccompanied. Spiritual text (O Mary, What You
Going to Name That Pretty Little Baby?). $2\frac{1}{2}$ min. Commis-
sioned by and first performed (1970) by the Spelman College
Glee Club, Aldrich Adkins, conductor.

COME ALONG IN JESUS' NAME (1974)
See CHORAL PRAYERS IN FOLK STYLE.

DANIEL, DANIEL SERVANT OF THE LORD (1952)
Chorus (SSAATTBB) unaccompanied. Arrangement of spiritual.

App. 1 min. 45 sec. M. Witmark, 1953. Recorded by the
Virginia State College Choir, Carl Harris, conductor (Rich-
sound 4112N10: The Undine Smith Moore Song Book); by the
Oberlin College Choir, Daniel Moe, conductor (Oberlin College
Choir Recordings, Series B, Volume 2: The Oberlin College
Choir); by the Oberlin College Choir, Robert Fountain, conduc-
tor (Empirical EM 17-18, Vol. 11: The Oberlin College Choir
1961 Concert Program); and by the Fisk Jubilee Singers, John
W. Work, conductor (Word Records W-4007: The Fisk Jubilee
Singers; Philips P76145R: Les Plus Beaux Negro-Spirituals
Par Les Fisk Jubilee Singers). First performance (1952) at
a faculty concert, Virginia State College (Petersburg, Va.).
Undine Smith Moore, conductor.

FARE YOU WELL (1950)
Chorus (SATB) unaccompanied. Arrangement of spiritual. App.
1½ min. M. Witmark, 1951. Recorded by the Virginia State
College Choir, Carl Harris, conductor (Richsound 4112N10: The
Undine Smith Moore Song Book). First performance (1951) by
the Virginia State College Choir, Robert Henry, conductor.

FUGUE IN F (1952)
String trio. Three-voice 18th century style fugue. 2½ min.
First performance (1952) at Virginia State College (Petersburg,
Va.).

GLORY TO GOD (1974)
A Christmas cantata for chorus (TTBB), narrator, flute, organ
and piano with optional brass and percussion. Text from St.
Luke, St. Matthew, and The Book of Common Prayer. 30 min.
Commissioned by the male chorus of the First Baptist Church
(Petersburg, Va.). First performance (1974) at the First Bap-
tist Church (Petersburg, Va.). Buckner Gamby, conductor.

GLORY TO GOD IN THE HIGHEST (1974)
See CHORAL PRAYERS IN FOLK STYLE.

HAIL! WARRIOR! (1958)
Chorus (SATB) unaccompanied. Arrangement of spiritual. App.
2 min. M. Witmark, 1958. Recorded by the Virginia State
College Choir, Carl Harris, conductor (Richsound 4112N10:
The Undine Smith Moore Song Book). First performance (1958)
by the Virginia State College Choir, Aldrich Adkins, conductor.

HEART, HAVE YOU HEARD THE NEWS? (1926)
Soprano and piano. Text by Christina Rosetti. App. 2 min.
First performance (1926) by Anna Lois Goodwin, soprano, and
Undine Smith Moore, piano.

HERE COMES ANOTHER ONE TO BE BAPTIZED (1973)
See TO BE BAPTIZED.

HOW I GOT OVER (1966)
Chorus (SATB) unaccompanied. Arrangement of spiritual.

App. 2 min. 50 sec.

I AM IN DOUBT (1975)
    Soprano and piano. Text by Florence Hynes Willett. App. 2
    min. 50 sec. First performance (1976) at Virginia State Col-
    lege (Petersburg, Va.). Carolyn Kizzie, soprano; Carl Harris,
    piano. This work and LYRIC FOR TRUE LOVE were written
    as companion pieces, but may be used separately.

I BELIEVE THIS IS JESUS (1974)
    See CHORAL PRAYERS IN FOLK STYLE.

I JUST COME FROM THE FOUNTAIN (1950)
    Chorus (SATB) unaccompanied. Arrangement of spiritual. App.
    1 min. 10 sec. M. Witmark, 1951. Recorded by the Virginia
    State College Choir, Carl Harris, conductor (Richsound 4112N10:
    The Undine Smith Moore Song Book). First performance (1951)
    by the Virginia State College Choir, Robert Henry, conductor.

I WANT TO DIE WHILE YOU LOVE ME (1975)
    Contralto and piano. Text by Georgia Douglas Johnson. First
    performance (1975) in Petersburg, Va., at the Beaux-Twenty
    Club program in honor of Undine Smith Moore. Marie Goodman
    Hunter, soprano; Clarence Whiteman, piano.

I WOULD BE TRUE (1958)
    Chorus (SAB) and piano. Text by Howard A. Walter. 2 min.
    20 sec. Written for the choruses of Ruffner and Jacox Junior
    High Schools (Norfolk, Va.).

I'M GOING HOME (1948)
    Chorus (SATB) unaccompanied. Arrangement of spiritual. $2\frac{1}{2}$
    min.

INTO MY HEART'S TREASURY (1950)
    Chorus (SATB) unaccompanied. Text by Sara Teasdale. App.
    $2\frac{1}{2}$ min.

INTRODUCTION AND ALLEGRO (1953)
    Clarinet and piano. Two movements. App. $2\frac{1}{2}$ min. This
    work was subsequently expanded into INTRODUCTION, MARCH,
    AND ALLEGRO (see next entry).

INTRODUCTION, MARCH, AND ALLEGRO (1958)
    Clarinet and piano. Three movements. 6 min. This work
    and THREE PIECES FOR FLUTE AND PIANO are identical with
    the exception of medium.

IS THERE ANYBODY HERE? (1949)
    Chorus (SSA) unaccompanied. Arrangement of spiritual. 3 min.
    First performance by the Women's Symphonic Choir of Virginia
    State College (Petersburg, Va.), Undine Smith Moore, conduc-
    tor.

THE LAMB   (1958)
    2-part canon for treble voices.   Text by William Blake.   App.
    $2\frac{1}{2}$ min.   H. W. Gray, 1958 (in Church Music Review).   Re-
    corded by the Virginia State College Choir, Carl Harris, con-
    ductor (Richsound 4112N10:   The Undine Smith Moore Song Book)
    and by the St. Stephen's Church Choir, Clarence Whiteman,
    conductor (Eastern ERS-542:   St. Stephen's Church Choir Sings).
    First performance (1958) by the Children's Choir of the Gillfield
    Baptist Church (Petersburg, Va.), Altona Trent Johns, conduc-
    tor.

LET US MAKE MAN IN OUR IMAGE   (1960)
    Chorus (SATB) unaccompanied.   Text by John Milton.   App. 2
    min. 20 sec.   M. Witmark, 1960.   Recorded by the Virginia
    State College Choir, Carl Harris, conductor (Richsound 4112N10:
    The Undine Smith Moore Song Book).   First performance (1960)
    by the Virginia State College Choir, Aldrich Adkins, conductor.

LONG FARE YOU WELL   (1960)
    Chorus (SATB) unaccompanied.   Arrangement of spiritual.   App.
    3 min. 10 sec.   M. Witmark, 1960.   First performance (1960)
    by the Virginia State College Choir, Aldrich Adkins, conductor.

LORD HAVE MERCY   (1974)
    See CHORAL PRAYERS IN FOLK STYLE.

LORD, MAKE US MORE HOLY   (1966)
    2-part canonic treatment of a spiritual with piano accompani-
    ment. $1\frac{1}{2}$ min.

LORD, WE GIVE THANKS TO THEE   (1971)
    Chorus (SATB) unaccompanied.   Biblical text.   2 min. 55 sec.
    Warner Brothers, 1973.   Recorded by the Virginia State College
    Choir, Carl Harris, conductor (Richsound 4112N10:   The Undine
    Smith Moore Song Book); by the Virginia Union University Choir,
    Odell Hobbs, conductor (Eastern ERS-549:   Lord, We Give
    Thanks to Thee); by the Massanetta Chorus, John Motley, con-
    ductor (Mark MC-8568C: Festival of Music--Virginia Music
    Camp 1975); and by the Fisk Jubilee Singers, Matthew Kennedy,
    conductor (Fisk University: The Eye of the Storm).   Commis-
    sioned by Fisk University for the 100th anniversary of the Fisk
    Jubilee Singers.   First performance (1971) at Fisk University
    by the Fisk Jubilee Singers, Matthew Kennedy, conductor.

LOVE, LET THE WIND CRY HOW I ADORE THEE   (1961)
    Soprano and piano or organ.   Text from Sappho rendered by
    Bliss Carman after the prose of T. W. Wharton.   App. 3 min.
    Written for and first performed at the wedding of Leon and
    Jewel Taylor Thompson (June 10, 1961).

LYRIC FOR TRUE LOVE   (1975)
    Soprano and piano.   Text by Florence Hynes Willett. $2\frac{1}{2}$ min.
    First performance (1976) at Virginia State College (Petersburg,

Va.).   Carolyn Kizzie, soprano; Carl Harris, piano.   This work
and I AM IN DOUBT were written as companion pieces, but may
be used separately.

MAMA, IS MASSA GOIN' TO SELL US TOMORROW?   (1973)
See WATCH AND PRAY.

MOTHER TO SON   (1955)
Chorus (SSAATTBB) unaccompanied.   Text by Langston Hughes.
App. 2½ min.   M. Witmark, 1955.   Recorded by the Virginia
Union University Choir, Odell Hobbs, conductor (Eastern ERS-
549: Lord, We Give Thanks To Thee).   First performance
(1955) by the Virginia State College Choir, Mozart Tevis Fraser,
conductor.

NO CONDEMNATION   (1935)
Chorus (TTBB) unaccompanied.   Arrangement of spiritual.   2
min.

O HOLY LORD   (1974)
See CHORAL PRAYERS IN FOLK STYLE.

O MARY, WHAT YOU GOING TO NAME THAT PRETTY LITTLE
BABY?   (1970)
See A CHRISTMAS ALLELUIA.

O SPIRIT WHO DOST PREFER BEFORE ALL TEMPLES   (1966)
Chorus (unison) and piano or organ.   Text by John Milton.   2
min. 50 sec.   First performance at the Gillfield Baptist Church
(Petersburg, Va.).   Undine Smith Moore, conductor.

O THAT BLEEDING LAMB   (1974)
See CHORAL PRAYERS IN FOLK STYLE.

ORGAN VARIATIONS ON "NETTLETON"   (1976)
3 min.   Commissioned by and first performed (1976) by Mayme
Maye at Christ and Grace Episcopal Churches (Petersburg, Va.).

REFLECTIONS FOR PIANO AND ORGAN   (1952)
3 min.   First performance (1952) at a faculty concert, Virginia
State College (Petersburg, Va.).   David Carroll, organ; Undine
Smith Moore, piano.

RISE UP SHEPHERD AND FOLLOW   (1970)
Chorus (TTBB) unaccompanied.   Arrangement of spiritual.
App. 4½ min.   Commissioned by the male chorus of the First
Baptist Church (Petersburg, Va.).   First performance (1970)
at the First Baptist Church (Petersburg, Va.).   Buckner Gam-
by, conductor.

ROMANCE FOR TWO PIANOS   (1952)
5 min.   First performance (1952) at a faculty concert, Virginia
State College (Petersburg, Va.).   Undine Smith Moore and Garland Butts, pianists.

ROMANTIC YOUNG CLOWN (1952)
Piano. App. 3 min. First performance (1952) at a faculty concert, Virginia State College (Petersburg, Va.). Undine Smith Moore, piano.

SCENES FROM THE LIFE OF A MARTYR (in progress)
For Dr. Moore's description of this work, see her response to II-7.

SCENES FROM THE LIFE OF A MARTYR (Excerpts)
The Voice of My Beloved (soprano); Arise, My Love, My Fair One (tenor); Set Me as a Seal on Thy Heart (soprano and tenor). Biblical texts. App. 5 min. These three pieces are a single unit from the larger work and were written in November 1975.

SCHERZO FOR PIANO (1930)
1 min. First performance (1930) at Columbia University. Undine Smith Moore, piano.

SET DOWN! (1951)
Soprano and piano. Arrangement of spiritual. 2 min.

SET ME AS A SEAL ON THY HEART (1975)
See SCENES FROM THE LIFE OF A MARTYR (Excerpts).

SINNER, YOU CAN'T WALK MY PATH (1958)
Chorus (SATB) unaccompanied. Arrangement of spiritual. App. 1 min. 40 sec. M. Witmark, 1958. Recorded by the Virginia State College Choir, Carl Harris, conductor (Richsound 4112N10: The Undine Smith Moore Song Book). First performance (1958) by the Virginia State College Choir, Aldrich Adkins, conductor.

SIR OLAF AND THE ERL KING'S DAUGHTER (1925)
Cantata for chorus (SSA) and piano. Text from a Scandinavian folk poem. App. 25 min. First performance (1925) at Fisk University by the Fisk University Girls' Glee Club, Mary E. Hellman, conductor. Undine Smith Moore, piano.

STRIVING AFTER GOD (1958)
Chorus (SATB) unaccompanied. Text by Michelangelo. App. 3 min. M. Witmark, 1958. Recorded by the Virginia State College Choir, Carl Harris, conductor (Richsound 4112N10: The Undine Smith Moore Song Book) and by the Virginia District Five All-Regional Chorus, John Motley, conductor (Mark MC-8458: The Virginia District Five All-Regional Chorus). First performance (1958) by the Virginia State College Choir, Aldrich Adkins, conductor.

TAKE ME TO THE WATER (1973)
See TO BE BAPTIZED.

TAMBOURINES TO GLORY (1973)
Chorus (SATB) unaccompanied. Text by Langston Hughes.

App. 1 min. Warner Brothers, 1973. First performance (1974) at the Mosque Auditorium (Richmond, Va.) by the Virginia Union University Choir, Odell Hobbs, conductor.

TEACH ME TO HEAR MERMAIDS SINGING (1953)
3-part canon for treble voices. Text by John Donne. 30 sec.

THOU HAST MADE US FOR THYSELF (1952)
Chorus (SATB) unaccompanied. Choral fugue. Text by St. Augustine. 5 min. First performance (1952) by the Virginia State College Choir, Undine Smith Moore, conductor.

THREE PIECES FOR FLUTE AND PIANO (1958)
Three movements. 6 min. This work and INTRODUCTION, MARCH, AND ALLEGRO are identical with the exception of medium. First performance (1973) at the Town Hall Gala Concert given in honor of Undine Smith Moore. Frank Wess, flute; Garland Butts, piano.

A TIME FOR REMEMBERING (1976)
Chorus (SATB) and piano. Text by Undine Smith Moore. 3 min. Commissioned by Dr. Keager of the Virginia State Board of Education, Music Department, in memory of the late Dr. C. J. Heoch, Supervisor of Music for the State of Virginia. First performance (1976) at the Loyola University Bicentennial Choral Festival by the Southern University Choir, Aldrich Adkins, conductor.

TO BE BAPTIZED (1973)
Soprano and piano. Arrangement of a combination of two spirituals: "Here Comes Another One To Be Baptized" and "Take Me To The Water." App. 2 min. 40 sec. Dedicated to and first performed (1973) by Camilla Williams at the Town Hall Gala Concert given in honor of Undine Smith Moore. This work and WATCH AND PRAY were written as companion pieces, but may be used separately.

UPHILL (1926)
Soprano and piano. Text by Dante Gabriel Rosetti. App. 2 min. First performance (1926) by Anna Lois Goodwin, soprano, and Undine Smith Moore, piano.

VALSE CAPRICE (1930)
Piano. 2 min. First performance (1930) at Columbia University. Undine Smith Moore, piano.

THE VOICE OF MY BELOVED (1975)
See SCENES FROM THE LIFE OF A MARTYR (Excerpts).

WALK THRO' THE STREETS OF THE CITY (1966)
Chorus (SATB) unaccompanied. Arrangement of spiritual. 3 min.

WATCH AND PRAY (1973)
    Soprano and piano. Arrangement of spiritual (Mama, Is Massa
Goin' to Sell Us Tomorrow?). App. 4 min. Dedicated to and
first performed (1973) by Camilla Williams at the Town Hall
Gala Concert given in honor of Undine Smith Moore. This work
and TO BE BAPTIZED were written as companion pieces, but
may be used separately.

WE SHALL WALK THROUGH THE VALLEY IN PEACE (1974)
    See CHORAL PRAYERS IN FOLK STYLE.

WEDDING SONG (1961)
    See LOVE, LET THE WIND CRY HOW I ADORE THEE.

WHEN SUSANNAH JONES WEARS RED (circa 1958)
    Chorus (SATB) unaccompanied. Text by Langston Hughes.
App. 1 min. 10 sec. Warner Brothers, 1975.

WHO SHALL SEPARATE US FROM THE LOVE OF CHRIST? (1953)
    Chorus (SATB) and piano or organ. Biblical text. 3 min.
First performance (1953) at the Gillfield Baptist Church (Peters-
burg, Va.) by the Gillfield Baptist Church choir, Undine Smith
Moore, conductor.

BIBLIOGRAPHY

Part I: Works about the composer

Beckner, Steve. "Composer and Teacher--Mrs. Undine Smith
    Moore." The Progress-Index (Petersburg, Va.), 5 January
    1975.

De Lerma, Dominique-René, ed. Reflections on Afro-American
    Music. Kent, Ohio: Kent State University Press, 1973.

Harris, Carl G. "A Study of Characteristic Stylistic Trends Found
    in the Choral Works of a Selected Group of Afro-American Com-
    posers and Arrangers." D.M.A. dissertation, University of
    Missouri-Kansas City, 1972.

_____. "Three Schools of Black Choral Composers and Arrang-
    ers 1900-1970." The Choral Journal 14 (April 1974): 11-18.

_____. "The Unique World of Undine Smith Moore." The Choral
    Journal 16 (January 1976): 6-7.

Herrema, Robert D. "Choral Music By Black Composers." The
    Choral Journal 10 (January 1970): 15-17.

Moore, James Edward. "Aspects of the Evolution of Music of the

Black Church as Shown Through Selected Works of Mrs. Undine
S. Moore." Master's thesis, Virginia Commonwealth University,
1975.

"Rare Treat for Retiree: Adieu by Concert." Clavier 11 (November 1972): 43.

Roach, Hildred. Black American Music: Past and Present. Boston: Crescendo Publishing Company, 1973.

Ryder, William Henderson. "Music at Virginia State College, 1883-
1966." Ph.D. dissertation, University of Michigan, 1970.

Thompson, Jewel Taylor. "Technical Practices of Negro Composers
in Choral Works for A Cappella Choir." Master's thesis, Eastman School of Music, 1960.

White, Evelyn, comp. Selected Bibliography of Published Choral
Music by Black Composers. Washington, D.C.: Evelyn White,
1975. Available from the Howard University bookstore.

Part II: Works by the composer

Moore, Undine Smith. Audiotapes, Videotapes, and Films Prepared
by Undine Smith Moore and Altona T. Johns for the Black
Music Center at Virginia State College. These materials are
available through Interlibrary Loan.

_____. A Recorded Supplement to Studies in Traditional Har-
mony. 1957. Unpublished.

CHAPTER VIII

OLIVER EDWARD NELSON

Oliver Edward Nelson was born June 4, 1932 in St. Louis,
Missouri. His educational background includes studies in theory
and composition at Washington University (St. Louis) and Lincoln
University (Mo.). Robert Wykes and George Trembly were among
those with whom Mr. Nelson studied composition. While involved
in an active performing career which included stints in the bands
of Erskine Hawkins, Count Basie, Quincy Jones, and others, he
achieved his first major success as a leader and composer with the
release of his album Blues and the Abstract Truth. This led to
considerable composing and arranging activities for the albums of
numerous artists in addition to those he did with his own groups.
He subsequently moved to Los Angeles, where his activities in television and film scoring brought him still wider recognition and ac-
claim. Mr. Nelson was also very active as a teacher, lecturer,
and clinician, and conducted classes in television and film scoring,
studio orchestra performance, arranging, and improvisation at a
number of universities. His improvisation book, Patterns for Jazz,
is widely used by both professionals and students.

Mr. Nelson was the recipient of numerous honors and awards,
both as a composer-arranger and as a performer. These include
the best instrumental performance award from the National Academy
of Recording Arts and Sciences for Full Nelson (1963), the Edison
Award for Blues and the Abstract Truth (1965), down beat's Jazz
Critics Poll award as New Star: Arranger (1962) and Readers Poll
awards in 1967 and 1968 as Best Arranger, Jazz & Pop's Best
Arranger award in both 1968 and 1969, a Pulitzer Prize nomination
for Concerto for Xylophone, Marimba, and Vibraphone in 1967, the
Jazz Cultural Award from Record World magazine for The Kennedy
Dream Suite, and an alumni citation from Washington University in
1971.

Oliver Nelson's considerable compositional output includes
works in the areas of concert music and jazz in addition to his
scores for television and film productions. Among his best-known
compositions are extended works such as Jazzhattan Suite, The
Kennedy Dream Suite, Berlin Dialogue for Orchestra, and Afro-
American Sketches as well as tunes like Stolen Moments, Hoe Down,
Dumpy Mama, Miss Fine, and Emancipation Blues. His television

Oliver E. Nelson (courtesy of the composer)

credits include Ironside, It Takes a Thief, The Name of the Game, Matt Lincoln, Longstreet, Chase, and Six Million Dollar Man; he also scored such feature films as Death of a Gunfighter, Skullduggery, and Zig Zag. In addition Mr. Nelson was very active as a composer-arranger-conductor for many recording artists, including Jimmy Smith, Johnny Hodges, Lena Horne, Count Basie, Cannonball Adderley, Nancy Wilson, and Richard "Groove" Holmes.

Oliver Edward Nelson died October 27, 1975, in Los Angeles, California. The interview which follows represents, to the best of our knowledge, the last extended discussion for publication in which Mr. Nelson participated.

Part I: General Questions

1. Q: What persons, events, and works (of art, literature, etc.) have influenced you in general as well as in terms of your musical activities?
   A: The biggest influence was that of my sister, Lucille Nelson. She was instrumental in introducing me to classical music-- the Nutcracker Suite, Beethoven, and other things--and she also introduced me to the music of Duke Ellington. I started taking piano lessons when I was six or seven years old, and later I started to play the saxophone. I was in Japan with the Marine Corps in 1952 and the records I found in the camp library, like the Mother Goose Suite by Ravel and Hindemith's Symphony in E Flat, opened my head up to a whole lot of things. After I got out of the Marine Corps, I went to college and studied as hard as I could. That was it. That's why I'm in music today (but I would have been in music somehow, no matter what). It was Ravel and Hindemith at first; then came Stravinsky and the rest. But it all started with Duke Ellington, really.
   Bartok was an influence later on. We had to analyze his six string quartets in college. Bartok and Stravinsky determined my total outlook on music because of what they managed to do in just one lifetime. There are so many composers that you'd like to know about, but there just isn't time for that. You have to settle on the composers you feel are really important to you and try to find a way to emulate them without imitating them. That's very difficult to do.

2. Q: How would you define black music?
   A: That is a very, very good question because I have been to Africa and I have heard the music. It's great when you listen to it and think about all the things that happen with African music because of the fact that it's usually music for an occasion--someone is born, someone dies, someone becomes old enough to be a man or a woman, and the rest of it. Most of the tribes are united in that one thing, that is, music accompanies practically everything.

My feeling about what black music is does not mean
what's happening in this country at all. If we want to define black music in this country, we say Motown, and we
say whatever it is is totally insignificant. The only black
music I know is the music that I heard in Africa. What we
have in this country is either Motown and the rest of that,
or what has been derived from the European sources, with
everybody wanting to write a symphony or a sonata or whatever. There are only a few black composers in this country. Hale Smith is a good friend of mine. Then there is
a pianist who is also quite a good composer, named George
Walker; he writes very well, very cleanly, utilizes his
roots, and gets a part of Europe, too. He is very significant. Another is Olly Wilson. We were in college together
and he's up at Berkeley now. His involvement is with electronic music and tapes and things. What makes me mad
about so many of the other people I've heard is that they
are so black!! They have the hair and the beads and all
these artifacts hanging around their necks and the rest of
that. And their music is usually mostly screaming about
down with whatever it is and up with blackism. I get sick
of it. If you're going to write music, then just write the
music. I finally found out that the only way I can function
is to function aside and apart from blackism. If I'm going
to write some music, then I'm going to write some music.
But please don't expect it to be black. It will be whatever
I want it to be. The only real black music is in Africa.
Everything else that happens in this country is either an
extension of Europe or Motown.

3. Q: What features of your own music do you see as uniquely
black (in terms of both musical and philosophical considerations)?

A: I would say that I have actually three kinds of music. First,
there is the music that I do for television. This year it's
The Six Million Dollar Man; last year it was Night Gallery,
Chase, Ironside, and I don't know how many others. That
music performs a certain function and is not black or white
or anything except what the film demands. You write music
to accompany a scene. It's not neutral music; it's just
music. Then there is the music that I write on commission.
These pieces can usually be whatever I want them to be.
Last, there is the semi-commercial music that I do as an
artist under contract to RCA. They want to sell records,
so that has to be music which will make people pat their
feet. What is uniquely black would probably be considered
that, I guess, because to make people pat their feet, there
has to be a great deal of emphasis on the rhythmic thing
and on the bass and the drums. So actually, in terms of
being black, I would say that only my commercial music
tries to reach that part of the audience. But I don't try to
contrive anything that will say, "Here! This is black, so
listen to it!" The only thing I do from time to time is try

to remind people of Duke Ellington because I use some of
his voicings in my commercial work, just so people will
say, "That's Oliver Nelson trying to look like Duke Ellington." I want to keep that alive.

4. Q: In what ways is your music a reflection of your personal
       philosophy (social, political, etc.)?
    A: I stay out of the philosophy part of it. If I get involved in
       all the social and political stuff, I can't write any music.
       I have to stay out of it. Otherwise, I can't get my own
       work done because it drains me too much.

5. Q: What do you see as the position or role of the black artist
       in contemporary society?
    A: It seems that there is no real role yet. Everything that is
       going on in the colleges and universities usually ends up as
       part of Black Studies programs. There's nothing wrong
       with that except that they are often so black that nobody can
       learn anything because they're so involved with the clothes
       and the hair and the rest of it.
          Now back to the role of the black artist. What black
       composer has his music performed on a regular basis by
       a major symphony orchestra? Usually Black History Week
       is the only time I get performed. The Los Angeles Phil-
       harmonic has done several things of mine, but it's usually
       connected with Black History Week or black this or black
       that. Black music is not really in the mainstream of any-
       thing. It just exists. There is a group in Minneapolis
       called AAMOA which is directed toward blackness and the
       rest of that, but for me that seems like a waste of time.
       If a composer is going to be a composer, let him compose.
       If a singer is going to be a singer, let he, she, or it sing.
       This is question five, but it all gets back to question two,
       which is blackness and nationalism. Every time it comes
       up, I will tell you that I prefer to be a living, working com-
       poser who does what he does for no other reason but out of
       a need to write music. None of it is part of a political
       or social thing.

6. Q: Please discuss any problems you may have encountered in
       getting your works performed, published, and recorded.
    A: A lot of my music is published, a lot of it is recorded,
       and a lot of it gets performed. The commissioned pieces
       are performed quite frequently, but it's still like Negro
       History Week. It's always that. Any time I get performed
       by the Los Angeles Philharmonic, what happens is that
       Zubin Mehta will call and say that he wants to do my piece
       and that it's going to be a tribute to the black community;
       then I have to go down there and pass out parts and all that
       stuff. But it never happens during the regular year.
          The music that is published is published by E. B.
       Marks, which is a very good firm. They are trying to
       reach kids in high school and college by publishing what I

guess you would call my commercial stuff, the stuff that is
recorded on my albums. Every time I go to a festival or
something, I hear my music. Of course, I say that I can't
be a judge so far as my music is concerned because I can't
judge it that way. If it's good, it's good, but let somebody
else do it. They should never do that to me. When I go
to a festival and hear all my music, what am I supposed to
do? Give them an A? Well, I just stay out of it. Anyway, I have no problems being published, performed, or
recorded.

Q: You have your own publishing company, too, right?
A: Yes. We publish a book that does quite well.[1] Actually,
we do very, very well in all of our endeavors. It's not
like the early music of Duke Ellington, which he gave to
Mills Publishing. They made a fortune off of it and Duke
never made anything. But that was typical of what happened
to the black artist coming up in the early years of this century. Scott Joplin was another composer who was never
really compensated for his music. But it's different now.
I have my own publishing company and I have my own production company. If I wanted to write a series of string
quartets, I could go into a studio with a string quartet and
record my own music if for no other reason than to beat
the government at tax time. (I got completely wiped out
last year!) Before I would give it to them, I would give it
to the symphony orchestra and the music center downtown.

6A. Q: How much of your actual output has ever been performed?
Published? Recorded?
A: Ninety per cent of everything I do is published. Almost
100% of it has been recorded. I have maybe four pieces--
commissioned pieces--that have not been recorded, but that
have been published. I don't have problems with performances, unlike a lot of guys who have to go around with their
scores under their arm and ask to have things performed.

6B. Q: Have you encountered difficulty in getting your works programmed?
A: No difficulty at all in getting anything programmed. I can
call Bob Boudreau from the American Wind Symphony or
Zubin Mehta or other people across the country and say
that I've written a new piece for symphony orchestra (or
whatever), that I'll send a score, and that I'd like to have
it performed. It would be easy.

6C. Q: Are there specific problems in getting a satisfactory performance? Exemplify and discuss.
A: The only problem is that symphony orchestras really don't
know what you have in mind a lot of the time. Often you
send a score and the parts, and when you hear a rehearsal
or the performance, you say, "No, that's not right." You
have to realize that conductors always view your music as

they see it. If you say that a quarter note equals 126, and you go there and find that they are playing it at 90, and you ask the conductor why he is doing the thing so slowly, he will probably say that he feels that it feels better there. You can say that it's not right and that the quarter note should be 126 as specified, but that's not always what you'll get.

Notation is a problem, too, because I am starting to use a new notation that I have developed for myself. It indicates how something should be played, and usually an explanation is necessary. Some things I don't even write any more, like col legno, which means that the string players use the wood of the bow on the strings. They don't want to do that because their bows usually cost over $1000. Why should they take a $1000 bow and beat it on a $12,000 violin? That's like driving your brand new Cadillac into a tree! That's how they feel about it. So when you say to play col legno, they say that they will play it hard arco style, but that's not the same sound. I know what I want, but I know that I have to make compromises because I understand about expensive instruments and all of that, so I don't write that any more.

There are really no problems in performance. It's just that you have to remember that string players can be very, very difficult, and when you want something a particular way, you have to explain it to them. That takes time (which I don't usually have), so I don't write it.

7. Q: What do you consider, at this point in your life, to be your most significant achievement(s) aside from your compositions?

 A: The only significant thing I've done is to father two boys. I am also kind of proud of my saxophone book, Patterns for Jazz, which was a book I wrote mainly for my own use. I got sick of all the books by French authors that were usually just

and all that, so I wrote my own. Now everybody's using it and it's in its third printing. They're asking me for Patterns for Jazz: Book 2, which I can't get to because of my work load. I want to do that plus an arranging book, which is also something that a lot of people have been asking me for. But the main thing for me with Patterns for Jazz is that it is very useful. Every time I get ready to go into the studio to record and I have to practice, I practice out of my own book. Just a couple of hours will be enough to get my fingers in shape so that I can go in and play like I've been playing all the time. I think that, outside of my compositions, Patterns for Jazz would probably be the most significant thing because everybody does not like my music. They say I'm too white, which is

weird, but that's what they say. The book has made it
over color lines. We have publishers in Germany, Bavaria,
and Austria. Every year we get orders for 200 or so copies
from Australia, so it's being used. It's being used because it's a good book.

8. Q: What do you see as the responsibilities and obligations of
the educational system (at all levels) to the study of black
music?

A: That is a loaded question because I think of the traditional
liberal arts college like the one I attended in St. Louis,
and the fact that the only music we got was Bach, Beethov-
en, and whatever. It was a good education because it prepared me for all the things I have to do now--write for
television, do pieces on commission from symphony orchestras, and all of that. But now the obligations of the educational system need to be dealt with. Take California,
for example. The question talks of obligations to black
music, but here we should probably include Mexican music
and all other music for that matter. Part of the problem
is that music is the last thing thought about. It comes
after the football team and the basketball team and all the
others. Right now they are trying to cut money from the
school budget, and the first things they are going to trim
will be music, drama, and art. Music should be a part
of the overall curriculum proper, because life would really
be dull if we didn't have organized sound. It should be a
part of everything, and for black people, it should cover
the whole gamut--history, performance, everything.
    When I was in school, they would mention Duke Elling-
ton's name, but then they would say that Stan Kenton was
greater. If somebody mentioned Charlie Parker, they
would say that Paul Desmond was greater. John Coltrane
has obviously got to be one of the greatest saxophone players who ever lived, but all you had to do was say that for
them to tell you about Stan Getz. And again we have a kind
of racial overtone. When black history is taught, it's usually taught by people who shouldn't be teaching it. That's
really unfortunate, but one day that will all change. The
only way it can happen is when black history is taught as
part of history as a whole.

9. Q: Do you feel that the people who write about your music
(critics in particular) understand what you are doing? Exemplify and discuss.

A: I have little or no feeling about what critics say about my
music because I really don't care. When you look into the
lives of these people, you find that most of them were
striving at one time to be something else. They didn't
have it, or couldn't make it, so they became critics. That's
what critics are--usually misfits. It isn't a question of what
they say about what you do; it's the fact that most critics
are people who never made it in their chosen field, and

ended up being critics because it was necessary for them to make a living.

10. Q: What advice would you give to the aspiring young black composer?

A: First, he should get a good liberal arts education. It is very important for him to be able to speak (that means English courses) and write down his thoughts (that means English composition courses). He should have contact with more than one foreign language. I would suggest German and Italian. Just about every mark in his field will be in Italian; there is a whole list of expressive terms to tell the performer how the music is to be played. And if you want to know history, you start with Bach. All of that stuff is in German. Italian and German would be the two primary languages to study. He should also learn others if possible.

He should take the theory courses and the composition courses and learn all the rules. I learned what they had to teach and that's why I'm on the top of the heap out here. I may have some talent, but I also know what I am doing. If they want a Baroque fugue or a Mozart symphony for a period piece, I can write all that stuff. I got it when I was a student at a university where I couldn't even use the cafeteria. I had to take a brown bag lunch, but I got the courses I needed.

Okay. We're talking about foreign languages, we're talking about theory and composition courses, and now we start on the music. He should write for whatever the school has. If he writes a piece for fifty-five bongo drums and conga drums and they don't have that, he'll never hear his pieces while he is a student. Most of my student pieces still hold up today because I heard them. In 1957 I wrote a saxophone sonata, in 1960 I did a piece for orchestra, and so forth. I haven't thrown them out because they're good music.

Mainly I would say to a young black composer, "If you can ever get away from trying to be black--down with white people and all that stuff--maybe you will become a good composer. You're wasting your time and energy trying to be black." And that's the way I feel. It robs me of the creative effort that I need to get things done. It soaks up the creative processes whether you realize it or not.

Part II: Music Questions

1. Q: When you sit down to begin a new composition on your own initiative or inspiration (as opposed to a commissioned work), what procedure or approach do you follow?

A: The only time I sit down and write music is when I have a deadline. Normally I'm pushed into that situation; the conductor will call me and say, "Where's the new piece?"

and I won't have started it yet. As far as procedure goes, the only thing I do is look in my book of themes and ideas, live with that material, and then sit down and do it. It's not like I go outside and an apple falls out of a tree and I say, "Eureka! I've got it!!" Writing music is work. Composition is work. There is no talk of inspiration. Once I get started, though, things happen.

2. Q: When composing a commissioned work or a work written for a specific occasion or person, does your procedure or approach differ from the one you described in question one? If so, in what way?

   A: I write for the American Wind Symphony almost every year. I must have written six or seven pieces for them, and these pieces are performed all the time. Now, this group is a wind orchestra; all it lacks is strings. It is also a group which performs outdoors, which means that you have to write for them in a particular way. If you have four flutes, you wouldn't dare give each of them a note in a four-voice chord because it won't work outside. You won't hear it; the wind will just blow the sound away. What I usually do is write two on a part. That's the only way it can be heard outside, even with the microphones and all that.

   Bob Boudreau is the conductor of this orchestra, and every time he commissions me to write a piece, he says something like this: "Oliver, I want you to do a piece for the orchestra, and I want it to start like this and I want it to end like that." Now why commission me at all if he's going to tell me how to write it? Then he says, "I want a piece that's going to arouse the audience, and I want them to jump up and down, and I want it to be jazz." That's the crusher!! And I say, "Why can't I just write a piece for your orchestra without making everybody happy?" But, for me, that's what he does.

   Sometimes I will be asked to write pieces that feature me with the orchestra, and I say, "Why should I have to play at all? If I'm going to do the piece, why can't I sit out in the audience and listen to it?" Well, that's my problem, and I guess maybe it's sort of a compliment to my ability to be involved as a participant.

   These pieces that I do for the American Wind Symphony are usually the last piece on the program. They will do a bunch of other pieces like the Stravinsky, and the last piece will be with me and my saxophone and the orchestra (and the people will jump up and down and that's what he wants, so it's not too bad).

3. Q: In general, with regard to your writing, what genre(s) do you prefer?

   A: I have no real preferences in terms of whatever it is that I like. I do occasionally like certain kinds of orchestral sounds, but there aren't very many orchestras around to write for.

Q: I was really curious about what your response would be to this question because you are one of the few people I know who is active in almost every conceivable genre.

A: That's why I should probably limit my activities to maybe one or two things.

Q: But would you want to restrict yourself like that?

A: No, not really. It's just that I made a lot of money last year and ended up paying a lot of it to the government. I've just about decided that maybe I don't need to make a lot of money because it doesn't make any sense. I'm just working for the government. Maybe before long--and I mean before two or three years--I will make some decisions which will allow me to do some of the things that I want to do. Right now I can't get to anything but my work.

Q: What would you like to do if you had the time?

A: You know, I just wonder because, when I do have the time, I don't do anything! Does that give you a clue? (laughter). Now, I'm sitting here in my studio and I'm looking around me. I have two huge five-foot 250-pound speakers, a Yamaha organ, two pianos (a grand and an upright), three synthesizers (a big Moog, an ARP, and a Japanese synthesizer), two sixteen-track mixers, one two-track Ampex with a reproducer on it, one Ampex reproducer and recorder, one eight-track Ampex, one four-track Sony, two two-track Teacs, four amplifiers, a total of eight speakers (six are JBL), a digital computer, tuners, reverb units, equalizers, echoplexes, all kinds of test devices to monitor sound, books, records, and all of this stuff, and I can't get to it! I can't get to anything because I'm too busy trying to make a living. Every time I come up here, the room demands that I do something with it and I can't because I'm too busy making money to pay the government. I'm not living, I'm existing. I'm existing in the kind of society that burns people like me but not Howard Hughes. I don't know how Howard does it, but there must be some other way!

4. Q: What do you consider your most significant composition? Please discuss.

A: I don't have a "most significant composition" because I haven't written anything that's any good yet. [2]

5. Q: Please comment on your treatment of the following musical elements and give examples from your compositions that illustrate the techniques you describe.

A. Melody

ON: For me, melody is very, very important because I use melody a lot. Maybe that's one of the things that makes my music playable. Often the conductor is humming the melody while he's conducting, and that's a good sign. Melody is important, and I don't feel that it should be a series of notes that runs from one to twelve and then every transposition of that twelve-note sequence turned upside down and the rest of it. That has no real meaning.

One of the things I really feel strongly about is electronic music. This does <u>not</u> mean the beeps and blops, or performing Bach, or "The Snow Is Dancing" from Debussy's <u>Children's Corner</u>, or <u>Pictures at an Exhibition</u>. I don't feel that that is what the synthesizer was invented for; its creation was for liberation from the keyboard and liberation from tonality. I've had people come here and I'll play an A natural on my synthesizer and they'll say that it's not an A. Well, A is relative; A is wherever I want to tune the thing. A can be anything. A is simply a place and you can tune the oscillator to do anything you want. I eventually intend to find the time to get involved with my three synthesizers, but not to do the music of Brahms because that, to me, is a waste. Brahms needs oboes and English horns, so what's the point of creating it on a synthesizer? Synthesizers should be free to do whatever they want. Synthesizer melodies can be whatever you want to make them, and you can make them sound like anything--English horns, oboes, trumpets, or whatever you want. I myself would prefer to spend more time trying to find something that I can't imitate. I want to hear something else. [3]

B. Harmony
ON: Harmony, of course, gets involved with the fact that you have twelve notes that you can deal with. Sometimes all you need is four notes. The last pieces that Stravinsky did for orchestra were written in a serial-like technique, but he didn't use all twelve tones; he'd use five, or sometimes seven. It's not necessary to arm yourself with a mortar or a magnum to take care of a mouse sitting on an apple; then you can't find the mouse or the apple ! You don't need that kind of power. I'm trying to be a little bit discriminating about what I will use. You can have an orchestra of eighty people, but maybe you don't need more than eight because you can hear more transparently.

C. Rhythm
ON: Rhythm is important. Rhythm should sometimes be free, but every performance should be almost the same; you should be able to guarantee an audience that every time you do a specific piece, it will sound pretty much the same. Some freedom will be necessary for a rhythm player, a

percussion player. There should be a section
where he can stretch out. He can be given notes
that can be played in any rhythm or in any kind of
format, but control will have to be exercised. So
I would say freedom of expression covering the
first three: melody, harmony, and rhythm. You
don't have to be tied down to tempered scales
with the synthesizer because it can be anything.
And harmony can be whatever the piece is all
about, not derived from twelve tones or sixteen
tones; on the synthesizer you can get much more
than that. And the rhythm should be free enough
to allow expression, but still maintain control.

D. Form
ON: It should have a beginning, a development section,
and an ending. That's very important.

E. Improvisation
ON: That should be a part of the whole thing. It
should be allowed, but controlled with certain
notes and certain rhythms depending on the player's talent. Every player does not have the same
talent. Some people have to have guidelines or
else they can't perform. So improvisation has to
be free, but depending on the player, the conductor should have the last word. Play, but be dis-
creet. The conductor should really be the judge.

F. Text
ON: It's a funny thing about that. When I was in college, you were expected to read James Joyce,
Poe, Emerson, Thoreau, and all those people.
Now that I think about it, I wasn't really that
interested in those poems. I wasn't interested in
reading. The only reading that I really do is
reading of a technical nature. I'm always reading
books about microphones, impediences between
microphones and tape recorders, and the rest of
that. The books are usually schematic diagrams
or electronic diagrams. I read for information;
I don't read for enjoyment. As a result, almost
all the books I have in my house are technical.
So now I wonder why I read those things in college and said to myself, "Hey, poems. I'll set
you to music," because it was really a bore.
Now Hale Smith likes to set things to music. But
I don't like singers, so I don't bother with them.
And I don't like reading poems; they bore me to
death. But a technical book will keep my interest
forever. If I were to set something, I would
probably set a schematic diagram for a tape recorder or something; that would be very interesting!

G. Instrumentation (both in terms of choice of particular combinations as well as how you treat them compositionally)

ON: I feel that I am actually an instrumental composer, and the reason for that is that I hate singers. I'm being truthful, all right? The reason I can't stand singers is because of the ego thing. There's one woman I can't stand to work with because she's had two piano lessons in her whole life, and she insists on sitting down at the piano and telling me what to do! She plays very badly, and I have to listen to that and put it down on paper. They are all a pain in the ass. I don't work for any of them any more. I don't know what that ego thing does for people, but obviously it's necessary for a singer to have it. The only singer I have ever worked for that I really liked was Lena Horne. She is a fantastic artist--no problems! But singers as a rule are off limits to me and they know it, so they never bother me. Anyhow, I would say that I'm mainly involved with instrumental music.

Q: You mentioned earlier something about consciously trying to remind people of Duke Ellington in your writing. Does that extend beyond voicings to include instrumental combinations as well?

ON: Yes. Combinations and those strange kinds of chords with the funny notes that remind people of Duke. But I don't do it all the time. I just don't want Duke's name to ever be forgotten. People have said that I have a tendency to remind them of Duke--not to imitate, only to remind. They'll say, "Hey. That voicing sounds a little like Duke." And to me, that is really a compliment.

Now, let's discuss combinations of instruments. I'll tell you what dictates that. The budget dictates that. It tells you what you can and can't have. There was a big writer's strike out here, and then there was a composer's strike. And when the musicians had a strike last year, they demanded this and that and they got it. Universal ended up having to pay all sorts of benefits to all these people, and as a result, they had to cut back on the size of the orchestra. That means I'm down to four woodwinds (which means a combination of English horns, flutes, and bass clarinets), four trumpets, four French horns, eight violins, four violas, four celli, two double basses, and four percussion. The price of every new agreement gets passed on to somebody else, and the composers end up being affected because you cannot make a lot of noise with eight violins.

No matter how much they raise the levels, eight
violins can't do what ten or twelve can do.
What really affects everything in my kind of
work is budgets. That's usually fixed with a
symphony orchestra or groups like the American
Wind Symphony, and I know what I have to work
for. But most of the time I work for smaller
groups. Say, for example, I am offered a commission to do a film for Tuskegee Institute, and
they only have a budget for three musicians.
What can I do? I write for flute doubling alto
flute, maybe for oboe doubling English horn, and
for a couple of keyboard instruments like piano
and electric harpsichord. But in the matter of the
three people, I am told what they can afford.
Then I have to write a sixty-minute score for a
motion picture using only three people, which
means I really have to make the sounds right;
otherwise, it will sound like a bore for an hour!
For me, instrumentation is usually dependent on
what people can afford to pay for, and that's very,
very awkward because, when you work for smaller
groups, they say, "This is what we have to pay
for the commission and this is the size of the
orchestra. That's it. Take it or leave it."

6. Q: Have difficulties with performance practice (inflection,
   phrasing, etc.) been a significant problem in having your
   works performed to your own satisfaction?
   A: If you're writing for symphony orchestra and you write four
   eighth notes and tie the last eighth to a half note--

   [musical notation: four eighth notes tied to a half note]

   --they will play it straight with no nothing. If you give
   that same thing to jazz players, they will play it like it's
   almost in a 12/8 kind of feel--

   [musical notation in 12/8]

   If I write that figure for symphony orchestra and I want it
   played with that 12/8 feel, I have to write it in 12/8.
   When you write for symphony orchestra, the notation has
   to be exact and it has to be clear. You can't just say
   "swing" or "get loose" to a symphony orchestra. Jazz
   players understand; that's no problem. But when you write
   things for symphony players, you have to write them out
   exactly like you want them to sound. "Get loose," "swing,"
   "lay it on," "you got it"--none of that is going to work.
   The notation has to be exact.

7. Q: What major works are currently in progress? Please de-
   scribe and discuss.
   A: Well, I'm supposed to be working on that saxophone book.
   I have had to turn down a number of commissions because

I can't take the time out of my so-called schedule to write a major work; that would mean not doing anything else for six months. What's in progress is twenty-two weeks of Six Million Dollar Man, which will start in about two weeks. They will start in about two weeks. They will start shooting the first week in June, and by the middle or end of June, they'll have one or two episodes for me to start. They want to stay on top of the schedule because last year I did about thirty-three shows at Universal--Ironside, Six Million Dollar Man, and two pilot films--and by the end of the season (which was only a month and a half ago), I could hardly move the little finger on my right hand because it was literally paralyzed! I know what writer's cramp is now! As long as they show the reruns, you're covered. But when they get ready to start the new season and the show has been bought for twenty-two weeks, it's going to be rough. And I haven't really had any time off because I've been busy with recording sessions with Shelly Manne and Groove Holmes.

8. Q: Given unlimited time and finances (and no restrictions whatsoever), what would you write?

    A: I'd probably write an electronic work for synthesizer or prerecorded tape and orchestra. That's not new; there are people who are doing it already. Hans Badings, who is coming to Pittsburgh in 1976, is doing a new piece for a group of tape recorders and orchestra. The tape recorders will all be in sync, and he'll have some kind of a unit where he can start them all at the same time and at the same place. So that's one thing I would do--get involved in my studio and do that piece.
    I would like to get involved in some kind of project dealing with notation. I saw a book on notation yesterday by Gardner Read, [4] who is also a composer. I run across so much music in which the notation differs so greatly from composer to composer that I wanted to see what this book was about, and it is a very very good book. What it does is show you the different ways in which a number of things are notated by different composers. Getting involved just in notation alone is a life's work. I don't know when this man found the time to gather up all this information, but he's done it. He's only devoted six pages out of four hundred to jazz, though. Jazz musicians have a different kind of notation that only works for them. But that's the kind of project I would be involved in if I wanted to sit down and do something. I would do something with all the stuff I have in this room. All the equipment is here, but I just haven't had the time to get involved.

9. Q: If given the opportunity would you choose to devote yourself to composition on a full-time basis? Why or why not?

    A: I doubt if I would do it full-time because I need contact with the outside world, so to speak. Teaching is very important to me. I learn a great deal from the students, and I like to teach because I need that kind of contact and I always find out something. I also feel that it's very important that students be exposed to more than one kind of attitude about music.

10. Q: How would you describe your compositional style?
    A: I have a couple of them: (1) television and film style, (2) jazz (usually large orchestra), and (3) serious (which is a drag to call it that because I am serious about all of it; let me change that to symphonic). They are all serious, all three. I can't stand composers who say that they are serious composers. What the hell does that mean? You either compose music or you don't. Everything I do I take as seriously as I can. People say to me, "Why don't you get some young student, teach him your style, break him in, and let him do some of the cues that aren't important?" and I say, "Every cue is important!" By the time I could take someone and break him in, I could have done the thing myself and been finished with it. I write all my own music. I don't use any ghost writers or anything. You establish a code for yourself and then you live up to it. The people that I work for know my sound and my style so well that if anyone tampered with it, they would know. If nothing else, they could tell from the writing because they know my hand. There was one composer out here who was doing two or three shows at the same time when he really couldn't handle even one. When the producers got the music, they would see four bars in one hand and more bars in a completely different hand, so they knew he wasn't doing it. He finally lost out on everything because he was delegating too much to other people. The producers told him that if he didn't have time to write their show, he could forget it.

11. Q: What have been the influences of other composers, styles, and other types of music on your compositional style?
    A: The main influences have been Duke, Stravinsky, Bartok, and Ravel. Maybe I should add Hindemith; he was one of the first composers I really found out about. There are a lot of other people, but if I named everybody, the list would be really long. I've tried to be very selective about it and only talk about the main influences. I have not been influenced at all by Schoenberg and Webern. I hate to be tied down to any kind of system; I just can't follow it.

12. Q: Has your style changed across your career? If so, what influenced these changes or developments?
    A: I don't think it has changed. I think that I have gotten better at what I do over the years, though. Basically, I still have not written opus one.
        Now this is something really weird. When I was a student at Washington University, the man I studied composition with told me that I would never really be any good

(Flying Dutchman CYL 2-1449: A Dream Deferred) and by
Count Basie (Flying Dutchman 10138: Afrique).

AFRIQUE
   Jazz ensemble. Nolsen Music. Recorded by Count Basie
   (Flying Dutchman 10138: Afrique).

AFRO-AMERICAN SKETCHES (1960)
   Jazz ensemble. Seven parts: Message; Jungleaire; Emanci-
   pation Blues; There's a Yearnin'; Goin' Up North; Disillusioned;
   Freedom Dance. App. 40 min. Nolsen Music. Emancipation
   Blues also published in an arrangement for stage band by E. B.
   Marks (1964) as part of their Oliver Nelson Stage Band series.
   Recorded by Oliver Nelson (Prestige 7225: Afro-American
   Sketches).

AFTERMATH
   Jazz ensemble. Nolsen Music. Recorded by Oliver Nelson
   (Flying Dutchman FDS-116: Black, Brown, and Beautiful).

ALPHA CAPER
   Film score. ABC Pictures/Universal Studios.

ALTOITIS
   Jazz ensemble. Nolsen Music. Recorded by Oliver Nelson
   (Prestige 8243: Screamin' the Blues; Prestige 24060: Images).

ANACRUSES
   Jazz ensemble. Nolsen Music. Recorded by Oliver Nelson
   (Prestige 7223: Soul Battle).

THE ARTISTS' RIGHTFUL PLACE
   See THE KENNEDY DREAM SUITE.

BAJA BOSSA
   Jazz ensemble. Nolsen Music. Recorded by Oliver Nelson
   (Flying Dutchman BDLI-0825: Skull Session).

BELOW ABOVE
   Co-written by Gail Fisher Levy. Edward Fisher Music.

BERLIN BEI NACHT
   See IMPRESSIONS OF BERLIN SUITE.

BERLIN DIALOGUE FOR ORCHESTRA (1970)
   Jazz ensemble. Four parts: Confrontation; Checkpoint Charlie;
   Relative Calm; Over the Wall. Nolsen Music. Recorded by
   Oliver Nelson (Flying Dutchman 10134: Berlin Dialogue for
   Orchestra). Commissioned by Berlin Jazztage (Berlin Jazz
   Days) for the city of West Berlin. First performance (1970)
   at Philharmonic Hall (Berlin) by the Berlin Dream Band,
   Oliver Nelson, conductor.

BLACK, BROWN, AND BEAUTIFUL (1969)
Jazz ensemble. Nolsen Music. Recorded by Oliver Nelson
(Flying Dutchman FDS-116: Black, Brown, and Beautiful; Fly-
ing Dutchman CYL 2-1449: A Dream Deferred; Flying Dutchman
FDS-10120: Three Shades of Blue). Commissioned by Flying
Dutchman Records.

A BLACK SUITE FOR NARRATOR, STRING QUARTET, AND JAZZ
ORCHESTRA (1970)
Text by Langston Hughes. Nolsen Music. Commissioned by
Flying Dutchman Records for Mayor Carl B. Stokes of Cleve-
land.

BLUES AND THE ABSTRACT TRUTH
Jazz ensemble. Nolsen Music. Recorded by Oliver Nelson
(Impulse AS-75: More Blues and the Abstract Truth).

BLUES AT THE FIVE SPOT
Jazz ensemble. Nolsen Music. Recorded by Oliver Nelson
(Prestige 7223: Soul Battle).

BLUES FOR M. F.
Jazz ensemble. Nolsen Music. Recorded by Oliver Nelson
(Prestige 7223: Soul Battle).

BOB'S BLUES
Jazz ensemble. Nolsen Music. Recorded by Oliver Nelson
(Moodville LP-13).

BOOZE BLUES
Jazz ensemble. Prestige Music. Recorded by Oliver Nelson
(Prestige 8244: Meet Oliver Nelson).

BOPOL
Jazz ensemble. Nolsen Music. Recorded by Oliver Nelson
(Impulse AS-9147: The Spirit of '67).

BUTCH AND BUTCH
Jazz ensemble. Nolsen Music. Recorded by Oliver Nelson
(Impulse AS-5: Blues and the Abstract Truth).

CASCADES
Jazz ensemble. Nolsen Music. Recorded by Oliver Nelson
(Impulse AS-5: Blues and the Abstract Truth) and by Freddie
Hubbard (Impulse AS-9237: Reevaluations: The Impulse Years).

CAT IN A TREE
Jazz ensemble. Nolsen Music. Recorded by Jimmy Smith
(Verve V-8652: Peter and the Wolf and the Incredible Jimmy
Smith).

CHASE
Television. Original theme and background music. Universal
Studios.

FREEDOM DANCE
    See AFRO-AMERICAN SKETCHES.

FUGUE AND BOSSA   (1973)
    Wind orchestra.   Commissioned by the American Wind Sym-
    phony.

FUNKY BUT BLUES
    Jazz ensemble.   Nolsen Music.   Recorded by Oliver Nelson
    and Hank Jones (Impulse AS-9132: Happenings/Hank Jones and
    Oliver Nelson).

A GENUINE PEACE
    See THE KENNEDY DREAM SUITE.

GIRL TALK
    Television.   Theme for Virginia Graham's series "Girl Talk."
    See also THE LADY FROM GIRL TALK.

GOIN' UP NORTH
    See AFRO-AMERICAN SKETCHES.

GOT TO GET LOOSE
    Co-published by Leeds Music and Duchess Music.   Co-written
    by Lionel E. Siegel.

A GROOVE
    Jazz ensemble.   Nolsen Music.   Recorded by Oliver Nelson
    (Prestige 8233: Takin' Care of Business).

GUITAR BLUES
    Jazz ensemble.   Nolsen Music.   Recorded by Oliver Nelson
    (Impulse AS-9153: Oliver Nelson's Big Band/Live in Los
    Angeles).

HAPPENINGS
    Jazz ensemble.   Nolsen Music.   Recorded by Oliver Nelson and
    Hank Jones (Impulse AS-9132: Happenings/Hank Jones and
    Oliver Nelson).

HEIDI
    See IMPRESSIONS OF BERLIN SUITE.

HO!
    Jazz ensemble.   Recorded by Oliver Nelson (Prestige 7236:
    Main Stem).

HOBO FLAT BLUES
    Co-written by Quincy Jones.   Nolsen Music.

HOBO FLATS
    Jazz ensemble.   Nolsen Music.   Recorded by Oliver Nelson
    (Argo LP-737: Fantabulous), by Jimmy Smith (Verve V6-8721:

The Best of Jimmy Smith; Verve V6-8544: Hobo Flats; Verve
2-V6S-8814: The History of Jimmy Smith; Verve single 133:
Hobo Flats), by Count Basie (Flying Dutchman 10138: Afrique),
and by Mel Brown (Impulse AS-9152: Chicken Fat).

HOE DOWN
Jazz ensemble. Nolsen Music. Also published in an arrange-
ment for stage band by E. B. Marks (1964) as part of their
Oliver Nelson Stage Band series. Recorded by Oliver Nelson
(Impulse AS-5: Blues and the Abstract Truth; Verve V-8508:
Full Nelson) and by Freddie Hubbard (Impulse AS-9237: Re-
evaluations: The Impulse Years).

I HOPE IN TIME A CHANGE WILL COME
Jazz ensemble. Nolsen Music. Recorded by Oliver Nelson
(Flying Dutchman FDS-116: Black, Brown, and Beautiful; Fly-
ing Dutchman CYL 2-1449: A Dream Deferred).

I SAW PINETOP SPIT BLOOD
Jazz ensemble. Unichappell Music. Recorded by Bob Thiele
(Flying Dutchman BDLI-0964: I Saw Pinetop Spit Blood).

I WONDER WHY
Co-written by Gail Fisher Levy. Edward Fisher Music.

IMAGES
Jazz ensemble. Nolsen Music. Recorded by Oliver Nelson
(Prestige 24060: Images).

IMPRESSIONS OF BERLIN SUITE   (1970)
Jazz ensemble. Four parts: Ku-damn; Wannsee; Heidi; Berlin
Bei Nacht. Nolsen Music. Recorded by Oliver Nelson (Flying
Dutchman 10134: Berlin Dialogue for Orchestra). Heidi has
also been recorded separately by Oliver Nelson on A Dream
Deferred (Flying Dutchman CYL 2-1449).

IN A JAPANESE GARDEN
Jazz ensemble. Nolsen Music. Recorded by Oliver Nelson
(Flying Dutchman BDLI-0825: Skull Session).

IN PASSING
Jazz ensemble. Nolsen Music. Recorded by Oliver Nelson
(Prestige 7223: Soul Battle).

IN TIME
Jazz ensemble. Nolsen Music. Recorded by Oliver Nelson
(Prestige 8233: Takin' Care of Business).

IN TIME
Piano. E. B. Marks (in Blues and the Abstract Truth: A
Folio of Original Piano Solos).

MAJORCA
    Jazz ensemble. Nolsen Music.

MAJORCA
    Piano. E. B. Marks (in Blues and the Abstract Truth: A
    Folio of Original Piano Solos).

MAMA LOU
    Jazz ensemble. Nolsen Music. Recorded by Oliver Nelson
    (Prestige 24060: Images).

MARTIN WAS A MAN, A REAL MAN
    Jazz ensemble. Nolsen Music. Recorded by Oliver Nelson
    (Flying Dutchman FDS-116: Black, Brown, and Beautiful; Fly-
    ing Dutchman CYL 2-1449: A Dream Deferred).

MATT LINCOLN
    Television. Original theme and underscore music. Universal
    Studios.

THE MEETIN'
    Jazz ensemble. Nolsen Music. Recorded by Oliver Nelson
    (Prestige 8243: Screamin' the Blues; Prestige 24060: Images)
    and by Count Basie (Pablo Records 2625701: Jazz at the Santa
    Monica Civic '72).

THE MEETIN'
    Piano. E. B. Marks (in Blues and the Abstract Truth: A
    Folio of Original Piano Solos).

MESSAGE
    See AFRO-AMERICAN SKETCHES.

MISS FINE
    Jazz ensemble. Lyric written by Pat Scott. Nolsen Music.
    Also published in an arrangement for stage band by E. B.
    Marks (1963) as part of their Oliver Nelson Stage Band series.
    Recorded by Oliver Nelson (Verve V-8508: Full Nelson; Impulse
    AS-9153: Oliver Nelson's Big Band/Live in Los Angeles).

MOLLY MALONE
    Nolsen Music.

MONEY TO BURN
    Film score. ABC Pictures/Universal Studios.

MORE BLUES AND THE ABSTRACT TRUTH
    Nolsen Music.

MORE SOUL
    Co-written by Curtis Ousley. Kilynn Music.

THE NAME OF THE GAME
Television. Original underscore music for various episodes.
Universal Studios.

NO
Nolsen Music.

NOCTURNE
Jazz ensemble. Nolsen Music. Recorded by Oliver Nelson
(Moodsville LP-13).

NOCTURNE
Piano. E. B. Marks (in Blues and the Abstract Truth: A
Folio of Original Piano Solos).

ONE FOR BOB
Jazz ensemble. Nolsen Music. Recorded by Oliver Nelson
(Impulse AS-75: More Blues and the Abstract Truth).

ONE FOR BRUCIE
Piano. E. B. Marks (in Blues and the Abstract Truth: A
Folio of Original Piano Solos).

ONE FOR DUKE
See JAZZHATTAN SUITE.

THE ONE I LOVE
Co-written by Gail Fisher Levy. Edward Fisher Music.

111-44
Jazz ensemble. Nolsen Music. Recorded by Oliver Nelson
(Prestige 24060: Images).

125TH STREET AND 7TH AVENUE
See JAZZHATTAN SUITE.

OSTINATO
Jazz ensemble. Prestige Music. Recorded by Oliver Nelson
(Prestige 8244: Meet Oliver Nelson).

OVER THE WALL
See BERLIN DIALOGUE FOR ORCHESTRA.

PATTERNS
Jazz ensemble. Nolsen Music. Recorded by Oliver Nelson
(Impulse AS-9129: Sound Pieces).

A PENTHOUSE DAWN
See JAZZHATTAN SUITE.

PETER PLAYS SOME BLUES
Jazz ensemble. Nolsen Music. Recorded by Jimmy Smith

(Impulse AS-5: Blues and the Abstract Truth; Flying Dutchman CYL 2-1449: A Dream Deferred), by J. J. Johnson (RCA Victor LPM-3350: The Dynamic Sound of J. J. with Big Band), by Eddie "Lockjaw" Davis (Prestige 7834: Stolen Moments), by Curtis Fuller (Trip Records 5580: Jazz Conference Abroad), by Paul Horn (Ovation 14-05: Paul Horn and the Concert Ensemble), by Freddie Hubbard (Impulse AS-9237: Reevaluations: The Impulse Years), and by Ahmad Jamal (Impulse AS-9194: Awakening; Impulse AS-9260: Reevaluations: The Impulse Years).

STOLEN MOMENTS (1960)
Piano. E. B. Marks (in Blues and the Abstract Truth: A Folio of Original Piano Solos).

STRAIGHT AHEAD
Jazz ensemble. Nolsen Music. Recorded by Oliver Nelson (Prestige 24060: Images).

THE SUN, THE SAND, AND THE SEA
Co-written by Gail Fisher Levy. Edward Fisher Music.

SWEET JAMIE
Co-written by Lionel E. Siegel. Co-published by Leeds Music and Duchess Music.

SWISS SUITE
Jazz ensemble. Nolsen Music. Recorded by Gato Barberi and Eddie Vinson (Flying Dutchman 10149).

TAKE ME WITH YOU
Jazz ensemble. Co-written by Willie Jean Tate. Nolsen Music. Recorded by Oliver Nelson (Argo LP-737: Fantabulous).

TEENIE'S BLUES
Jazz ensemble. Nolsen Music. Recorded by Oliver Nelson (Argo LP-737: Fantabulous; Impulse AS-5: Blues and the Abstract Truth; Impulse AS-9284: The Bass; Impulse D-9228: Energy Essentials).

THERE'S A YEARNIN'
Jazz ensemble. See AFRO-AMERICAN SKETCHES.

THERE'S A YEARNIN'
Piano. E. B. Marks (in Blues and the Abstract Truth: A Folio of Original Piano Solos).

THERE'S A YEARNIN' DEEP INSIDE ME
Co-written by Frank H. Stanton and John Locke Stanton. Alameda Music.

THREE PLUS ONE
Jazz ensemble. Nolsen Music. Recorded by Oliver Nelson (Argo LP-737: Fantabulous).

THREE SECONDS
Jazz ensemble. Nolsen Music. Recorded by Oliver Nelson
(Prestige 8243: Screamin' the Blues; Prestige 24060: Images).

THREE SECONDS
Piano. E. B. Marks (in Blues and the Abstract Truth: A
Folio of Original Piano Solos).

3, 2, 1, 0
Jazz ensemble. Nolsen Music. Recorded by Oliver Nelson
(Flying Dutchman FDS-116: Black, Brown, and Beautiful; Fly-
ing Dutchman CYL 2-1449: A Dream Deferred).

TIPSY
Jazz ensemble. Nolsen Music. Recorded by Oliver Nelson
(Prestige 7236: Main Stem).

TOLERANCE
See THE KENNEDY DREAM SUITE.

TOP STUFF
Jazz ensemble. Unichappell Music. Recorded by Oliver Nelson
(Flying Dutchman CYL 2-1449: A Dream Deferred).

TRANS EUROPA EXPRESS
Film score. Universal Studios.

A TYPICAL DAY IN NEW YORK
See JAZZHATTAN SUITE.

WALK AWAY
Nolsen Music.

WANNSEE
See IMPRESSIONS OF BERLIN SUITE.

WHOLE NELSON
Jazz ensemble. Nolsen Music. Recorded by Eddie "Lockjaw"
Davis (Prestige 7834: Stolen Moments).

WONDERING WHERE IS LOVE
Co-written by Gail Fisher Levy. Edward Fisher Music.

WOODWIND QUINTET   (1965)

YEARNIN'
Jazz ensemble. Nolsen Music. Recorded by Oliver Nelson
(Impulse AS-5: Blues and the Abstract Truth; Flying Dutchman
10120: Three Shades of Blue).

YOUR LAST CHANCE
Nosnibor Music.

Coleridge-Taylor Perkinson (courtesy of the composer)

CHAPTER IX

COLERIDGE-TAYLOR PERKINSON

Coleridge-Taylor Perkinson was born June 14, 1932 in New York City. He received his B. M. (1953) and M. M. (1954) degrees in composition from the Manhattan School of Music and continued his education with studies in conducting at the Berkshire Music Center, the Mozarteum, and the Netherlands Radio Hilversum. Among those with whom Mr. Perkinson studied composition were Vittorio Gianni- ni, Charles Mills, and Earl Kim.

Mr. Perkinson has been a member of the faculties of the Manhattan School of Music and Brooklyn College in addition to serv- ing as music director of the Professional Children's School in New York City from 1952 to 1964. He was the first composer-in-resi- dence for the Negro Ensemble Company and wrote the music for several of its productions, including Man Better Man and Song of the Lusitanian Bogey. Mr. Perkinson has held conducting positions with the Desoff Choirs, the Brooklyn Community Symphony Orchestra, and the Symphony of the New World, for which he also served as acting musical director from 1972 to 1973.

Mr. Perkinson's compositional output demonstrates his ability to function in a variety of musical contexts. In addition to his work in the areas of concert music and jazz, he has written a consider- able number of compositions for television, motion pictures, the ballet, and the theater. Among his best-known works are Attitudes, a cantata commissioned by the Ford Foundation for tenor George Shirley; Commentary, a work for violoncello and orchestra commis- sioned by the National Association of Negro Musicians; and the scores for the motion pictures A Warm December, Amazing Grace, and The Education of Sonny Carson. Mr. Perkinson's television credits include Ceremonies in Dark Old Men, Room 222, and The Barbara McNair Show, for which he was musical director for two seasons. He has also written and/or arranged materials for the albums of such outstanding artists as Max Roach, Marvin Gaye, Harry Bela- fonte, Donald Byrd, Barbara McNair, Leon Bibb, and Melvin Van Peebles as well as for recordings in the Music Minus One series.

Mr. Perkinson's current projects include albums for Marvin Gaye and Jimmy Owens in addition to his involvement in the National Black Theater production Soul Journey into Truth.

239

offered a job with the Philharmonic provided that he would not reveal his racial origin, at which point he told them exactly what he thought about that idea and thereby curtailed his career. I'm sure that was one of the heartbreaks of his life. Of course, the situation has changed today; it has not changed very much, but it has changed.

There were a number of teachers I had in high school[2] who should be mentioned. Everything was taught to me very well in that high school; I literally learned nothing academically about music after leaving there because the training was so thorough. There were four major people for me: Alexander Richter, Abraham Klotzman, Alfred Weiss, and Isadore Russ.[3] They all encouraged me to continue and helped me in trying to come up with definitive musical answers that made sense in terms of what I was endeavoring to do.

There were a few events that influenced me in terms of what I care about doing in music and with my life. One of them was a trip that I took to Europe in 1960. At that point I had had a very flourishing career as a young man. Even though I had been in school, I had done practically everything. I had conducted orchestral and choral concerts, I had written music that had been well-received, and then all of a sudden, the bottom dropped out; whatever plateau I should have reached next simply disappeared. Thinking that perhaps I was wrong and that everyone else was right (everyone else being the social structure that I was living in), I decided to go to Europe for further study. It was there that I found out just how much I knew and how much I didn't know. How much I knew almost frightened me, and I'm not saying that out of ego; it really came out in the situation there. It was the reverse of what I had experienced in America, where the barriers had been placed for me. In Europe I became a curiosity item. Everybody wanted to know what a black American was doing over there studying conducting. They had been exposed to a few other black musicians involved in the Western classical music tradition, the best-known being Dean Dixon. Everyone would ask me, "Do you know Dean Dixon?" I didn't know him, but I had heard him speak before he left America; he had spoken at our high school graduation exercises in 1948. At any rate, when I was studying in Europe, I found out how far advanced my technique and my craft were, and it did wonders for me. It allowed me to try to develop a career while no longer doubting myself in terms of my ability to have a career. It allowed me to deal with things in a totally different manner. That trip and subsequent trips to Europe did a lot for me. I met a number of Americans who were there, but never developed the expatriate mentality myself. It's very understandable why a number of creative people have left here and gone elsewhere in order to have the opportunity of practicing their craft. When that is shut off from you here in America, it becomes extremely difficult to live with oneself. In my own case, it almost turned me into another kind of person in that I began not to have the confidence with which I had started. Everything had seemed so promising, and then the promises were not kept. That became a very acute problem, and going to Europe helped me in a number of ways.

I was in Europe at the time of the march on Washington. I was really impressed with European awareness of what was going on in this country. We American students all bought American papers when they were available and one day saw an ad in the Times that said that you could support the march on Washington provided you showed up in Bonn and signed a form. A number of us formed a caravan, drove to Bonn, and went to the American Embassy to file these forms. What we found there was a total lack of awareness; the people with whom we had to deal didn't know what was going on. When the actual march took place, I was in Amsterdam. A group of people started marching spontaneously in the street to support the march on Washington and it literally turned into a sea of people; thousands of people were jamming traffic and marching to the square to parallel the march on Washington. It was heartwarming to know that people in other parts of the world cared about what was happening in America.

The death of Dr. Martin Luther King was another major event. I think that his death was a traumatic experience for almost every black person. I still fight the bitterness. I am not a very group-oriented person; the nature of what I do requires that I spend a lot of time privately. Consequently, I did not participate in the King movement and, as a result, did not truly understand the magnitude of the man at that time. I was subsequently assigned to do the music for Memphis to Mobile, the Martin Luther King film. It is one of the things that I am the most proud of and the most humble about. It was also one of the most difficult assignments I've ever had, not so much in terms of what it took technically to accomplish the work but in terms of the emotional involvement. I didn't write the music; I compiled music that had to do with the situations presented in the film, which was made up primarily of newsreel footage. The editors and I worked on the film every day, but it was very difficult work for long periods of time because each one of us had to periodically excuse himself to go out of the room and cry. There was no way to have been aware of everything that had taken place. There are people who were more conversant with Dr. King's activities than I was at that time, but when we talk about the major influences that have colored my creativity, I would have to say that his life and death were certainly major influences on my musical activities.

In terms of art and literature, I was exposed to a lot of black poetry in my youth. I'm very glad that I learned

of Harlem called <u>Ode to Otis</u>, and what I used were two
Otis Redding tunes, "Dock of the Bay" and "Happy Song."
I felt that I was hearing something more in Otis Redding's
music than just what was on the surface, and I thought that
by putting these two tunes together in the manner that I
imagined them in my mind's eye, I could show people what
it was that I heard and go on from there to create whatever
was necessary for the ballet. Arthur Mitchell and I talked
about Otis and it turned out that we were both hearing the
same thing, so we decided to do the work. I can't say that
writing the ballet and using Otis Redding as the inspiration
was not a conscious effort on both my part and Arthur's
because we were involved with blackness; at the same time,
the main criterion was to come up with a work of art, a
work of art that had its inspiration in something that was a
part of black life in America, and of course Otis Redding
was a large part of that.

All of the theater things that I've done have been about
some part of black life with the exception of the Strindberg
play.[6] My creative output over the years has been definitely involved in black subject matter and this has happened
through no design of my own; that's just the way it's happened. Maybe the design is there in that I only get involved
in things that I'm interested in.

If I were to write about things in terms of my personal
philosophies, <u>Grass</u> had to do with my involvement or anyone's involvement in war. I have a solo cantata for tenor,
<u>Attitudes</u>, which is really about attitudes; its whole point is
that a person can have many different attitudes about things
and the question is the coming toward a point of understanding where we can coexist. I think that's a major problem.
Two pieces that I did for the sake of doing them were <u>Blue
Forms</u> for unaccompanied violin and <u>Lamentations</u>, which is
a black/folk song suite for unaccompanied cello. I can't
say why my involvement with black materials is that way,
but it is. Even when I want to get away from it and use
something like serial technique (which I am doing in the
piano sonata I'm currently working on for the Bicentennial),
I think that the selection of notes for the tone row has to
do with what I hear as being an acceptable row, and I think
my row says something about my being black as opposed to
being somebody else. I know that there are people who will
challenge me on that and I can't blame them. I know that
my row is an arbitrary choice of notes and that their sequence is arbitrary, but somehow what comes out doesn't
sound like a serial piece. All you have to do is take the
microscope and go over it and you will see how the notes
fit together. There is no question that the technique is
serial, but you can take the technique and bend it and make
it say whatever you want and somehow that comes out. I
feel this way because this is how I hear it.

4. Q: In what ways is your music a reflection of your personal
philosophy (social, political, etc.)?

A: The only thing that I try to do in my music is to try to be excellent in my craft. My concepts are really classic in nature. Who is to say who writes the perfect piece as opposed to who doesn't? Yet I have a tendency to think of Bach, Mozart, and Brahms as being perfect composers as opposed to Beethoven, in whose music you will find things which are effective as opposed to being compositionally correct. My tendency is to try and write what is musically correct. My tendency is to try and live socially in terms of what I think is correct social behavior. I don't know how successful I am at either of them (laughter); I'm sure that there would be as many opinions as there are people who know me as to what degree I'm successful in doing any of that. That's about as much as I can say about what reflects my personal philosophy, except that I really believe that if you have something to say, how well you say it is in direct proportion to how well you will be understood and how effective it will be.

5. Q: What do you see as the position or role of the black artist in contemporary society?

A: I think that there are no mandates that can be handed down to someone else creatively. I think the main purpose, especially for the black artist, is to be excellent. I keep coming back to that because I think it's terribly important, especially for black artists. I think we have less leeway; the margin of error is very, very narrow for us, as it should be for anyone who considers himself an artist. I would simply like for him to be aware of the fact that he is black and how unique that is. Depending on his understanding of that, he will be a successful black artist regardless of the milieu in which he functions. Stevie Wonder is excellent; Gladys Knight is excellent; Dean Dixon is excellent--it adds up to things of that sort. It doesn't make any difference how you're trying to function; you simply have to try to do the best you can, hopefully without losing sight of who you are in the total scheme of things. It is very easy to get into the ivory tower existence of one's artistry and forget about what everything else means to you. That is a luxury a black artist cannot afford because, whether he's aware of it or not, whatever it is that he is doing is being viewed in that context, so he is better off if he remains aware. I personally would like to be able to influence people to function that way, but you cannot control them or demand that they function in any way other than the way that they see fit. I've seen a lot of people make mistakes because they are not in control of their awareness of who they are and are not in control of their craft; that can happen out of ignorance or it can happen out of lack of craftsmanship. But if they are excellent and strive toward that kind of perfection (and it's always a striving towards and never an arriving at, because perfection is an unattainable goal) and set their sights in that direction, they will certainly

A: Yes, there are. It's like what I was saying about Stravinsky with regard to Le Sacre. It is only by virtue of the fact that the piece has become familiar that the problems of performing his music have lessened. It has become a part of every musician's capabilities to handle the problems that he is confronted with in Stravinsky. If there are problems in your music, orchestras and performers will never become familiar with them if they only have the opportunity for one performance now and maybe another in five years and so on.

I really think the opportunity to be familiar with any composer's work is what will bring about more satisfactory performances. If that's not available to you, you're always going to have problems and that's been the case for myself. I have encountered some very strange situations.

Whatever kind of music you write is a constant problem because it's never familiar to the player. We look at someone's playing in terms of his understanding of the style of music that he's playing. You have to know that you play a scale in a different way in Mozart than you do in Brahms. If you are confronted with the contemporary literature, the whole approach is different. Even within the similarity of styles there is a difference; if you don't have that understanding or awareness, it creates great problems. I had a work premiered in New York where the conductor was so unfamiliar with it that the critics would not even review it. [9] It is a very costly and hurting experience to get a premiere of a major work (which represents hours and months--literally your life's blood!) and have it be said that the piece as played by Mr. X cannot be reviewed. What do you do the next time? There can only be one first performance. The next time the piece is of less interest because, unless you want to falsify the records, you are no longer offering the public and the critics a first performance. It takes a lot out of you when you are confronted with problems like that.

There is never enough time to prepare a new work as is required unless you have unlimited funds. The economics of music are what they are. It's no fault of the musicians; everybody has to earn a living. If you take up their time, you should pay them for it, because time is money and is valuable. At the same time, you know that a limited income is going to be available from any performance, so it becomes virtually impossible with some new works to get a definitive performance. Even if it's not a new work, the fact that it is something totally unfamiliar presents peculiar kinds of problems which are going to make it very difficult for you to get a satisfactory performance.

For instance, there are things in my own music that I have a tendency not to indicate. I must admit that in some instances I've been in such a hurry to get it all down on paper that I simply don't take the time to put in everything, or it might often be a case of not having really made up

my mind about it.   However, I do not make a lot of markings in the music because I think that the music should
show what it is.   In a score where there are many markings, the musician can do very little other than execute the
work exactly as it is.   I would like for the musician to be
able to bring his musical and intellectual understanding to
whatever he plays.   You pick up the music of Bach and
there are no markings, with the exception of a piano or a
forte here and there; it is up to the musician to understand
what the music is all about.   I think that the success of the
music depends on the performer's ability to do that; if you
lay everything out for him, then it becomes very mechanical
--just the execution of notes.   No <u>music</u> comes out; just
<u>notes</u> come out.   I leave a lot for performers to find.

7. Q: What do you consider, at this point in your life, to be your
        most significant achievement(s) aside from your composi-
        tions?

    A: My ability to survive without being bitter.   It's something
        that I really didn't know about myself until after I had done
        a radio program on which they played a lot of my works
        and I spoke.   I didn't hear the broadcast because I was
        away, but when I returned to New York, one person called
        me and said, "Perk, it really was nice to know what you've
        been through and that it never shows up in your work or in
        what you had to say.   There was no bitterness there."[10]
            I know that I have survived and that I am not <u>yet</u> bitter.
        It is a little difficult every now and then to control the
        momentary emotional outbursts that may come, but I think
        I have maintained a healthy perspective in terms of dealing
        with whatever it is that I have to deal with.   It does not
        get in the way of my accomplishing my primary objective,
        which has to do with craft and music.
            There have been some extremely frustrating moments,
        however.   For example, the premiere of <u>Commentary</u>, a
        piece that represented a year's work, was really a waste.
        That was the incident I was describing in response to the
        previous question.   <u>Commentary</u> was my first attempt at a
        large-scale serial piece.   Serial technique was relatively
        new to me; my involvement came late, but I was interested
        in it and saw the possibility of doing some things that I
        wanted to do with that technique.   I don't know if it's one
        of the crosses I bear, but as a black creative artist, I
        don't want it to be said that black composers can only
        write <u>this</u> kind of music or <u>that</u> kind of music or <u>any</u> kind
        of music.   If I didn't think that serial technique would work,
        I would throw it away; I would not involve myself.   The
        <u>Ode to Otis</u> ballet is not serial, but I think the style is as
        severe or as accomplished as is whatever I may do in seri-
        al technique, even though the basis for composing is totally
        different.   I am just very concerned that the output of black
        composers--whatever it is--not be looked down upon, and
        that people do not say, "Yes, they are good, but they can't

do this, that, or the other." I know that I cannot accomplish all of it, but I certainly want to try my hand at that portion of it that is acceptable to me, that makes sense, and that I am interested in and see how good I can be at it.

8. Q: What do you see as the responsibilities and obligations of the educational system (at all levels) to the study of black music?

A: One of the first responsibilities and obligations is to help define black music. I don't know exactly where to begin, but each person at each level of the system has to begin somewhere. They could start by exploring the music of black composers in comparison to any other composers-- white, Oriental, or whatever--but I think that what should not be done is to try to cram anything--<u>absolutely anything</u> --that has to do with blackness down a person's throat. You cannot take it and put it up on a pedestal and say that <u>this</u> is black music. Like it! I know that some individuals want to embrace any and everything that is black. I can appreciate the sincerity of their gesture, but I think that, especially in the educational system, one has to be a little more methodical and careful regarding procedures. You can't talk about Leadbelly in the same way you talk about Stravinsky; you talk about Leadbelly and other comparable artists who function in that realm. You talk about one jazz artist as opposed to another jazz artist, not about a jazz artist as opposed to a classical artist. The basic responsibility is to define it and to make people familiar with it so that they can go out and explore things on their own, which is basically the purpose of <u>all</u> education. Education should not be an end in itself; education should prepare you to really be educated.

We have this problem: all of the history books have to be rewritten to include us. Until that has been done, supplementary materials should be put together and used at all levels of the educational system as required addenda to texts in the various subject areas--science, music, art, and so forth.

It is very difficult to get people to change. First of all, we have to influence people to the point that they at least understand the necessity of it. Once they understand, we can move on to the problem of how to go about doing it. In some instances, people don't even see the necessity of it. They may even figure that there is enough information available and that it isn't necessary for them to add it to their educational program.

The one thing that I would like to see is for it not to be limited to Negro History Week. Negro History Week really served a good purpose, as did the Negro baseball league. I think it is unnecessary today, but we had to start somewhere. The best way to begin to really make people aware at all levels is through the media--television, radio, film, theater, etc. If the educational process could start there, I think everything else would fall into line.

9. Q: Do you feel that the people who write about your music (critics in particular) understand what you are doing? Exemplify and discuss.

A: I have no way of knowing. I definitely appreciated the critic not criticizing my piece when he understood that what I had done was not what was coming out of the orchestra. [11] At the same time, I remember a very favorable review of the String Quartet No. 1 (the Calvary Quartet) in which the reviewer was describing as jazz-influenced what for me was a folk idiom. That's a question of a person being able to hear the difference between one and the other. If there had been jazz influences, it would have been a totally other kind of piece of music.

I find that I don't pay too much attention to the critics. This is not because I don't think music criticism is necessary, but rather because I don't think that my particular problems with music criticism are any different than anybody else's. I have been to concerts and read reviews by different people and you would not believe that they were at the same concerts. It's very peculiar what the end result is.

It is possible to simply be criticized as a composer and a piece of music on a program. At the same time, it is important that people know that you are a black composer; until everything is on an even keel, we need that to help the people who are coming along behind us as well as those who are our contemporaries. It works both ways. It would be marvelous if critics could just walk in and say, "I heard a piece of music last night and it was this, this, and this." But as soon as you say it was by a black composer, they either become condescending or overly critical. The word black added to whatever your creativity is gives them a perspective. It would be good if we could do without it, but at the same time it is important for other reasons.

I don't know whether or not critics understand what it is that I'm about. I hope so. It's important in terms of them telling someone else what it's about, but music criticism has gotten into a realm beyond what it was originally intended to be. It's perfectly fine for someone to have an opinion about what it is that he hears, but unless the person is the kind of music critic that, especially with a new work, takes out the time to attend rehearsals and puts forth the effort to get a copy of the music so that it can be looked at, [12] his opinion isn't likely to be particularly significant. I think I hear extremely well, and if I go to a performance of a new work or a piece that is totally unfamiliar, I come away with an opinion of it, but there is a limited amount of what I can say about the piece. Being a musician (and a number of critics are not musicians), I feel as though I'm in a better position to say what I have heard

or what the music was about than they are. They come up
with some things that are beyond their own capabilities to
grasp. If music criticism is gone into seriously, then I
think it's fine. But I think that the best attitude is not to
worry too much about it. If you're involved with your own
creativity, you won't worry too much about what people are
writing about you because you don't have time for it.

10. Q: What advice would you give to the aspiring young black
    composer?
    A: The best advice I can give is for him to expose himself to
    as much as possible. One of the reasons I love living in
    New York is because there is so much going on that if my
    creative juices run dry, I can go out and hear or experience
    something that will inspire me. It may not be done in the
    way that I would do it, but something that is interesting to
    my ear will send me off on another avenue. Exposure has
    to do with more than just listening; it also has a great deal
    to do with analysis. If you live in a cocoon, you don't
    really get a total picture of where you are in the scheme
    of things. It has happened to me. There have been in-
    stances in which someone will have already done what I
    was setting out to do, and I could have saved myself a lot
    of trouble had I been aware of his creative output. We can
    really help one another. Someone's music helps me and in
    turn I hope that my music helps or inspires someone else
    to want to investigate other areas.
        Young black composers should expose themselves to as
    much music as possible. At the same time, since inspira-
    tion is really rare, they should look to their own roots for
    something generic to build music on. It doesn't make any
    difference which part of their roots they draw from; it is
    what they're the most familiar with, and possibly what they
    will be able to write best about. However, the notion of
    doing one's own thing with a lack of craft is the one thing
    that I'm set against. I'm not against people trying to be
    unique and doing their own thing, but it cannot be done
    without having attained a level of craftsmanship that enables
    them to do whatever they set out to do without having to
    skirt the stumbling blocks (i.e., problems) simply because
    of a lack of technique.
        When we stop and think about it, the music of some of
    the most successful composers came right out of whatever
    it was that they were most familiar with. We somehow
    know the music of Norway through Grieg, just as we know
    the music of Hungary through Bartok. Another example is
    Aaron Copland. Here is a composer who cannot write an
    unquotable melody, and the melodic invention in his works
    comes right out of the folk music of this country. For a
    long time, the notion was propagated that black music (or
    what was understood as being black music, mainly the folk
    music such as it was) was not suitable for serious under-
    taking in the realm of composition. That's one of my pet

peeves, and was why I took something as simple as an
Otis Redding tune and constructed a ballet on it. [13] If Copland can do it with those Billy the Kid-type tunes, I don't
see why it can't be done with any kind of music. The truth
of the matter is that it can; it simply poses another set of
problems. It is important for skilled black composers to
try and show an awareness of black achievements in music.
People may not know who Paganini was, but his name gets
into their consciousness by virtue of the fact that Brahms,
Rachmaninoff, and recently Blacker wrote works based on
his caprices. [14] This same premise would hold true in
reaching for an understanding and appreciation of black
music and its creators.

Inspiration is rare. We can't all write great melodies
every day. If one is stuck, there is no reason why one
cannot draw on one's background. It is a great challenge.
When I am teaching, I put the task to my students, just
as I do when I ask them to solve a compositional problem
in the style of Bach, Handel, or Brahms. I tell them to
solve the problem with a certain kind of melody and see
what happens when they try to be inventive. That's not
advice; that's something I would like for them to do. I
think that they will help their own uniqueness by doing so,
unless the melodies are flowing forever and ever and the
muse is on their shoulder. In that case, they should do
whatever they feel like because they've nothing to worry
about. Anyone should be that lucky!!

Part II: Music Questions

1. Q: When you sit down to begin a new composition on your own
initiative or inspiration (as opposed to a commissioned
work), what procedure or approach do you follow?

2. Q: When composing a commissioned work or a work written for
a specific occasion or person, does your procedure or approach differ from the one you described in question 1?
If so, in what way?

(Ed. note: Mr. Perkinson chose to answer questions one
and two together.)

A: For me, it's exactly the same. It's the same whether I
write a piece for myself or I'm writing a film score or
something for television. I have to come up with the idea.
That's the kind of composer I am. The procedure depends
on what the piece is. I generally know what it is that I'm
writing about, even if it involves an abstract piece and I
can't verbalize it. It becomes even more simple if you
give a piece a title right away because then you know exactly what it is that you're writing about. I begin by wanting
to write a piece about something; then it's a question of
finding the general format to hang the piece on and the ingredients that will go into it. I have changed on a couple
of occasions and started by saying, for instance, that I was

going to write a sonata. Now you can start out by saying that you're going to write in the sonata form, but you may change because you may find that the musical material simply does not warrant it. By your craft, you can make music do whatever you want it to. But you must also realize that, in some cases, it's like attempting to make an elephant fit into a Volkswagen. You have to put something else in that kind of car!

When I am writing on my own initiative, I am inspired to write about things with which I am concerned. For me, art is a reflection of that. It says "I think this way," or "I don't think this way," or "This is the way things are," or "This is the way things should be."

It's been quite a while since I sat down to write music simply in order to write; it's a luxury that I haven't been able to afford. I sometimes will get a commission to write something that will not be specified, as was the case when I was asked to write a piece for the New York All-City High School Chorus. The conductor told me, "The kids are tired of singing Bach, Beethoven, and Brahms. These are young people. They're a very well-trained choir. Write a piece of music for them." That was the assignment given to me. At the same time, I was thinking, "These are young people. They're inspired by music, so why throw away a golden opportunity?" It took a year of just reading poetry before I stumbled onto the things that I wanted to write about. One of the texts I decided to use turned out to be a poem I had known for a long time and had forgotten, a poem entitled "Fredome" by the fifteenth-century English poet John Barbour. I found that poem, a poem by James Russell Lowell, and a line from a spiritual for the text of this piece. All the subject matter was about freedom. When the kids learned the piece, they came to me and said, "Mr. Perkinson, this piece is about what's happening today." The subject matter is something that I am very concerned about. By giving that material to a choir of 300, I got 300 people singing the same thing and thinking pretty much the same way for a period of time. That is influencing people. I don't want to throw away any opportunity I have to help make the world a place that I think is better.

I really like to write about something. Commentary was based on "Troubled Waters" and man's age-old quest for equality. That's what the piece is about; whether or not you find that in the music is something else, but that's what inspired me. How does this differ from a commission? It doesn't. The only difference with a commissioned work is that perhaps the medium or duration or something like that might be set for you. In the case of my writing for the kids, I might have written another kind of piece had I been writing for some other adult choir. I knew, however, that this piece was to be written for and performed by young people; my musical approach was colored

by the medium for which I was writing. The same thing
happens when I write for the theater. If I know that actors
are going to be singing the music, I simplify what it is that
I ask of them. Of course, my preference is to write for
the artists for whom performing in this milieu is what they
do. You cannot write for both in the same way.

3. Q: In general, with regard to your writing, what genre(s) do
you prefer?

A: It's hard to say that I have a preference. I would enjoy
the luxury of being able to write for orchestra. When I
was younger I did a lot of that, but then I got to the point
where I refused to write music and put it in the drawer
any more. That has to do with whether or not I'm on commission or writing for a specific purpose. If somebody calls
me up and asks me to write a piece for them, I know that
it will be performed so I sit down and write whatever it is.

What I enjoy is solving the problem of saying what I
have to say with whatever performing medium is accessible
to me. My preference? It's difficult to say. I used to
love to write songs, but I found that texts were always difficult to come by. I've gotten a little spoiled in that once
I solve certain problems for myself, I don't want to deal
with those problems any more unless there are specific
reasons for doing so. Some of my first endeavors were in
art song writing; once I knew that I knew how to write art
songs, they just didn't interest me. If there were a reason
for me to do it or if I read something that particularly inspired me, then I would try my hand at it again. These
last two unaccompanied string pieces still offered challen-
ges. [15] I will probably go back to the unaccompanied solo
instrument form many times because it is practical to get
a performance and because it still offers a challenge to me.

The orchestra is really an enjoyable medium to work
in. I would guess that my preference is for orchestra, but
it's very difficult for me to say, because it really depends
on what it is that I'm trying to say. There are some things
that can only be said with a large orchestra, which is why
I talked about orchestrating Attitudes, the solo cantata for
tenor. I didn't give it as large a framework as it needed,
but at the time what I set out to do was to write that piece.
I might think that it works now, but still in the back of
my mind there are sections of it that would work better
with orchestra.

4. Q: What do you consider your most significant composition?
Please discuss.

A: There are significant compositions by virtue of what I
arrived at, at the time. I feel that way about Commentary,
which was my first really large serial work. Before that,
I had just done exercises in serialism and a lot of small
pieces, all of which I have thrown away. Then I think
about something like Fredome-Freedom and its significance

in terms of what the end result of its performance was; if the idea of the text of that piece catches on, then it has yet another kind of significance. When I think about the first play that I did for the Negro Ensemble and the kind of response that it got (positive and negative!), that was also significant for me.

Asking a question like this is like asking someone which one of their children they like the most. I don't have a bunch of kids, but I certainly hope that as a parent I would not ever say that I liked one child better than another; I would want to be the same parent to all of them. It's like that with pieces, but at the same time I think I could say that I like each of them for different reasons. Of the pieces that I've written for the theater, I really loved the first one that I did for the Negro Ensemble. That was Song of the Lusitanian Bogey. I love it for a lot of reasons. Of all the things that I would like to see chronicled of my creative output, that for me is one of the most important ones. I can't really say why. It says a lot, because in a couple of hours in the theater, you can get a lot done. It also gave me the chance to do many many things, which is the opportunity that theater affords one. Of the theater pieces, I think Song of the Lusitanian Bogey is probably the best one.

But there are other things. Of the films that I've done, I like each for different reasons. Some are better than others by virtue of this and that. One of my favorite pieces is a piece for violin and piano, Variations and Fugue on "The Ash Grove." I have been in love with that piece for a long time; it is probably one of my favorite pieces. But it's hard to say that any one piece is more dear to you than any other; they were all firsts.

5. Q: Please comment on your treatment of the following musical elements and give examples from your compositions that illustrate the techniques you describe.

   A. Melody

   CTP: I cannot say what makes a good melody except that I know when it is right and I know when it is not complete. I think that the kind of melodies that I personally enjoy the most are the ones that are very concise but complete, and allow themselves to be metamorphosed to whatever format I'm working in at the time. Some melodies like that are a bar in length or four bars in length; then there are some that become longer melodies by virtue of whatever work I do with the materials. They expand themselves, which has to be a natural consequence regardless of how hard I work at it. I am not terribly concerned with melodies being hummable. My criterion for what makes a melody is whether or not it works for me. It's difficult for me to go beyond that.

B. Harmony
CTP: It has to do with my inner hearing and the things that ring true to my ear. I have on occasion written things that, when I went to the piano to play them, did not sound as I had thought they would sound. I think that is always true when one is trying to be inventive and to reach out for something other than the familiar. I don't like staying on familiar ground. Once I have solved the compositional problems of format, medium, etc., I move on to something else. It's not that I'm not interested in them; I will probably come back to them when I find something new to do with them, but I keep trying to reach for the unknown. I want to keep expanding. It's fine to say that this is the style you write in and that everybody recognizes your style and knows it right away when they hear it, but that's almost like writing the same piece over and over and over again, which is what I prefer not to do. In my own mind, I am constantly searching for new things to do. Even after I've worked out the new things and they've become cold, I often look back on them and find that they no longer seem new any more. It's a question of constantly searching for the next thing to do.

C. Rhythm
CTP: I am fascinated by some things that I have experienced rhythmically. One of my most rewarding experiences was meeting eight royal court drummers from Upper Volta. When I heard them play, I realized that what I wanted to do rhythmically was close to the kind of music they were playing. I can't say that my concept of what to do with rhythm is especially unique. I'm sure that there are other people who have the same idea, although their approach to notation might be different from mine. And there are so many kinds of rhythm--harmonic rhythm, melodic rhythm, rhythm rhythm. My approach to rhythm is to get out of the metric system. There has to be some kind of common denominator, but the ability to change that common denominator and still make the work sound like a cohesive unit is something that I'm interested in and investigating. How successful I've been is for other people to say, but it was a very rewarding experience for me to realize that I was not that far off base from something

I thought was unique and very special. In all
the recordings of African music that I'd heard
and all the organized pulse forms I was familiar
with, I had never heard anything like what they
did with the royal court drumming. They played
it for me in my apartment in New York. They
didn't mind playing in a house, but they were
somewhat concerned because there is just no
other way to play the royal court drumming
other than to play it; you cannot soft-pedal your
way through it. When they played it for me, I
understood why they were apprehensive about
playing it indoors, but it fascinated everyone
within earshot. People were even standing in
the street outside my window, listening!

That approach to rhythm and metrics is something that I'm very interested in. I have found
it in some of my earlier works, but not as clearly defined as it is when I'm working with it now.
Some people might think that I'm being overly
complicated, but if that's what the inner hearing
is, there can be no argument with that. The
problem is codifying it and making it work, compositionally and creatively.

D. Form
CTP: I like to be extremely clear. With a few exceptions, the music I've done is pretty clear in
terms of what the structures are.

E. Improvisation
CTP: I love to include improvisation and aleatoric concepts in my writing, but only when they work.
There are times when I really want the precision
of what's on the page, and there are times when
I can allow the players some freedom within a
given format, which is actually what I'm doing
when I write it all out note for note. Within
the framework of the written page, there is a
certain amount of expressive freedom in terms
of improvisation. I have seen both successful
and unsuccessful attempts. For the most part,
I find not as much use for this in some works
as I do in others. For example, if I'm working
on a film score or a recording or something of
that sort, I naturally depend on the ability of the
musician to improvise, and I will give him only
a general frame of reference. That's why I ask
certain people to play--because of their creativity.
At the same time, I would like for the player
to be able to pick up the written note and play
it as though it were his own creation because,
for me, composition is written improvisation.

It's a little bit more thought out; I cannot write as fast as I can hear. But improvisation is really what composition is about, except that you have to be more careful with the science of it because you go back to it again and again as opposed to its passing the ear once and being lost to posterity.

F. Text
CTP: In terms of approach, I think what I really try to find in the text is the speech pattern that makes it say whatever it is that I want it to say. In each instance I have to deal with text differently. The performing medium has to be taken into consideration, though. For a solo performer, it's one thing; for a large ensemble, it's something else. For example, with a large ensemble, the ability to do something on a speech pattern that is metrically complex or against a pulse that is not discernible is something of a problem.

Q: How do you select the texts that you decide to set?

A: Fredome-Freedom took me a year of just reading and what did I find? Two poems. Attitudes also took me a while. I just read and read and read. Sometimes I find things that I know I will want to set to music at some future time. I'll have something that I'm familiar with and once I get an idea about a piece and how it should go together, I'll go back and find that particular piece of poetry and utilize it within the piece. It invariably never happens that I just find a piece of poetry and set it at that moment. The only time that I have to set a piece of poetry at the moment I get it is when I'm writing the music for a lyric that someone is writing for a song. But that, too, is the same kind of problem for me. I don't compose any differently for a film or a record date in the popular medium than I do for works on a larger scale.

G. Instrumentation or medium
CTP: I have no preferences, except to say that I like large orchestras.

6. Q: Have difficulties with performance practice (inflection, phrasing, etc.) been a significant problem in having your works performed to your own satisfaction?

A: Definitely, and that has to do with what we were talking about earlier in terms of people's familiarity with the kind of music I write. [16] There are some performers in New York who have played most of what I have written and who understand what I'm about musically. We have experienced a great deal of the same music together and have done a lot of playing together--sonatas, jazz, theater pieces, and what have you. Their understanding of what I'm doing musically is instantaneous; I have very little trouble communicating.

Generally whatever problems there are involve notation. Even if I write things that people have heard before (and that happens, because a lot of what I do comes out of my own experience), they are often notated in such a way that they appear unfamiliar. In cases where we have to record right away, this unfamiliarity shows up. In subsequent performances, however, it disappears. All it takes is familiarity.

It takes time to communicate what your music is about, but this must also come out of the player's understanding; it isn't all up to you. You can't explain a word to somebody if you use a bunch of words that they don't understand. You have to keep trying to find things that make sense to them, but at the same time, they have to have enough background to be able to grasp what it is that you're saying.

If I'm involved in the performance as a conductor, I have fewer difficulties in getting performances to my own satisfaction. If I'm not involved, it depends on the other person's familiarity with what I've written. I know what my music should sound like, but my attitude sometimes has to be to accept what is correct under the circumstances. I can live with that when the music is playing a secondary role, as is the case when it's music for the theater or for a film, and I know that the attention of the audience is not going to be directed totally toward the music. Nobody hears the other things that I hear. If the music were just to be played on its own, I would go back and redo, that is, re-record it the way I want it to be done.

One difficulty I find that people have involves changing of meters. I thought that by the time Stravinsky became familiar territory, dealing with the kinds of problems posed by my music would be very simple. I think it really depends on a person's training; if they aren't trained well, they're going to have those kinds of problems. It's the same as singing strange pitches. Most singers can sing things that are tonally oriented with great ease, but if they have to do something like Webern (which is, in that sense, totally unfamiliar territory), the learning process takes much longer; however, once they have done it, the rest is gravy. I feel that there is a direct ratio between the amount of exposure a performer has had to different kinds of music and the ease with which that person is able to deal effectively with performing my music.

7. Q: What major works are currently in progress? Please describe and discuss.

    A: There's a piano sonata that I'm writing for the Bicentennial

which I should have completed by now, but I find working
in California very difficult. I think I would have been
finished with it had I been in New York.[17] Then there is
a work about justice and the judicial system. It's really
an opera, or perhaps a large-scale theater piece. The full
title is <u>The Passion of Justice According to Judicial Docu-
mentation</u>. The major body of the text is the transcript
of the Panther 13 trial. In reading the transcript I found
situations that paralleled other historical trials, so that the
total text is the Panther 13 court transcript plus a series
of other excerpts which are either interpolated or super-
imposed. It's a major project, but I am determined to get
at least this one opera written. I am fascinated with the
theater as a performance vehicle, and I am writing about
something that I want to write about. It was my own idea
to choose that subject matter. I don't know how long it is
going to take me; it depends on the amount of time that I
can devote to it.

I have a piece in mind that I have sketched called <u>Blues
Forms II.</u> The first <u>Blues Forms</u> was for solo violin.
<u>Blues Forms II</u> is a piece for solo trumpet and either cham-
ber orchestra or large orchestra. It will be based on famous blues choruses of trumpet players. I'm going to use
something of Miles's, something of Dizzy's, something of
Clifford Brown's, and so on. In essence what I will do is
to take a blues chorus from one of them and write a movement for solo trumpet and orchestra around it. There will
probably be four or five movements.

Do I have anything else in mind? Yes, a piece called
<u>Dunbar.</u> I put it aside for a long time, but I'm sure I'll
get back to it. It's about Paul Laurence Dunbar. The text
will be a poem by Countee Cullen about Paul Laurence Dunbar and a series of Dunbar poems. It will probably be for
solo voice, chorus, and orchestra.

Are you familiar with the <u>Musical Offering</u> of Bach?
Another kind of offering I have in mind is a piece for jazz
ensemble (improvisational) and large orchestra. I don't
like what is generally called thirdstream music, and I've
heard a lot of pieces that are for jazz ensemble and orchestra. Either the jazz ensemble doesn't really sound like
a jazz ensemble and the orchestra is brilliant, or the jazz
ensemble is good and the orchestral fabric is lousy. I
really haven't seen the proper marriage; I don't know that
I'll make it either, but that's certainly what I intend to do.
I want to do a large-scale contrapuntal composition because
that is the way it will work best.

Those are my main projects. Those are my <u>pet</u> projects. Whether or not I can get them done is a whole other
thing, which I think gets into the next question about considerations of time and finances.

8. Q: Given unlimited time and finances (and no restrictions whatsoever), what would you write?

A: Those are the things that I would write. There is one other thing; I am very concerned about writing in the symphonic form. If I could, I would sit down and just start writing symphonies. There was a time (I think it was at my graduation) that it was required and I refused to write one. I didn't care whether I graduated or not; I had learned what I had gone to school to learn. But the symphonic form is probably the most serious for a composer, and working on that size canvas is very difficult. At this stage in my life I am ready to write about whatever it is that I want to write about; I have the equipment to deal with it. When I was younger, I had the technical knowledge but I didn't have anything to put in it. I would have produced thousands of pages of notes that would have been relatively without significance, I think. That is why the Sinfonietta for Strings is a little symphony. I did not consider myself capable of writing a symphony at that time. When you title a piece a sonata or a symphony or something like that, then you have an obligation to write whatever it is that you set out to do. That's personal on my part. There are tiny sonatas and there are chamber symphonies, but you have to call them that. I want to write the big full-blown work. No, I don't want to write the big work; I want to write a bunch of them! I want to write as many of them as I can between now and my demise!

9. Q: If given the opportunity would you choose to devote yourself to composition on a full-time basis? Why or why not?

A: When you say composition, I think you mean the act of sitting down with a pencil and just composing. If I had to choose which activity I would do to the exclusion of everything else ... if it came down to that kind of a decision, I think I would rather compose than do anything else; however, I would not want to give up conducting because I find that when I am conducting I am actively composing, in that I work on a piece by actually recreating whatever it is that I'm dealing with. The activity of composing is more than sitting with a pencil. I have many approaches to it and I learn a lot from dealing with other people's music. If I had to just compose, I would like to couple it with teaching because I get a great deal of inspiration from young people who are not set in their ways. They have what is new and inventive and creative; they come in with a whole new perspective. They always think that they learn from me, but I think that the teacher (in any instance) learns more than the pupils.

I would not like to be limited just to composing. I enjoy conducting; it's the one performing medium that I like being involved in. I don't have the patience to sit and practice and keep my performing ability at the keyboard up to the caliber that I expect it to be. If given the opportunity to be a composer full-time, I would do it but I would really not like for it to exclude other things.

10. Q: How would you describe your compositional style?

A: Impossible question!!! I don't know, because it has to do with whatever it is that I'm working on at a given time. It's different with almost every piece I do. Some people say that they know my music when they hear it, but I think that in a number of instances they are talking about the things I write for films or record dates or things of that sort; I think that that is more clearly defined. Maybe my music is recognizable, but I really don't have that per- spective in terms of what it is that I do.

If I am just writing for myself--noncommissioned works out of my own inspiration and on my own initiative--I would say that the style is a little severe, that is, severe in terms of being able to grasp the logic of it immediately; I don't think it's difficult to enjoy. I remember the first time I played Ode to Otis for someone who had nothing whatsoever to do with music. I thought he was going to say that the piece was really strange, but he simply said, "This is beautiful." I was totally unprepared for that comment as a response to this piece because I had written the work in great haste and there were sections of it that were even a little perplexing to my ear. But then I'm dealing with it differently. I guess he just took in the total effect, which is the way I listen to other music. I have my critical faculties working, but I always try to respond to what is emotional in the music; if it doesn't say anything to me emotionally, then I consider it not such a good piece.

But you asked me how I would describe my style. I'm trying to put myself in the lay person's chair to figure out what the response to the kind of music I write is. I think of it as being severe. If it's not severe, I could say that it's difficult. If it's not difficult, I hope I can say that it's enjoyable. In any case, I hope that it's enjoyable both for the performer and the listener. (As an afterthought, I know that the most informative musical description for my style would be linear.)

11. Q: What have been the influences of other composers, styles, and other types of music on your compositional style?

A: I've mentioned Bach, Mozart, and Brahms. I know that I've talked enough about Stravinsky to give you an indication that I know a lot of his music. What I'm really talking about is the music of those eras, but they are the people to whom I look for guidance. Of course, there are the Renaissance composers. Monteverdi was also very influ- ential. One cannot get through Christmas and Easter from year to year without having experienced a lot of Handel simply because The Messiah is there to be reckoned with. There are some contemporary English composers whose choral music I became familiar with; they changed what I thought about the criteria for writing one kind of music as opposed to another. Everyone I've listened to has provided some degree of influence.

The tendency to compare my music to that of other composers is always there. After hearing the Sinfonietta for Strings, Paul Freeman asked me if I had studied with Hindemith. Well, nothing could be farther from the truth! Someone else told me that one of the movements sounded like the Barber Adagio for Strings. I can't say what the specific influences are. When I say that Mozart is an influence, I mean that the influence is there because I cannot find any wrong notes in his music. Not that I'm looking for wrong notes! I'm examining his craft just as I do that of any composer whose works I am analyzing. But there are no mistakes; here is a composer capable of solving all the problems.

I don't think it's all intellectual. I have tried to develop my craft to the point that even though I'm solving problems (and trying to be musical at the same time), I'm also doing a great deal by instinct. There are no questions about simple compositional procedures like correct voice leading or the correct way for this to progress to that. In retrospect I find that I've either successfully solved most of the problems or I haven't. There are no mistakes in Bach. From what I hear, there is just one set of parallel fifths in Mozart. I haven't found anything wrong in Brahms, and I've only found one wrong note in Stravinsky. That's the direction I'm bent in.

12. Q: Has your style changed across your career? If so, what influenced these changes or developments?

A: I exhaust whatever it is that I am about and then move on to something else. Two of my early pieces, Grass and the Sinfonietta for Strings, were written in a very contrapuntal style and are stylistically the same. Once I finished them, I was no longer interested in writing that kind of music because it would have meant just staying in the same place. The major thing for me has been continuing to try and find my own voice. This has pushed me into other avenues. The flirtation that I'm having with serialism goes on and off; sometimes it works for me and sometimes it doesn't. I just hope that my voice shows through it. I would like for people to say, "That's a piece of Perkinson's and he's writing using serial technique," rather than something like "That's a serial piece."

Yes, my style has changed. The influences have been mainly the number of kinds of music I have been exposed to and a social awareness of the necessity of communicating with the masses. I do not think that one should write down to the lowest common denominator; I am very much against that. However, I do think it is possible to write music that communicates something to the musicologists without excluding the general public of music lovers.

13. Q: When you are listening to music for your own enjoyment, what are your preferences?

A: I really love to listen to music, and I listen to lots of different kinds. I've named my favorite composers, and there are a host of others I listen to because I find different things in different people. I'm also involved in the folk music of as many places in the world as appeal to my ear. I've listened to a lot of jazz and a lot of rock. I try to listen to everything. I don't really care what kind of music it is; I just try to get the best out of it that it has to offer, not necessarily meaning that I will get involved myself in that kind of creativity. When I listen to music, I'm really listening for what it's trying to communicate. For me, being able to find that is the criterion for deciding that the music is good. It's like the difference between one person singing "The Way We Were" and Gladys Knight singing "The Way We Were."

I can't really pick a favorite composer or type of music. All I can say is that Bach, Mozart, and Brahms get all my votes. I find that my mind is free when I listen to them. Their music is not specific in terms of what it tries to say; it says more because it allows me the freedom of a wide range of emotional responses. I could listen to the unaccompanied sonatas of Bach forever.

I like finding as much unadulterated music from Africa as I can; the Crossroads Africa film was what really got me bent in that direction. The music of that continent is so diverse from one place to another that it is virtually inexhaustible. I don't think that anyone will ever (or can ever) comprehend African music because there is no such thing as African music (which is almost like saying that there is no such thing as black music because it covers too many different areas). I enjoy listening to African music in all its forms, provided that it has not been tampered with. I found some recordings in the library at Columbia University, but in examining the tapes, I found that the people running the recording equipment had tried to engineer some things. After a period of time, you begin to be able to tell what is authentic and what is not.

I like hearing music performed by the countrymen of the composer. That might sound like a strange answer, so let me give you some examples of what I mean. I heard a German orchestra play Rodeo and Billy the Kid and it was obvious to me that they didn't know anything about cowboys. Maybe they feel the same way about how we play their music, which is why I have spent a lot of time trying to assimilate what is stylistically correct in terms of their culture. On the other hand, when I heard a broadcast of a Hungarian orchestra playing Bartok's Music for Strings, Percussion, and Celeste, it was as if I were hearing the piece for the very first time! I knew what the notes were; I had played the piece, had studied it, and had listened to many recordings of it. But it was as if I had never heard the music in it before! The creativity of every group of people is unique. That is why I would like to encourage

young black composers to get involved in finding their own
voice--the thing that is really unique to them--because it
needs to be heard. It needs to be recognized and placed in
its proper perspective. It needs to be shared with the
world.

Notes to Chapter IX

1.   The French Six or "Les Six" was the designation given to a
group of young French composers active in an early twentieth-century movement which proposed utilizing popular styles as models for
composition. For further information on the movement itself and the
composers involved see Donald Jay Grout, A History of Western
Music (New York: W. W. Norton, 1960), pp. 625-630, and Eric
Salzman, Twentieth-Century Music: An Introduction, 2nd ed.
(Englewood Cliffs, New Jersey: Prentice-Hall, 1974), pp. 55-59.

2.   Mr. Perkinson attended the High School of Music and Art in
New York City.

3.   In a subsequent conversation, Mr. Perkinson asked that Mr.
Weber, another of his teachers at the High School of Music and Art,
be added to the list of persons from that school who were influential
in his development.

4.   Although Mr. Perkinson was born in New York City and lived
there much of his early life, he also spent a considerable amount
of time with relatives in Winston-Salem, North Carolina.

5.   Mr. Perkinson's remarks on defining black music are continued
in his response to I-3.

6.   The title of the play to which Mr. Perkinson is referring is
To Damascus.

7.   The Afro-American Music Opportunities Association. This organization, founded in 1969 by C. Edward Thomas, supports a variety of projects and activities in the area of black music. The
program to which Mr. Perkinson is referring resulted in the Black
Composers Series issued by Columbia Records.

8.   Mr. Perkinson has since changed publishers. Tosci Music is
now being administered to his satisfaction by Belwin-Mills.

9.   Mr. Perkinson is referring to his composition Commentary.

10.   Mr. Perkinson asked that a note be made identifying the caller
as Camilla Williams.

11.   Mr. Perkinson's discussion of this incident appears in his response to I-6C.

12.   Mr. Perkinson asked that Alfred Frankenstein of the San Francisco Chronicle be cited as a critic who prepares thoroughly and carefully.

13.   Mr. Perkinson is referring to Ode to Otis.

14.   Mr. Perkinson asked that a reference be made to the fact that a recently completed work for violin and piano by David Baker (entitled Ethnic Variations on a Theme of Paganini) is also based on material from the caprices.

15.   Mr. Perkinson is referring to his compositions Blue Forms and Lamentations.

16.   See Mr. Perkinson's response to I-6C.

17.   This interview took place on June 25, 1975; the piano sonata has since been completed.

LIST OF COMPOSITIONS

ABSTRACT BLUES   (late 1960s)
   See THIRTEEN LOVE SONGS IN JAZZ SETTINGS.

AD LIB + CHANGES   (late 1960s)
   See THIRTEEN LOVE SONGS IN JAZZ SETTINGS.

AD LIB + TUNE   (late 1960s)
   See THIRTEEN LOVE SONGS IN JAZZ SETTINGS.

AMAZING GRACE   (1974)
   Film score.   United Artists.

ATTITUDES   (1962-63)
   Solo cantata for tenor, violin, violoncello, and piano.   Five
   movements: Sinfonia (Introduction) (text by the composer);
   Ricercare I (On Aloneness) (texts by Tu Fu, Lawrence Ferling-
   hetti, and e. e. cummings); Ricercare II (On Death) (texts by
   Dylan Thomas, John Donne, Mei Tao Ch'en, and Langston
   Hughes); Ground (On Love) (texts by John Dryden and Charles
   Cotton); Finale (On Freedom) (texts by Langston Hughes, Thomas
   Paine, Margaret Walker, e. e. cummings, and Boris Pasternak).
   Tosci Music.   Commissioned by the Ford Foundation.   Dedicated
   to and first performed (1964) by George Shirley at the Metro-
   politan Museum of Art.

BACK BEAT   (late 1960s)
   See THIRTEEN LOVE SONGS IN JAZZ SETTINGS.

BALLAD (late 1960s)
See THIRTEEN LOVE SONGS IN JAZZ SETTINGS.

THE BARBARA McNAIR SHOW (1970, 1971)
Television. Opening and closing theme and incidental original
music. Winters-Rosen production, syndicated.

BLUE FORMS (1972)
Solo violin. Three movements: Plain Blue/s; Just Blue/s;
Jettin' Blue/s. Tosci Music. Dedicated to and first performed
(1972) by Sanford Allen at Carnegie Hall.

BLUE/S FORMS II (in progress)
Solo trumpet and either orchestra or chamber orchestra. Projected as a four- or five-movement work, the movements of
which will be based on famous blues choruses of such trumpet
players as Miles Davis, Dizzy Gillespie, and Clifford Brown.

BLUES (late 1960s)
See THIRTEEN LOVE SONGS IN JAZZ SETTINGS.

BLUES WITH A TAG (late 1960s)
See THIRTEEN LOVE SONGS IN JAZZ SETTINGS.

CALVARY (circa 1952)
See STRING QUARTET NO. 1.

CALVARY OSTINATO (1973)
See LAMENTATIONS: A BLACK/FOLK SONG SUITE FOR UN-
ACCOMPANIED CELLO.

CANONS (circa 1965)
See SONATINA FOR PERCUSSION.

CEREMONIES IN DARK OLD MEN (1974)
Television. Negro Ensemble Company production, ABC television network. Tosci Music.

COMMENTARY (1964)
Violoncello and orchestra. Composer describes the work as a
concert piece in two parts. Tosci Music. Commissioned by
the National Association of Negro Musicians. Dedicated to Kermit Moore. First performance (1967) by the Symphony of the
New World, Benjamin Steinberg, conductor; Kermit Moore,
violoncello.

CONCERTO FOR VIOLA AND ORCHESTRA (1953)
Three movements, but performed without pauses. Tosci Music.
Dedicated to Selwart Clark. First performance (1964) by the
Orchestra of America, Coleridge-Taylor Perkinson, conductor;
Selwart Clark, viola. This work was the composer's Master's
thesis.

CROSSROADS AFRICA (circa 1962)
Film score.   United States Information Agency production.
Tosci Music.

DUNBAR (in progress)
Solo voice, chorus, and orchestra.   Texts by Countee Cullen
and Paul Laurence Dunbar.   Dedicated to Paul Laurence Dunbar.

THE EDUCATION OF SONNY CARSON (1974)
Film score.   Paramount.

FORCES OF RHYTHM (1972-73)
Ballet score.   Tosci Music.   Commissioned by the Dance Theater of Harlem.

FREDOME-FREEDOM (1970)
Chorus (SATB) with chamber ensemble or piano (chamber ensemble consists of two pianos, electric bass, and percussion).
Texts by John Barbour and James Russell Lowell in addition to
lines from a traditional spiritual.   Tosci Music, 1970.   Dedicated to and first performed (1971) by the New York All-City
High School Chorus, John L. Motley, conductor.

FUGUE (circa 1965)
See SONATINA FOR PERCUSSION.

FUGUING TUNE (1973)
See LAMENTATIONS: A BLACK/FOLK SONG SUITE FOR UN-
ACCOMPANIED CELLO.

GOD IS A (GUESS WHAT)? (1968)
Music for Ray McIver's play God Is a (Guess What)?   Negro
Ensemble Company production.   Tosci Music.

GRASS: A POEM FOR PIANO, STRINGS, AND PERCUSSION (1956)
Three movements, but performed without pauses.   Tosci Music.
Inspired by and based on Carl Sandburg's poem "Grass."

THE GREAT MACDADDY (1974)
Music for Paul Carter Harrison's play The Great MacDaddy.
Negro Ensemble Company production.   Tosci Music.

HAPPY BIRTHDAY MRS. CRAIG (circa 1971)
Film score.   Belafonte Enterprises production.

HUNDREDTH PSALM (circa 1949)
Chorus (SSA), brass, and strings.   Biblical text.   Tosci Music.
First performance (1951) at Town Hall by the St. Cecelia Club,
Hugh Ross, conductor.

IN 4 (late 1960s)
See THIRTEEN LOVE SONGS IN JAZZ SETTINGS.

J. T. (1972)
Music for the television pilot J. T.

JETTIN' BLUE/S (1972)
See BLUE FORMS.

JUST BLUE/S (1972)
See BLUE FORMS.

LAMENTATIONS: A BLACK/FOLK SONG SUITE FOR UNACCOM-
PANIED CELLO (1973)
Four movements: Fuguing Tune; Song Form; Calvary Ostinato;
Perpetual Motion. Tosci Music. First performance (1973) at
Alice Tully Hall. Ronald Lipscomb, violoncello.

THE LOU RAWLS SPECIAL (1971)
Television. Winters-Rosen Production, syndicated.

LULLABY (early 1950s)
See THREE SONGS OF ROBERT HILLYER.

THE MACMASTERS
Film score. Jayjen Productions.

MADRIGAL (early 1950s)
See THREE SONGS OF ROBERT HILLYER.

MALCOCHON (1969)
Music for Derek Walcott's play Malcochon. Negro Ensemble
Company production. Tosci Music.

MAN BETTER MAN (1969)
Music for Erroll Hill's play Man Better Man. Negro Ensemble
Company production. Tosci Music.

MEMPHIS TO MOBILE (1969)
Film score. Mr. Perkinson created the score for this film,
but did not write the music. See his discussion of this as a
portion of his response to I-1.

NIGHTSIDE (1972)
Music for the television pilot Nightside.

NINE ELIZABETHAN LOVE LYRICS (circa 1952)
Voice and piano. Nine songs. Texts by William Shakespeare,
Ben Jonson, and other Elizabethan poets. Tosci Music.

ODE TO OTIS (1971)
Ballet score. Based on two Otis Redding tunes: "Dock of the
Bay" and "Happy Song." Tosci Music. Commissioned by and
first performed (1971) by the Arthur Mitchell Dance Company
(Dance Theater of Harlem).

THE PASSION OF JUSTICE ACCORDING TO JUDICIAL DOCUMEN-
TATION (in progress)
Opera or large-scale theater piece. Libretto to be based on the
transcript of the Panther 13 trial, with excerpts from other historical trials.

PERPETUAL MOTION (1973)
See LAMENTATIONS: A BLACK/FOLK SONG SUITE FOR UN-
ACCOMPANIED CELLO.

PIANO SONATA NO. 1 (circa 1965)
Three movements. Tosci Music.

PIANO SONATA NO. 2 (1975)
Alternate title: STATEMENTS. Three movements. Tosci Music. Commissioned by the Washington Performing Arts Society
with a grant from the Edyth Bush Charitable Foundation, Inc.
Dedicated to Armenta Adams, who will give the first performance of this work November 27, 1976 at the Kennedy Center as
part of the Washington Performing Arts Society Bicentennial
Piano Series.

PLAIN BLUE/S (1972)
See BLUE FORMS.

PSALM 23 (late 1960s)
Chorus (SSATB) unaccompanied. Biblical text. Tosci Music.

RIFF NO. 1 (late 1960s)
See THIRTEEN LOVE SONGS IN JAZZ SETTINGS.

RIFF NO. 2 (late 1960s)
See THIRTEEN LOVE SONGS IN JAZZ SETTINGS.

RIFF NO. 3 (late 1960s)
See THIRTEEN LOVE SONGS IN JAZZ SETTINGS.

ROOM 222 (1970)
Television. Original underscore music for various episodes.
Twentieth-Century Fox, ABC television network.

SCHERZO (early 1950s)
Piano. Tosci Music. First performance (1976) at the New
York Historical Society. Sylvia Walton, piano.

SERENADE (early 1950s)
See THREE SONGS OF ROBERT HILLYER.

SEVENTH SONG (late 1960s)
See THIRTEEN LOVE SONGS IN JAZZ SETTINGS.

A SHORT MOVEMENT FOR TREBLE INSTRUMENT AND PIANO
(early 1950s)
Tosci Music.

SINFONIETTA NO. 1 FOR STRINGS (1956)
   String orchestra. Three movements. Tosci Music. First
   performance (1966) in Hilversum, Netherlands by the Radio
   Kammer Orchest.

SONATINA FOR PERCUSSION (circa 1965)
   Percussion (8 players). Three movements: Canons; Song Form;
   Fugue. Tosci Music.

SONG FORM (circa 1965)
   See SONATINA FOR PERCUSSION.

SONG FORM (1973)
   See LAMENTATIONS: A BLACK/FOLK SONG SUITE FOR UN-
   ACCOMPANIED CELLO.

SONG OF THE LUSITANIAN BOGEY (1967)
   Music for Peter Weiss's play Song of the Lusitanian Bogey.
   Negro Ensemble Company production.

SONGS TO SPRING (late 1960s)
   Voice and piano. Text by Diane di Prima. Tosci Music.

STATEMENTS (1975)
   See PIANO SONATA NO. 2.

STRING QUARTET NO. 1: CALVARY (early 1950s)
   Three movements. Tosci Music. First performance (early
   1950s) at Carnegie Hall by the Cumbo Quartet.

THIRTEEN LOVE SONGS IN JAZZ SETTINGS (late 1960s)
   Voice and piano. Text by Diane di Prima. Blues with a Tag;
   Blues; Ad Lib + Tune; Riff No. 1; Riff No. 2; To Be?; Seventh
   Song; In 4; Back Beat; Riff No. 3; Ballad; Ad Lib + Changes;
   Abstract Blues. Tosci Music.

THOMASINE AND BUSHROD (1974)
   Film score. Warner Brothers.

THREE SONGS OF ROBERT HILLYER (early 1950s)
   Voice and piano. Text by Robert Hillyer. Serenade; Madrigal;
   Lullaby. Tosci Music. First performance (early 1950s) at
   Town Hall. Eugene Brice, baritone.

TO BE? (late 1960s)
   See THIRTEEN LOVE SONGS IN JAZZ SETTINGS.

TO DAMASCUS (1960)
   Incidental music for Strindberg's play To Damascus.

TOCCATA (early 1950s)
   Piano. Tosci Music. Dedicated to and first performed by
   Samuel Dilworth.

TOGETHER FOR DAYS   (circa 1972)
    Film score.   This film was an independent production.

VARIATIONS AND FUGUE ON "THE ASH GROVE"   (early 1950s)
    Violin and piano.   Tosci Music.

A WARM DECEMBER   (circa 1972)
    Film score.   Verdon Productions Limited.

---------------   (in progress)
    Jazz ensemble (improvisational) and large orchestra.

BIBLIOGRAPHY

Claghorn, Charles E.   Biographical Dictionary of American Music.
    West Nyack, N.Y.:   Parker Publishing Company, 1973.

Roach, Hildred.   Black American Music: Past and Present.   Boston:
    Crescendo Publishing Company, 1973.

Southern, Eileen.   The Music of Black Americans.   New York:
    W. W. Norton, 1971.

George A. Russell (courtesy of the composer)

CHAPTER X

GEORGE ALLAN RUSSELL

George Allan Russell was born June 23, 1923 in Cincinnati,
Ohio.　He attended Wilberforce University for a short time, but
was forced to withdraw because of illness.　In 1945 and 1946 he
was hospitalized for sixteen months, and it was during this period
that he formulated the principles behind his theoretical masterwork,
The Lydian Chromatic Concept of Tonal Organization.

George Russell's initial compositional success was Cubana
Be Cubana Bop, a work written for Dizzy Gillespie.　This composition, acknowledged as the first to combine jazz and Latin influences,
was given its premiere performance at Carnegie Hall in December
of 1947 by the Dizzy Gillespie Big Band under the direction of the
composer.　Mr. Russell wrote sporadically for the next several
years, studying with composer Stephan Wolpe and producing such
compositions as Ezz-thetic (commissioned by Lee Konitz) and A
Bird in Igor's Yard (commissioned by Buddy DeFranco).　In 1950
he dropped all his compositional and performing activities for four
years in order to devote himself totally to the production and refinement of the lydian concept, which was published for the first
time in 1953.　The Lydian Chromatic Concept of Tonal Organization
is the first theoretical treatise to come from jazz, and is one which
points directions for the future of the music as well as codifying,
justifying, and explaining the past and present.　Entire bodies of
music currently utilize the harmonic and melodic implications of the
lydian concept, and the now pervasive modal school received its
initial impetuses from the concept as early as 1953.　The Lydian
Chromatic Concept of Tonal Organization has been revised and expanded several times since its initial publication, and Mr. Russell
is presently involved in writing what will eventually become books
two and three of the concept.　He has taught the lydian concept for
over twenty years, both privately and at such institutions as the
School of Jazz (Lenox, Mass.), Lund University (Sweden), Vaskilde
Summerschool (Denmark), Tanglewood, and the New England Conservatory of Music, where he has been a member of the faculty
since 1969.

Mr. Russell has been the recipient of numerous awards and
grants, including Metronome's Outstanding Composer Award (1958),
down beat's Best Composer award (1961), France's Oscar Du Disque

277

De Jazz (1961) for his album New York, N.Y., two Guggenheim
Fellowships (1969, 1972), grants from the National Endowment for
the Arts in 1969 and 1976, and the 1976 National Music Award
recognizing Mr. Russell as one of 121 people having made substantial and significant contributions to American music from 1776 to
1976.

Mr. Russell's best-known works include All About Rosie
(commissioned for the Brandeis University Festival of Fine Arts),
Ezz-thetic, Cubana Be Cubana Bop, Stratusphunk, New Donna and
The Lydiot, in addition to extended compositions such as Living
Time (commissioned by Columbia Records), Listen to the Silence
(commissioned by the Norwegian Cultural Fund for the 1971 Kongsberg Jazz Festival), and Electronic Sonata for Souls Loved by Nature.

Part I: General Questions

1. Q: What persons, events, and works (of art, literature, etc.)
      have influenced you in general as well as in terms of your
      musical activities?
   A: Those who have shown me the way not to go have contrib-
      uted most in my life, that is, those who have chosen a
      path that has caused them to die in life before physical
      death--the manipulators of all shades and colors.

2. Q: How would you define black music?
   A: Terminology like "black music" might be suspected as slick
      Madison Avenue terminology, so therefore I suppose it de-
      serves a slick question like this. It assumes, first of all,
      that the term is freely and universally accepted beyond
      question by all. It is loaded with the heavy hand of styli-
      zation. It begs to be answered on that level. I believe
      black music does exist, but its definition can be on the
      parochial level of the mangled terms "soul" and "roots" or
      it can be on the level of the lost high knowledge of ancient
      Abyssinian civilization. It should have to do with the world
      struggle between conscious and mechanical forces. It should
      have to do with the richness of experience, not money.

3. Q: What features of your own music do you see as uniquely
      black (in terms of both musical and philosophical considera-
      tions)?
   A: The substitution of the tone F$\sharp$ (instead of F natural) as
      the fourth degree of a diatonic C scale, and the conviction
      that the lydian scale is a much more scientifically profound
      scale upon which to base a world of music. The construc-
      tion of a seven-note scale by using a succession of inter-
      vals of fifths (lydian scale structure) has been the basis for
      scalar structure in certain non-Western cultures from be-
      fore Pythagorean times.

4. Q: In what ways is your music a reflection of your personal philosophy (social, political, etc.)?

   A: It reflects the idea that freedom exists only in higher law. Everything is under a law; therefore, freedom does not exist. The higher the level of law a thing exists in ... the more objective the law, the greater degree of freedom.

5. Q: What do you see as the position or role of the black artist in contemporary society?

   A: To show a new path to human evolution based upon his ancient high African heritage.

6. Q: Please discuss any problems you may have encountered in getting your works performed, published, and recorded.

   (Ed. note: Mr. Russell chose not to address himself to the general portion of question six; he moved directly to the specifics of 6A, 6B, and 6C.)

6A. Q: How much of your actual output has ever been performed? Published? Recorded?

   A: All.

6B. Q: Have you encountered difficulty in getting your works programmed?

   A: Of course.

6C. Q: Are there specific problems in getting a satisfactory performance? Exemplify and discuss.

   A: No. I've gotten great performances from musicians of countries as remote as Finland.

7. Q: What do you consider, at this point in your life, to be your most significant achievement(s) aside from your compositions?

   A: The lydian chromatic concept of tonal organization. [1]

8. Q: What do you see as the responsibilities and obligations of the educational system (at all levels) to the study of black music?

   A: Again, it depends on how one defines black music. The aim of the educational system should be to awaken from a deep sleep in general, not just wake up to one more slogan that it will pretend to understand but in reality does not understand at all.

9. Q: Do you feel that the people who write about your music (critics in particular) understand what you are doing? Exemplify and discuss.

   A: Jazz, or Afro-American music (as it should be known), is the only serious music which is at the mercy of fans (old and new) who have the nerve to dare to criticize an art music without "knowing do from re, " as a friend of mine has explained. [2] This is all because of the American attitude toward the Negro as a relaxed, happy fellow. Still, there are some people who take their jobs as critics seriously and are artists in their own right.

At the roots of this ignoble state of affairs lies the attitude of the Western World toward art in general as a form of entertainment. I believe that in ancient times music was viewed as an expression of universal laws. It served as a catalytic agent through which one was brought into contact with these higher laws. This is objective as opposed to subjective art. The function of objective art is to inform the highest centers of one's being rather than entertain the senses.

10. Q: What advice would you give to the aspiring young black composer?
    A: Make the richness of experience your aim.

Part II: Music Questions

1. Q: When you sit down to begin a new composition on your own initiative or inspiration (as opposed to a commissioned work), what procedure or approach do you follow?
   A: This question assumes that one works under different laws when there is no money involved. Slightly ridiculous!

2. Q: When composing a commissioned work or a work written for a specific occasion or person, does your procedure or approach differ from the one you described in question one? If so, in what way?
   A: Again, the answer to this question is married to the previous answer. It assumes that one's musical philosophy changes to meet the occasion.

3. Q: In general, with regard to your writing, what genre(s) do you prefer?
   A: Black music. Just black music.

4. Q: What do you consider your most significant composition? Please discuss.
   A: Listen to the Silence. The reason is that it is complete for me.

5. Q: Please comment on your treatment of the following musical elements and give examples from your compositions that illustrate the techniques you describe:
   A. Melody
   B. Harmony
   C. Rhythm
   D. Form
   E. Improvisation
   F. Text (both choice and treatment)
   G. Instrumentation or medium (both in terms of choice of particular combinations as well as how you treat them compositionally)

GR: All the above listed elements behave according to certain modes of behavior. If one can categorize how they behave, then one will obtain the possibility of finding the scales of these elements which leads to the composition of form itself.

6. Q: Have difficulties with performance practice (inflection, phrasing, etc.) been a significant problem in having your works performed to your own satisfaction?
   A: Each performance has its own inflections, phrasing, etc. Why should one be a connoisseur of only one way to have a work sound?

7. Q: What major works are currently in progress? Please describe and discuss.
   A: Books two and three of the Lydian Chromatic Concept. Book two will be the ultimate finality of the tonal part of the Lydian Chromatic Concept and book three will deal with rhythm and form.

8. Q: Given unlimited time and finances (and no restrictions whatsoever) what would you write?
   A: Nothing. There must be struggle to evolve.

9. Q: If given the opportunity would you choose to devote yourself to composition on a full-time basis? Why or why not?
   A: No. Composition is only the medium through which I speak of musical law. It is this researching of musical law that I consider my chief task in my life's work.

10. Q: How would you describe your compositional style?
    A: I have never settled on one style, and I don't think I ever will.

11. Q: What have been the influences of other composers, styles, and other types of music on your compositional style?
    A: I listen to everything and everybody who has a new musical law to offer. I repeat: I have no style. But I might add that I am particularly interested in those artists who change the musical aesthetic, such as Charlie Parker, Thelonious Monk, Louis Armstrong, and Ornette Coleman. You might add György Ligeti and Stockhausen to that.

12. Q: Has your style changed across your career? If so, what influenced these changes or developments?
    A: I have never had a style, but I feel that my music has evolved over the years, that it has never stayed the same.

13. Q: When you are listening to music for your own enjoyment, what are your preferences?
    A: Those few musicians who are in touch with the depth of musical law and who make it their life.

Notes to Chapter X

1. In the introduction to his book The Lydian Chromatic Concept
of Tonal Organization for Improvisation Mr. Russell describes the
lydian concept as follows: The Lydian Chromatic Concept is an
organization of tonal resources from which the jazz musician may
draw to create his improvised lines. The Lydian Chromatic Concept of Tonal Organization is a chromatic concept providing the
musician with an awareness of the full spectrum of tonal colors
available in the equal temperament tuning. There are no rules, no
"do's" or "don'ts." It is, therefore, not a system, but rather a
view or philosophy of tonality in which the student, it is hoped,
will find his own identity.
    For Mr. Russell's explanation of how he formulated the lydian
concept see Pat Wilson, "George Russell's Constant Quest," down
beat 39, no. 8 (April 27, 1972): 15, 28-29.

2. Mr. Russell specified that at this point in the interview a ref-
erence should be made to Meetings with Remarkable Men by Georges
I. Gurdjieff. Meetings with Remarkable Men is the second part of
Gurdjieff's three-part work All and Everything, of which Harcourt,
Brace and Company has published parts one and two (New York:
1950).

LIST OF COMPOSITIONS

ALL ABOUT ROSIE (1956)
    Jazz ensemble. Russ-Hix Music. Recorded by George Russell
    (Columbia WL-127: Modern Jazz Concert); by Gerry Mulligan
    (Verve V-8415: Gerry Mulligan Presents a Concert in Jazz);
    and by an ensemble which included Bill Evans and Art Farmer
    (Columbia C2S-831: Outstanding Jazz Compositions of the 20th
    Century). Commissioned by Brandeis University. First per-
    formance (1957) at the Brandeis University Festival of Fine
    Arts.

THE BALLAD OF HIX BLEWITT (1956)
    Jazz ensemble. Russ-Hix Music. Recorded by the George
    Russell Smalltet (RCA Victor LPM-1372: George Russell--The
    Jazz Workshop).

BIG CITY BLUES (1958)
    Jazz ensemble. Russ-Hix Music. Recorded by George Russell
    (Decca DL-79216: New York, N.Y.; MCA 2-4017: New York,
    N.Y. and Jazz in the Space Age).

A BIRD IN IGOR'S YARD (1949)
    Jazz ensemble. Beechwood Music Corporation. Recorded by
    Buddy De Franco (Capitol M-11060, Capitol Jazz Classics
    Series, Vol. 14: Cross-Currents). Commissioned by Buddy
    De Franco.

BLUES IN ORBIT (1962)
Jazz ensemble. Russ-Hix Music. Recorded by the George
Russell Septet (Riverside RLP-9412: The Stratus Seekers;
Riverside RS-3043: 1, 2, 3, 4, 5, 6extet) and by Gil Evans (Atlan-
tic SD-1643: Svengali).

CHROMATIC UNIVERSE: PARTS 1, 2, and 3 (1959)
Jazz ensemble. Russ-Hix Music. Recorded by George Russell
(Decca DL-79219: Jazz in the Space Age; MCA 2-4017: New
York, N.Y. and Jazz in the Space Age).

CONCERTO FOR BILLY THE KID (1956)
Jazz ensemble. Russ-Hix Music. Recorded by the George
Russell Smalltet (RCA Victor LPM-1372: George Russell--The
Jazz Workshop).

CONCERTO FOR SELF-ACCOMPANIED GUITAR (1962)
Russ-Hix Music. Recorded by Rune Gustafsson (Sonet SLP-
1411/1412: The Essence of George Russell).

CUBANA BE CUBANA BOP (1946)
Jazz ensemble. Robbins Music. Recorded by Dizzy Gillespie
(RCA Victor LPM-2398: The Greatest of Dizzy Gillespie; RCA
Victor 731068, Black & White Series, Vol. 34: Dizzy Gillespie
and His Orchestra, Vol. II). Commissioned by Dizzy Gillespie.

D. C. DIVERTIMENTO (1962)
Jazz ensemble. Russ-Hix Music. Recorded by the George
Russell Sextet (Riverside RM-440: The Outer View; Riverside
RS-3016: The Outer View).

THE DAY JOHN BROWN WAS HANGED (1956)
Jazz ensemble. Russ-Hix Music. Recorded by the Hal
McKusick Quartet (RCA Victor LPM-1366: Hal McKusick--
The Jazz Workshop). Commissioned by Hal McKusick.

DIMENSIONS (1958)
Jazz ensemble. Russ-Hix Music. Recorded by George Russell
(Decca DL-79219: Jazz in the Space Age; MCA 2-4017: New
York, N.Y. and Jazz in the Space Age).

ELECTRONIC ORGAN SONATA NO. 1 (1969)
Russ-Hix Music. Recorded by George Russell (Flying Dutchman
FDS-122; Sonet SLP-1409).

ELECTRONIC SONATA FOR SOULS LOVED BY NATURE (1968)
Jazz ensemble and electronic tape. Russ-Hix Music. Recorded
by George Russell (sextet version is on Flying Dutchman FDS-
124; big band version is on Sonet SLP-1411/1412: The Essence
of George Russell). First performance (1969) at the Hennie/
Onstad Center for the Arts in Oslo, Norway.

EZZ-THETIC (1949)
Jazz ensemble. Russ-Hix Music. Recorded by Lee Konitz

(Prestige 116: Ezz-thetic; Prestige 7827: Ezz-thetic); by the George Russell Smalltet (RCA Victor LPM-1372: George Russell --The Jazz Workshop); by the George Russell Sextet (Riverside RLP-9375: Ezz-thetics; Milestone M-47027: Outer Thoughts); and by Max Roach (Trip 5522: Max Roach Plus Four). Commissioned by Lee Konitz.

FELLOW DELEGATES (1956)
Jazz ensemble. Russ-Hix Music. Recorded by the George Russell Smalltet (RCA Victor LPM-1372: George Russell--The Jazz Workshop).

FREEIN' UP (1965)
Jazz ensemble. Russ-Hix Music. Recorded by the George Russell Sextet (SABA SB-15059: The George Russell Sextet at Beethoven Hall; MPS MC-25125: The George Russell Sextet at Beethoven Hall).

A HELLUVA TOWN (1958)
Jazz ensemble. Russ-Hix Music. Recorded by George Russell (Decca DL-79216: New York, N.Y.; MCA 2-4017 (New York, N.Y. and Jazz in the Space Age).

JACK'S BLUES (1955)
Jazz ensemble. Russ-Hix Music. Recorded by the George Russell Smalltet (RCA Victor LPM-1372: George Russell--The Jazz Workshop).

KNIGHTS OF THE STEAMTABLE (1956)
Jazz ensemble. Russ-Hix Music. Recorded by the George Russell Smalltet (RCA Victor LPM-1372: George Russell--The Jazz Workshop).

LISTEN TO THE SILENCE (1971)
Jazz ensemble, chorus (SATB), and bass soloist. Text is drawn from the following sources: Newsweek magazine (2/2/71); Dee Brown's Bury My Heart at Wounded Knee; The New York Times (7/8/70); Maurice Nicoll's The Mark; and Ranier Maria Rilke's Duano Elegies. Russ-Hix Music, 1970. Recording (Concept Records CR-002) is of the first performance. Commissioned by the Norwegian Cultural Fund for the 1971 Kongsberg Jazz Festival. First performance (1971) at the Kongsberg Church (Kongsberg, Norway). Chorus of the Musikk Konservatoriet of Oslo, Norway, Arnuv Hegstad, conductor; Dan Windham, bass.

LIVING TIME: EVENTS I-VIII (1972)
Jazz ensemble. Russ-Hix Music. Recorded by George Russell and Bill Evans (Columbia KC-31490). Event V also appears on Columbia CG-31574: The Progressives. Commissioned by Columbia Records.

LIVINGSTONE I PRESUME (1955)
Jazz ensemble. Russ-Hix Music. Recorded by the George

Russell Smalltet (RCA Victor LPM-1372: George Russell--The Jazz Workshop).

A LONELY PLACE   (1962)
    Jazz ensemble.   Russ-Hix Music.   Recorded by the George Russell Septet (Riverside RLP-9412: The Stratus Seekers).

LYDIA AND HER FRIENDS   (1965)
    Jazz ensemble.   Russ-Hix Music.   Recorded by the George Russell Sextet (SABA SB-15059: The George Russell Sextet at Beethoven Hall; MPS MC-25125: The George Russell Sextet at Beethoven Hall).

LYDIAN LULLABY   (1955)
    Jazz ensemble.   Russ-Hix Music.   Recorded by the Hal McKusick Quartet (RCA Victor LPM-1366: Hal McKusick--The Jazz Workshop).   Commissioned by Hal McKusick.

LYDIAN M-1   (1955)
    Jazz ensemble.   Russ-Hix Music.   Recorded by the Teddy Charles Tentet (Atlantic 1229: The Teddy Charles Tentet). Commissioned by Teddy Charles.

THE LYDIOT   (1959)
    Jazz ensemble.   Russ-Hix Music.   Recorded by George Russell (Decca DL-79219: Jazz in the Space Age; MCA 2-4017: New York, N.Y. and Jazz in the Space Age; Riverside RLP-9375: Ezz-thetics).

MANHATTAN-RICO   (1958)
    Jazz ensemble.   Russ-Hix Music.   Recorded by George Russell (Decca DL-79216: New York, N.Y.; MCA 2-4017: New York, N.Y. and Jazz in the Space Age).

MAY IN DECEMBER   (1951)
    Jazz ensemble.   Lyric by Hix Blewitt.   Russ-Hix Music.

MISS CLARA   (1956)
    Jazz ensemble.   Russ-Hix Music.   Recorded by the Hal McKusick Octet (RCA Victor LPM-1366: Hal McKusick--The Jazz Workshop).   Commissioned by Hal McKusick.

THE NET   (1967)
    See OTHELLO.

NEW DONNA   (1960)
    Jazz ensemble.   Russ-Hix Music.   Recorded by the George Russell Sextet (Riverside RLP-9341: Stratusphunk).

NIGHT SOUND   (1956)
    Jazz ensemble.   Russ-Hix Music.   Recorded by the George Russell Smalltet (RCA Victor LPM-1372: George Russell-- The Jazz Workshop).

NITA (1958)
    Jazz ensemble. Russ-Hix Music. Recorded by Art Farmer
    (Contemporary 7027: Portrait of Art Farmer). Commissioned
    by Art Farmer.

NITA (1958)
    For melody and chord symbols see Russell, The Lydian Chro-
    matic Concept of Tonal Organization for Improvisation, p. 21.

NOW AND THEN (1965)
    Jazz ensemble. Russ-Hix Music. Recorded by George Russell
    (Sonet SLP-1411/1412: The Essence of George Russell).

ODJENAR (1949)
    Jazz ensemble. Russ-Hix Music. Recorded by Lee Konitz
    (Prestige 116: Ezz-thetic; Prestige 7827: Ezz-thetic).

OH JAZZ, PO' JAZZ (1965)
    Jazz ensemble. Russ-Hix Music. Recorded by the George
    Russell Sextet (SABA SB-15060: The George Russell Sextet at
    Beethoven Hall, Part 2; MPS MC-25125: The George Russell
    Sextet at Beethoven Hall).

OTHELLO (1967)
    Ballet score. Russ-Hix Music. Commissioned by Norwegian
    television as music for the ballet THE NET.

OTHELLO BALLET SUITE (1967)
    Jazz ensemble. Russ-Hix Music. Recorded by George Rus-
    sell (Flying Dutchman FDS-122; Sonet SLP-1409).

THE OUTER VIEW (1962)
    Jazz ensemble. Russ-Hix Music. Recorded by the George
    Russell Sextet (Riverside RM-440: The Outer View; Riverside
    RS-3016: The Outer View; Milestone M-47027: Outer Thoughts).

PAN-DADDY (1962)
    Jazz ensemble. Russ-Hix Music. Recorded by the George
    Russell Septet (Riverside RLP-9412: The Stratus Seekers;
    Milestone M-47027: Outer Thoughts).

ROUND JOHNNY RONDO (1956)
    Jazz ensemble. Russ-Hix Music. Recorded by the George
    Russell Smalltet (RCA Victor LPM-1372: George Russell--The
    Jazz Workshop).

THE SAD SERGEANT (1956)
    Jazz ensemble. Russ-Hix Music. Recorded by the George
    Russell Smalltet (RCA Victor LPM-1372: George Russell--The
    Jazz Workshop).

THE STRATUS SEEKERS (1962)
    Jazz ensemble. Russ-Hix Music. Recorded by the George

Russell Septet (Riverside RLP-9412: <u>The Stratus Seekers</u>;
Riverside RS-3043: <u>1, 2, 3, 4, 5, 6extet</u>; Milestone M-47027:
<u>Outer Thoughts</u>).

STRATUSPHUNK (1958)
Jazz ensemble. Russ-Hix Music. Recorded by the Hal McKu-
sick Sextet (Decca DL-79209: <u>Cross Section--Saxes</u>); by the
George Russell Sextet (Riverside RLP-9341: <u>Stratusphunk</u>;
Milestone M-47027: <u>Outer Thoughts</u>); by J. J. Johnson (RCA
Victor LPM-3350: <u>The Dynamic Sound of J. J. with Big Band</u>);
and by Gil Evans (Impulse AS-4: <u>Out of the Cool</u>).

STRATUSPHUNK (1958)
For melody and chord symbols see Russell, <u>The Lydian Chromatic Concept of Tonal Organization for Improvisation</u>, p. 36.

SWINGDOM COME (1960)
Jazz ensemble. Russ-Hix Music. Recorded by the George
Russell Sextet (Decca DL-79220: <u>The George Russell Sextet
at the Five Spot</u>).

TAKIN' LYDIA HOME (1965)
Jazz ensemble. Russ-Hix Music. Recorded by the George
Russell Sextet (SABA SB-15059: <u>The George Russell Sextet at
Beethoven Hall</u>; MPS MC-25125: <u>The George Russell Sextet at
Beethoven Hall</u>).

THEME (1961)
Jazz ensemble. Russ-Hix Music. Recorded by the George
Russell Sextet (Decca DL-74183: <u>The George Russell Sextet
in Kansas City</u>).

THINGS NEW (1960)
Jazz ensemble. Russ-Hix Music. Recorded by the George
Russell Sextet (Riverside RLP-9341: <u>Stratusphunk</u>).

THOUGHTS (1961)
Jazz ensemble. Russ-Hix Music. Recorded by the George
Russell Sextet (Riverside RLP-9375: <u>Ezz-thetics</u>; Riverside
RS-3043: <u>1, 2, 3, 4, 5, 6extet</u>; Milestone M-47027: <u>Outer Thoughts</u>).

VOLUPTE (1964)
Jazz ensemble. Russ-Hix Music. Recorded by the George
Russell Sextet (SABA SB-15060: <u>The George Russell Sextet at
Beethoven Hall, Part 2</u>; MPS MC-25125: <u>The George Russell
Sextet at Beethoven Hall</u>).

WALTZ FROM OUTER SPACE (1959)
Jazz ensemble. Russ-Hix Music. Recorded by George Russell
(Decca DL-79219: <u>Jazz in the Space Age</u>; MCA 2-4017: <u>New
York, N.Y. and Jazz in the Space Age</u>).

WEST OF BENCHAZI (1949)
Jazz ensemble. Beechwood Music Corporation.

WITCH HUNT (1956)
   Jazz ensemble. Russ-Hix Music. Recorded by the George Russell Smalltet (RCA Victor LPM-1372: George Russell--The Jazz Workshop).

YE HYPOCRITE, YE BEELZEBUB (1956)
   Jazz ensemble. Russ-Hix Music. Recorded by the George Russell Smalltet (RCA Victor LPM-1372: George Russell--The Jazz Workshop).

BIBLIOGRAPHY

Part I: Works about the composer

Brooks, John Benson. "George Russell." Jazz Review 3 (February 1960): 38-39.

Cerulli, Dom. "George Russell." down beat, 29 May 1958.

Crane, Genevieve Sue. "Jazz Elements and Formal Compositional Techniques in 'Third Stream' Music." Master's thesis, Indiana University, 1970.

Feather, Leonard. The Encyclopedia of Jazz in the Sixties. New York: Horizon Press, 1966.

_____. The New Edition of the Encyclopedia of Jazz. New York: Horizon Press, 1960.

Jones, Olive. "Conversation with George Russell: A New Theory for Jazz." The Black Perspective In Music 2 (Spring 1974): 63-74.

Kraner, Dietrich H. "George Russell: A Discography Compiled by Dietrich H. Kraner." Matrix 69 (February 1967): 3-8.

Linden, Ken. "George Russell." Jazz & Pop, April 1970.

McCarthy, Albert; Morgan, Alun; Oliver, Paul; and Harrison, Max. Jazz on Record. A Critical Guide to the First 50 Years: 1917-1967. New York: Oak Publications, 1968.

"Random Thoughts from George Russell." down beat, 29 July 1965.

Riley, John Howard. "A Critical Examination of George Russell's Lydian Chromatic Concept of Tonal Organization for Improvisation." Master's thesis, Indiana University, 1967.

"Tangents." down beat, 18 June 1964. This is a panel discussion on the problems of small jazz bands. The persons involved in

the discussion are George Russell, Oliver Nelson, Cannonball
Adderley, Gary McFarland, and Don De Michael.

Who's Who Among Black Americans, 1st ed. (1975-76), s.v. "Russell, George A."

Who's Who in America. 39th ed. (1976-77), s.v. "Russell, George
Allen." [sic]

Wilson, Pat. "George Russell's Constant Quest." down beat, 27
April 1972.

Part II: Works by the composer

Russell, George. The Lydian Chromatic Concept of Tonal Organization for Improvisation. New York: Concept Publishing Co.,
1959.

_____. "Where Do We Go from Here?" In The Jazz Word,
edited by Dom Cerulli, Burt Korall, and Mort Nasatir. New
York: Ballentine Books, 1960.

Russell, George, and Williams, Martin. "Ornette Coleman and
Tonality." Jazz Review 3 (June 1960): 7-10.

CHAPTER XI

ARCHIE VERNON SHEPP

Archie Shepp was born May 24, 1937 in Fort Lauderdale, Florida. He was raised in Philadelphia where he studied piano, clarinet, and alto saxophone as a child before switching to tenor saxophone. Upon graduation from high school he was awarded a full academic scholarship to Goddard College, where he majored in theater. He received his B. A. from Goddard in 1959 and continued his education with further studies at the New School for Social Research and Hunter College.

Mr. Shepp has taught in the New York City public school system and has worked for the city's department of welfare and for New York's Mobilization for Youth. Prior to accepting his current position on the faculty of the University of Massachusetts (Amherst), he was a lecturer in music and assistant director of the black studies program at the State University of New York at Buffalo, where he also served as associate director of the Experimental Program for Independent Study.

Mr. Shepp has been the recipient of numerous honors and awards, including the Grand Prix du Jazz for his album Mama Too Tight and the 1964 New Star Award from down beat magazine. He has been named Jazz Man of the Year in both England (1965) and Holland (1966). Among his best-known compositions are "Wherever June Bugs Go, " "Mama Too Tight, " "Hambone, " "Rufus, " "Malcolm, Malcolm--Semper Malcolm, " and "A Portrait of Robert Thompson. "

In addition to his prodigious activities as a performer and recording artist, Mr. Shepp is a well-known writer whose output includes a number of plays and dramatic works in addition to poetry and short stories. He has also written a number of articles which have appeared in such publications as down beat, Jazz, and The New York Times. He is very active as a lecturer on a variety of subjects and is considered by many to be one of black music's most eloquent spokesmen.

Part I: General Questions

1. Q: What persons, events, and works (of art, literature, etc.)

Archie Shepp (courtesy of BMI/Archives)

have influenced you in general as well as in terms of your musical activities?

A: Well, I would say first my father and mother. My father was a banjo player and my mother sang very beautifully. They provided me with an opportunity to listen to the great masters: Duke Ellington, Oscar Pettiford, Panama Francis, Ben Webster, and Illinois Jacquet. They very graciously provided me with music lessons and with a piano and later a clarinet to practice on. My aunt and my grandmother later bought me a saxophone. I consider these the primary influences because they are the most practical ones.

There are other people who have influenced me: Lee Morgan, Cal Massey, John Coltrane, Clarence Sharp, Hank Mobley, Benny Golson, Lucky Thompson, Edward Kennedy Ellington, Billy Strayhorn, Fletcher Henderson, Don Redman, Langston Hughes, Richard Wright, Ralph Ellison, and Imamu Baraka. I've been influenced by a lot of people.

Q: Are there any events or works of art and literature you'd like to discuss?

A: The book <u>Native Son</u> had a great effect on me.

2. Q: How would you define black music?

A: I think that the definition is oral; I don't think there's a literary definition. For example, I'm beginning to question the pedagogy that is being developed for teaching it at the university level, largely because it seems to me that the structure is designed for failure. The average institution has five or six specialists on Bach or Beethoven alone. The University of Massachusetts, for example, has me and Professor Max Roach (who is a university unto himself!) to teach black music, and they have no intentions of expanding the faculty--quite the contrary. So a definition of black music to me would first have to assume a certain economic foundation and community strength in support of the artist which seem to me not to exist. Black music right now is an apparition. It's a shadow. It is a reality only in the living presence of the work of the Lester Youngs, the Charlie Parkers, and the Louis Armstrongs.

How would you define black music? How can you? Can you touch it? Where do they teach it? They teach it in the streets, but the streets have no credibility in our society. I first met Bud Powell in a basement in Willow Grove, Pennsylvania, where I was rehearsing with a group called The Jolly Rompers--Carl Holmes, Lee Morgan, Reggie Workman, and myself. And Bud, who lived just across the way, walked in with his nurse. He didn't say a word, as was his wont at the time. He had sustained a very savage beating and it was after that that he began to have mental trouble. In fact, it was described to me thusly: a gentleman who had been in his company said that you could almost see his scalp breathing! So when you ask me how I would define black music, I say it's <u>murder</u>! Genocide! They're trying to kill us! There is a cultural genocide that I'm addressing myself to! I think that there will be a point at which we do define black music, but the implications are that at that time we must have a system and an economic basis to provide that this music is taught adequately and permanently.

3. Q: What features of your own music do you see as uniquely black (in terms of both musical and philosophical considerations)?

A: Ironically, this is a questionnaire for composers. I've never given that much attention to writing music. I have always put writing music in a certain context, largely because I think that most of the great body of black music is not what is written down. Take, for example, the great Count Basie orchestra of the 1930s with its unique rhythm, swing, drive, harmony, and imagination. Most of what they did involved head arrangements, things like "Royal Garden

Blues, " "One O'Clock Jump, " "Prince of Wales, " and all
of those things. I think that a great deal of what goes into
composition, at least in this idiom, is intuitive. I found
that out through working with people like Cecil Taylor,
people who you would think would be top-heavy with written
notes but who are not. Once they derive the formula, they
discard the visual image.

4. Q: In what ways is your music a reflection of your personal
       philosophy (social, political, etc.)?

5. Q: What do you see as the position or role of the black artist
       in contemporary society?
       (Ed. note: In the course of responding to question four, Mr.
       Shepp also addressed himself to question five.)
    A: It's always hard to say. Music is another language. I
       think that black people are quite fortunate. Perhaps it was
       even through this other language that we survived slavery.
       In my work, both in terms of shaping the notes and the
       texts (where there have been poems or songs), I have at-
       tempted to address myself to what I consider the plight of
       African-American people here in the diaspora. I'm deeply
       influenced in this way by people like Charlie Mingus, Max
       Roach, and especially Duke, because in his works we have
       a running chronicle of the history of black people here in
       the United States: "Harlem Air Shaft, " "Black and Tan
       Fantasy, " "Black Beauty. " He expressed negritude and
       black consciousness at a time when very few people even
       dared to deal with it, at least so openly. In terms of my
       own social-political being, I've tried for example to include
       poetry as an adjunct to the music because I feel that at
       some point we have to be more specific in addressing our-
       selves to a racist society. It seemed very easy for people
       to go and hear John Coltrane and come away with all sorts
       of strange notions about what he was playing. And yet when
       I hear Jean Carn singing the lyrics to those songs, it's
       precisely what you would think. I think of John Coltrane as
       one of the most militant of people, as one who addressed
       himself to many things through the medium of his horn.
       People like John and their music have obviously influenced
       me very greatly in numerous ways. To the extent that I
       express socio-political ideas, I am influenced by them.
       Not that they verbally told me to do this! I think black
       music is an unselfconscious affirmation. In fact, we don't
       really have to say anything; just play the music! We have
       enough Eldridge Cleavers and Imamu Barakas now to define
       that socio-political thing out there. By a musician being
       too outspoken, he can get himself blacklisted (no pun in-
       tended). It's a fact that some of the things I've said in
       print have already been used against me by many of the
       entreprenuers. For example, we did the Newport tour in
       1967, and it was very successful. [1] That's where the
       Donaueschingen album came from. That long applause

section went on for half an hour; that's how successful we were when we went there in 1967. But do you know that we were never asked by the promoter of that concert to go back again? I have not worked for him in Europe since 1967 even though we were playing with the best groups in the country and following Miles and Monk and groups like that. That was no mean feat over there because these groups quite naturally had followings that had been built up since the 1940s. We had a highly successful tour and yet we were never asked to go back again. You know, I've always questioned that because they tell you about things like supply and demand and about how this is really a free society. It's not. It's a slave society, and anyone who has been outspoken will certainly find that he can't find a job.

In one way, I'm answering both questions four and five because the role of the black artist in contemporary society is directly related to what is happening socially, politically, and so on. I'm questioning how free a black person is to say just what he or she feels in this society without severe repercussions. There were people who spoke out before me. I think of Max Roach and Charlie Mingus, who had gone out much earlier and had not only said things, but had also tried to form a recording label. Although I was not the first person to speak out and to write things, I certainly felt like I was coming from somewhere. After all, the whole critical establishment is essentially a white, Anglo-Saxon clique. I was helped as a writer by the fact that I have some style, but it was mostly the content that the critics objected to. I think they also objected to black people being verbal and articulate about this music because the assumptions about what the music is have been so wrong. I think Max is perfectly right in saying that we should dispense with the use of the term jazz because it is too ambiguous in the social-political context. The critics were quite obviously threatened, not so much by my eloquence or my articulateness as a black person, but by the fact that I perhaps represented something that they had always miscalculated. Maybe this was what Charlie Parker had been saying to them all the time. It's not popular to go on record against war in a country which is fighting a war. It is not popular to be anti-racist in a country that spends all its money fomenting racism. These things can be dangerous for an individual.

6. Q: Please discuss any problems you may have encountered in getting your works performed, published, and recorded.

   A: To some extent I have answered number six. What problems have I encountered in getting my works performed, published, and recorded? I'll also add to this the problems of getting grants and so on, because we did stage a demonstration at the Guggenheim Foundation several years ago. I had applied for a grant and had been turned down, and so

in concert with Brother Rahasaan Kirk and Beaver Harris
and a number of other people who supported me, we had a
play-in at the Guggenheim Foundation. We brought our
instruments and went to their offices and sat down in the
main office and played music until we got them to sit down
with us. The following year, Mr. Ornette Coleman was
put on their jury, which was a significant step for them.

But obviously there are problems. I think that we have
been proscribed through racism from getting the real grant
money, like from the National Endowment and agencies like
that. We just get a drop in the bucket compared to what
the others get. I think it's due to an attitude and a predilection for academic phenomena and closed systems, all
of which boils down to a racist ethic as far as I'm concerned. There's five hundred years of slavery behind this.
It's a question now if these people are going to, in the words
of the spiritual, let our people go, and allow black youngsters to achieve anything they're capable of achieving, and
to provide equality of opportunity, and so on.

Yes; I've had a number of problems in getting my
works performed and published. I'll give you an example.
When I started to use singers on recordings, the producers
at the company I was working for became very upset. They
said, "Listen. You're spending $25,000-$30,000 a year and
you're a jazz outfit. You're bringing too many musicians
into the studio, all these strings and all that." Now I was
being put down on the other hand by a number of kids who
accused me of turning my back on the avant-garde. I never
went for that title anyway; it's essentially white, and it's
like having to step over your father's body to keep going,
you know? On the one hand, I couldn't accept myself as
being different from the people who came before me. But
when I went into the studio and I took Joe Lee Wilson in,
the first thing the producer said to me was, "Hurry up and
get him out! Get him out of here! He's costing me money!
He's costing me money!" Now do you think that when they
take the Beatles into the studio, that's what they say?

I worked for Epic Records for a time as an A & R
trainee, a job which ironically I got through the Welfare
Department! And it just so happened that the guy I worked
for, Dave Kapralik, was producing Sly and the Family
Stone and Peaches and Herb. Dave liked me because he
knew that I was sort of different from the other guys. I
wasn't really cut out for that kind of work. I only stayed
there a couple of weeks, but I got to know something about
the business. At that time, Dave was recording Dino Valen-
ti, a guy he was very hot on. He had spent close to
$100,000 on Dino and Dino had not put out a single record-
ing because he wasn't satisfied with any of the things he
had heard in the studio. They called Dave in on the carpet
because he had something like a half-million dollar budget
and he had spent almost every dime of it. When this thing
came up about Dino, I thought back to the times when I

had tried to take singers into the studio and had been told to get them out because I was taking up too much time and costing the company too much money.

When we got around to doing things like Attica Blues and The Cry of My People, the A & R man at the time, Ed Michel, said to me, "Listen. If we could call you Archie and His Rock Band, we could make a lot of money. But this way, you're costing us too much." And the next year they dropped my contract because I was getting out of the jazz category. That's why I say that jazz is a pernicious word; it's being used against us! They told Miles that the reason he wasn't making any money was because he plays jazz, so he said, "Well, shit! I don't play no more jazz then!" He automatically started to make more money. It's a fact. He used to come to the Jazz Workshop here in Boston; now he goes next door to Paul's Mall, which is owned by the same people, but is where all the slick groups go. See, he's no longer just a jazz man. I'm not questioning what black folks mean by the term jazz, but I am questioning what white folks mean by it. It's like the term avant-garde. Once you've been locked into that kind of a phony label, they've got you blacklisted. Entrepreneurs will say, "He's a troublemaker. He loses money. He plays that noise." That's how they talk about you. And I'm going to tell you, it keeps you from working. All it's designed to do is keep you out of a job. Even the universities are nests of racist attitudes. It's amazing! I've really seen the face of America at the University of Massachusetts, and if these are the kinds of institutions that are manufacturing our morality and ethics, this country is in sad shape.

6A. Q: How much of your actual output has ever been performed? Published? Recorded?

A: I don't know; I've never figured that out. I've had pretty good success with performance. I've written for two or three shows, including Lady Day and Slave Ship. I've written for my own productions June Bug Graduates Tonight and A Trilogy of One-Act Plays. These have not been recorded commercially, but they have been performed. June Bug, a play I wrote and composed the music for, was done at the Chelsea Theater in 1965 under a Rockefeller grant. Incidentally, June Bug was originally entitled The Communist, but they didn't think that would go over too big. Changing the name apparently didn't help, either. After June Bug, I really began to question the efficacy of compromise on any level, because it didn't do a damn bit of good. I might as well have called it The Communist. It lasted two weeks, anyway.

6B. Q: Have you encountered difficulty in getting your works programmed?

A: Yes, there have been certain difficulties. I think that, as

jazz musicians, we are stigmatized by the very name because of its many implications. Stephen Longstreet's book
Sportin' House is really a bombshell; it ought to be required
reading. I don't endorse all of Longstreet's observations.
He seems to be a little too clinical and objective. But one
thing he does tell you is exactly what New Orleans was.
Aside from all that beautiful music that was being made,
there was nothing happening except prostitution. There was
no real culture outside of that of the black people there in
Congo Square. Time and time again it is overlooked that
the real cultural basis in this country is not white but black.
Do I have problems getting things performed? All over the
place! Problems getting things programmed? All over the
place!

6C. Q: Are there specific problems in getting a satisfactory performance? Exemplify and discuss.
   A: Writing a satisfactory contract. That says it all.

7. Q: What do you consider, at this point in your life, to be your
most significant achievement(s) aside from your compositions?
   A: My family.

8. Q: What do you see as the responsibilities and obligations of
the educational system (at all levels) to the study of black
music?
   A: Tenure; that's the magic word. Max says that all students
should get $10,000 a year to go to college, because if they
were suddenly to be turned loose on the world, they would
constitute the biggest unemployed group in the country.
Figure it out; what does the government spend on unemploy-
ment compensation and all that? I'm advising my students
to stay in school, to get that Ph.D., and then go for a
master's in some other field because the government has got
to fund education and they know it. Like it or not, that is
somehow part of the system.
      We can't determine exactly what we want to see educa-
tion doing every moment, but certainly, as a strategy, I
think that every student ought to decide to remain a student
for the time being and not put himself in the job market,
because that, to me, is tantamount to being unemployed.
The market has been satiated. It's bloated. There's too
much of a good thing. There is too much money in too
few hands, and the people who've got it don't feel like
spending it.
      And now, back to tenure. Tenure has a lot of impli-
cations, and what it seems to indicate is that there is a
white academic establishment. I was at the University of
Buffalo for three or four years and I've been here now for
three years. [2] From what I've seen, there is a white establishment. Take the union, for example. We don't have
a teachers' union here, but we're trying to get one and I

opted to join. I'm not going to withdraw my initial opting, but I really feel that the situation is so discouraging and frustrating for black people. I'm dissatisfied with the university system as I see it functioning, but at the same time, if I want to join or try to build a teachers' union, that is also very frustrating. You would be amazed at just how middle-of-the-road the union is in its opinions, racial and otherwise. It's almost like being a part of another lily-white group. It's very frustrating, and I think that the black teacher at the white university has a hard row to hoe. It reminds me of something I heard Mr. Roy Eldridge, one of the great musicians of our people, say in a radio interview. When he was working with the Gene Krupa band, they would travel to Las Vegas and places like that. He said that when they would finish playing, all the other guys would go out into the audience and to the bar and socialize. But the racial laws were so strict that he either had to go to his room or sit in a corner. And he said at one point in the interview that no matter how much money they paid him, it just was not worth that kind of indignity. I think that's what we're up against.

9. Q: Do you feel that the people who write about your music (critics in particular) understand what you are doing? Exemplify and discuss.

A: Well, some do and some don't. I think that when you talk about people writing about music, you're discussing a very tenuous phenomenon. You can't put your finger on it too well because most of them are liars. They're liars! They lie! I know it! They lie; they never told the truth unless they were forced to! That may sound very pessimistic to you. In fact, it may even sound paranoid. But that doesn't mean I'm wrong. It doesn't mean that we're wrong because, in that sense, I don't want to be right, but I hope we're right. I want to be right, but I hope we're right together.

10. Q: What advice would you give to the aspiring young black composer?

A: I would tell him to treat music as an integral aspect of his life. I would tell him not to look to make money playing black music; I would tell him not to expect to make a dime. It may make him cry, but that'll make his blues stronger. There's not much in it by way of fame or fortune. It's something one has to love the way we loved the gods we sang to: Ogun, Shango, Legba, and Damballa.

Part II: Music Questions

1. Q: When you sit down to begin a new composition on your own initiative or inspiration (as opposed to a commissioned work), what procedure or approach do you follow?

A: I start with a feeling--or maybe an experience--and I try to get that feeling into music.

Q: Do you work at the piano?

A: I do now. I didn't used to have a piano, except when I was a kid and living at home with my parents. When I went to New York, I didn't have a piano because I didn't have an apartment that would have held a piano. Even if I had had a piano, I would have had to pay for it. Living away from home was quite different from living at home. That's why I credit my parents with much of the musical development I've been able to experience. When I got away from home, I realized how bereft and starved I was.

2. Q: When composing a commissioned work or a work written for a specific occasion or person, does your procedure or approach differ from the one you described in question one? If so, in what way?

A: Well, usually the money is different. I think you have to deal with that. That has become so endemic to our relationship. How does it affect me when somebody pays me money? I feel better! It means that I'm not being treated in the same old way. I know what it feels like to be a slave, believe me!

3. Q: In general, with regard to your writing, what genre(s) do you prefer?

A: I like to write anything that the song calls for.

4. Q: What do you consider your most significant composition? Please discuss.

A: I see my work as a total body. The purpose of what I'm doing seems to me far more significant than merely defining the reality in terms of Aristotelian logic. In other words, how could I do this work if that work hadn't helped me do it? I wouldn't put anything I've done down. Why would I do that? Would I put my big toe down because my little toe is smaller? The little toe might have helped the big toe to grow. I wouldn't want to be without either of them!

5. Q: Please comment on your treatment of the following musical elements and give examples from your compositions that illustrate the techniques you describe.
   A. Melody
   B. Harmony
   C. Rhythm
   D. Form
   E. Improvisation
   F. Text (both choice and treatment)
   G. Instrumentation or medium (both in terms of choice of particular combinations as well as how they are treated compositionally)

A: That sounds very technical, but what it all adds up to is economics. Can you afford it? You may be the best writer in the world, but if you can't afford strings, what difference does it make? I saw this happen recently with the Andrew

White concert here at this college. The French horn players never showed up for rehearsals because they were too
busy, and they were white at that. Why were they white?
Because black kids are not encouraged to play that instrument. Go to communities like South Philadelphia and southside Chicago. You're not going to find a plethora of harps
and harpsichords and those kinds of instruments. You're
not even going to find music teachers kicking around there.
They think they're doing enough for the niggers already.
These niggers are doing all right if they get peanut butter
sandwiches for lunch, and I know what I'm talking about
because I taught public school in New York. Do you think
they're teaching these kids <u>music</u>? My father said to me
when I was a boy, "Music is a hobby, son." That, to me,
is a challenge. Is black music just something you do on a
Saturday night? That answers this question on melody,
harmony, rhythm, form, and improvisation: it's just something you do on a Saturday night. Ultimately, you have to
answer that question when you look into your children's
faces and they say, "Daddy, I need lunch money. Daddy,
I need a new pair of shoes." My Daddy told me that music
is a hobby. So maybe it's a hobby. If it's a hobby, then
Lord, I've given my life to a hobby! Maybe that's what
I've done.

I think we've got to do something, and we've got to
do something <u>now</u>! It's been going on too long. They've
hurt too many of us. I've watched them kill my people,
and I'm not going to stand by any longer, at least without
saying that I think this is a hobby. Music for a nigger <u>is</u>
a hobby! White folks make a lot of money playing black
music. A nigger will never make a dime; if he makes a
dime, he's lucky. But that's good, because this country
is giving up less and less. I'm opposed to what I see, and
I'll go on record as being opposed to what I see being done
to my people!

6. Q: Have difficulties with performance practice (inflection, phrasing, etc.) been a significant problem in having your works
performed to your own satisfaction?

   A: No, because I've been learning a lot about notation and
things like that. Basically, I feel like what would be called
a folk musician. I remember reading in Mr. Ellington's
autobiography about a time when he was writing something
which was giving him problems musically. He ran into
Mr. Will Marion Cook, whom he called Dad Cook because
Mr. Cook was one of the deans of black composers, like
Mr. William Grant Still. And Mr. Cook said to him, "Well,
you really ought to go to music school and learn these things
another way, but since I know you're not going to do that,
I'll tell you what's happening."[3]

7. Q: What major works are currently in progress? Please describe and discuss.

   A: I want to write a play, but I've got no money.

Q: Have you written to the National Endowment for the Arts? Maybe they could provide you with some financial assistance.

A: Well, I doubt it. They're usually looking for a certain approach, and I write very traditionally, but not in a standard way. That's why I went through the thing with the Guggenheim Foundation that I told you about. 4 I sent them reams of scores, which probably made them think that I didn't know how to write music. That's why I sent the recordings with the scores, so that they could see that even if they thought I didn't know how to write, other people thought I could. They couldn't have played the music if I hadn't been able to write it, right? I would have had to hum it to them or sing it to them; although that was possible, that wasn't how it was done. The thing I resented was their telling me that there is only one way to write music and that is by using standard notation. I don't buy that!

I have a play in mind that I'd like very much to write. It would deal with a black family that moves from the South to the North, and with their struggle to buy a home. They have a son who is a musician. He goes off to college and never really comes back home. He's the oldest son, and when he comes back, he finds things very different than when he left. He doesn't feel needed. It goes on like that.

8. Q: Given unlimited time and finances (and no restrictions whatsoever), what would you write?

A: I'd like to write that play, and not only that one because I've got quite a few others that I'd like to write. I'm not trying to write the great American drama or no shit like that, because I don't believe in that. I don't think of America that way. I don't think there's much that is "American." America is really like a patchwork quilt.

9. Q: If given the opportunity would you choose to devote yourself to composition on a full-time basis? Why or why not?

A: Yes, because I think Bird is one of the greatest composers that America has produced. Haiku; seventeen syllables. That's what I'm talking about. A cameo, a beautiful flower, a dove, its call. It may be only a moment, but it's such a beautiful moment. People in this country tend to think that if a person writes 5,000 pages of music, it's worth more than if someone writes 50 songs, and that's silly. That's like going to a junk shop and finding out that 50,000 pounds of paper are worth more than a rag.

Yes, I would be a composer--a composer and a performer. They are one in the same. What I want to do is play music.

10. Q: How would you describe your compositional style?

A: I feel like I'm a folk musician. I don't make much about myself. Whatever I am, I hope it's worth something, but there isn't much I can say about it. I love music. I

always have. If people like my music and I can make somebody happy with it, that's a wonderful thing. It's a wonderful thing to make somebody happy with music, because there
are not many things in life that can make you happy, you
know. People talk a lot about happiness, but there are
very few things that can make you happy. Music is one
of them. It can take you literally and dramatically from a
sorrowful state to a happy state. It can make you feel better. It's a healing force. I go along with Brother James
Brown and Aretha and Stevie and all of them on that; I'm
with them on that!

11. Q: What have been the influences of other composers, styles,
and other types of music on your compositional style?

A: Cecil Taylor was the first composer I met, and he helped
me immensely. He helped me play my horn. Mr. Ellington and Mr. Strayhorn were the first composers I heard,
but Cecil was the first composer I met. Ornette is a fine
composer, too.

Q: Have any other types of music been influential?

A: African music. I've been listening to that, to West Indian
music (particularly music from Haiti and Trinidad), and to
music from Brazil.

12. Q: Has your style changed across your career? If so, what
influenced these changes or developments?

A: I hope it has changed. My style is the same, but I hope
that I've grown and I've learned. Style is a word I don't
like to use much because it is sort of an English language
word; it means that you put on a new shirt or new shoes
and suddenly you're something different. I don't deal much
with style.

13. Q: When you are listening to music for your own enjoyment,
what are your preferences?

A: All of it. All of it! I love music!! I just want to say a
word about Mr. Sonny Clark and Mr. Bobby Timmons--
beautiful piano players. I happen to have had the privilege
of hearing both of them. They are my Stravinskys, my
Bachs, my Beethovens.

Notes to Chapter XI

1. The album to which Mr. Shepp is referring is Live at the
Donaueschingen Music Festival (SABA SB 15 148 ST).

2. Mr. Shepp is a member of the faculty of the Afro-American
Studies Department at the University of Massachusetts (Amherst
Campus).

3. The incident to which Mr. Shepp is referring can be found in

Edward Kennedy Ellington, Music Is My Mistress (Garden City, New
York: Doubleday & Co., 1973), p. 97.

4. See his response to I-6.

LIST OF COMPOSITIONS

ABSTRACT
Jazz ensemble. Dawn of Freedom. Recorded by Archie Shepp
(Impulse AS-9188: For Losers).

ANON
ABC Dunhill Music.

ATTICA BLUES
Jazz ensemble. Text by William G. Harris. Co-published by
Dawn of Freedom and Becabiverip. Recorded by Archie Shepp
(Impulse AS-9222: Attica Blues).

AU PRINTEMPS
Pab Music.

AUCTION BLOCK SONG
Dawn of Freedom.

BACK BACK
Jazz ensemble. Dawn of Freedom. Recorded by Archie Shepp
(Impulse AS-9262: Kwanza).

BALLAD FOR A CHILD
Jazz ensemble. Text by William G. Harris. Co-published by
Dawn of Freedom and Becabiverip. Recorded by Archie Shepp
(Impulse AS-9222: Attica Blues).

BASHEER
Jazz ensemble. Dawn of Freedom. Recorded by Archie Shepp
(Impulse AS-9134: Mama Too Tight; Impulse AS-9267: No
Energy Crisis).

BEELZEBUB
Merpine Music.

BLASE
Jazz ensemble. Dawn of Freedom.

BLUE SOAP
Music for Lenox Raphael's play Blue Soap.

BLUES FOR BROTHER GEORGE JACKSON
Jazz ensemble. Dawn of Freedom. Recorded by Archie Shepp
(Impulse AS-9222: Attica Blues).

A BLUES TRIBUTE TO STEAM MINCER
Pab Music.

BUGALOO YORUBA
Dawn of Freedom.

CALL ME BY MY RIGHTFUL NAME
Jazz ensemble. ABC Dunhill Music. Recorded by Archie
Shepp (Impulse AS-94: New Thing at Newport).

CAPTAIN MARVEL JR.
ABC Dunhill Music.

THE CHASED
Jazz ensemble. ABC Dunhill Music. Recorded by Archie
Shepp (Impulse AS-9101: The Definitive Jazz Scene; Impulse
AS-9284: The Bass).

CONSEQUENCES
Jazz ensemble. Crossroads Music. Recorded by Archie Shepp
(Savoy MG-12184: Bill Dixon 7-tette/Archie Shepp and the New
York Contemporary Five).

UN CROQUE MONSIEUR (POEM: FOR LOSERS)
Jazz ensemble. Text by the composer. Dawn of Freedom.
Recorded by Archie Shepp (Impulse AS-9188: For Losers).

DANGEROUS GAMES
Ballet score. Text by Brian MacDonald. Commissioned by the
Ballets Theatre Contemporain.

DEDICATION TO JAMES BROWN
See THREE FOR A QUARTER.

DELICADO
Jazz ensemble. Merpine Music. Recorded by Marion Brown
(Impulse AS-9139: Three for Shepp).

DOIN' THE THING
ABC Dunhill Music.

ET MOI
ABC Dunhill Music.

EXACTEMENT
Merpine Music.

FAT BACK
ABC Dunhill Music.

FESTIVAL SONG
Dawn of Freedom.

FIESTA
Jazz ensemble. Dawn of Freedom. Recorded by Archie Shepp
(Impulse AS-9170: The Way Ahead).

THE FLASH
ABC Dunhill Music.

FOR MODS ONLY
Jazz ensemble. Dawn of Freedom. Recorded by Chico Hamil-
ton (Impulse AS-9130: The Dealer; Impulse AS-9213: Chico
Hamilton--His Greatest Hits).

FRANKENSTEIN

THE FUNERAL
Jazz ensemble. Crossroads Music. Recorded by Archie Shepp
(Delmark DS-9409: Archie Shepp in Europe--Volume 1--With
the New York Contemporary Five. Dedicated to Medgar Evers.
This composition was later re-written and re-titled MALCOLM,
MALCOLM--SEMPER MALCOLM.

GINGERBREAD, GINGERBREAD BOY
Jazz ensemble. Pab Music. Recorded by Archie Shepp (Impulse
AS-97: On This Night).

HAMBONE
Jazz ensemble. Embassy Music. Recorded by Archie Shepp
(Impulse AS-86: Fire Music; Impulse AS-90: New Wave in
Jazz).

INVOCATION TO MR. PARKER
Jazz ensemble. Text by Bartholomew Gray. Dawn of Free-
dom. Recorded by Archie Shepp (Impulse AS-9222: Attica
Blues).

IT IS THE YEAR OF THE RABBIT
Jazz ensemble. Recorded by Archie Shepp (Arista/Freedom
AL-1016: There's a Trumpet in My Soul).

LADY DAY: A MUSICAL TRAGEDY
Music for the two-act drama Lady Day: A Musical Tragedy by
Aishah Rahman. First performance (1971) at the Brooklyn Aca-
demy of Music (Brooklyn, N.Y.).

LIKE A BLESSED BABY LAMB
Jazz ensemble. Crossroads Music. Recorded by Archie Shepp
(Savoy MG-12184: Bill Dixon 7-tette/Archie Shepp and the New
York Contemporary Five).

THE MAC MAN
Jazz ensemble. ABC Dunhill Music. Recorded by Archie
Shepp (Impulse AS-97: On This Night).

THE MAGIC OF JU-JU
  Jazz ensemble. Dawn of Freedom. Recorded by Archie Shepp
  (Impulse AS-9154: The Magic of Ju-Ju; Impulse AS-9272: The
  Drums).

MALCOLM, MALCOLM--SEMPER MALCOLM
  Jazz ensemble. Text by the composer. Pab Music. Recorded
  by Archie Shepp (Impulse AS-86: Fire Music). Dedicated to
  Malcolm X. This work is a revision of an earlier composition
  entitled THE FUNERAL.

MAMA ROSE
  Jazz ensemble. Dawn of Freedom. Recorded by Archie Shepp
  (BYG 529.311: Poem for Malcolm).

MAMA TOO TIGHT
  Jazz ensemble. Dawn of Freedom. Recorded by Archie Shepp
  (Impulse AS-9272: Mama Too Tight; Impulse D-9228: Energy
  Essentials).

LE MATIN DES NOIRE
  Jazz ensemble. Pab Music. Recorded by Archie Shepp (Impulse
  AS-94: New Thing at Newport).

MONEY BLUES
  Jazz ensemble. Co-written by William G. Harris. Co-published
  by Dawn of Freedom and Becabiverip. Recorded by Archie
  Shepp (Impulse AS-9212: Things Have Got To Change).

MY ANGEL
  Dawn of Freedom.

LOS OLVIDADOS
  Jazz ensemble. ABC Dunhill Music. Recorded by Archie Shepp
  (Impulse AS-86: Fire Music).

ON THIS NIGHT (IF THAT GREAT DAY WOULD COME)
  Jazz ensemble. Text by the composer. Pab Music. Recorded
  by Archie Shepp (Impulse AS-97: On This Night). Dedicated
  to W. E. B. DuBois.

ONE FOR A DIME
  Jazz ensemble. Embassy Music. Recorded by Archie Shepp
  (Impulse AS-9162: Three for a Quarter: One for a Dime).

ONE FOR THE TRANE
  Jazz ensemble. Dawn of Freedom. Recorded by Archie Shepp
  (SABA SB-15148-ST: Live at the Donaueschingen Music Festival; MPS 20651: One for the Trane). Dedicated to John Coltrane.

THE ORIGINAL MR. SONNY BOY WILLIAMSON
  Jazz ensemble. ABC Dunhill Music. Recorded by Archie
  Shepp (Impulse AS-97: On This Night).

THE OUIJA MAN
Merpine Music.

THE PAWN
Pab Music.

THE PELOPONNESIAN WAR
Ballet score. Co-composed with Eric Salzman. Commissioned
by Daniel Nagrin. First performance (1968) at New York State
University College at Brockport.

THE PICKANINNY (PICKED CLEAN--NO MORE--OR CAN YOU
BACK BACK DOODLEBUG)
Jazz ensemble. Embassy Music. Recorded by Archie Shepp
(Impulse AS-97: On This Night).

POEM FOR MALCOLM
Jazz ensemble. Dawn of Freedom. Recorded by Archie Shepp
(BYG 529.311: Poem for Malcolm).

A PORTRAIT OF ROBERT THOMPSON AS A YOUNG MAN
Jazz ensemble. Dawn of Freedom. Recorded by Archie Shepp
(Impulse AS-9134: Mama Too Tight).

RAIN FOREST
Jazz ensemble. Dawn of Freedom. Recorded by Archie Shepp
(BYG 529.311: Poem for Malcolm).

RUFUS (SWUNG HIS FACE AT LAST TO THE WIND, THEN HIS
NECK SNAPPED)
Jazz ensemble. ABC Dunhill Music. Recorded by Archie Shepp
(Impulse AS-94: New Thing at Newport; Impulse AS-71: Four
for Trane; Impulse AS-9272: The Drums).

SAMBA DA RUA
Jazz ensemble. Recorded by Archie Shepp (Arista/Freedom
AL-1016: There's a Trumpet in My Soul).

SCAG
Jazz ensemble. Text by the composer. ABC Dunhill Music.
Recorded by Archie Shepp (Impulse AS-94: New Thing at New-
port).

THE SECOND JUBA LEE
Merpine Music.

SHAN A LAN A LING
Pab Music.

SHAZAM
Jazz ensemble. Dawn of Freedom. Recorded by Archie Shepp
(Impulse AS-9154: The Magic of Ju-Ju).

SLAVE SHIP
    Incidental music for LeRoi Jones's play <u>Slave Ship</u>. Co-com-
    posed with Gilbert Moses. First performance (1969) in Brook-
    lyn, New York.

SLOW DRAG
    Jazz ensemble. Dawn of Freedom. Recorded by Archie Shepp
    (Impulse AS-9262: <u>Kwanza</u>).

SORRY 'BOUT DAT
    Jazz ensemble. Dawn of Freedom. Recorded by Archie Shepp
    (Impulse AS-9154: <u>The Magic of Ju-Ju</u>).

SPOO PEE DOO
    Jazz ensemble. Dawn of Freedom. Recorded by Archie Shepp
    (Impulse AS-9262: <u>Kwanza</u>).

SPOOKS
    Jazz ensemble. Mention Music. Recorded by Marion Brown
    (Impulse AS-9139: <u>Three For Shepp</u>).

STEAM
    Jazz ensemble. Text by the composer. Dawn of Freedom.
    Recorded by Archie Shepp (Impulse AS-9222: <u>Attica Blues</u>).

STICK 'EM UP
    Jazz ensemble. Lyric by the composer. Dawn of Freedom.
    Recorded by Archie Shepp (Impulse AS-9188: <u>For Losers</u>).

THREE FOR A QUARTER
    . Jazz ensemble. Embassy Music. Recorded by Archie Shepp
    (Impulse AS-9162: <u>Three for a Quarter; One for a Dime</u>).
    This work was originally entitled DEDICATION TO JAMES
    BROWN.

TOUAREG
    Jazz ensemble. Dawn of Freedom.

U-JAMAA
    Jazz ensemble. Recorded by Archie Shepp (Arista/Freedom
    AL-1027: <u>Montreux One</u>).

VESPERS
    ABC Dunhill Music.

THE VILLAIN
    ABC Dunhill Music.

THE WEDDING
    Jazz ensemble. Text by the composer. ABC Dunhill Music.
    Recorded by Archie Shepp (Impulse AS-9118: <u>Archie Shepp Live
    in San Francisco</u>).

WEST INDIA
Jazz ensemble. Mention Music. Recorded by Marion Brown (Impulse AS-9139: Three for Shepp).

WHERE POPPIES BLOOM
Jazz ensemble. Crossroads Music. Recorded by Archie Shepp (Savoy MG-12184: Bill Dixon 7-tette/Archie Shepp and the New York Contemporary Five).

WHEREVER JUNE BUGS GO
Jazz ensemble. Embassy Music. Recorded by Archie Shepp (Impulse AS-9118: Archie Shepp Live in San Francisco).

YASMINA
Jazz ensemble. Dawn of Freedom.

YOU'RE WHAT THIS DAY IS ALL ABOUT
Jazz ensemble. Dawn of Freedom. Recorded by Archie Shepp (Impulse AS-9154: The Magic of Ju-Ju).

BIBLIOGRAPHY

Part I: Works about the composer

"Archie Shepp." Melody Maker, 7 August 1965.

BMI: The Many Worlds of Music, April 1967. See page 20 of the "Theater" section for information on Mr. Shepp's play June Bug Graduates Tonight.

Cooke, Jack. "The Avant-Garde." Jazz Monthly 12 (June 1966): 2-9.

Feather, Leonard. "Archie Shepp: Some of My Best Friends Are White." Melody Maker, 30 April 1966.

_____. The Encyclopedia of Jazz in the Sixties. New York: Horizon Press, 1966.

_____. "Shepp: Look Forward in Anger." Music Maker 1 (October 1966): 25-26+.

Heckman, Don. "Archie Shepp." BMI: The Many Worlds of Music, May 1967.

Hentoff, Nat. "Archie Shepp: The Way Ahead." Jazz & Pop 7 (June 1968): 16-17.

_____. "Archie Shepp: The Way Ahead." In The Black Giants, edited by Pauline Rivelli and Robert Levin, pp. 118-121. New

York: The World Publishing Company, 1970. Same as Nat
Hentoff's "Archie Shepp: The Way Ahead" in Jazz & Pop (June
1968).

Hunt, David C. "Coleman, Coltrane, and Shepp: The Need for an
Educated Audience." Jazz & Pop 7 (October 1968): 18-21.

_____. "Coleman, Coltrane, and Shepp: The Need for an Edu-
cated Audience." In The Black Giants, edited by Pauline Rivelli
and Robert Levin, pp. 89-94. New York: The World Publishing Company, 1970. Same as David Hunt's "Coleman, Coltrane,
and Shepp: The Need for an Educated Audience" in Jazz & Pop
(October 1968).

"Jazz and Revolutionary Black Nationalism." This is a panel discussion published in fourteen installments in Jazz. The participants are Archie Shepp, Frank Kofsky, Steve Kuhn, George
Wein, LeRoi Jones, Robert Farris Thompson, Nat Hentoff, and
Father Norman O'Connor. The installments of this discussion
were published as follows: Jazz 5 (April 1966): 28-30; (May
1966): 27-29; (June 1966): 28-30; (July 1966): 34-35; (August
1966): 28-29; (September 1966): 29-30; (October 1966): 39-41;
(November 1966): 37-38; (December 1966): 43-45; Jazz 6 (January 1967): 38; (April 1967): 30; (May 1967): 38; (June 1967): 30;
(July 1967): 37-38.

Jones, LeRoi. "Archie Shepp Live." Jazz 4 (January 1965): 8-9.

_____. "Voice from the Avant Garde: Archie Shepp." down
beat, 14 January 1965.

Levin, Robert. "The Third World." Jazz & Pop 10 (June 1971): 10-11.

_____. "The Third World. Archie Shepp II." Jazz & Pop 9
(December 1970): 12.

_____. "The Third World. Archie Shepp: A Period of Reflec-
tion." Jazz & Pop 9 (November 1970): 12.

_____. "The Third World." Jazz & Pop 10 (January 1971): 12.

Litweiler, John B. "Archie Shepp: An Old Schoolmaster in Brown
Suit." down beat, 7 November 1974.

Long, David. "Archie Shepp--Jazz Playwright." Jazz 5 (January
1966): 26.

McCarthy, Albert; Morgan, Alun; Oliver, Paul; and Harrison, Max.
Jazz on Record. A Critical Guide to the First 50 Years: 1917-
1967. New York: Oak Publications, 1968.

McRae, Barry. "Archie Shepp." Jazz Journal 21 (January 1968):34-5.

_____. "Avant Courier. No. 21: Things Have Got to Change." Jazz Journal 27 (February 1974): 26+.

_____. "The Traditionalism of Archie Shepp." Jazz Journal 28 (September 1975): 14-16.

"The New Jazz." Newsweek, 12 December 1966.

Patterson, Michael. "A Profile-Interview: Archie Shepp." Black World, November 1973, pp. 58-61.

"Point of Contact: A Discussion." down beat Music '66 (11th yearbook), pp. 19-31+. This is a panel discussion on the jazz avant-garde. The participants are Archie Shepp, Cannonball Adderley, Art D'Lugoff, Roland Kirk, Sonny Murray, Cecil Taylor, and Dan Morgenstern.

Raben, Erik, comp. A Discography of Free Jazz. Copenhagen: Karl Emil Knudsen, 1969.

Spellman, A. B. "Introducing Archie Shepp." Metronome 78 (November 1961): 26.

Walker, Malcolm. "Archie Shepp." Jazz Monthly 12 (June 1966): 30-31.

Who's Who Among Black Americans, 1st ed. (1975-76), s.v. "Shepp, Archie Vernon."

Who's Who in America. 38th ed. (1974-75), s.v. "Shepp, Archie Vernon."

Williams, Martin. "The Problematic Mr. Shepp." Saturday Review, 12 November 1966.

Wilmer, Valerie. Jazz People. Indianapolis: Bobbs-Merrill Company, 1970.

_____. "Shepp the Teacher." Melody Maker, 16 October 1971.

_____. "The Tenorist Playwright Who Speaks for Black Expressionism." Melody Maker, 14 October 1967.

Part II: Works by the composer

Shepp, Archie. "An Artist Speaks Bluntly." down beat, 16 December 1965.

_____. "Black Jazz and Black Power." The New York Times.

_____. A Cellwalk to Celestine. Play.

Shepp, Archie. The Communist (later re-titled June Bug Graduates Tonight). Play.

_____. June Bug Graduates Tonight (originally entitled The Communist). Play.

_____. "On Jazz." Jazz 4 (August 1965): 24.

_____. "On Pugilism." Jazz 5 (July 1966): 7.

_____. Revolution. One-act play.

_____. 69. One-act play.

_____. Skulls. One-act play.

_____. "A View from the Inside." down beat Music '66 (11th yearbook), pp. 39-44.

CHAPTER XII

HALE SMITH

Hale Smith was born June 29, 1925 in Cleveland, Ohio. His educational background includes B. M. (1950) and M. M. (1952) degrees from the Cleveland Institute of Music, where he studied theory with Ward Lewis and composition with Marcel Dick. A post-graduate grant enabled him to continue his studies with Professor Dick, his only composition teacher, for an additional two years. Currently a member of the faculty at the University of Connecticut (Storrs), Mr. Smith also taught at the C. W. Post College of Long Island University.

Mr. Smith has received a number of awards and honors including BMI's Student Composers Award (1952) and the prestigious Music Award of the Cleveland Arts Prize (1973). Among the artists and organizations from which he has received commissions are Kermit Moore, Broadcast Music Inc., the Thorne Music Fund, Frank Music Corporation, the Karamu Theater (Cleveland), and Tougaloo College.

Mr. Smith's activities as a composer and arranger have produced music in a wide variety of genres. He has written a number of works in both the areas of concert music and jazz, and has also been active in creating scores for films, commercials, and theatrical productions. His best-known compositions include Contours (recorded by the Louisville Orchestra), In Memoriam--Beryl Rubenstein (recorded by the Kulas Choir and Chamber Orchestra), The Valley Wind (recorded by Hilda Harris and Zita Carno), Evocation (recorded by Natalie Hinderas), and Ritual and Incantations (recorded by the Detroit Symphony for release in Columbia's Black Composers Series).

In addition to his activities as a composer and teacher, Mr. Smith has served as editor for the E. B. Marks Corporation, editor and general musical advisor for the Frank Music Corporation, editor for Sam Fox Music Publishers, and musical consultant for the C. F. Peters Corporation. He is also an expert investigator in the area of music copyrights. Mr. Smith is quite active as a lecturer and consultant on black music and has participated in a number of projects and conferences in that capacity. He has also published several articles dealing with various aspects of Afro-American music and culture.

313

Hale Smith (courtesy of the composer)

Part I: General Questions

1. Q: What persons, events, and works (of art, literature, etc.)
        have influenced you in general as well as in terms of your
        musical activities?

    A: That's a loaded question, but I could start by saying that
        the most specific influences in terms of individuals have
        been my composition teacher Marcel Dick and my theory
        teacher Ward Lewis. Then there was a musician out of
        Chicago (who is still active there) named William Randall;
        he was a very great influence on me when I was in the
        Army and afterward, when he taught me the basic princi-
        ples of orchestration and things like that. Of course, all
        of this takes for granted such things as one's environment,
        parentage, etc. Now, getting a little farther afield, I was
        influenced to a very great extent by the philosophy (more
        than the music) of Charles Ives. I was influenced to a great
        extent by Frank Lloyd Wright. I was also influenced great-
        ly by Duke Ellington, Art Tatum, and other jazz musicians.
        I was not so strongly influenced by the likes of Charlie
        Parker because by that time I had already been formed.
        Schoenberg and Stravinsky were influential, and I'd say that
        Mozart was one of the great influences for me.
            In terms of literature, Samuel Butler, with his book
        The Way of All Flesh, was a great influence on my thoughts
        as far as being a parent is concerned. Then there is the
        book Genji Monogatari, or The Tale of Genji, by Murasaki
        shikibu.[1] I guess that's another way of saying something
        that I've said on a number of occasions, and that is that I
        tend to view all of the accomplishments of man as my own
        basket to dip into.

2. Q: How would you define black music?
3. Q: What features of your own music do you see as uniquely
        black (in terms of both musical and philosophical considera-
        tions)?
    (Ed. note: Mr. Smith chose to answer questions two and three
    together.)
    A: How do I define black music? Well frankly, I think that
        the second and third questions are very closely related. I
        have a joke that I think I might have told once or twice up
        there at I. U. that has to do with defining black music in
        terms of the major practitioners of it. I do this by making
        a contrast between what I would consider black music and
        white music. Now for me the major practitioner of white
        music was Paul Hindemith and the major practitioner of
        black music was (and is) Roger Sessions--Hindemith be-
        cause he tended toward using larger note values (half notes,
        whole notes, and so on), giving his pages a rather light or
        white appearance, and Roger Sessions because he tends to-
        wards notes of smaller values (sixteenths and thirty-seconds),
        causing his pages to tend to look darker. Frankly, when
        we come down to what I call formal music, I think that's

about as far as we're going to get in terms of a definition, except for those elements that come out of one's own background which may or may not be easily discerned. For instance, as I indicated in Black Music in Our Culture, [2] there tend to be rhythms out of ragtime and also Charleston rhythms that pop up in my pieces. Then also, regardless of the type of structure, very frequently there are harmonic progressions reminiscent of the blues, and other jazz idioms. But I don't know whether these things are specifically or uniquely black or not. I think that when we are dealing with popular music, things of this nature can be more easily discerned.

Now it has been said that Contours and some other pieces of mine show signs of call and response patterns, but I couldn't say that they are uniquely black because all we're talking about there is antiphony. So I couldn't really say. Farther than that, I'm not even sure that judgments of this kind are all that valid, except to say that people like me are writing this music. Here's another thing that again would not be uniquely black except in terms of much that is being done today, and that is that the black creative artist in this particular period seems to be closer to the human scale than many non-black creative people. Translated into musical terms, I'd say that there is still a greater concern on the part of the average black creative personality to relate to an audience of some sort than is evident in the more advanced or maybe even average output of his white peers. Even though a black musician like Olly Wilson deals with the electronic medium, he doesn't have the same approach that someone like Milton Babbitt would have to it, Milton being someone who seems to be satisfied with going into a studio and coming out with his complete piece on a roll of tape under his arm, that being the be-all and end-all except that he would like to have the approbation of his colleagues. In contrast, Olly has tied electronics very definitely into a way of trying to reach a larger public and he has gone out of his way to establish an aesthetic position in support of his efforts. I, myself, happen to like the business of dealing with live musicians; I just happen to like that particular game.

4. Q: In what ways is your music a reflection of your personal philosophy (social, political, etc.)?

   A: When I'm working on a piece, I don't have any political or social philosophy whatsoever that gets involved, except perhaps when I might be setting a text. In the cantata I wrote for Tougaloo College a couple of years ago, I ended up writing my own text. [3] They wanted something related to the black experience in some way, so I dealt with certain social questions and philosophical questions in the writing of that text. But the writing of the music had to do with musical problems. In other words, I don't try to make the music relate to a philosophical position, unless you can say that

the fact that I am concerned with the human element is a
philosophical position. OK--I'll go that far. But to say
that my work has to represent my position as a black artist
and that it has to have a certain position vis-à-vis the black
community--blah, blah, blah, blah--is baloney!

5. Q: What do you see as the position or role of the black artist
in contemporary society?

A: The role I see of the black artist is the same as any artist,
frankly. From where I stand, that is an essentially non-
political role. I don't find any value for myself in trying to
relate my work to the struggle. If a person happens to feel
that way about his work, that's his business; I don't think
that the artist can really subordinate his work to a political
or social issue and have it remain valid as a work of art.
In other words, my position is diametrically opposed to
those who say that unless a work of art is slanted towards
the social struggle, it is valueless. I say exactly the op-
posite. My position has not changed since "Here I Stand";[4]
I don't think the situation has changed. The evidence in
support of my position can be found just about any place you
want to look, namely the Soviet Union, Nazi Germany, or
any other place where it is decreed that art shall support
any political or social philosophy. In the societies where
art is an integral part of the social system, that's something
different. Take the arts as they have been used in various
African cultures or other non-European cultures; I can see
that. But there the artist is a part of a cog in the wheel
of a piece of social machinery, where his position is very
clearly defined to the point that art takes on not an individual aspect but a tribal or regional aspect. You can identify
the tribe from which an artist comes, roughly in the same
way that you can identify the nationality of a composer
through hearing his music, in that a piece of music written
by a Frenchman would normally sound different from a
piece written by a German, or a piece written by a Russian,
or a piece written by an American.

6. Q: Please discuss any problems you may have encountered in
getting your works performed, published, and recorded.

A: For me that's easy. In the pop/jazz area I've had difficulties in having recordings and getting involved on a regular basis in recordings; that's in my more commercial
activities, except in recent years when I've been doing
music for TV commercials in collaboration with Chico
Hamilton. But the business of just doing jazz things and
having them recorded has been a problem. Other than that,
I have had no problems. In other words, in the area of my
formal music, I have never really had any performance
problems. I have never had to go out of my way to ask
anybody to perform anything. Since I've been in the position of being a published composer, which really came as
a result of getting into the field as an editor, I've never

had any publishing problems. In fact, the only problem I
have had along those lines is keeping up with the demand.
As far as recording is concerned, I don't really have a bad
recording record. I think that now there are about four
things recorded: Contours, In Memoriam--Beryl Rubenstein, Evocation, and The Valley Wind. And, although I
can't really go into detail, there is something in the wind
relative to the recording of my Ritual and Incantations.

6A. Q: How much of your actual output has ever been performed?
Published? Recorded?

A: All of my works have been performed. That is literally
true. The last major thing that had not been done was a
piece of mine called Orchestral Set, which I wrote in 1952;
it was finally done last fall. I'll qualify it this far--every-
thing that I think is worth performing has been performed.
And almost everything has been published, either in print
or on rental; I can usually call my own shots there. In
fact, everything that I've done, unless I have withdrawn it,
is available in some way or another. Most of my summer[5]
is going to be devoted to preparing things for publication
because I'm well behind. In other words, anything that I
want to be published is publishable.

6B. Q: Have you encountered difficulty in getting your works programmed?
(Ed. note: Mr. Smith addressed this question in his response
to I-6.)

6C. Q: Are there specific problems in getting a satisfactory performance? Exemplify and discuss.

A: I would say that that depends on the quality of the players
and the amount of time available. Sometimes there is just
not enough time. For instance, when Paul Freeman did
Ritual and Incantations, there were a number of things that
I was dissatisfied with, but I could not blame Paul except
to say that there just wasn't enough time. But I think the
main problem had to do with the orchestra itself; this was
just prior to the beginning of the season, so the orchestra
didn't have the proper discipline and had gotten a little
slack over the summer--I'll give them the benefit of the
doubt. But aside from problems like that, I couldn't say
that I have had serious problems. I've gone into this in
some detail in the article in The Black Perspective; I've
forgotten the exact page, but it deals with the question of
how I relate to musicians.[6]

7. Q: What do you consider, at this point in your life, to be
your most significant achievement(s) aside from your compositions?

A: I don't know how to answer that question. I'm not trying
to avoid it; I just don't know how to answer it. What do I
say--parenthood or what? I don't know. I've done a lot

of things. One thing I have made a point of doing is opening
doors for people that I was able to open doors for, people
I felt were worthy of having those doors opened. That might
well be it. Whether it's my most significant or not I don't
know; I don't even know that it is an achievement. I happened to be instrumental in getting the first recording for
T. J. Anderson, getting a recording for Olly Wilson, and
the same thing for William Grant Still--his Festival Overture. But I wouldn't say that that was an achievement; I
just happened to be in a certain place at a certain time when
I was able to influence things along those lines.

8. Q: What do you see as the responsibilities and obligations of
the educational system (at all levels) to the study of black
music?

A: I touched on that in Black Music in Our Culture. [7] I think
that the educational system has an obligation to present a
rounded view of our entire culture, and in saying "our" I
mean the human culture. The only reason I think that there
should be any particular differentiation in the presentation of
courses relative to black issues is simply the fact that these
issues have been neglected and relegated to Siberia in the
past, so the overall picture should be balanced out. Now,
as I indicated in Readings in Black American Music, [8] I
really don't think very much of the idea of separating. I
think that the example of the Black Music Center at Indiana
University and the current situation with that center is beautifully illustrative of my position, which is simply that if
something is considered (or can be considered) separate, it
can be separated, cut off, or dropped on the grounds that it
is not really an integral factor. It is no secret that as
far as T. J. Anderson and I are concerned, the Black
Music Center should be a part of the School of Music. But
the School of Music, as soon as it got into a position to
drop it, dropped it. Am I wrong? This is again because
of its being considered something separate, and I object to
that.

   I think that schools all over the country should have
courses, possibly similar to a course that I run at the
University of Connecticut. I didn't start the course, but I
run it now. It's called "The Black Experience in the Arts,"
and each semester we have ten outstanding practitioners
(some of whom are not very well-known and some of whom
are actually quite famous) come up simply to talk with the
students. The first semester deals more with the personal
element, and the second more with the historical. But I
think it is clear that, in many of these cases, the people
who are doing the talking are also the ones making the history. We have had difficulties with certain members of the
advisory faculty and the student body taking this thing a
little too lightly, so this past semester we tightened it up
some. We went contrary to one of our objectives and
started giving computerized exams rather than essay exams,

but we did that in order to emphasize that we weren't going to be trifled with in taking this stuff seriously.

I think that it's not enough to have a course called "The Black Experience in the Arts" where we have just creative people. There should be room to have scientists come in, and literary people, inventors, and business people--people in all of these areas of activity in a situation where they can actually be seen and where they can become real factors in the lives of the students. That, I think, is an obligation on the part of education.

9. Q: Do you feel that the people who write about your music (critics in particular) understand what you are doing? Exemplify and discuss.

   A: No. I don't. I don't think they know what they are talking about for the most part. [9] And I'm not sure that a musician would do much better, simply because a creative person usually has to take a line in accordance with the path that he is following in his own creative work. But the critics do not seem to understand; even when they give me good reviews they don't seem to know what I'm talking about. Let's put it this way: those that make more sense to me, whether they are favorable or unfavorable, are those who do not try to deal with the meaning I am trying to project, because very frequently that is where they go off. I am not interested in establishing a social position musically and I'm not really interested in protest music as such. If I use a dissonance it does not mean that I am mad at somebody!

   Q: I remember reading something in which you mentioned a gentleman who had written a review of In Memoriam--Beryl Rubenstein for Saturday Review. You commented that he seemed to be sympathetic to what you were trying to do in that work. Would you want to include this in your discussion of problems with critics?

   A: The review appeared in Saturday Review. [10] That particular individual didn't get into the meaning so much, even though he may have touched on the fact that it was a memorial piece. And it is a memorial piece, but it is very secular. In fact, the poem by Langston Hughes makes reference to ... well, it might not have been prostitutes, but there is some secular love going on in the poem! But the poem, all in all, is something that I felt could project an elegiac quality. This reviewer happened to have been a person who knew me quite well, and who furthermore had a very definite personal interest in helping me along. I'm not saying that he went beyond the bounds of critical propriety in what he wrote, but put it this way: he was sensitive enough to my position to ask me beforehand if I had any objections to his referring to my race. Of course the article was written before this current black business, so that was something that I could really appreciate. [11] Have

you seen that review? This person's major activity is not
being a music reviewer. He has a very powerful position
in American music and he is known to have helped a number of musicians.

10. Q: What advice would you give to the aspiring young black
composer?
   A: First of all, I'd say learn as much as one could learn
about as much as one could learn. You can refer the
reader to the portion of the interview in The Black Perspective that relates to my attitude about craftsmanship. [12]
I happen to think that developing craftsmanship is one of
the basic considerations. To me that is more valuable
at the beginning than having something to say. I think that
if a person has something to say, it is going to come out.
Having the craft is going to enable that person to say what
he wants. Further than that, just having a technical knowledge of music itself is not enough. This relates more to
the business of having something to say, because I think
that a composer should have a very broad cultural background in terms of his attainment of knowledge and his
awareness of the world around him--the contents of the
great cultural "grab bag" that the human animal has created. I also mentioned in The Black Perspective interview
that one should be able to dip into the well of human pro-
ductivity and utilize all of this; it helps give one a broader
point of view.

Part II: Music Questions

1. Q: When you sit down to begin a new composition on your own
initiative or inspiration (as opposed to a commissioned
work), what procedure or approach do you follow?
2. Q: When composing a commissioned work or a work written
for a specific occasion or person, does your procedure or
approach differ from the one you described in question one?
If so, in what way?
(Ed. note: Mr. Smith chose to answer questions one and two
together.)
   A: Let's tie in the first two; they go together so much as a
pair for me that I don't see any difference. I personally
for years have not just sat down without having a specific
reason to sit down and write. In other words, just about
everything that I have done has been commissioned unless
I was just going to write a tune or something, which I
don't really consider seriously at all. I don't see any
reason why a person should have a different point of view
in writing a work that is a commission than writing a work
that just might pop into his cranium sometime. As far as
I'm concerned, the musical problems should be the same.
When I accept a commission, I never accept conditions except that I would be thinking in terms of the specific group

or type of group for which I would be writing (perhaps a
certain instrumentation or certain personnel in the group)
and/or I would be thinking in terms of total duration. I
think if someone asks me to write a piece, they have the
right to say that they would like, for example, a piece for
string quartet which would be ten to fifteen or twenty minutes in duration. (And for that amount of money I would
not write them a forty-five minute piece for string orchestra!) Beyond that, they have absolutely nothing whatsoever
to say about what I do. And I have never yet had anybody
who tried to infringe on that. [13]

3. Q: In general, with regard to your writing, what genre(s) do
        you prefer?
    A: I'd say that I don't have any preference, and it's true. [14]
        I imagine there are certain things that I would much rather
        not write for. Imagine a combination like accordian, mouth
        harp, and bagpipes--I would really have to get sort of drunk
        to deal with that!

             As far as preferences go, I really don't have any. I
        enjoy doing all of it. Some things are easier than others.
        The purely formal writing for me is the most difficult be-
        cause, for one thing, there is nothing to hang a hat on ex-
        cept one's own imagination. But if I'm working with a film
        or with a commercial, much of that is already taken care
        of because the visual images suggest certain things. It is
        easy for me to write like that, just like it is easy for me
        to write tunes. I have often demonstrated this. One of the
        reasons I differentiate song writing (or tune writing) from
        composition is that the norm in writing a tune is the writing
        of a lead sheet, which is the melodic line with chord sym-
        bols and maybe words. I have very frequently written tunes
        like this to stop watches, often writing a number of tunes
        back to back. My quickest time has been around six min-
        utes; my slowest time was about ten. In other words, I
        would sit down cold and within an average of 7 to $7\frac{1}{2}$ min-
        utes, I would write a piece in lead sheet form that would
        be from 32 to 40 measures long; then, in certain cases, I
        would start right over again and write another one, and so
        on.
             About two years ago, Lofton Mitchell was up at the
        school and he had four students with him. After he fin-
        ished his talk, we went up the road for a liquid dinner.
        One of the students kept challenging my authority, asking
        what authority I had to say this or that. Well, Lofton told
        me that he had some words he wanted me to look at, so we
        went to my office. Lofton sat down at the desk across
        from mine, and started writing on one of those $8\frac{1}{2}$ by 11
        yellow legal pads. When he finished the first sheet, he
        handed it to me; I just skimmed it quickly and began work-
        ing on one of my little sketch pads. Fifteen minutes later
        I was at the piano playing the finished song, using the ac-
        companiment that I later wrote out in a fuller piano part.

All of the students were stunned. Lofton knew what I would do; he didn't know how fast I would do it, but he knew that I could write very quickly because my first experience with him came when I was called in at the last minute to do a show for which he and John Killens had written the book. I ended up writing the music for a full doggone show within a week's time! That flabbergasted everybody, because at the same time I was working with Frank Loesser and was taking care of his business during the day. That's why I say that tune writing is different from formal composition, which is much more complex and much more difficult.

4. Q: What do you consider your most significant composition? Please discuss.

 A: I don't really know what that means. I happen to think that Contours and Ritual and Incantations are among the best things I've ever written in terms of quality. There's a piece more recent than Ritual called Introduction, Cadenzas, and Interludes for Eight Players which I happen to like a great deal. Then there's another piece that I did back in March for woodwind quintet and piano; I'm just now settling in on it. I projected it as a twelve-minute piece and it came in under the wire at eight, so now I'm having to psychologically deal with that missing four minutes. But the piece evidently is satisfactory the way it is. This is one of the few times I've really had other people listen to a piece to carefully measure their responses. Howard Swanson listened to it, and my former teacher listened to it, and some other people listened to it as well. They all felt that it was satisfactory and should be left as it stood. There is a piece I did for concert band called Somersault, which to me was a training kind of piece. It has evidently become quite significant in the areas of educational music and concert band music in that it is already considered a band classic by some people. In that sense it might be significant, but as far as its relationship to my other writing is concerned, it is far surpassed even by other band pieces that I have written. There is one for solo trumpet and concert band called Exchanges which I think is a far stronger piece. Faces of Jazz, a piece for solo piano, could be considered significant in that teachers all over the country have been picking it up and using it; evidently it is quite highly regarded as a means of presenting certain jazz idioms to students of piano. So I really don't know how to answer this question; it depends upon what it is that we consider significant. In Memoriam --Beryl Rubenstein could very easily be considered significant because it was the first of my pieces ... no, it was not the first of my pieces to be recorded. Contours was the first piece to be recorded. All things considered, I think that Contours is probably my most significant composition.

5. Q: Please comment on your treatment of the following musical

elements and give examples from your compositions that
illustrate the techniques you describe:
A. Melody
B. Harmony
C. Rhythm
D. Form
E. Improvisation
F. Text (both choice and treatment)
G. Instrumentation or medium (both in terms of choice of
    particular combinations as well as how they are treated
    compositionally)

(Ed. note: Mr. Smith chose not to address each of the above
            elements individually. Instead, he presented a gen-
            eral discussion of compositional procedure and tech-
            niques.)

A: I've got a comment on this and the comment is "few." I
    don't really know how I could comment on these things.
    I'd say that there are certain things in each of these areas
    that are characteristic of me. There are certain ways that
    I hear music; I hear certain vertical and certain horizontal
    combinations and those are the things that I think give what-
    ever I do a particular smell. I very rarely use improvisa-
    tion in my formal music, perhaps because I am an impro-
    viser myself and I work out my improvisational impulses
    when I'm improvising; very little of it has ever filtered
    over into my other writing. Now, when it comes to text,
    I'm very careful. Sometimes I'll read a text and the musi-
    cal setting will be suggested immediately. More often,
    though, the text is something that I analyze on a number of
    different levels. Usually I find that there are several lay-
    ers of meaning in the text. Then I analyze it from the
    point of view of prosodic values, which involves rhythm,
    the various points of word stress and syllable stress, and
    things like that. I analyze all the aspects very carefully
    to the point that I understand the text even on a subjective
    level; that way, when I'm writing, I don't have to deal
    consciously with those elements.
        I suppose I could say that, when dealing with questions
    of melody and harmony and rhythm, I do similar things in
    that I'll write a couple of pages of music and then I'll stop
    and analyze very carefully from the melodic point of view,
    the harmonic point of view, and the rhythmic point of view,
    just to see what I have. What I very frequently will do is
    establish a set or a tone row based on the melodic and
    harmonic values, just to see what they are. I may very
    likely not use this set as a structural thing; the piece more
    than likely will not be a serial piece but the set will serve
    as a motivic source. Down underneath I am what you would
    call a motivic composer, a motivic thinker. I isolate the
    various melodic, harmonic, and rhythmic elements, which I
    study separately and together to the point that they become
    second nature. In doing that, the overall shape or form of
    the piece will gradually become clear. I'm one of those

composers who has to see where a piece is going before I
can do too much. As far as instrumentation is concerned,
part of this was covered earlier in one of the other questions. [15] If I'm asked to do a piece for orchestra, I'll
understand that that might mean woodwinds in pairs and so
on. But if I'm going to use doublings within that framework, that's my business. Or whatever percussion I want
to use, that's my prerogative. From the very beginning
I'm thinking in terms of the instrumentation actually indicated. I think there are certain combinations of instruments that are characteristic of me. There is a person
named Malcolm Breda, the head of the Music Department
at Xavier University in New Orleans, who is doing his
doctoral dissertation on me. [16] Part of his study involves
analyzing my works and finding points in common, so it's
very possible that he could tell you a whole lot more about
this than I could.

6. Q: Have difficulties with performance practice (inflection,
      phrasing, etc.) been a significant problem in having your
      works performed to your own satisfaction?

   A: OK. Now, for instance, I've found that the most wide-
      spread practice (or mis-practice) among string players is
      their lack of precision when they see such markings as sul
      ponticello, where they'll put the bow somewhere in the gen-
      eral neighborhood of the bridge rather than putting it on the
      bridge. But generally I find players to be very cooperative.
      With regard to phrasing and notation, I do my best to write
      out the precise values and so forth that I want. One could
      write one way for people who have come up in the jazz tra-
      dition, but one would also have to write another way to get
      the same effect when writing for someone who did not come
      up in that kind of tradition. I recognize these differences,
      so I don't find problems there. I do think that, in general,
      if players had jazz backgrounds, they would have greater
      rhythmically inflectional authenticity when playing things of
      mine. This is not to say that my things should be played
      as if they were jazz. After all, jazz is something that is
      a part of my background and my rhythms are influenced by
      that fact. If a person understood how to deal with that,
      there would be less of a problem. However, I find that in
      nearly every case I've dealt with, especially in dealing with
      professionals, it only involves me having to talk with them.
      I just go up to the podium and tell the players what I want,
      and with one exception, I've had a lot of cooperation. Even
      in that case I had cooperation; the problem was that the
      orchestra was just incompetent. [17]

7. Q: What major works are currently in progress? Please de-
      scribe and discuss.

   A: I have two works in progess, only in the sense that I'm
      working on the master sheets now; these would be the sextet
      for woodwinds and piano and the octet, the two pieces that

I mentioned a few moments ago. The octet is called Introduction, Cadenzas, and Interludes for Eight Players and the other piece is called Variations for Six Players, although I'm not so sure that it's a good title or that it's even altogether accurate. I'm not really sure what I'm going to call the doggone thing! I'm thinking about it while I'm working on the master sheets.

Q: How long before the first performance?
A: Both of them have been played. Again it was a case of having to squeeze them out and deliver the parts the day before the performance, which is usual with me.

8. Q: Given unlimited time and finances (and no restrictions whatsoever), what would you write?
A: Probably nothing. I tend to need pressure. If I had unlimited time and finances, I'd probably just go to pot. I have to have a deadline of some kind--one that I can't squeeze out of!

9. Q: If given the opportunity would you choose to devote yourself to composition on a full-time basis? Why or why not?
A: As it stands now, probably not. I happen to agree with the point of view that the person who functions in more than one area has greater chances, vitality, and so forth. I just like being a professional musician and doing all the things that it involves. I don't do too much editorial work now, but that's still a part of it, too.

10. Q: How would you describe your compositional style?
A: I don't think in terms of style; I really don't. I think Breda is in a better position to discern whatever stylistic elements there are in my work because he's looked at it from that point of view. But I really can't say. Part of this is semantic. If style is defined as the outward appearance of something that has an internal growth pattern, fair enough. I tend to think contrapuntally; I tend to think motivically. I think those ways when I am writing. In other words, I tend to think horizontally rather than vertically, although the vertical has a very great importance in my writing in that I tend to use vertical structures as one means of achieving structural clarity. I notice that my recent things have tended more and more toward the most laconic, abbreviated statement I could get out, to the extent of having only one or two instruments going at a time. I don't know whether that's style or not; someone else would have to answer that.

11. Q: What have been the influences of other composers, styles, and other types of music on your compositional style?
A: Except for the business of absorbing underlying principles, I couldn't say anything. Everybody has been influenced by somebody else. I tend to think more in terms of principles.

For instance, a lot of people might have a question mark in their minds when I say that the three greatest influences on my orchestration have been Duke Ellington, Mozart, and Mahler, in that order. And there are certain things that I have learned about tonal distribution from Stravinsky, but I'm quite sure that very little of my work has a Stravinskian sound. I've learned a lot about handling materials from Bartok. You name them, I've learned from them. But I couldn't say that they were stylistic influences at all.

12. Q: Has your style changed across your career? If so, what influenced these changes or developments?

A: I think that the changes (and I would like to think that there have been changes) have been not so much stylistic or even changes in approach, but rather have been refinements of my basic impulses. I'm inclined to think that whatever changes may have come about have come about through my refinement of my own thought processes. I think there is a great deal of difference between, on the one hand, these last two pieces that I've done[18] and, on the other, my Sonata for Violoncello and Piano, which I mention because I know that David's working with it.[19] But not very far beneath the surface of both pieces I think it could be discerned that the same person or the same thought processes were involved. One is full of notes and "sturm und drang" and the other two pieces are not like that; yet there are certain things that hold common, such as certain details in the piano writing (even though the piano writing here is much more sparse than in the cello sonata).

13. Q: When you are listening to music for your own enjoyment, what are your preferences?

A: These past few years I find that I tend more and more to listen to the old masters rather than the current thing, whatever the current thing might be. I listen to very little current popular music except that which I'm forced to hear because it's on the radio and I can't escape. That's not for my own enjoyment! If I had my choice, I just wouldn't turn on the radio to listen to much of any music, and that includes jazz and everything else. It also includes much of the non-popular music that is being produced today. The things I really turn to most are by Mozart, Mahler (to a somewhat lesser extent), and Duke; the things Duke did between 1938 and 1943 are the ones that I turn to even more often. I love listening to Art Tatum and a few other great players. And I'll go out and listen to friends of mine who are jazz musicians that I happen to admire a great deal, whereas I wouldn't necessarily pick up a record and play it.

Notes to Chapter XII

1. Murasaki shikibu, The Tale of Genji, trans. Arthur Waley (Boston and N.Y.: Houghton Mifflin Company, 1935). This two-volume edition includes all six parts of the novel.

2. Dominique-René de Lerma, ed., Black Music in Our Culture (Kent, Ohio: Kent State University Press, 1970), p. 75.

3. Mr. Smith is referring to his composition Comes Tomorrow.

4. Hale Smith, "Here I Stand," in Readings in Black American Music, ed. Eileen Southern (New York: W. W. Norton and Company, Inc., 1971), pp. 286-289.

5. The interview with Mr. Smith took place May 28, 1975.

6. Hansonia Caldwell, "Conversation with Hale Smith," The Black Perspective in Music 3 (Spring 1975): 63-64.

7. De Lerma, Black Music in Our Culture, p. 23.

8. Smith, "Here I Stand."

9. For additional remarks by Mr. Smith on the subject of critics and criticism see Caldwell, "Conversation with Hale Smith," pp. 65-66.

10. Oliver Daniel, "Ten from Cleveland," Saturday Review, 28 November 1964, p. 58.

11. Mr. Smith discusses this review and the problems of racial categorization in Caldwell, "Conversation with Hale Smith," p. 66.

12. Caldwell, "Conversation with Hale Smith," pp. 59-61.

13. For additional material relating to these questions see Caldwell, "Conversation with Hale Smith," for Mr. Smith's remarks on the concept of inspiration (pp. 60-61) and on the subject of commissions (pp. 70-71).

14. Mr. Smith also discusses the various genres (and media) in which he has written in Caldwell, "Conversation with Hale Smith," pp. 69-70.

15. See Mr. Smith's responses to II-1/II-2, and II-3.

16. Malcolm Breda, "Hale Smith: The Man and His Music" (Ph.D. diss., University of Southern Mississippi, 1975).

17. For additional remarks by Mr. Smith relating to his experiences with musicians and performance problems see Caldwell, "Conversation with Hale Smith," pp. 63-64.

18.   Mr. Smith is referring to <u>Introduction, Cadenzas, and Inter-</u>
<u>ludes for Eight Players</u> and the sextet for woodwinds and piano
(discussed under the working title <u>Variations for Six Players</u>).

19.   Mr. Smith is referring to David Baker.

LIST OF COMPOSITIONS*

ANTICIPATIONS, INTROSPECTIONS, AND REFLECTIONS   (1971)
       Piano.   App. 6 min.   E. B. Marks, rental.   Dedicated to
       Marcel Dick.   First performances (1971) by Natalie Hinderas
       (at the International Piano Festival, University of Maryland) and
       Zita Carno (New York City).

AN ASPHODEL FOR MARCEL   (1968)
       See FACES OF JAZZ.

BEYOND THE RIM OF DAY   (1950)
       High voice and piano.   Text by Langston Hughes.   Three songs:
       March Moon; Troubled Woman; To a Little Lover-Lass, Dead.
       7 min. 40 sec.   E. B. Marks, 1970.   Dedicated to and first
       performed (1955) by Gladys Tiff, soprano, at the Karamu The-
       ater (Cleveland, Ohio); accompanied by Charles Baskerville,
       piano.

BLOOD WEDDING   (1953)
       Chamber opera.   (Main characters are non-singing parts.)   Play
       by Garcia Lorca.   App. 90 min.   Commissioned by and first
       performed at the Karamu Theater (Cleveland, Ohio).   Benno
       Frank, director.

BLOOZ   (1968)
       See FACES OF JAZZ.

BOLD NEW APPROACH   (1966)
       Music for a documentary film on mental health.   App. 60 min.
       Irving Jacoby, producer.

THE BROKEN SAXOPHONE   (1968)
       See FACES OF JAZZ.

BY YEARNING AND BY BEAUTIFUL   (1961)
       String orchestra.   6 min.   E. B. Marks, rental.   Dedicated to
       Russell Atkins and suggested by his poem "By Yearning and By
       Beautiful. "   First performance (1972) by the Richmond Symphony
       Orchestra, Joseph Kennedy, Jr. , conductor.

---

*Mr. Smith has also written numerous jazz compositions, including
ALISON (recorded by Benny Bailey and also by Ahmad Jamal) and
FEATHER (recorded by Eric Dolphy).   He felt that their inclusion in
the following list was unnecessary, but requested that a note be made
to the effect that he has written a number of pieces of this nature.

COME TO MY PARTY (1968)
See FACES OF JAZZ.

COMES TOMORROW (1972; revised in 1976)
Jazz cantata. Chorus (SATB), soloists (soprano, contralto, tenor, and bass-baritone), and jazz ensemble. Text by the composer. Four movements: Exhortation; How Lucky I Am; Every Day Is a New Day; What Good Is a World? App. 20-21 min. E. B. Marks, 1976. Commissioned by Tougaloo College with the assistance of the National Endowment for the Arts. First performance (1972) at Tougaloo College (Tougaloo, Mississippi) by the Tougaloo College Concert Choir, A. Lovelace, conductor; the Jackson College instrumental ensemble, K. Holly, conductor; and soloists Gwendolyn Sims, Melvin White, Hattie Johnson, and Larry Robinson.

THE COMPUTATION (1958)
See TWO LOVE SONGS OF JOHN DONNE.

CONCERT MUSIC FOR PIANO AND ORCHESTRA (1972)
App. 14 min. C. F. Peters, rental. Commissioned by Undine Smith Moore and Altona T. Johns. Dedicated to Jewel and Leon Thompson. First performance (1972) by the Richmond Symphony Orchestra, Leon Thompson, conductor; Jewel Thompson, piano.

CONFINED LOVE (1958)
See TWO LOVE SONGS OF JOHN DONNE.

CONTOURS (1962)
Orchestra. 9 min. C. F. Peters, 1962. Recorded by the Louisville Symphony Orchestra, Robert Whitney, conductor (Louisville LOU-632). Commissioned by Broadcast Music Inc. in celebration of its 20th anniversary and dedicated to Carl Haverlin. Also dedicated to the memory of Clarence Cameron White and Wallingford Riegger. First performance (1962) by the Louisville Symphony Orchestra, Robert Whitney, conductor.

DAY'S END (1968)
See FACES OF JAZZ.

DUO FOR VIOLIN AND PIANO (1953)
Three movements. App. 15 min. C. F. Peters, rental. First performance (1955) at the Karamu Theater (Cleveland, Ohio). Jeno Antal, violin; Betty Oberacker, piano.

ELEGY (1953; 1958)
See IN MEMORIAM--BERYL RUBINSTEIN.

ENVOY IN AUTUMN (1955)
See THE VALLEY WIND.

EPICEDIAL VARIATIONS (1956)
Violin and piano. App. 12 min. E. B. Marks, rental. First

performances in Cleveland, Ohio by Elliott Golub, violin, and John Ferritto, piano; and James Barrett, violin, and Jane Corner Young, piano.

EVERY DAY IS A NEW DAY (1972; 1976)
See COMES TOMORROW.

EVOCATION (1965)
Piano. 3 min. 10 sec. C. F. Peters, 1966; International Library of Piano Music. Recorded by Natalie Hinderas (Desto DC-7102/7103: Natalie Hinderas Plays Music by Black Composers). First performance (1965) in Cleveland, Ohio. Nancy Voigt, piano.

EXCHANGES (1972)
Trumpet and band. App. 8 min. E. B. Marks, rental. Commissioned by Robert Nagel. First performance (1972) by the Lehigh University Band (Bethlehem, Pa.), Jonathan Elkus, conductor; Robert Nagel, trumpet.

EXCHANGES (1972)
Trumpet and piano. App. 8 min. E. B. Marks, 1976. Commissioned by Robert Nagel.

EXHORTATION (1972; 1976)
See COMES TOMORROW.

EXPANSIONS (1967)
Band. App. $7\frac{1}{2}$ min. E. B. Marks, 1967. Recorded by the Symphonic Band of Southern Illinois University at Edwardsville, C. Dale Fjerstad, conductor (Educational Record Reference Library, Band Program, Vol. 7, BP-107; Century Records: Dimension 27361). Commissioned by and dedicated to the Symphonic Band of Southern Illinois University at Edwardsville, C. Dale Fjerstad, conductor. First performance (1967) by the Symphonic Band of Southern Illinois University at Edwardsville, C. Dale Fjerstad, conductor.

FACES OF JAZZ (1968)
Piano. 12 parts: My Scarf Is Yellow; The Broken Saxophone (for Eric [Dolphy]); Pooty's Blues; Day's End (for Eric [Dolphy]); Off-Beat Shorty; Blooz (for Ahmad Jamal); Following (for John Lewis); Scrambled Eggs and Ernie (for Ernie Wilkins); That's Mike; An Asphodel for Marcel; Goin' in a Hurry (for Ahmad Jamal); Come to My Party (for William Randall). Published as a set, but can be used as separate pieces. E. B. Marks, 1968.

FOLLOWING (1968)
See FACES OF JAZZ.

FOR ONE CALLED BILLY (1975)
Piano. App. 2 min. E. B. Marks, 1975; The Black Perspective in Music 3 (May 1975): 224-225. Dedicated to William

Grant Still. Described by the composer as one of a projected set of pieces to be written during the summer of 1976.

GOIN' IN A HURRY (1968)
See FACES OF JAZZ.

HOW LUCKY I AM (1972; 1976)
See COMES TOMORROW.

I'M COMING HOME (1974)
Chorus (SATB) with optional piano and/or rhythm section ac-companiment. Text by the composer. 4 min. 10 sec. E. B. Marks, 1974. Dedicated to the memory of Hall Johnson.

IN MEMORIAM--BERYL RUBINSTEIN (1953; orchestrated 1958)
Chorus (SATB) and chamber orchestra or piano. Three move-ments: Moderato (text is a vocalise); Poème D'Automne (text by Langston Hughes); Elegy (text by Russell Atkins). $10\frac{1}{2}$ min. Highgate Press (Galaxy Music), 1959 as part of the Cleveland Composers Guild Publication Series. Recorded by the Kulas Choir and Chamber Orchestra, Robert Shaw, conductor (Com-posers Recordings Inc. CRI SD-182: The Cleveland Composers' Guild, Vol. I).

INTRODUCTION, CADENZAS, AND INTERLUDES FOR EIGHT
PLAYERS (1974)
Flute/alto flute, oboe, clarinet, harp, piano, violin, viola, and violoncello. App. 12 min. E. B. Marks, 1976. Commissioned by the Nassau County Office of Cultural Development, John Maerhofer, director. First performance (1974) by the Sea Cliff Chamber Players.

LYSISTRATA (1952)
Incidental music for Aristophanes's play Lysistrata. Commis-sioned by and first performed (1952) at the Karamu Theater (Cleveland, Ohio). Kurt Cerf, director.

MARCH MOON (1950)
See BEYOND THE RIM OF DAY.

MUSIC FOR HARP AND ORCHESTRA (1967)
Harp and chamber orchestra. Two movements. 13 min. E. B. Marks, rental. Commissioned by the Symphony of the New World. First performance (1967) at Carnegie Hall by Symphony of the New World, Benjamin Steinberg, conductor; Gloria Agos-tini, harp.

MY SCARF IS YELLOW (1968)
See FACES OF JAZZ.

NUANCES OF HALE SMITH (circa 1967-1968)
TV and radio background music. Small orchestra. Seven short pieces. 15 min. Sam Fox Music Publishers. Sam Fox

SF 1022 (side A), Synchrofox Music Library. Commissioned by Sam Fox Music Publishers.

OFF-BEAT SHORTY (1968)
See FACES OF JAZZ.

ORCHESTRAL SET (1952)
Orchestra. Four pieces. 15 min. C. F. Peters, rental. First performance (1974) by the Symphony of the New World, Everett Lee, conductor. This work was part of the composer's Master's thesis.

POEME D'AUTOMNE (1953; 1958)
See IN MEMORIAM--BERYL RUBINSTEIN.

POOTY'S BLUES (1968)
See FACES OF JAZZ.

RITUAL AND INCANTATIONS (1974)
Orchestra. 15-18 min. C. F. Peters, rental. Recorded for Columbia by the Detroit Symphony Orchestra, Paul Freeman, conductor; to be released in 1976 as part of Columbia's Black Composers Series. Commissioned by the Thorne Music Fund and dedicated to Francis Thorne. First performance (1974) by the Houston Symphony Orchestra, Paul Freeman, conductor. Other performances (1976) by the Detroit Symphony, Paul Freeman, conductor, and the American Symphony, Kazuyoshi Akiyama, conductor.

SCRAMBLED EGGS AND ERNIE (1968)
See FACES OF JAZZ.

SOMERSAULT: A TWELVE TONE ADVENTURE FOR BAND (1964)
App. 4 min. Frank Music, 1964. Recorded by the Baldwin-Wallace Symphonic Band, Kenneth Snapp, conductor (Educational Record Reference Library, Band Program, Vol. 2, BP-102). Commissioned by Frank Music Corp. as part of their Adventures in Form series. First performance (1964) in Chicago at the Midwest Band Clinic. John Paynter, conductor.

SONATA FOR VIOLONCELLO AND PIANO (1955)
Three movements. 22 min. C. F. Peters, rental. Commissioned by and dedicated to Kermit Moore. First performances were done in Europe by Kermit Moore. First American performance (1958) in the Donnell Auditorium (New York City). Benar Heifitz, violoncello; Ward Davenny, piano.

TAKE A CHANCE: AN ALEATORIC EPISODE FOR BAND (1964)
Duration variable due to the nature of the piece. Frank Music, 1965. Commissioned by Frank Music Corp. as part of their Adventures in Form series.

THAT'S MIKE (1968)
See FACES OF JAZZ.

THREE BREVITIES (1960)
Solo flute. 5 min. 15 sec. E. B. Marks, 1969. Recorded by
D. Antoinette Handy (Eastern ERS-513: Contemporary Black
Images in Music for the Flute). Originally written for Eric
Dolphy and Jerome Richardson. First performance (circa 1961)
in Cleveland, Ohio. Thomas Nyfenger, flute.

TO A LITTLE LOVER-LASS, DEAD (1950)
See BEYOND THE RIM OF DAY.

TRINAL DANCE (1968)
Band. 3 min. 20 sec. Duchess Music/MCA, 1968. Commissioned by Lewis Roth.

TROUBLED WOMAN (1950)
See BEYOND THE RIM OF DAY.

TWO KIDS (1950)
Chorus (SATB) unaccompanied. Text by Nicholas Guillén (trans-
lated by Langston Hughes and Ben Frederic Carruthers from
"Cuba Libre"). 5½ min. E. B. Marks, 1973. Dedicated to
Russell and Rowena Jelliffe, founders of Karamu House.

TWO LOVE SONGS OF JOHN DONNE (1958)
Soprano, string quartet, and woodwind quintet. Text by John
Donne. Confined Love; The Computation. App. 8 min. E. B.
Marks, rental. Dedicated to Adele Addison. First performance
(1958) at the Donnell Library Composer's Forum (New York
City). Bethany Beardslee, soprano; Arthur Winograd, conduc-
tor.

THE VALLEY WIND (1955)
Medium voice and piano. Four songs: The Valley Wind (text
by Lu Yŭn, translated by Arthur Waley); When Daisies Pied
(text by Shakespeare); Envoy in Autumn (text by Tu Fu, translated by Powys Mathers); Velvet Shoes (text by Elinor Wylie).
App. 15 min. E. B. Marks, 1974. Recorded by Hilda Harris,
soprano, and Zita Carno, piano (Composers Recordings Inc.
CRI SD-301). Dedicated to Hilda Harris and Zita Carno. First
performance (1955) at the Karamu Theater (Cleveland, Ohio).
Judith Faris, soprano; Gerald Snyder, piano. Envoy in Autumn
and Velvet Shoes were part of the composer's Master's thesis.

VARIATIONS FOR SIX PLAYERS (1975)
Woodwind quintet and piano. App. 9 min. E. B. Marks, 1976.
Commissioned by William Scribner. First performance (1975);
Bronx, New York.

VELVET SHOES (1955)
See THE VALLEY WIND.

WHAT GOOD IS A WORLD? (1972; 1976)
See COMES TOMORROW.

WHEN DAISIES PIED   (1955)
   See THE VALLEY WIND.

YERMA   (1951)
   Incidental music for Garcia Lorca's play <u>Yerma</u>.   Commissioned
   by and first performed (1951) at the Karamu Theater (Cleveland,
   Ohio).   Benno Frank, director.

BIBLIOGRAPHY

Part I: Works about the composer

"Black Composers."   <u>Newsweek</u>, 15 April 1974.

Breda, Malcolm Joseph.   "Hale Smith: A Biographical and Analytical Study of the Man and His Music."   Ph. D. dissertation,
   University of Southern Mississippi, 1975.

Brooks, Tilford.   "A Historical Study of Black Music and Selected
   Twentieth Century Black Composers and Their Role in American
   Society."   Ed. D. dissertation, Washington University, 1972.

Caldwell, Hansonia L.   "Conversation with Hale Smith: A Man of
   Many Parts."   <u>The Black Perspective in Music</u> 3 (Spring 1975):
   58-76.

Claghorn, Charles E.   <u>Biographical Dictionary of American Music</u>.
   West Nyack, N. Y.:   Parker Publishing Company, 1973.

"The Commercial Composer Enters the School Music Field: A
   Phenomenon of Our Times."   <u>Instrumentalist</u> 22 (November
   1967): 87-89.

De Lerma, Dominique-René, ed.   <u>Black Music in Our Culture:</u>
   <u>Curricular Ideas on the Subjects, Materials, and Problems</u>.
   Kent, Ohio: Kent State University Press, 1970.

Erickson, Frank.   "A Composer Discusses Band Music."   <u>The</u>
   <u>School Musician, Director and Teacher</u> 39 (October 1967): 64-65.

"Hale Smith."   <u>BMI: The Many Worlds of Music</u>, March 1963.

Harris, Carl G.   "A Study of the Characteristic Stylistic Trends
   Found in the Choral Works of a Selected Group of Afro-American Composers and Arrangers."   D. M. A. dissertation, University of Missouri-Kansas City, 1972.

_____.   "Three Schools of Black Choral Composers and Arrang-
   ers 1900-1970."   <u>The Choral Journal</u> 14 (April 1974): 11-18.

Music and Artists 4 (April-May 1971): 10.

Roach, Hildred. Black American Music: Past and Present. Boston: Crescendo Publishing Company, 1973.

Southern, Eileen. "America's Black Composers of Classical Music." Music Educators Journal 62 (November 1975): 46-59.

_____. The Music of Black Americans. New York: W. W. Norton, 1971.

"Sterling Staff International Competition (SSIC) Composers Offer Works for Auditions." The Triangle of Mu Phi Epsilon 66 (Spring 1972): 13-14.

Who's Who in the East. 15th ed. (1975-76), s.v. "Smith, Hale."

Yestadt, Sister Marie. "Song Literature of the 70's: A Socio-Musical Approach." The NATS Bulletin 29 (May-June 1973): 22-27.

Part II: Works by the composer

Smith, Hale. "Black America, 1976." WFLN Program Guide (Philadelphia, Pa.), February 1976, pp. 11-12.

_____. "Creativity and the Negro." African Forum 1 (Summer 1965): 117-120.

_____. "Here I Stand." In Readings in Black American Music, edited by Eileen Southern, pp. 286-289. New York: W. W. Norton, 1971.

CHAPTER XIII

HOWARD SWANSON

Howard Swanson was born August 18, 1909 in Atlanta,
Georgia. At the age of twenty, he entered the Cleveland Institute
of Music where he studied composition with Herbert Elwell. In
1937 Mr. Swanson was awarded a Rosenwald Fellowship for study
in Europe and chose to go to Paris, where he continued his composition studies with Nadia Boulanger. Following his return to the
United States in 1940, Mr. Swanson was employed for a time by the
Internal Revenue Service. In 1945 he made the decision to devote
himself to composing on a full-time basis, regardless of the ensu-
ing financial hardship. He has continued to follow this policy for
over thirty years, and is presently involved in completing a chamber work and two piano sonatas.

Mr. Swanson has been the recipient of a number of awards
and grants including a Guggenheim Fellowship, a grant from the
Academy of Arts and Letters, and the 1951 New York Music Critics
Circle Award for his composition Short Symphony. The Thorne
Music Fund, the Symphony of the New World, and the New World
Trio are among those from whom he has received commissions.

Mr. Swanson's compositional output includes works for orchestra, solo voice, chamber ensemble, piano, and various other
solo instruments. He is perhaps best-known for his Short Symphony (recorded by the American Recording Society Orchestra and
by the Vienna State Opera Orchestra) and for his many song settings, particularly "The Negro Speaks of Rivers," which, when
performed by Marian Anderson in 1950, first drew national attention
to his considerable compositional talents.

Part I: General Questions*

1. Q: What persons, events, and works (of art, literature, etc.)
      have influenced you in general as well as in terms of your

---

*Howard Swanson is by nature a very private individual. For this
reason, the following interview was done on behalf of The Black
Composer Speaks by Mr. Swanson's long-time friend and colleague,
Hale Smith.

337

Howard Swanson (courtesy of ASCAP)

musical activities?

A: That's a rather general question. In the first place, my mother had a tremendous influence because she always tried to make us aspire to what people call the better things. She also made us feel that we could accomplish anything regardless of our circumstances. Outside of the family, my first music teacher in Cleveland, a lady by the name of Eugenia B. Crayton, really introduced me to music and to the great composers. She tried to instill in all her pupils the respect which she felt was due all the great composers. After teaching thirty or forty pupils a week, she would gather seven or eight of us every Saturday and take us to a concert in Cleveland. When I started studying at the Cleveland Institute, Mr. Herbert Elwell, along with Mr. Ward Lewis, made me feel that I really could make it.

2. Q: How would you define black music?

A: That's a tough one. I suppose black music is music written by black composers. I would classify it in that general way although I realize and understand that there are people who insist that so-called black music has to have elements of Afro-Americanism in it, including things with some kinship to African rhythms or to developments in Afro-American music as it has evolved here in the United States. There are so many different ideas and opinions about what black music is. My opinion, more or less, is that it is music which is composed by black composers.

3. Q: What features of your own music do you see as uniquely black (in terms of both musical and philosophical considerations)?

A: I feel that my compositions are simply my own self-expression. Being an Afro-American, I can't see how my music could be anything but that, regardless of what I write. The most important thing for me is to try to write something which is genuine and in which I feel that I'm expressing myself in terms of my ideas, my feelings, and my reactions to the events and historical processes through which I have passed during my lifetime.

Q: If I may, I'd like to interject something which relates to my own reaction to a number of your pieces with which I am acquainted. On a number of occasions, I've suggested that performers have misunderstood or misread your intentions in thinking of you as being neo-classic in a sense, or influenced by the Boulanger or Stravinsky neo-classic musical aesthetic. My attitude is that the performance would be much closer to your intentions if the performers would think in terms of Southern tent and camp meeting religious services. In this context, do you think that this is misleading, or do you think that this is closer to the reality of your musical thinking than the so-called neo-classic label that you've been stuck with?

A: I think that there are certain elements of religious music
in my music. I come from a family of church people and
I have a background in that. All Southerners, especially
Southern Negroes, have a history of churchgoing. There
have always been tremendously creative things happening in
Southern black churches, especially in the music and the
oratory. As a child I can remember extraordinary experiences and feelings about what went on in the religious ceremonies. But I think that when people speak about the neo-
classic aspects of my music, they are talking about it in
terms of French music versus German music. My music
has a tendency to be sparse and contrapuntal. I don't
write the fat chords and the generally fat music that people
usually think of as Germanic. I think that perhaps some
attention is brought to that because generally the antecedents
of American music have been Germanic; the interest in and
influence of French music are recent, actually since the
Second World War. I did study in Paris with Nadia Boulanger and my teacher also studied in Paris with Nadia
Boulanger, but I don't think of my music as French at all.

Q: In other words, it's a mistake to think of you in terms of
European precedents rather than the precedents of your own
cultural mileau.

A: I think it's very difficult to make a differentiation. After
all, the whole American culture is European. We speak of
Afro-American, but what we really are is Afro-European.
Afro-American music is a mixture of African and European
music which grew out of America. It's a strange sort of
happening. European music doesn't seem like an alien thing
to me. I don't feel that it's completely my tradition, but
I certainly don't see it as alien. I understand it. It's not
like going to China or to India, for instance, where I might
not understand the music because I don't have any historical
reason for being able to understand it. I can admire it;
I can regard it in all kinds of ways and fashions, but when
I go to Europe, it's like home away from home.

4. Q: In what ways is your music a reflection of your personal
philosophy (social, political, etc.)? Does this question
seem to have been answered by what you said before?

A: I think so, to a great extent, because I don't think in those
terms. I have never thought in those terms from a creative
standpoint. I think that I can best express my viewpoint by
saying that my music is very personal; I could almost say
that it's private. I don't feel that it's necessary to try to
portray events or even to be consciously influenced by them
because that's going to be there anyway. No one can escape
what he experiences.

5. Q: What do you see as the position or role of the black artist
in contemporary society?

A: I feel that the black creative artist has, to a great extent, been excluded from American history and the American cultural scene. In a certain way he has a mission to rectify this situation, which in the end will wipe out the whole racial thing. There will come a time when designations such as black music will be ridiculous; everything will just be called American music. Let's look at a country like Brazil, for instance. I've heard Brazilian music and I've heard about Brazilian music. I've heard about African influences on Brazilian music, but I can't ever remember hearing the term Afro-Brazilian music used. The Brazilians don't think in those terms. They think of any music that is produced there as Brazilian music. It is only in America where race has been dramatized so much that we are confronted with this kind of situation.

6. Q: Please discuss any problems you may have encountered in getting your works performed, published, and recorded.

   A: At the time when my Short Symphony was played, blacks were generally excluded from opportunities to have their music performed and published. [1] I think that now these are things of the past, not that the black composer has suddenly gained a lot of new friends and support from people who are going to bend over backwards to do things for him. The black composer of today is in about the same position as the white composer; it's difficult for all composers. There were incidents and events that perhaps I could recall, but I don't think that they are really that important. What I would say generally is that it's much better now than it used to be.

   Q: This particular question deals with works performed, published, and recorded. You have had a rather longstanding relationship with a single publisher which, at least on the surface, would indicate that you are one of those rare composers who has not had to go out looking for someone to handle that aspect of his work. You are in a somewhat different situation than many composers, regardless of their origins, who do not have serious relationships with publishers. Does this extend into the area of performance? I am aware that in recent years major orchestras have not been knocking at your door, in spite of the fact that you are one of the major composers. Is that one of the ways in which your creative life is comparable to that of most composers, in that orchestras, conductors, and performers are not necessarily coming to you all the time, or do you get a fair number of requests for your works?

   A: This question is a little bit difficult for me to answer, for the simple reason that I was outside the country for almost fourteen years, which means that in a way I was cut off. I wasn't here, so I really can't judge what would have happened had I been here. Since I've been back I've had pieces done. The New York Philharmonic has not played pieces of mine, but other orchestras have. None of the so-called

great five[2] have played any of my music,[3] but then I am not
a prolific symphonic composer. Along with you, I feel very
fortunate that the Symphony of the New World exists. I've
had four or five performances by them in the last six or
seven years. The Symphony of the New World is not considered one of the great five, but it's a very good orchestra.
It's right here in New York City and it gets coverage by the
most important critics and newspapers, so I don't feel frustrated in that respect.

With regard to the point you made about the publisher,
I was very fortunate in the fact that when Eugene Weintraub,
who had been with Leeds for years and had accepted five
pieces of mine for Leeds, decided to set up his own company, he told me that he was going to build his company
around my music and that I should bring it all down; he was
going to publish everything. I was fortunate in being at the
right place at the right time. That was after years and
years of going around to different publishers and showing
them my works and then being turned down, so that if that
opportunity had not come along, I would perhaps feel very
frustrated. I can understand how many composers feel
that way. I don't think that this is limited to black composers, however; all composers face this.

Q: I think you're absolutely right. If I can interject myself in
here even though this is your interview, the fact that Eugene Weintraub chose to make a comprehensive publication
venture with regard to your works proved to be of great
value to me as an individual because I was one of those
people who was able to benefit directly from that exposure
to your work. I'm mentioning this because I think that the
point you made about Mr. Weintraub is very important, at
least as far as my own development is concerned. Let's
go on.

6A. Q: How much of your actual output has ever been performed?
Published? Recorded?
A: Of the music that I'm willing to let go out into the world,
the better part of it falls into one of those three categories.

6B. Q: Have you encountered difficulty in getting your works programmed?
A: That's kind of difficult for me to answer. It would be the
same thing as asking William Grant Still that. He has
encountered all kinds of difficulties but, at the same time,
he has had a lot of performances. I think that question is
better suited to the younger composer.

6C. Q: Are there specific problems in getting a satisfactory performance? Exemplify and discuss.
A: To a certain extent, that has something to do with the kind
of music one writes. If one writes very very difficult
avant-garde music, one needs very special and highly

trained people to play it. On the other hand, if one's music is much more accessible and falls to a great extent into the general tradition, it is much easier to have performers perform it. My music falls sort of in between there somewhere. I've had people who have been enthusiastic about my music and have worked very hard and have given excellent performances of it. On the other hand, I have sat in concerts where I twitched in my chair and crossed my legs and twiddled my fingers. But every composer goes through that; it's one of the hazards of the occupation.

Q: I've heard it said that the more difficult and avant-garde a piece is, the easier it is to get it played because the audience knows less about what's happening and the performer can get away with more!

A: That's very true.

7. Q: What do you consider, at this point in your life, to be your most significant achievement(s) aside from your compositions?

A: The only achievements I've made are my compositions. I haven't made any other kind of achievements.

Q: I don't know. I'm inclined to think that considering where you and I are chronologically, simply waking up the next morning is an achievement; living the number of days we've managed to live already is an achievement!!

A: The only thing I live for is my music. I don't want to make any other achievement. That's enough for me, and I don't think that I will ever be able to make the kind of achievement in my music that I have dreamed of making.

I have a job and that job is to write the best music that I can. I have been struggling and struggling with these notes and musical forms night and day all my life. I don't see how I can do any more. If I am going to be a composer, that's my job. If I'm going to be a teacher, that's something else. I don't call myself a teacher; I call myself a composer. I haven't refused to teach, because I have never been asked to teach. I have always felt that if anyone really wanted me to teach, they would ask me. I know that a lot of people teach who don't wait to be asked; they go out and get jobs themselves. I have tried not to put myself in that position because I feel that to be a composer, you need all the time you can possibly get. You need more than twenty-four hours; you need forty-eight hours a day. And you work all your life. To be a creator, one is cursed. People say that it's a gift, but it's also a curse because you can never get away from it. You can't close up on a Friday afternoon and lock your desk and go home and forget about it until Monday morning. You can't do that! Even when you go to a social affair, your mind is on it. It has to be on it. You can never let that thought go; you must keep the line of thought forever. And when you finish one piece, you start another one. In fact, you only write one piece anyway, one continuous piece. You may cut it off in various places and call it different things, but it's the same piece.

8. Q: What do you see as the responsibilities and obligations of the educational system (at all levels) to the study of black music?

    A: Black studies is something that is very necessary. Black studies, as I understand it, deals with those facts and events which have been deliberately left out of the history books. For instance, all my life I have heard about Paul Revere, but the whole time I was in public school I never heard about Crispus Attucks. I knew about him because I learned about him in my home. Crispus Attucks, a black man, was the first person to fall for American independence. There is a plaque in the Boston Common which marks the place where he is supposed to have fallen. It seems to me that he is far more important than Paul Revere. I can't understand why he has been left out of all the history books. We are just now gradually getting him into the history books so that people are beginning to know that there was a man named Crispus Attucks and who he was. When we get facts like this included in the history books and included in our culture, black studies will have done its job.

9. Q: Do you feel that the people who write about your music (critics in particular) understand what you are doing? Exemplify and discuss.

    A: I think the critics understand very little about what's going on. I don't think that it's completely their fault because expecting them to go to a concert and hear a piece for the first time (and only one time) and then write a comprehensive and intelligent analysis of what actually took place is asking a little too much of the human mind. I don't really take music criticism seriously. I think it should be entertaining. We still read and cherish the music criticism of George Bernard Shaw even though we don't know anything about most of the people he wrote about and could care less! The music criticism of Virgil Thompson is highly entertaining, and one feels that what he is writing about is one man's honest reaction to some event that took place at a particular time in the concert hall. If criticism is entertaining, it's worthwhile; other than that, I really don't think it's that important.

10. Q: What advice would you give to the aspiring young black composer?

    A: Speaking from my most sincere thoughts, the only thing I would say to him is try to be the best composer he can be regardless of whether he's black, green, gray, white, or whatever. That seems to me to be the only advice you can give anyone.

Part II: Music Questions

1. Q: When you sit down to begin a new composition on your own initiative or inspiration (as opposed to a commissioned work), what procedure or approach do you follow?
   A: The same procedure.

2. Q: When composing a commissioned work or a work written for a specific occasion or person, does your procedure or approach differ from the one you described in question one? If so, in what way?
   A: I've answered that except for the fact that if the work is a commissioned work, it's usually going to be for a particular group of instruments or in a particular form; one has to take that into consideration. If I am commissioned to do a work for chamber orchestra, I obviously will not be thinking in terms of three tympani or three trombones. But as far as the actual musical content is concerned, I don't believe that there is much difference.

3. Q: In general, with regard to your writing, what genre(s) do you prefer?
   A: I find any genre a challenge. I like writing for the piano, I like writing for solo voice, I like writing chamber music, and I adore the orchestra. I don't think I've left anything out. Each one is a different sort of challenge. I have said (and to a great extent I still believe) that writing a successful piano piece is perhaps the most difficult in a way because, as my good friend Hale Smith says, you can't hide there.

4. Q: What do you consider your most significant composition? Please discuss.
   A: Well, I could say the Short Symphony since it won the New York Critics Circle Award and has been played by so many different orchestras at so many different times. I received a tremendous amount of recognition from that piece, so I suppose it would be considered the most significant one.

   Q: I found that question rather difficult myself because, as you've indicated here, the answer depends upon the area in which a piece might be significant.
   A: Exactly, and it also depends on which way you are thinking about it, that is, whether it was significant for you or significant for the public. It's rather difficult to pin down.

5. Q: Please comment on your treatment of the following musical elements and give examples from your compositions that illustrate the techniques you describe:
   A. Melody
   B. Harmony
   C. Rhythm
   D. Form

E. Improvisation
F. Text (both choice and treatment)
G. Instrumentation or medium (both in terms of choice of particular combinations as well as how they are treated compositionally)

A: I don't see how you can isolate those elements and I don't attempt to. I don't think in those terms.

Q: I'm personally not aware that you've dealt with texts in recent years, but I do know that of the songs of yours of which I am aware (and I might even be aware of some that have not gone into print), your choice of texts is remarkable because of the quality of the poems that you have chosen to use. Would you say that there is any particular reason that you chose the type and quality of poetry to which you have gravitated?

A: In terms of text, that's a legitimate question. I can only write the song if I am inspired by the poem. I also have to feel that the poem is suitable for musical treatment, and by that I mean that the language must be simple enough for the singer to get some of the ideas across to the audience. Then one has to think about tessitura and the type of voice to be used. Some texts immediately suggest a low voice or a high voice and so forth and so on. I know of composers who can take any poem or even the daily newspaper and set it to music, but I really have to be inspired. I haven't written songs for some time now, but when I was writing songs, I would sometimes think about a song for two or three months. I would carry the text around in my head and gradually the rhythm would form; then the formal structure of the song would come about in a nebulous sort of way. When I would sit down and write a song in two days, it would be because I would have worked it out to a great extent in my mind before doing that.

I think that there is one other thing that could be said here. English poetry, in my opinion, presents a real challenge to a composer. English is an extraordinarily expressive language, and English poetry is one of the great wonders of literature. However, the poetry is so strong that a lot of it defies musical settings. I think that French and even German to some extent are easier to set to music than English. The English pronunciation of words is very difficult. Also, after the Elizabethan period, there was no tradition of setting English to music. Once the Puritans got control of England, the whole music thing went out. Except for Handel and Gilbert & Sullivan, there was virtually no setting of English to music until we got to people like Vaughn Williams and Benjamin Britten. That has something to do with it, too, I think.

Q: I have two questions that I would interject relating to this: (1) might that have any bearing on what I think is your lack of involvement with the choral media? and (2) how does

this relate to your very sensitive settings of the poems of
Langston Hughes?

A: Do you mean the fact that I've written very little choral
music? Well, I wrote one choral piece for Leonard De
Paur and his chorus which they sang with seemingly great
success. I have not exploited the choral thing too much because my music is very chromatic and I feel that with regard to choral music, things get very difficult when you begin to introduce a lot of chromaticism in the line. That's
a problem for all modern composers. One can write like
Berg and Schoenberg, where the chromaticism takes over
the whole style and becomes a very special thing. But I
have felt that there was another way of doing it in my music and I haven't completely discovered yet exactly what
that is. There is a great choral tradition among Afro-
Americans which comes out of the church and somehow I
feel that I ought to exploit that marvelous kind of a tradition
in sound; maybe I'll get around to it one day.

Q: That's the first part. Now, how about your involvement with
the poems of Langston Hughes?

A: I think that the poetry of Langston Hughes has been recognized by many composers as a marvelous vehicle for writing
songs. I remember once being in Langston's home and seeing him pull out a very large bureau drawer which was full
of songs that people had set to his poems and had sent to
him. I would say that Langston Hughes and probably Emily
Dickinson are the two American poets who have been most
frequently set to music by different composers.

6. Q: Have difficulties with performance practice (inflection, phrasing, etc.) been a significant problem in having your works
performed to your own satisfaction?

A: I have always had the opinion that a composition is nothing
more than a guideline. The composer hopes that he puts it
down precisely enough that the performing artist produces
what he thought about and imagined. I've always felt that it
takes quite a few performances to find out how a piece really goes. I don't believe that all the nuances can possibly be
realized to the best advantage in a first performance. I
don't mean that there shouldn't be nuances projected; I don't
mean that there shouldn't be phrasing and a sense of form.
The problem is whether or not they are correct, and that
has to be worked at.

7. Q: What major works are currently in progress? Please describe and discuss.

A: I am in the process now of finishing a trio for flute, oboe,
and piano. I have two commissions for piano works which
will probably be the second and third piano sonatas. I also
have a dozen more compositions lying around which one day
I hope I will get to.

Q: Flute, oboe, and piano--that's an intriguing combination.

A: I wrote it for the New World Trio, which is a trio from the Symphony of the New World.

Q: In this case you are dealing with some remarkable performers: Harold Jones, flute; Harry Smyles, oboe; and Alan Booth, piano.

8. Q: Given unlimited time and finances (and no restrictions whatsoever), what would you write?

A: I'd just go off somewhere and write pieces without having to think about performances. The whole business of showing off before the public or trying to convince people to play my music has never interested me. One wouldn't have to send in applications or send out examples of one's work and so on; one could just go ahead and work. Then someday people could come around and say that they wanted to play this or that. Good! Marvelous!! Beautiful!!! Then music takes on the right process. We have a problem in that the truly great music of the 17th, 18th, and 19th centuries was created in the salons of rich and powerful Europeans. These people hired the most talented musicians, provided for their needs, and asked them to produce the best music that they possibly could. In our modern democracies, we are trying to incorporate the idea that the great arts can somehow or another be connected with the broad mass of people. Since none of these people as individuals have enough money or power to engage artists themselves, it has to be a joint affair which then becomes a commercial venture. As soon as that happens, something happens to the whole thing. I'm not sure we've really solved that problem yet.

9. Q: If given the opportunity, would you choose to devote yourself to composition on a full-time basis? Why or why not?

A: I would, and that's what I try to do. I don't know how much longer I'll be able to keep at it because it entails being poverty-stricken, but that's what I have chosen to do.

10. Q: How would you describe your compositional style?

A: That's very difficult for me to say. When people ask me that question, I answer that I write in the style of Swanson. That's not a cop-out; what I'm trying to do is write in my own style.

11. Q: What have been the influences of other composers, styles, and other types of music on your compositional style?

A: There is no doubt that our teachers have a tremendous influence on us. My very wonderful teacher Mr. Elwell said one day in class that we would have to choose some musical ancestors in order to get started, and I think we all had to do that; we had to start somewhere. When I was a young student at the conservatory, everybody was playing Sibelius; Wagner was still around to a great extent; and of course Debussy and Ravel were very much alive. Schoenberg was just beginning to be recognized as a leading force in the musical activity of the world. I think that music has become more diffuse now, but at that time there were different and precise styles like the Hindemith style, the Schoenberg style, and the modern French style which was exemplified by the works of Debussy and Ravel. I imagine Sibelius also had quite an influence among American composers, although I can't say that I know of anyone who actually fashioned his music after Sibelius.

I think this is a difficult question because oftentimes we are influenced by composers and artists without even realizing it. If we are sensitive enough, we are influenced by anything that comes along; we have our tentacles out. It's a question of taking advantage of any opportunity that comes along.

12. Q: Has your style changed across your career? If so, what influenced these changes or developments?

A: No, I don't think my style has changed fundamentally. I think it has evolved. The style of any artist, whether he is a musician, a painter, or a writer, evolves as he grows older; it _has_ to evolve.

13. Q: When you are listening to music for your own enjoyment, what are your preferences?

A: I don't listen to much music these days except my own.

Q: That is, unless he comes over to my house and is stuck and can't get away!

A: Then I listen to Hale Smith!!

Notes to Chapter XIII

1. The Short Symphony was given its first performance November 23, 1950.

2. By tradition, the designation "great five" refers to the following group of orchestras: Boston, Chicago, Cleveland, New York, and Philadelphia.

3. Mr. Swanson is referring to the fact that none of these orchestras has performed his works since his return to the United States in 1966; however, prior to that time, his orchestral compositions were being performed by a number of American orchestras, including members of the "great five." The Short Symphony, one of Mr. Swanson's best known and most frequently performed works, was given its first performance by the New York Philharmonic under the direction of Dmitri Mitropoulos.

LIST OF COMPOSITIONS

CAHOOTS (1950)
    Voice and piano. Text by Carl Sandburg. App. 3 min. Weintraub Music, 1951. Dedicated to William Warfield.

CONCERTO FOR ORCHESTRA (circa 1957)
    Three movements. App. $19\frac{1}{2}$ min. Weintraub Music, 1970. Recorded by the Budapest Philharmonic Orchestra, Benjamin Steinberg, conductor (Silhouettes in Courage SIL-K5001/5002: The Long Quest). Commissioned by and first performed (1957) by the Louisville Symphony Orchestra, Robert Whitney, conductor.

THE CUCKOO (1948)
    Piano. App. 3 min. Leeds Music, 1949.

DARLING, THOSE ARE BIRDS (1952)
    Voice and piano. See SONGS FOR PATRICIA.

DARLING, THOSE ARE BIRDS (1952)
    Voice and string orchestra. See SONGS FOR PATRICIA.

A DEATH SONG (1943)
    Voice and piano. Text by Paul Laurence Dunbar. Estimated duration: app. 2-3 min. Weintraub Music, 1951.

FANTASY PIECE FOR SOPRANO SAXOPHONE AND STRINGS (1969)
    One movement. Estimated duration: app. 18-20 min. Weintraub Music, rental. Commissioned by the Thorne Music Fund and dedicated to Francis Thorne. This work is listed in the Weintraub catalogue as FANTASY PIECE FOR CLARINET AND STRINGS; however, Mr. Swanson specifies soprano saxophone.

FOUR PRELUDES (1947)
    Voice and piano. Text by T. S. Eliot. Four songs, no titles. First lines are as follows: The winter evening settles down; The morning comes to consciousness; You tossed a blanket from the bed; His soul stretched tight across the skies. App. 6 min. 5 sec. Weintraub Music, 1952.

GHOSTS IN LOVE (1950)
    Voice and piano. Text by Vachel Lindsay. App. 1 min. 55 sec. Weintraub Music, 1950. Recorded by Helen Thigpen, soprano, and David Allen, piano (Desto DC-6422).

GOODNIGHT (1952)
    Voice and piano. See SONGS FOR PATRICIA.

GOODNIGHT (1952)
    Voice and string orchestra. See SONGS FOR PATRICIA.

HIS SOUL STRETCHED TIGHT ACROSS THE SKIES (1947)
See FOUR PRELUDES.

I WILL LIE DOWN IN AUTUMN
Voice and piano. Text by May Swenson. Estimated duration:
2-3 min. Weintraub Music, 1952.

IN TIME OF SILVER RAIN (1947)
Voice and piano. Text by Langston Hughes. App. 3 min. 45
sec. Weintraub Music, 1950.

JOY (1946)
Voice and piano. Text by Langston Hughes. App. 45 sec.
Weintraub Music, 1950. Recorded by Helen Thigpen, soprano,
and David Allen, piano (Desto DC-6422).

THE JUNK MAN (1950)
Voice and piano. Text by Carl Sandburg. App. 2 min. 45 sec.
Weintraub Music, 1950. Recorded by Helen Thigpen, soprano,
and David Allen, piano (Desto DC-6422).

THE MORNING COMES TO CONSCIOUSNESS (1947)
See FOUR PRELUDES.

MUSIC FOR STRINGS (1952)
String orchestra. 12 min. Weintraub Music, rental. First
performance (1952) at Town Hall by the Little Orchestra Society,
Thomas Scherman, conductor.

THE NEGRO SPEAKS OF RIVERS (1942)
Voice and piano. Text by Langston Hughes. App. 4 min. 5 sec.
Weintraub Music, 1950. Recorded by Helen Thigpen, soprano,
and David Allen, piano (Desto DC-6422).

NIGHT MUSIC (1950)
Chamber orchestra (flute, oboe, clarinet, bassoon, F horn, and
strings). 9 min. Weintraub Music, rental. Recorded by the
New York Ensemble of the Philharmonic Scholarship Winners,
Dimitri Mitropoulos, conductor (Decca DL-8511; Decca DCM-
3215). First performance (1950) at the Locust Valley Music
Festival. Clara Roesch, conductor.

NIGHT SONG (1948)
Voice and piano. Text by Langston Hughes. App. 2 min. 15
sec. Weintraub Music, 1950. Recorded by Helen Thigpen,
soprano, and David Allen, piano (Desto DC-6422).

NIGHTINGALES
Chorus (TTBB) unaccompanied. Text by Robert Seymour
Bridges. Weintraub Music, 1952. Commissioned by Leonard
De Paur.

NO LEAF MAY FALL (1952)
Voice and piano. See SONGS FOR PATRICIA.

NO LEAF MAY FALL (1952)
Voice and string orchestra. See SONGS FOR PATRICIA.

NOCTURNE (1948)
Violin and piano. App. 3 min. 20 sec. Weintraub Music, 1951.

ONE DAY (1952)
Voice and piano. See SONGS FOR PATRICIA.

ONE DAY (1952)
Voice and string orchestra. See SONGS FOR PATRICIA.

PIERROT (1946)
Voice and piano. Text by Langston Hughes. App. 2 min. 15 sec. Weintraub Music, 1950.

SAW A GRAVE UPON A HILL
Voice and piano. Text by May Swenson. App. $3\frac{1}{2}$ min. Weintraub Music, 1952.

SHORT SYMPHONY (1948)
Orchestra. Three movements. App. 11-$12\frac{1}{2}$ min. Weintraub Music, rental. Recorded by the Vienna State Opera Orchestra, Franz Litschauer, conductor (Composers Recordings Inc. CRI SD-254) and by the American Recording Society Orchestra, Dean Dixon, conductor (American Recording Society ARS-116). Dedicated to Dimitri Mitropoulos. First performance (1950) at Carnegie Hall by the New York Philharmonic, Dimitri Mitropoulos, conductor. This composition won the 1951 New York Critics Circle Award for the best orchestral work of the 1950-51 season.

SNOWDUNES
Voice and piano. Text by May Swenson. App. 3 min. 45 sec. Weintraub Music, 1955.

SONATA FOR VIOLONCELLO AND PIANO (1973)
Three movements. Estimated duration: 20-25 min. First performance (1973) at Alice Tully Hall. Ronald Lipscomb, violoncello; Zita Carno, piano.

SONATA NO. 1 (1948)
Piano. Three movements. App. $9\frac{1}{2}$ min. Weintraub Music, 1950.

SONATA NO. 2 (in progress; to be completed by summer 1976)
Piano. Three movements.

SONATA NO. 3 (in progress; to be completed by summer 1976)
Piano. Three movements.

SONGS FOR PATRICIA (1952)
Voice and piano. Text by Norman Rosten. Four songs:
Darling, Those Are Birds; No Leaf May Fall; One Day; Good-
night. App. 6 min. 25 sec. Weintraub Music, 1952.

SONGS FOR PATRICIA (1952)
Voice and string orchestra. Text by Norman Rosten. Four
songs: Darling, Those Are Birds; No Leaf May Fall; One Day;
Goodnight. App. 6 min. 25 sec. Weintraub Music, rental.

SOUNDPIECE FOR BRASS QUINTET (1952)
App. $5\frac{1}{2}$ min. Weintraub Music, 1953.

STILL LIFE (1950)
Voice and piano. Text by Carl Sandburg. App. 1 min. 25 sec.
Weintraub Music, 1950. Recorded by Helen Thigpen, soprano,
and David Allen, piano (Desto DC-6422).

SUITE FOR VIOLONCELLO AND PIANO (1949)
Four movements: Prelude; Pantomine; Dirge; Recessional.
App. 13 min. 45 sec. Weintraub Music, 1951. Recorded by
Carl Stern, violoncello, and Abba Bogin, piano (Society of Par-
ticipating Artists SPA-54). Commissioned by and dedicated to
Bernard Greenhouse.

SYMPHONY NO. 1 (1945)
Orchestra. Four movements. 25 min. Weintraub Music,
rental. First performance (1969) at Lincoln Center. Symphony
of the New World, Benjamin Steinberg, conductor.

SYMPHONY NO. 2 (1948)
Orchestra. See SHORT SYMPHONY.

SYMPHONY NO. 3 (1970)
Orchestra. Three movements. Estimated duration: 30 min.
Weintraub Music, rental. Commissioned by and first performed
(1970) by the Symphony of the New World, Benjamin Steinberg,
conductor.

TO BE OR NOT TO BE
Voice and piano. Anonymous text. App. 3 min. Weintraub
Music, 1951.

TRIO FOR FLUTE, OBOE, AND PIANO (1975)
Three movements. 13 min. 45 sec. Weintraub Music, rental.
Recorded by the New World Trio (Harold Jones, flute; Harry
Smyles, oboe; and Alan Booth, piano) on Folkways FTS-33903
(record jacket carries incorrect title TRIO FOR FLUTE, CLARI-
NET, AND PIANO). Commissioned by and dedicated to the New
World Trio.

TWO NOCTURNES (1967)
Piano. App. 10 min. Weintraub Music, rental.

THE VALLEY
  Voice and piano. Text by Charles Edwin Markham. App. 1
  min. 50 sec. Weintraub Music, 1951. Recorded by Helen
  Thigpen, soprano, and David Allen, piano (Desto DC-6422).

VISTA NO. II (1969)
  String octet. App. 15 min. Weintraub Music, rental.

THE WINTER EVENING SETTLES DOWN (1947)
  See FOUR PRELUDES.

YOU TOSSED A BLANKET FROM THE BED (1947)
  See FOUR PRELUDES.

BIBLIOGRAPHY

Baker, Theodore. Baker's Biographical Dictionary of Musicians.
  5th ed. (1958) completely revised by Nicholas Slonimsky, s. v.
  "Swanson, Howard."

Brooks, Tilford. "A Historical Study of Black Music and Selected
  Twentieth Century Black Composers and Their Role in American
  Society." Ed. D. dissertation, Washington University, 1972.

Claghorn, Charles E. Biographical Dictionary of American Music.
  West Nyack, New York: Parker Publishing Company, 1973.

Ennett, Dorothy Maxine. "An Analysis and Comparison of Selected
  Piano Sonatas by Three Contemporary Black Composers: George
  Walker, Howard Swanson, and Roque Cordero." Ph. D. disserta-
  tion, New York University, 1973.

Grove's Dictionary of Music and Musicians. 5th ed. (1954), s. v.
  "Swanson, Howard," by Peggy Glanville-Hicks.

"Howard Swanson." Pan Pipes 44 (January 1952): 45-46.

Jackson, Raymond. "The Piano Music of Twentieth Century Black
  Americans as Illustrated Mainly in the Works of Three Composers." D. M. A. dissertation, Juilliard School of Music, 1973.

Nolan, Robert L. "The Music of Howard Swanson." Negro History
  Bulletin 34 (December 1971): 177-178.

Roach, Hildred. Black American Music: Past and Present. Boston: Crescendo Publishing Company, 1973.

Sims, D. Maxine. "An Analysis and Comparison of Piano Sonatas
  by George Walker and Howard Swanson." The Black Perspective in Music 4 (Spring 1976): 70-81.

Southern, Eileen. "America's Black Composers of Classical Music." Music Educators Journal 62 (November 1975): 46-59.

_____. The Music of Black Americans. New York: W. W. Norton, 1971.

"The Swanson Story." Music News 43 (October 1951): 11.

Thompson, Oscar. The International Cyclopedia of Music and Musicians. 9th ed. (1964) edited by Robert Sabin, s.v. "Swanson, Howard."

Yestadt, Sister Marie. "Song Literature of the 70's: A Socio-Musical Approach." The NATS Bulletin 29 (May-June 1973): 22-27.

Yuhasz, Sister Marie Joy. "Black Composers and Their Piano Music, Part I." The American Music Teacher 19 (February/ March 1970): 24+.

George T. Walker (courtesy of the composer)

CHAPTER XIV

GEORGE THEOPHILUS WALKER

George Theophilus Walker was born June 27, 1922 in Washington, D. C. In 1937 he graduated from Dunbar High School and, at the age of fifteen, entered Oberlin College on a scholarship. He later became the first black graduate of the Curtis Institute.

His educational background includes a B. M. in piano with highest honors (1941) from Oberlin College, an Artist Diploma in piano (1945) from the Curtis Institute, a diploma in piano (1947) from the Conservatoire Americaine in Fontainebleau, and a Doctor of Musical Arts degree and Artist Diploma in piano (1957) from the Eastman School of Music. He studied piano with Rudolph Serkin, Clifford Curzon, and Robert Casadesus; chamber music with William Primrose and Gregor Piatigorsky; orchestration and opera with Gian-Carlo Menotti; and composition with Rosario Scalero and Nadia Boulanger.

Dr. Walker's Town Hall debut recital in 1945 marked the beginning of his long and distinguished career as a concert pianist, during which he has performed extensively throughout the United States and Europe. Prior to his 1975 appointment to the faculty of the University of Delaware as Distinguished Visiting Professor, he held positions at Dillard University, the Dalcroze School of Music, the New School for Social Research, Smith College, University of Colorado, Rutgers University (Newark), and Peabody Conservatory.

Dr. Walker has been the recipient of numerous awards and grants including a Fulbright Fellowship (1958), a John Hay Whitney Fellowship (1958), a MacDowell Colony Fellowship (1966), a Guggenheim Fellowship (1969), a Bennington Composers Conference Fellowship (1967), a Yaddo Fellowship (1973), Rockefeller Fellowships (1972-1975), and grants from the University of Colorado (1968) and the Rutgers University Research Council (1969-1974). He won the Religious Arts Festival Award (1961) for Psalm 84, the Harvey Gaul Prize (1964) for Sonata for Two Pianos, and an award in the Rhea Sosland Chamber Music Contest (1967) for his String Quartet No. 2. The National Endowment for the Arts, the Cleveland Orchestra, the David Ensemble, the Washington Society for the Performing Arts, the Atlanta Symphony Orchestra, the Symphony of the

New World, and the Hans Kindler Foundation are among the organizations from which he has received commissions.

Dr. Walker has written works for a number of vocal and instrumental combinations including orchestra, chamber ensemble, piano, chorus, voice and piano, and various solo instruments in combination with piano or orchestra. Among his best-known compositions are Address for Orchestra, Concerto for Trombone and Orchestra, Lyric for Strings, Sonata No. 1 for Piano, and Sonata No. 2 for Piano. In addition to his activities as a composer, pianist, and educator, Dr. Walker is also a writer. He has contributed articles to several music periodicals and has had two of his poems published in Grecourt Review.

Part I: General Questions

1.   Q: What persons, events, and works (of art, literature, etc.) have influenced you in general as well as in terms of your musical activities?

   A: First of all, I have to give an enormous amount of credit to my parents, to my mother for having actually started me with piano when I was five and to my father for having financed virtually my entire career as a pianist. This provided me with enormous stability and confidence. Beyond my parents, my first piano teachers have to be credited with making me aware of my talent to the point where they were very encouraging and very supportive. There were two teachers with whom I studied prior to going to the conservatory at Oberlin. My first teacher's name was Mamie Pinkney Henry. My second teacher, Lillian Allen, is still living. I think the one event that was the most significant in influencing me as a pianist was the first time I heard Horowitz, when I was a student at the Oberlin Conservatory; that really convinced me of what I wanted to do. Subsequently I had the opportunity of studying with Serkin and I was very much impressed by the traditions of the Curtis Institute. I was impressed by my composition teacher Rosario Scalero, primarily because of his approach; he worked from the most elementary aspect of theory to the most complicated technical aspects of composition by having each student, regardless of his previous experience, work through every technique in counterpoint, fugue, canon, and harmony as if he had never studied it before, with the primary objective of becoming a complete master of these compositional techniques. Toscanini was perhaps the most towering musical figure at that time, and I felt an enormous attraction to his musical approach. There aren't any other particular persons who have had quite the same impact as those I've mentioned. I do want to mention, however, that receiving my first MacDowell Colony fellowship was a very significant event for me, because prior to that time I had never sought to have any musical connection with other composers. The fellowship provided me with my first real opportunity for social intercourse with a number of composers in an artist's environment. At the same time this fellowship gave me a stamp of approval, so to speak--the recognition that I was a legitimate composer. Another thing I want to mention in connection with this part of the question is that I feel that I have learned a great deal from my association with my fellow black colleagues in the various symposiums. Each symposium has had a very meaningful effect on both myself and my work; they are very stimulating experiences and I look forward to them with great excitement.

Now we come to art and literature. I am quite fascinated by art because as a student of fifteen I had a very excellent course in art which stimulated my interest in art. In terms of literature, I've read extensively in both fiction and philosophy. I don't have any personal favorites among painters or authors.

2. Q: How would you define black music?
    A: This is really problematic. Although the term black music is currently being used as a subject for discussion about music by black composers or music which shows influences of black music, it is virtually impossible to define to any degree of satisfaction, either in a narrow sense or a general sense. In the broadest sense which I would prefer to consider it, it refers to music by black composers, or music that has been influenced by idioms associated with black musicians in their music, or music which suggests the influence of black idioms on white composers. This definition is too broad to be dealt with, if only because its scope is never completely comprehended. In particular I would like to refer to a review written by Michael Anthony for the Minneapolis Tribune; it is dated May 27, 1975 and reviews a concert of symphonic works by black composers.[1] He states: "With some exceptions, however, the music was no more 'black' than 'white'." He goes on to say that an artist's ethnic background is only one of the many influences from which he draws. But then he deduces that some of the music sounds rather like Bartok, or Schumann, or Prokofiev. The danger in referring to black music is that it makes it possible for this type of critic to make his own interpretation of what he thinks black music is on the basis of his own experience. This often results (as it did in this case) in the critic trying to relate what has been performed --what he has heard as music by a black composer--to what he associates with other music. It's natural for a person to start from a point of reference and make certain deductions from that point; the trouble is that this type of critic never gets beyond his point of reference. It becomes easy for him to say that pieces by black composers sound like Bartok or William Schumann or Prokofiev because these are the

closest stylistic references that he knows. [2] At the same time, this is somewhat understandable because it is in fact true that an exclusively black idiom is not consistently related to any performer or any type of composition; we are all influenced by things outside our own closest affinities.

3. Q: What features of your own music do you see as uniquely black (in terms of both musical and philosophical considerations)?

    A: Following my own loose interpretation of black music, I don't really find anything in my music that is uniquely black. I have made use of some of the techniques associated with black folk music. I've used spirituals both in choral arrangements and incorporated in orchestral compositions; I make use of blues intervals, and I make use of ostinato that is associated with jazz. But I would really hesitate to say that, with the exception of the spirituals, there is anything in my music that is uniquely black.

4. Q: In what ways is your music a reflection of your personal philosophy (social, political, etc.)?

    A: I think it's probably a reflection only from the point of view of my concern for doing the job well. Certainly there is nothing political in the music, and I'm not too certain that there's anything particularly social except what I have used of the spirituals, which I feel to be extraordinary in their musical content and emotional depth. I have done that with a purpose because I think that the spirituals are a treasure that black people should always be aware of, proud that it has emanated from a scorched earth tradition.

5. Q: What do you see as the position or role of the black artist in contemporary society?

    A: I think of the artist as an individual. At times I think he is a lost soul crying in the wilderness to be heard. I'm always reminded of Countee Cullen's poem "Yet Do I Marvel," the last lines of which are "Yet do I marvel at this curious thing/To make a poet black and bid him sing."[3] I think that the black artist is trying for legitimacy in both the artistic and social environment which surrounds him; he is striving first of all to make himself visible so that he can be understood.

6. Q: Please discuss any problems you may have encountered in getting your works performed, published, and recorded.

    A: I had a great deal of difficulty initially in getting my works published. I wasn't, for quite a long time, interested so much in having my works performed. I was more interested in getting recitals and concerts as a pianist than I was in being known as a composer. Then, about six years ago, the problems of getting published seemed to become less formidable. About three years ago I met my present publisher--Paul Kapp of General Music--and since then I have virtually resolved the problems of being published. In terms of recordings, I wasn't as concerned initially with being recorded as a composer as I was being recorded as a pianist. Most composers feel that they would like to have more of their works recorded, and I'm certainly no exception.

6A. Q: How much of your actual output has ever been performed? Published? Recorded?

A: Actually, the greater part of my output has been performed, although not as well as I would have liked. I don't really have an enormous catalogue. At this point in my career I am almost totally unaware of many performances that do take place, but I would say that certainly the greater part of my output has been performed.

Published? I have some new works which will be available by next month. With these new works, I will have probably thirty published works. These are basically the smaller works, not the large orchestral works. The greater part of my smaller works have been published; most of the large works have not been published.

Only a very small percent of my compositional output has been recorded. There are recordings of my second piano sonata, two piano pieces, 4 the trombone concerto, the Lyric for Strings (which was actually the slow movement of my first string quartet), and the Passacaglia from the Address for Orchestra. These represent really a minuscule total of the published works.

6B. Q: Have you encountered difficulty in getting your works programmed?

A: That's a very difficult question for me to answer because I don't make a great deal of effort to get my works played. The main problem I have now is getting orchestral works played in their entirety; they are usually segmented. The usual excuse given for this is that there is not enough rehearsal time to prepare the entire work. Another problem (and this is a common complaint of many contemporary composers) is getting one performance of a work and not being able to get subsequent performances.

6C. Q: Are there specific problems in getting a satisfactory performance? Exemplify and discuss.

A: Lack of rehearsal time seems to be the chief problem relating to orchestral compositions. It sometimes affects the chamber works as well. But the fact that the performers may have a great deal of difficulty putting something together is sort of preconditioned; it relates in part to the lack of time but it also relates to the difficulty of some of the pieces, in fact, most of the pieces. I hate to be too hard on the performer; I'm always flattered when someone wishes to do a work of mine, but it's seldom that the work has the finish that I would like it to have. I can think of exceptions to this. I refer to my sister, Frances Walker,

who plays both my piano sonatas beautifully. I have a new
work for clarinet and piano (four hands) that received an
excellent first performance by the David Ensemble. [5] I always feel as if I would like to collaborate in preparing the
performance, but this is not always possible. Even when
I am working with the performers, I sometimes encounter
the kind of resistance that comes from prima donnas (both
male and female) being totally subjective about what they
want to do with the work.

7. Q: What do you consider, at this point in your life, to be your
        most significant achievement(s) aside from your composi-
        tions?
    A: There are certain performances I did as a pianist, begin-
        ning with my Town Hall debut recital in 1945, which I
        look back on with some degree of satisfaction. As a teach-
        er I look back on some of the fine piano students I've had
        and on the particular kind of pleasure I've had in teaching.

8. Q: What do you see as the responsibilities and obligations of
        the educational system (at all levels) to the study of black
        music?
    A: I feel that there has simply not been enough emphasis in
        the public schools or even in the colleges on the contribu-
        tions of black musicians to the history of music. Oddly
        enough, at this point I am able to look back to the Saturday
        classes which I attended (and resented!) at the preparatory
        school at Howard University when I was ten or so. I was
        taking piano in the music department there, and the Satur-
        day class was a supplement to the piano lessons. There
        was a lady who was a very well-known authority on Creole
        music, Camille Nickerson, and she used to speak with great
        conviction about the great black singers, composers, and
        performers. As I look back on this I realize that it was
        the kind of experience that very few black youngsters have
        now. They simply are not aware of what happened ten
        years ago, certainly in the field of classical music. They
        may be au courant about what is happening in jazz or rock,
        but this is only one side of the coin and the other side is
        certainly as important, even to youngsters. I think that on
        the college level we have to insist that seminal figures in
        black music be incorporated into the white history books of
        Grout and the other major historians. The educational
        system must be made responsive to the cultural achieve-
        ments of all black artists. I know that in today's schools
        our teachers are so intent upon being relevant that they
        stress what is happening now on the jazz or rock scene.
        That's very superficial--there is much more to that scene
        than what exists today. There really ought to be a major
        effort made to develop a sense of cultural history from a
        point well beyond that of the present.

9. Q: Do you feel that the people who write about your music

(critics in particular) understand what you are doing? Exemplify and discuss.

A: I sympathize with the job that critics have to do, especially New York critics, going out every night whether they want to or not. It would seem to be an attractive job, but it's really such an enormous task for even the most competent person. But it's really depressing to experience a review from a critic who is not capable of being reasonably competent in his judgment. Part of the problem is aural; another part is the matter of criteria. In view of the fact that aesthetic standards are really depressingly low at this time, it is certainly no wonder that one finds a critic either refusing to commit himself or expressing a view which is either provincial or subject to personal whim based on his limitations. I am perhaps not so much concerned with the critic understanding what I'm doing in the sense of incorporating ethnic materials or elements; I'm more concerned about whether a critic can comprehend the total organization of the piece. That's asking a lot. It is making an enormous demand upon any listener to hear something for the first time and be musically astute and knowledgeable--to sense the total direction of the piece as well as whatever details happen to make up the piece. Some critics get lost in the stylistic aspect of the piece; others have their personal preferences as to idiom, and still others simply sit on the fence for fear of either making a substantial faux pas or offending some portion of their readers. So they are a necessary evil, necessary only because they contribute to publicizing works being performed (and I've been told that publicity is a good thing).

10. Q: What advice would you give to the aspiring young black composer?

A: Whatever advice I would offer would be in part conditioned by my own experience as a student. I feel that it's terribly important that one should try to achieve a high degree of technical facility and be able to manipulate ideas both harmonically and contrapuntally. It is also very important that a young composer be an avid listener of music and a knowledgeable student of music history. I think that composition should be based on an awareness of the many choices that one has stylistically and the critical awareness of what one chooses to reject if one is to select.

Part II: Music Questions

1. Q: When you sit down to begin a new composition on your own initiative or inspiration (as opposed to a commissioned work), what procedure or approach do you follow?

2. Q: When composing a commissioned work or a work written for a specific occasion or person, does your procedure or approach differ from the one you described in question one?

If so, in what way?

(Ed. note: Dr. Walker chose to answer questions one and two together.)

A: I don't treat the writing of a commissioned work any differently from the writing of a non-commissioned work. I approach both with a sense of dread! (laughter) I hope that I can somehow make a beginning, and have it blossom into something worth continuing. I try to make my approach vary. There was a time in the past when I decided that I was going to write, for example, a sonata or a sonata-like movement or a set of variations; now it's become more haphazard if only because of the fact that I'm always trying to do something a little different from what I've done before, although that may not always be apparent. It happened in the past that I would not always start out with a clear idea of what a piece was going to be, but within a few measures I would know what it was going to be in terms of form. Now I discourage that in my thinking. I'd say that for the most part I begin with an idea that is essentially melodic. It may not always be the beginning, though, because after working on the composition I might find something that I would like to have precede it. In fact, I've been acutely conscious lately of a predilection for introductions; sometimes these introductions are related to the principal idea, but more often than not, they are unrelated.

3. Q: In general, with regard to your writing, what genre(s) do you prefer?

A: I don't really have any preference. Without any qualification, I love to hear performances of my orchestral music, and since I have been fortunate in getting more performances of these works, I look forward to both the rehearsing of the work and the performance.

4. Q: What do you consider your most significant composition? Please discuss.

A: That's really a hard question. It is an interesting question from another aspect, that is, the interpretation of the word "significant." For me it could mean "most completely satisfactory" in the sense that I've managed to achieve pretty much of what I thought I would not be able to achieve (which is normally the way I feel about my compositions). Basically, I look at my compositions in the same way that I look at the compositions of other composers. If someone were to ask me who my favorite composers were I would be completely nonplussed because I don't have any. Instead I would probably say that I like one movement of this work or one movement of that work. In the same way, I look at the things in my works which for me were the most successful. These are things which I doubt most people would know about. For example, from my point of view some of my most successful things have been fugues, particularly the fugue from my second string quartet, the fugue from my cello sonata, and the fugue from my violin sonata. In terms of overall impact, I'd probably select the ending of my violin sonata. I think I would also have to include the piano concerto and the first piano sonata, as well as some of the songs ("Bereaved Maid" in particular) and some of the choral pieces which aren't really known.

5. Q: Please comment on your treatment of the following musical elements and give examples from your compositions that illustrate the techniques you describe:

   A. Melody

   GW: I have been concerned for a fairly long time with melodic content which is oriented toward twelve-tone considerations. By that I mean to say that the actual tones of the melody will be represented by from nine to twelve notes without actually being part of a totally serialized system. By making use of this type of melody I am able to achieve a less tonally oriented type of harmonic implication. My pieces are intended to be melodic in a freely singable sense without being conventional in either a diatonic or a chromatic sense. Let me give you some examples. In the Passacaglia from the Address for Orchestra there are ten or eleven notes making up the theme itself. In the piano concerto the second theme of the first movement is ten or eleven notes. In the trombone concerto the trombone entrance in the first movement is nine notes.

   B. Harmony

   GW: To talk about harmony is much more difficult. I don't have any preconceived ideas of what I'm trying to do harmonically, partially because I have a strong tendency to think linearly. I have at times been fascinated by harmonic structures involving fourths; I am fond of harmonies in which the tritone appears. But I try to evolve harmonic structures which are not symmetrical. The one exception is the second piano sonata, which was one part of my doctoral dissertation. The thesis behind it was to write a composition that was wholly dominated by the presence of thirds (or their inversion--sixths); there is a high degree of consistency in that work, which is intentional.

   C. Rhythm

   GW: That's an interesting question. Conductors regard me with a certain amount of vehement displeasure because of my meter changes. Complaints, for example, have been registered about the meter structure of the first movement of the Address for Orchestra. After the introduction, the fugue begins in 3/8 and then goes 4/8, 5/8, 6/8; that's really part of the structure of the fugue itself.

What has interested me since the writing of that composition has been the possibility of creating a linearity of unpredictable lengths, particularly with apparent cadential effects, but certainly going well beyond any classical or romantic concept of phrase (which has implicit with it whatever theorists have determined to be the norms for length). My fascination with linearity has led me to become interested in a free kind of meter that often ends up being irregular. Since it is not desirable from a conductor's point of view to incorporate an uneven number of beats into the conventional 3/4 or 4/4 measure, it would be better not to have a measure of 11/8 but rather a measure of 4/4 plus a measure of 3/8. This of course means that both the conductor and the performers have to be on their toes, and that's not popular, I'm afraid. There is no answer to this problem in terms of orchestral writing, but in writing for a solo instrument the answer is simply to leave out all meters. This has been done, and I will probably be doing it in my next piece. It really doesn't present any problems for the solo performer; he has to count all of the eighths and quarters anyway.

D. Form
GW: I have really been a strong advocate of traditional forms simply because they provide stability to a work. The moment one ventures into a less well-defined organizational procedure, one creates the possibility of a dangerous imbalance. That's just a possibility; it need not be that way. In my works I have tried to mix up structures which adhere to classical or Baroque concepts and have treated these structures somewhat freely, although the basic aspects of these forms are still evident. On the other hand, I have worked with forms which are somewhat improvisatory; one of the best examples of that is Spektra.

I keep coming back to traditional forms because they provide a base from which I can incorporate new and more contemporary content into my music. I can also create more deviations than one would normally associate with the more classical aspects of these forms.

In retrospect, I think I have shown a partiality to variation forms, sonata forms, and fugues. But the point is that I try to mix these classically derived systems with other things that are sometimes a little hard to grasp readily. I feel that it's possible to befuddle even the average musician with what one does with the classical forms.

E. Improvisation
(Ed. note: Dr. Walker was informed that the question
also addressed the use of aleatoric devices
and chance music as well as improvisation.)

GW: Considering my unrelenting concern for the observation of the printed page, especially in my music,
I have no real use for aleatoric music. I'm sure
that there are other composers who feel as I do
about aleatoric music; there's quite a bit of the
ego involved! But I do feel rather strongly that
I get enough surprises hearing prepared performances of my works. I am sympathetic to the performer; I think the risks involved in performance
have to be understood by both the composer and
the audience. These risks are determined in
part by the very nature of performance, but I
don't really care to have them enlarged by chance
operations. This is not only because one may not
be totally familiar with what notes might be played
or how they might be played; it is possible for us
to work those things out. What concerns me is
the total organization of the work and its cohesive-
ness.

F. Text
GW: My early songs made use of poems that at that
time I felt a particular affinity with. Subsequently I have had greater difficulty in finding poems
that I feel capable of setting, as well as poems
I especially like, which have a different kind of
content than those I've set in the past. The love-
lyric type, which is what I've primarily set in the
past, is something I would like to avoid, with the
hope that I would be able to achieve other effects
besides the purely lyrical. I am sort of at a
standstill in trying to find texts that I think I can
work effectively with, so I have not written much
in this area recently. I have one new song coming out next month, [6] but the treatment of the text
involves the imposition of a style on the lyric itself. It's one of the few times that I have incorporated a decidedly blues element into the music
in an improvisatory way, so I was able to deal
with a conventional text in a different way by
utilizing this type of musical material. But it's
not really what I would like to do; I would really
like to find a different type of text to challenge
me.

Q: Once you have selected a text, how do you go
about deciding how you want to realize it?
GW: Normally it's defining the melodic element in
conjunction with the phrase length of both the text

and the music. Sometimes I actually work against the natural phrase lengths, and sometimes I conform to them.

G. Instrumentation or medium

GW: I don't have any particular combinations that I like to work with. Sometimes if I have discovered a particular effect that I like, I catalogue it so that I can either avoid it or make some slight deviation from it; this is because the pursuit of fresh timbres involves, to a certain extent, trying to stay away from effects one knows one can produce and taking a risk in treating something slightly differently. But there are certain basic things that one is always working with in terms of instrumentation. It's something that fascinates me, but more in terms of the particular harmonic structure that I'm working with rather than purely considerations of instrumentation.

6. Q: Have difficulties with performance practice (inflection, phrasing, etc.) been a significant problem in having your works performed to your own satisfaction?

A: Not really. It is something that I think is not pertinent to any performances I've had, although some composers I have observed in the past become quite wrathful when the drum is struck in the middle of the head rather than on the edge. I must say that I really haven't had any problems other than worrying about whether the orchestra was going to fall apart in the middle of the piece, which has happened! And then there's the problem of having only portions of a work performed--that's so infuriating! It's by no means something that happens to just one composer. I've reached the point that I recognize the stone wall when I see it now. I've literally been told that if I didn't agree to have part of a work played, none of it would be played. What can you say? The solution is not as simple as the composer would like to have it.

7. Q: What major works are currently in progress? Please describe and discuss.

A: I worked earlier in the summer on a work for cello and orchestra that was commissioned by the Cleveland Orchestra for performance in April 1976. [7] I was working on it in Europe and since I've been back I haven't looked to find out whether it's going to be long enough; it's not supposed to be a long work. I put it aside to work on another commission, a work for solo piano. [8] Leon Bates commissioned it through the Washington Society for the Performing Arts, and he is scheduled to play it at the Kennedy Center in Washington in January. Those are the two works in progress now. In addition, I have a chamber work which I am writing for brass quintet, but since I'm considering using some older material, I haven't quite decided whether it's going to work.

8. Q: Given unlimited time and finances (and no restrictions what-
      soever), what would you write?

   A: I'd probably say that I'd really prefer to go fishing. That's
      a fairly sincere response because the only thing that I have
      actually written off as a possibility is an opera. I was ac-
      tually much more interested in writing an opera ten or fif-
      teen years ago than I am now. If I were to be put in a sit-
      uation where I wouldn't have to make a deadline and I
      wouldn't have to be worried with other commissions, I
      might possibly write an opera, or I might also write an-
      other extended orchestral work. But since I do in fact
      have another commission for a work for orchestra and cho-
      rus, which I think will be a liturgical work, I probably
      would not be ready to write an opera after finishing that
      work.

9. Q: If given the opportunity would you choose to devote yourself
      to composition on a full-time basis? Why or why not?

   A: No, I definitely would not. I think it's too stifling. Giving
      up teaching would be kind of a welcome relief in a way, but
      teaching does provide a stimulus and creates a routine
      around which one has to work, constituting a discipline for
      one's other activities. I've never been particularly sold on
      the idea of writing an enormous amount of music anyway.
      I think there are very few composers with the kind of talent
      that enables them to have a high output quantitatively and
      also write a large proportion of interesting music. I defi-
      nitely would prefer to play. In fact, I think the ideal situa-
      tion for me would probably involve doing a limited amount
      of concerts (twenty or thirty a year), composing, and teach-
      ing a few gifted, advanced piano students.

10. Q: How would you describe your compositional style?

    A: I think the so-called style varies somewhat; however, I
       think that the style does vary from the relatively simple
       diatonic idiom to an idiom that is more complex. I think
       it really depends on the piece. Of course, the question of
       any consistencies throughout my output always arises and
       I like to think that the lyrical quality may be the most con-
       sistent element. My more recent work in general has be-
       come somewhat more dramatic, but again I think a descrip-
       tion of style is dependent more or less on the individual
       piece.

11. Q: What have been the influences of other composers, styles,
       and other types of music on your compositional style?

    A: At my first composition lessons, when I was eighteen, my
       teacher introduced me to Stravinsky and Ives. My com-
       position teacher, whose name was Norman Lockwood,
       showed me some Ives songs and a piano reduction of Stra-
       vinsky's Symphony of Psalms. Considering the giants living
       in this country in the 1950s, I preferred Stravinsky to
       Schoenberg or Hindemith. Although everybody was flocking
       to study with Hindemith at Yale, I never really wanted to

study with him. I shunned that particular path although I have always had a great admiration for a few of his pieces. I was fascinated by the open quality of much of Copland's music (as opposed to some of the elements in Schoenberg's works), and I think I consciously attempted to arrive at this kind of openness in certain passages. But I think that basically, even in my earlier works, my music is more complex than Copland's.

I think that when I was searching for a linear kind of phrasing I was immediately drawn to Gregorian chant. I am still extraordinarily fond of Gregorian chant, and I consider it quite a strong influence. I admire the slight inflections in the line; in relation to the stepwise motion, these enormously subtle inflections are so expressive!

Subsequent influences haven't been anything more than a passing interest in a particular disposition of instrumentation or a particular harmony. On the other hand, I have become more interested in color (in terms of orchestration) than I had been.

Some people have said that my music reminds them of Barber, and have found similarities between myself and Barber in certain pieces. This may very well be. We studied with the same teacher, Rosario Scalero, whom I consider my principal composition teacher even though our work involved very little composition; it was really working with counterpoint, fugue, canon, and other techniques, but it was his approach which permeated my early works. One critic in particular has made reference to the Address for Orchestra being reminiscent of Barber; I think he was probably referring to the last movement. I anticipate that once Columbia has released the Lyric for Strings, there will be more comments about how similar my music is to Barber's, especially with reference to the Adagio for Strings. I think that my Lyric is really quite different, but since it has something of an elegiac quality I know that I can expect comments that it sounds sort of like Barber.

12. Q: Has your style changed across your career? If so, what influenced these changes or developments?

A: I think the stylistic changes relate more to the incorporation of diverse elements. I have utilized twelve-tone technique as well as elements of jazz and the blues in an effort to keep my music fresh and free of repetition of any sort. I think my style reflects the kind of selectivity every composer engages in when he hears something that is particularly interesting or appealing to him. He has to somehow find his own way to make use of it. Since composition is really organization, I feel that selectivity is a very strong part in the organization of any piece. I do a lot of listening to determine what I like in any particular idiom; I want to find out how things work and if they can be made to work better.

13. Q: When you are listening to music for your own enjoyment, what are your preferences?

A: It's a more complex question for me because of my addiction to hi-fi. It's more than a joke with some people; I have become extremely retiring and don't discuss it except with a few close friends. I'm fairly well-known here in the New York area because of my interest in hi-fi. Well, all of this is to say that I like to scan the radio columns of the Sunday Times to see what works of interest are programmed; I especially look for contemporary works that I don't know. And in the past I was a great borrower. I would take records from the university library and keep them for an interminable period!

Actually, my listening tastes are quite catholic. But primarily I'm interested in whatever contemporary music is around and, at the same time, whatever seems to provide me with a reference for judging top quality hi-fi. I'm terribly picky in the classical area and with regard to jazz; I haven't yet been educated to rock.

Notes to Chapter XIV

1. Minneapolis Tribune, 27 May 1975, p. 8B.

2. See the last paragraph of Dr. Walker's response to II-11 for his discussion of the comparisons which have been made between his works and the compositions of Samuel Barber.

3. Arna Bontemps, ed., American Negro Poetry (New York: Hill and Wang, 1963), p. 88.

4. Actually, four of Dr. Walker's compositions for solo piano have been recorded. Sonata No. 1 for Piano was recorded on Desto's Natalie Hinderas Plays Music by Black Composers (Desto DC-7102/ 7103). Sonata No. 2 for Piano, Spatials, and Spektra were recorded by Dr. Walker for Composer's Recordings, Inc. (CRI SD-270).

5. Five Fancys for Clarinet and Piano (Four Hands).

6. A Red, Red Rose.

7. Dialogus for Cello and Orchestra.

8. Sonata No. 3 for Piano.

LIST OF COMPOSITIONS

ADDRESS FOR ORCHESTRA (1959)
Three movements. 22 min. MCA Music, 1970. Third move-

ment recorded under the title PASSACAGLIA by the Oakland Youth Orchestra, Robert Hughes, conductor (Desto DC-7107: The Black Composer in America). Commissioned by the Symphony of the New World. First performance (1971) at the Mons Festival (Mons, Belgium), James DePriest, conductor. Although the Symphony of the New World (Benjamin Steinberg, conductor) performed movements I and III of this work at Lincoln Center in 1968, the Belgian performance was the first performance of the work in its entirety.

ANTIPHONYS FOR CHAMBER ORCHESTRA (1968)
Chamber orchestra (flute, oboe, B♭ clarinet, bassoon, F horn, C trumpet, trombone, percussion, and strings). 5 min. 50 sec. First performance by the Bennington College Chamber Orchestra, E. Guigi, conductor.

ANTIPHONYS FOR STRING ORCHESTRA (1968)
5 min. 50 sec. General Music, agent. This work is a transcription for string orchestra of ANTIPHONYS FOR CHAMBER ORCHESTRA. First performance (1968) at the New England Chamber Festival (Univ. of Mass.) by the New England Festival Chamber Orchestra, Paul Olefsky, conductor.

THE BEREAVED MAID (1953)
Medium voice and piano. Anonymous text. 6 min. General Music, 1971. Distributed by Frank Music. First performance (1958) in Paris. Sylvia McDonald, soprano; Boyd McDonald, piano.

THE BEREAVED MAID (1958)
Chorus (SATB) with piano. See THREE LYRICS FOR CHORUS.

CAPRICE (1941)
See PRELUDE AND CAPRICE.

CONCERTO FOR TROMBONE AND ORCHESTRA (1957)
Three movements. 16 min. General Music, agent. Recorded by Denis Wick, trombonist, and the London Symphony Orchestra, Paul Freeman, conductor (Columbia M-32783: Vol. 3, Black Composers Series). First performance (1957) by the Rochester Philharmonic, Howard Hanson, conductor; P. Poindexter, trombone.

CONCERTO FOR TROMBONE AND ORCHESTRA (1957)
Trombone and piano; reduction made by the composer. Three movements. 16 min. To be published by General Music in 1976.

DIALOGUS FOR CELLO AND ORCHESTRA (in progress)
App. 12 min. Commissioned by the Cleveland Orchestra. First performance projected for April 1976.

EV'RY TIME I FEEL DE SPIRIT (1975)
See THREE SPIRITUALS FOR VOICE AND PIANO.

FIVE FANCYS FOR CLARINET AND PIANO (FOUR HANDS) (1974)
Theme and five variations. 8½ min. General Music, agent.
Commissioned by the David Ensemble. First performance (1975)
at Alice Tully Hall by the David Ensemble, Warren Wilson, director.

GLORIA (IN MEMORIAM) (1963)
Chorus (SSA) with organ. Latin text. 4 min. New Valley
Music Press, 1963. First performance (1964) by the Smith
College Choir, Charles Fassett, conductor.

I GOT A LETTER FROM JESUS (1975)
See THREE SPIRITUALS FOR VOICE AND PIANO.

I WENT TO HEAVEN (1953)
Medium voice and piano. Text by Emily Dickinson. 2 min.
General Music, 1971. Distributed by Frank Music. First
performance (1958) in Paris. Sylvia McDonald, soprano; Boyd
McDonald, piano.

LAMENT (1971)
Medium voice and piano. Text by Countee Cullen. 5 min.
General Music, 1975.

LAMENT FOR ORCHESTRA (1946)
See LYRIC FOR STRINGS.

LYRIC FOR M. K. (1946)
See LYRIC FOR STRINGS.

LYRIC FOR STRING ORCHESTRA (1946)
See LYRIC FOR STRINGS.

LYRIC FOR STRINGS (1946)
String orchestra. 5 min. General Music, 1975. Recorded by
the London Symphony Orchestra, Paul Freeman, conductor
(Columbia M-33433: Vol. 7, Black Composers Series). This
work is an arrangement of the slow movement of STRING QUAR-
TET NO. 1. It has undergone several title changes; previous
titles include LAMENT FOR ORCHESTRA, LYRIC FOR M. K.,
and LYRIC FOR STRING ORCHESTRA. First performance (1958)
in Paris by the American Foundation Orchestra, George Walker,
conductor.

MARY WORE THREE LINKS OF CHAIN (1975)
See THREE SPIRITUALS FOR VOICE AND PIANO.

MUSIC FOR BRASS (SACRED AND PROFANE) (1975)
Brass quintet. Four movements: Invocation; Dance; Chorale;
Dance. App. 13 min. Commissioned by the Hans Kindler
Foundation. First performance to be given January 1976.

MUSIC FOR THREE (1970)
Violin, violoncello, and piano. 5 min. General Music, 1972.

First performance (1970) at the National Gallery of Art by the University of Maryland Trio.

O WESTERN WIND (1958)
See THREE LYRICS FOR CHORUS.

PERIMETERS FOR CLARINET AND PIANO (1966)
Three movements. 9 min. General Music, 1972. Commissioned by Leroy Johnston. First performance (1966) at the Juilliard School of Music. Leroy Johnston, clarinet; Frances Walker, piano.

PIANO CONCERTO (1975)
Three movements. 23 min. Piano score to be available from General Music in 1976. Recorded for Columbia by Natalie Hinderas, pianist, and the Detroit Symphony Orchestra, Paul Freeman, conductor; to be released in 1976 as part of Columbia's Black Composers Series. Commissioned by the National Endowment for the Arts and the Atlanta Symphony Orchestra. First performance (1975) by the Minneapolis Symphony Orchestra, Paul Freeman, conductor; Natalie Hinderas, piano.

PRELUDE AND CAPRICE (1945, 1941)
Piano. Two movements: Prelude; Caprice. 7 min. General Music, 1975.

PSALM 84 (1960)
Chorus (SATB) with organ. Biblical text. $5\frac{1}{2}$ min. General Music, 1975.

PSALM 96 (1963)
Chorus (SATB) unaccompanied. Biblical text. App. $2\frac{1}{2}$ min. General Music, 1975. First performance (1976) by the Morgan State College Choir, Nathan Carter, conductor.

PSALM 105 (1963)
Chorus (SSA) with organ. Biblical text. App. 3 min. General Music, 1975. First performance (1976) by the Morgan State College Choir, Nathan Carter, conductor.

PSALM 117 (1953)
Chorus (SATB) with organ. Biblical text. 4 min. General Music, 1975. First performance (1975) at Riverside Church (New York), F. Swann, conductor.

PSALM 148 (1963)
Chorus (SATB) with organ. Biblical text. App. $2\frac{1}{2}$ min. General Music, 1975. First performance (1971) by the Montclair State College Choir.

A RED, RED ROSE (1971)
Medium voice and piano. Text by Robert Burns. 4 min. General Music, 1975.

RESPONSE (1953)
Medium voice and piano. Text by Paul Laurence Dunbar. 3 min. General Music, 1971. Distributed by Frank Music. First performance (1968) at Bennington College. Antonia Lavanne, soprano; George Walker, piano.

SO WE'LL GO NO MORE A-ROVING (1953)
Medium voice and piano. Text by Lord Byron. 3 min. General Music, 1971. Distributed by Frank Music. First performance (1968) at Bennington College. Antonia Lavanne, soprano; George Walker, piano.

SONATA FOR CELLO AND PIANO (1957)
Three movements. 15 min. General Music, 1972. First performance (1965) by Paul Olefsky, violoncello; American Cello Society series (Kosciusko Foundation).

SONATA FOR TWO PIANOS (1957)
Four movements. 9 min. 45 sec. Adaptation of SONATA NO. 2 FOR PIANO. Received the Harvey Gaul Prize (1963).

SONATA FOR VIOLIN AND PIANO (1958)
One movement. App. 10 min. Associated Music, 1970. First performance (1964) at the Hartt College of Music. B. Lurie, violin; H. Chatsky, piano.

SONATA NO. 1 FOR PIANO (1953)
Three movements. 15 min. General Music, 1972. Recorded by Natalie Hinderas (Desto DC-7102/7103: Natalie Hinderas Plays Music by Black Composers). First performance (1960) at the National Gallery of Art. George Walker, piano.

SONATA NO. 2 FOR PIANO (1957)
Four movements. 9 min. 45 sec. Galaxy, 1966. Recorded by George Walker (Composers Recordings Inc. CRI SD-270). First performance (1958) at the Eastman School of Music. George Walker, piano.

SONATA NO. 2 FOR PIANO (1957)
Two pianos. See SONATA FOR TWO PIANOS.

SONATA NO. 3 FOR PIANO (1975)
Three movements. App. $9\frac{1}{2}$ min. General Music, 1975. Commissioned by the Washington Society for the Performing Arts and Leon Bates. First performance (1976) at the Kennedy Center. Leon Bates, piano.

SPATIALS (1961)
Piano. Theme and six variations. 4 min. General Music, 1972. Recorded by George Walker (Composers Recordings Inc. CRI SD-270). First performance (1965) at Brandeis University. George Walker, piano.

SPEKTRA (1971)
   Piano. $5\frac{1}{2}$ min. General Music, 1972. Recorded by George
   Walker (Composers Recordings Inc. CRI SD-270).

SPIRITUALS FOR ORCHESTRA (1974)
   Introduction and four sections. $8\frac{1}{2}$ min. General Music, agent.
   First performance (1974) by the Houston Symphony Orchestra,
   Paul Freeman, conductor.

STARS (1953)
   Chorus (SATB) unaccompanied. Text by Susan D. Keeney. 3
   min. Associated Music, 1968. First performance (1969) at the
   University of Colorado (Boulder) by the University of Colorado
   Chamber Singers.

STRING QUARTET NO. 1 (1946)
   Three movements. App. 14 min. First performance (1946)
   at the Juilliard School of Music.

STRING QUARTET NO. 2 (1967; revised in 1968)
   Four movements. 15 min. General Music, agent. First performance (1967) at the Library Museum of Lincoln Center. Received the Rhea Soslund Chamber Music Competition Award
   (1967).

SWEET, LET ME GO (1954)
   Medium voice and piano. Anonymous text. $2\frac{1}{2}$ min. General
   Music, 1971.

SYMPHONY FOR ORCHESTRA (1961)
   Four movements. 18 min. General Music, agent. First per-
   formance (1969) at the University of Colorado (Boulder) by the
   University of Colorado Symphony, H. Chavez, conductor.

TAKE, O TAKE THOSE LIPS AWAY (1958)
   See THREE LYRICS FOR CHORUS.

THREE LYRICS FOR CHORUS (1958)
   Chorus (SATB) with piano. The Bereaved Maid (anonymous text);
   Take, O Take Those Lips Away (text by Shakespeare); O Western Wind (anonymous text). 14 min. General Music, 1971.
   Published separately, but constitute a set. First performance
   (1969) at the University of Colorado (Boulder) by the University
   of Colorado Chamber Singers.

THREE SPIRITUALS FOR VOICE AND PIANO (1975)
   Medium voice and piano. Arrangements of the following spirit-
   uals: Ev'ry Time I Feel de Spirit; I Got a Letter from Jesus;
   Mary Wore Three Links of Chain. Traditional spiritual texts.
   App. 10 min. General Music, 1975.

VARIATIONS FOR ORCHESTRA (1971)
   Introduction and eight variations. 10 min. General Music,

1972. Recorded by the New Philharmonia Orchestra, Paul Freeman, conductor (unreleased). First performance (1974) by the Baltimore Symphony Orchestra, Paul Freeman, conductor.

WITH RUE MY HEART IS LADEN (1953)
Medium voice and piano. Text by A. E. Housman. 3 min. General Music, 1972. Distributed by Frank Music. First performance (1968) at Bennington College. Antonia Lavanne, soprano; George Walker, piano.

WITH THIS SMALL KEY (1971)
Chorus (SATB) unaccompanied. Text by Sister M. Therese. $4\frac{1}{2}$ min. General Music, 1975.

BIBLIOGRAPHY

Part I: Works about the composer

"Black Composers." Newsweek, 15 April 1974.

Brooks, Tilford. "A Historical Study of Black Music and Selected Twentieth Century Black Composers and Their Role in American Society." Ed. D. dissertation, Washington University, 1972.

Claghorn, Charles E. Biographical Dictionary of American Music. West Nyack, N. Y.: Parker Publishing Company, 1973.

Delphin, Wilfred. "A Comparative Analysis of Two Sonatas by George Walker: Sonata No. 1 (1953) and Sonata No. 2 (1958)." D. M. A. dissertation, University of Southern Mississippi, in progress.

Ennett, Dorothy Maxine. "An Analysis and Comparison of Selected Piano Sonatas by Three Contemporary Black Composers: George Walker, Howard Swanson, and Roque Cordero." Ph. D. dissertation, New York University, 1973.

Furie, Kenneth. "Columbia's Black Composers Series." High Fidelity/Musical America 24 (June 1974): 71-73.

Hildreth, John. "The Keyboard Works of a Select Group of Black Composers." Ph. D. dissertation, Northwestern University, in progress.

Jackson, Raymond. "The Piano Music of Twentieth Century Black Americans as Illustrated Mainly in the Works of Three Composers." D. M. A. dissertation, Juilliard School of Music, 1973.

Newson, Roosevelt. "The Solo Piano Music of George Walker." D. M. A. dissertation, Peabody Conservatory of Music, in progress.

Roach, Hildred. Black American Music: Past and Present. Boston: Crescendo Publishing Company, 1973.

Sims, D. Maxine. "An Analysis and Comparison of Piano Sonatas by George Walker and Howard Swanson." The Black Perspective in Music 4 (Spring 1976): 70-81.

Southern, Eileen. "America's Black Composers of Classical Music." Music Educators Journal 62 (November 1975): 46-59.

_____. The Music of Black Americans. New York: W. W. Norton, 1971.

Who's Who Among Black Americans, 1st ed. (1975-76), s.v. "Walker, George T."

Who's Who in Colored America. 7th ed. (1950), s.v. "Walker, George Theophilus."

Part II: Works by the composer

Walker, George T. "It Is Clear That We Must End This." Grecourt Review 6 (November 1962): 31.

_____. "Let's Consider the Listener." Music Journal 19 (January 1961): 40+.

_____. "Piano Sound in Reproduction." Music Journal 22 (May 1964): 40+.

_____. Review of The Music of Black Americans, by Eileen Southern. Journal of Research in Music Education 20 (Fall 1972): 410-411.

_____. "Rise From Your Curled Position." Grecourt Review 6 (November 1962): 30.

CHAPTER XV

OLLY WOODROW WILSON

Olly Wilson was born September 7, 1937 in St. Louis, Missouri. His educational background includes a B.M. (1959) from Washington University (St. Louis), an M.M. (1960) from the University of Illinois, and a Ph.D. (1964) from the University of Iowa. Among his composition teachers were Robert Wykes, Robert Kelley, and Philip Bezanson. In 1967 Dr. Wilson studied electronic music at the Studio for Experimental Music at the University of Illinois. During the 1971-1972 academic year he was in Ghana, studying West African music. Prior to his appointment as Professor of Music at the University of California at Berkeley, he held positions at Florida A&M University, West Virginia University (Graduate Division), Indiana University, and Oberlin College.

Dr. Wilson has been active as a performer in both the jazz and classical idioms. He played piano and bass with several jazz groups in the St. Louis area and was also a member of several orchestras, including the St. Louis Philharmonic, the St. Louis Summer Players, and the Cedar Rapids Symphony Orchestra.

Dr. Wilson has received a number of awards including the 1968 Dartmouth Arts Council Prize for his composition Cetus and an award for outstanding achievement in music composition from the American Academy of Arts and Letters and the National Institute of Arts and Letters (1974). He has been awarded commissions by the Boston Symphony Orchestra and the Fromm Foundation (for Voices), the Oakland Symphony Orchestra (for Spirit Song), and Pitzer College (for Black Martyrs). In 1972 he received a Guggenheim Fellowship for composition.

Among Dr. Wilson's compositions are works for orchestra, chorus, piano, chamber ensemble, and electronic sound. His music has been performed by a number of artists and ensembles including Natalie Hinderas, Richard Bunger, the Oberlin College Choir, the Dallas Symphony Orchestra, the Baltimore Symphony Orchestra, the Oakland Symphony Orchestra, the Atlanta Symphony Orchestra, the Minneapolis Symphony Orchestra, and the San Francisco Symphony Orchestra. Recordings of his compositions appear on the Columbia, Desto, Turnabout, Oberlin College Choir, and CRI labels.

379

Olly W. Wilson (courtesy of the composer)

Part I: General Questions

1.   Q: What persons, events, and works (of art, literature, etc.)
          have influenced you in general as well as in terms of your
          musical activities?

     A: There are a wide variety of events, works of art, and
          individuals that have influenced my musical activity. Some
          time ago, in an article I wrote for The Black Perspective
          in Music, [1] I attempted to discuss some of these influences.
          I said: "The source of the black composer's music lies
          deeply embedded in the collective consciousness of his
          people. Along with a heightened sensitivity to motion,
          qualitative rhythm, and immediateness of expression, it
          includes a dimension which encompasses the wordless moans
          of a mid-week poorly attended prayer meeting, the Saturday-
          night ecstatic shrieks of a James Brown, the relentless
          intensity of the modal excursions of a John Coltrane, and
          the tonal word-songs of the teenage brothers rappin' on the
          corner, full of the pride of new-found self respect." Then,
          later in the same article: "It should not be deduced from
          what I have said that the black American composer is un-
          influenced by music that comes from non-black traditions.
          Nothing could be further from the truth. The black com-
          poser is like any contemporary composer who is constantly
          stimulated by a bombardment of diverse musical sources.
          As a matter of fact, one of the general characteristics of
          twentieth-century music of any type is the pervasiveness of
          cross-cultural influences. This has led one observer of
          contemporary music to refer to this eclectic period as one
          in which the norm was one of constant stylistic diversity--
          or a period of 'fluctuating stasis.' There is no such thing
          in the world of today as complete cultural isolation. One
          need only turn on the radio to hear the mixtures of various
          musical cultures. Aretha Franklin is 'big' in Japan, Indian
          ragas are popular on American college campuses, the Ed-
          win Hawkins singers were a smashing success in Europe."
              So in terms of people who have influenced me there
          have been a number of different sources, including my
          teachers and including a number of jazz performers, most
          notably Charlie Parker. Although I never met Charlie
          Parker or knew him personally, his music has influenced
          me in terms of the way I approach the musical process.

2.   Q: How would you define black music?
     A: I usually avoid those kinds of questions--they're too com-
          plicated. I would never be able to go into this in the
          amount of time and space we have here. [2]

3.   Q: What features of your own music do you see as uniquely
          black (in terms of both musical and philosophical considera-
          tions)?
     A: O.K. I spoke about that in the article. [3] The first para-
          graph that I quoted in response to question one relates to

this question as well. Later in the article I stated: "In other works these factors[4] may be more subtle, but nonetheless are equally as important. They are used to determine internal factors, such as pacing, intensity, and formal development. In the works of such composers as T. J. Anderson, David Baker, and Wendell Logan[5] may be found examples of this." And I was talking about myself as well as the people that I mentioned.[6]

4. Q: In what ways is your music a reflection of your personal philosophy (social, political, etc.)?

    A: That's answered in the article:[7] "My approach to the electronic media is similar to my approach to any musical media. I use it as a means of projecting the musical idea I am trying to convey in a particular piece. It is illogical to assume that different composers using the same media will produce similar works, as it is to assume that different artists using the same plastic media will produce works that look alike. Both Scott Joplin and Arnold Schoenberg wrote pieces for the piano about the same time, but there any similarity ends. Each man was expressing something out of his personal experience, and those experiences were culturally light-years apart. Nevertheless, each man created something that was universal in that it reflected universal sentiments from a discernible cultural perspective. My approach to electronic media, like my approach to the orchestra or any instrument, carries with it the sensibilities of a black man in the latter half of the twentieth century.

    "The attitude I hold toward media is also applicable to my approach to compositional techniques. I will use any technique or device which will enable me to project my musical ideas. It is debilitating to limit oneself a priori to any system or style. For me, questions of musical technique are meaningless outside the context of a specific piece and should not limit one's appreciation of the musical ideas. A response to any music ultimately must be on the basis of the communicability of that music. One should ask himself, 'Does this affect me in a meaningful way?', not 'Does it use this or that technique?'"

5. Q: What do you see as the position or role of the black artist in contemporary society?

    A: The black composer reflects the unique black experience. In the article[8] I stated: "In conclusion, I would like to make a final statement on the role of the black composer in the struggle for Black Liberation. I am sometimes asked by students and others how I am able to justify my activity as a composer at this crucial historical moment. The question betrays a fundamental lack of understanding of the role of music in the traditional black community, both in the United States and in Africa. In traditional West African cultures music is not an abstraction, separate from life, a distillation of experience. It is, rather, a force by which man communicates with other men, the gods, and nature. In this sense it is obligatory and vital to existence.

"The ideal I strive toward as a composer is to approach music as it is approached in traditional African cultures. In that sense my music is directly related to the struggle in that it aspires to inform, motivate, and humanize my fellow men in their aspirations."

6. Q: Please discuss any problems you may have encountered in getting your works performed, published, and recorded.
   A: Most of my works have been performed; as a matter of fact, in recent years I've had quite a few performances. In general, I have experienced some difficulty in getting works published. Part of that has to do with the fact that I insist on having them published by certain companies that have wide distributions. I don't have anything published by anybody other than myself, at present. I don't have an incorporated publishing company. All of my music is in manuscript, which I reproduce; people have to write directly to me for copies of my pieces. [9]

6A. Q: How much of your actual output has ever been performed?
    A: Most of my output has been performed.

    Q: Published?
    A: None of my output has been published. I've had opportunities to have it published by various companies, but those weren't the companies that I wanted to publish it because of the distribution. In fairness I have to say that. There are several large publishing companies--Universal, etc.-- that I would like to publish my works simply because they have an international distribution, as opposed to some smaller units here that are relatively new and don't have an international distribution but are interested in publishing my works.

    Q: Recorded?
    A: Currently there are five recordings of mine available. Cetus is available on Turnabout recordings. In Memoriam Martin Luther King is available on Oberlin College Choir Recordings with Robert Fountain as conductor. Piano Piece (1969) was recorded by Natalie Hinderas; it's on the Desto record Natalie Hinderas Plays Music by Black Composers. [10] Piece for Four is recorded on Composers Recordings (CRI). Akwan is recorded on Columbia Records as volume 8 of the Black Composers series. Richard Bunger is the piano soloist with the Baltimore Symphony; Paul Freeman conducts.

6B. Q: Have you encountered difficulty in getting your works programmed?
    A: Not really. I guess it's a mixed bag; it depends on which work and it depends on where it's programmed. Among

my chamber works are several smaller works that are performed quite frequently--the piece for piano and electronic sound,[11] an earlier sextet[12] which has been performed very frequently, and a number of electronic pieces that are performed very frequently. In general my chamber music is performed very often and I don't have any difficulty getting that programmed at all.

Though I've had a number of orchestral performances, I would have preferred having more performances of certain specific works. For example, I just finished a big work for soprano solo, double chorus, orchestra, and electronic sound; it's called Spirit Song. Of course, that is a work I want to try and have performed again, but that's difficult. Part of it has to do with the fact that it's for a large ensemble, and so forth.

I guess, at a certain level, I've had a number of performances. It's a difficult kind of question to answer because what it really means is what's not in the question. What one thinks of when one attempts to answer it is really this: Have you encountered difficulty in getting your work performed enough? Most people will say yes to that. On the other hand, for example, let's say a young composer (or a composer who's not so young) who has not had many performances at all could answer that with a resounding YES. In all honesty, I can't say that I've had a great deal of difficulty getting performances of my works. I have been concerned with the frequency of getting specific works performed. I guess a proper response to this question depends upon how one judges oneself; in short, though I have had frequent performances, I am not performed as often as I think I should be.

6C. Q: Are there specific problems in getting a satisfactory performance? Exemplify and discuss.

A: Again, it depends on the situation. In those instances where a work of mine has been programmed by an excellent chamber ensemble with ample rehearsal time available, the result is usually an outstanding performance. One of the things that might speak to this question has to do with the practice that has arisen in the last few years of various organizations, orchestras, and institutions setting up special concerts of the music of black composers. One of the problems that happens all too often here is that there is not enough rehearsal time for these pieces, mainly because the orchestra or the sponsoring institution doesn't have money to pay for the rehearsal time. As a result, if your music happens to be difficult to perform and involves special kinds of things, like mine tends to do--that is, either because the notation is unusual, or because it uses electronic devices or amplification, or involves the players in spatial relationships or in movement or something which is a little outside of the range of most literature that the orchestra plays--it is usually difficult to get a satisfactory performance.

On the other hand, if the conductor looks at my score and decides to do it on his regular subscription concerts, he has taken into account the difficulty of the piece and will give it enough rehearsal time. Unfortunately, too often my orchestral works have been programmed on special concerts, i.e., black composers' concerts where each work is given about thirty minutes rehearsal. This just doesn't work for most of my music. Ample rehearsal time has remained one of my problems.

7. Q: What do you consider, at this point in your life, to be your most significant achievement(s) aside from your compositions?

A: That's very difficult. I would think basically trying to live in harmony with my fellow men and trying to develop a sense of universal love for everybody. I think that would be the most important achievement.

8. Q: What do you see as the responsibilities and obligations of the educational system (at all levels) to the study of black music?

A: It appears to me that black music is an output of black people, and if an educational system exists to help man understand his existence, then it's obligatory for educational institutions to include the artistic output of a significant segment of humanity. It is absolutely necessary for educational institutions to include this music in their curriculum.

9. Q: Do you feel that the people who write about your music (critics in particular) understand what you are doing? Exemplify and discuss.

A: Again, that's another one of those questions that it's difficult to give a simple yes or no answer. Obviously some people have more insight than others. I could talk about individuals; in another sense that article[13] I referred you to does speak to that in its criticism of Kolodin, but he's not talking about me--he's talking about other composers. In terms of people who have some insight, I think that what Eileen Southern has to say is good, although it was not her intention to deal with it from an analytical point of view.[14] At this point, nobody has; it is still too early for that.

10. Q: What advice would you give to the aspiring young black composer?

A: The only thing I can advise is for him to be honest with himself and to express what he feels is true.

Part II: Music Questions

1. Q: When you sit down to begin a new composition on your own

initiative or inspiration (as opposed to a commissioned
work), what procedure or approach do you follow?

2. Q: When composing a commissioned work or a work written
for a specific occasion or person, does your procedure or
approach differ from the one you described in question 1?
If so, in what way?

(Ed. note: Dr. Wilson chose to answer questions one and two
together.)

A: Not really; the reason I'm answering both these questions
together is because for me there's not much difference.
Usually in beginning a new work, what has to happen is
that there has to be some kind of spark--some kind of
source of inspiration or something--to get me going. That
might come in a number of different ways, and it's independent of whether or not the work is a commissioned
work or a noncommissioned work. If it's a commissioned
work, I simply try to force myself to get that spark of
inspiration. If it's not a commissioned work, then it's
self-generated. But I don't have a set procedure or approach. In some instances I might improvise before I begin a piece, but I might improvise when I'm not even thinking about a piece at all! Or the act of improvisation might
bring on a spark or an idea which might be the germinal
idea for a piece that's developed later on. Or it may be a
piece the very nature of which suggests something to me.
For example, I remember doing the piece Spirit Song,
which called for a couple of choirs and was designed for
a specific hall. 15 I knew when I saw the hall that there
were certain kinds of things that I wanted to do in the
piece. Because the piece was based on spirituals, that
also suggested certain kinds of musical things about the
piece. So it depends on the piece. With other pieces, it
didn't depend on that at all. It was just a matter of waiting
until I got that spark and then trying to develop it.

Q: Does the medium you choose--electronic sound, conventional
instruments, combinations, etc.---affect the way you approach the compositional process?

A: Not really. It varies from composition to composition. I
hope there are certain stylistic consistencies, but those are
generally at an unconscious level. There are certain kinds
of things to consider; if it's going to be an electronic piece,
there are certain limitations and there are certain qualities
that are suggested by the medium itself, just as if you're
doing a piano piece there are certain things you can and
can't do. I don't think that I approach the piano in one
way, nor do I think I approach the electronic media in one
way.

Q: Do you work at or away from the piano?

A: It's a combination of things. Sometimes at the piano and
sometimes away from the piano. It depends on what I'm
doing. Obviously if it's an electronic piece I don't work

at the piano at all. If it's an orchestral piece, I might try
out certain basic things at the piano, but I don't consciously work at the piano all the way through on any composition.

3. Q: In general, with regard to your writing, what genre(s) do
      you prefer?
   A: Actually there aren't any particular genres that I prefer.
      I've written chamber music for set chamber groups like
      string quartets, I've written for mixed chamber ensembles,
      and I've written for large orchestra and for chorus and
      orchestra as well as electronic music alone and the elec-
      tronic media with live instrumental media. Those are the
      media I've done; there's no particular genre that I seem to
      favor. I think it depends on the particular time that I was
      writing a piece. Recently I've written several pieces which
      call for the electronic media and live performance, includ-
      ing In Memoriam Martin Luther King for electronic media
      and mixed chorus, and Piano Piece for electronic media
      and amplified electronic piano. 16 Then I recently finished
      a piece for clarinet and electronic sound, 17 which I'll say a
      few words about later on. There are other media for which
      I have never composed. I have never done an opera; I
      just have never been particularly interested in that medium
      as something for me. I've talked with several people at
      different times about possibly doing an opera, although if
      I did, it would be a very unusual kind of opera--an opera
      which used space and other elements in a different way.

4. Q: What do you consider your most significant composition?
      Please discuss.
   A: It's hard to say; I like different pieces for different reasons.
      But among the most successful pieces in terms of capturing
      what I sought to capture are In Memoriam Martin Luther
      King; Akwan, which is the piece for piano, electronic piano,
      and orchestra; and Spirit Song. Interestingly enough, all
      of those are relatively large works and all of them involve
      either some kind of electronic sound or amplification.

5. Q: Please comment on your treatment of the following musical
      elements and give examples from your compositions that il-
      lustrate the techniques you describe:
      A. Melody
      B. Harmony
      C. Rhythm
      D. Form
      E. Improvisation
      F. Text (both choice and treatment)
      G. Instrumentation or medium (both in terms of choice of
         particular combinations as well as how they are treated
         compositionally)
   (Ed. note: Dr. Wilson chose not to address each of the above
   elements individually. Instead, he presented a general discussion of compositional style and techniques.)

A: That's very difficult for me to do, mainly because I don't try to think analytically about my music. I think analytically about other people's music but I don't really try to think analytically about my own music, although I can talk somewhat analytically about specific pieces. In general, it is very difficult for me to comment about the techniques that I use because I regard them as sort of private craft kinds of questions, and perhaps they are. I also know that composers are notorious for misleading people in this regard. I suggest that perhaps one might look at analyses of my works other people have done. One such analysis I can cite is an analysis that Wendell Logan did of my Piece for Four in Perspectives of New Music, Fall/Winter 1970, volume 9, number 1.

Now, I could say a couple of general words about some of the various compositional techniques that I have used at various times. For example, my earliest music was sort of pan-tonal, that is, essentially tonal but not functionally tonal in the traditional sense. There is a tonal center which emerges at various times and one is concerned about the relationship of this tonal center to other tonal centers which may emerge; the harmony is not based on traditional modes of harmonic structure. That's in the earlier works. Shortly thereafter I used serial technique in some pieces. As I look back over the list of my compositions the pieces that are serial are the Sextet of 1963 (parts of it are serial), Three Movements for Orchestra (1964), and Piece for Four, which is at least partially serial; Logan[18] discusses that work and how it's constructed. My approach to serialism was never classical Schoenbergian serialism; it was serial, but with a great deal of flexibility. There were reasons when and where I would move away from the series I was using. Now, following that, I found myself using not so much a 12-tone set but rather segments of a set--a hexachordal segment or, more often, trichords--three-note intervallic cells. What then happened was that in the course of a piece or in the course of a section of a piece there might have been a gradual movement from one intervallic set of three-note cells to another, and this was the means of determining pitches in a particular piece. Pieces which use portions of this technique are Piece for Four and Biography. You can find this technique being used throughout my compositional output, even in later works, for example, in segments of In Memoriam Martin Luther King.

Following that, from time to time one might see movement or usage of those intervallic cells in one way or another in a particular piece or in a section of a piece. I began to use not so much predetermined intervallic cells or predetermined sets but a basic static harmonic quality where the specific intervallic relationships were not as important as other parameters of the music. For example, changes in such factors as texture, timbre, and density became the more preeminent ones to determine progress,

to determine movement as opposed to changes in pitch or
changes in tonal centers. That probably resulted from my
involvement with electronic music. I think one can see that
clearly in a piece like In Memoriam Martin Luther King
(particularly the last section of the piece--the women's
voices), and also in Piano Piece and in most of the music
following that up to the present time. When I said "static
harmonic quality" a moment ago, I did not mean that my
sense of time is one in which movement is not important;
on the contrary, movement is extremely important. I'm
very much interested in what has been referred to as tele-
ological time--progressive time, time which moves, linear
time. But this sense of progression, this sense of a beginning and a middle and an end, is achieved mainly through
changes in texture, changes in timbre, and changes in density as opposed to changes in pitch relationships. Pitch
relationships are important too, but these other three factors take a more fundamental position.

Q: How do you choose your texts?
A: Basically it's sort of an intuitive approach. What I'll do if
I'm working on a piece in which I want to use a text is read
through a great deal of poetry and find something that sets
off that spark I referred to earlier. If I'm able to find
something that excites me and it seems to be well-fitted to
a musical setting, then I'll go ahead and try to use it. In
other instances (for example, In Memoriam Martin Luther
King) I started out with a concept where I knew that I didn't
want to use any poetry in the traditional sense of the word;
I wasn't so much interested in the semantic meaning of the
words as I was in the musical and symbolic meaning of the
text. That's why I wanted to use refrains from Dr. King's
speeches in In Memoriam Martin Luther King. In thinking
about a requiem, I wanted something that would have direct
symbolic reference not only in terms of the meaning of the
words--"How long? Not long" or "Freedom" or "Free
at last!"--but also in terms of the repetition which is
an integral part of the sermon and the speaking style
of a Martin Luther King. That was what I was interested
in in that particular case. I was interested in the sound
quality as sound and I was interested in the symbolic im-
port of the piece. In Memoriam Martin Luther King is a
piece that involves electronic media and a chorus, and I
wanted to merge these two media as close as possible.
That's why frequently in the piece the chorus is simply
singing a vowel or is producing some other sound which is
indistinguishable from that being produced on the electronic
media. One of the things I look for in writing music for
electronic instruments and live performers is that sort of
a merger, that interaction; the two become one, as opposed
to the artificial quality of the electronic sound and the live
and immediate quality of the live sound. I try to merge
those two, and that's been a guiding principle for me in my

approach to all electronic and live music.   Another thing
about instrumentation or medium is something I spoke
of when we were talking about genre.   Timbre is
extremely important to me.   It's important to me not only
for its sensual quality and for its immediate effect, but it's
important to me as a structural component of the music.
I attempt to explore the various timbral qualities of an
instrument very very carefully.   As to the reason why, I
think perhaps it is a direct effect of the Afro-American
tradition on my music. [19]   As you know, one of the important aspects of Afro-American music is the usage of a
wide variety of timbres.   Traditionally, the value system
allows for a very very wide variety of timbres.   In singing,
for example, there is not A single absolute timbre which is
to be sought after; it is rather what one does with a wide
variety of timbres.   That's why voices as diverse as Louis
Armstrong's and Smokey Robinson's can be accepted in the
same genre.   It has to do with the fact that although Louis
Armstrong has a very raspy voice, the way he uses his
voice--the kinds of nuances, the kinds of timbral differences
that he makes in his voice--is highly valued within that
musical tradition.   Somebody like Smokey Robinson, who
has a very high, clear voice (almost bel canto-like), is
successful because of his ability to make timbral nuances.
Of course, timbral nuances are well-known in terms of
wind instruments which are commonly used in Afro-American tradition.   I think that consciously (or sub-consciously)
the propensity for timbral differences has affected my approach to composition and my insistence on exploiting timbral nuances in unusual ways in my music.

6.   Q: Have difficulties with performance practice (inflection,
phrasing, etc.) been a significant problem in having your
works performed to your own satisfaction?

   A: It depends on the piece; a lot depends on who's doing the
piece, what the piece is about, and so forth.   To give you
an example I'll talk about my latest piece, Spirit Song.
The piece was commissioned by the Oakland Symphony Orchestra to be performed when they moved into their new
hall, a magnificent renovated theater called the Paramount
Theater.   One of the interesting things about that theater
is that it has a very large grill in the ceiling.   When I
explored the theater I noticed that there was a very large
area at the top of the theater, so I decided that one of the
things I wanted to do was use the entire space of the theater, because I've been interested in the full utilization of
space in my music for some time, even going back to In
Memoriam Martin Luther King.   So I designed the piece for
two choirs, one of which would be a predominantly black
choir and the other of which would be the women's voices
of the Oakland Symphony Chorus.   The members of the
orchestra were asked to use their voices as well as play.
I also had certain instruments, specifically the first desk

of each of the string sections--first violins, second violins,
violas, celli, and basses--amplified and the speakers placed
all around the hall so that the sound sources engulfed the
audience; sound was coming from behind them, it was coming from above them from that grill, it was coming from
the stage, and it was also coming from within the audience
itself because the entire first movement of the piece is essentially a procession by the black choir down the aisles and
up to the stage. The women of the Oakland Symphony
Chorus were performing from the ceiling, so that the sound
was emanating from a number of different sources. Now, I
should explain something else about the piece: Spirit Song
is about the evolution and development of the black spiritual.
The first movement starts out with the wordless moans,
hollers, and chants which preceded the development of the
spiritual proper; eventually this moves to the association
of text with these moans. That happens near the end of the
piece. The first movement involves a procession because
an important aspect of the spiritual is the association of
motion or movement with music. In the spiritual this is
associated symbolically in many of the texts as well as
directly in terms of the fact that in most Afro-American
music, motion is an intrinsic aspect of the music--one
tends to move when one performs the music, one tends to
move to the music. So the choir is involved in this procession as they're moving down the aisles, singing these
moans and chants. Later on in the piece (in the second
movement), a soprano soloist emerges. Then there's a
gradual development to text associated with the chant-like
statement that she gives initially. The text is taken from
fragments of spirituals, the most prominent of which is
"O Lord, O Lord, keep me from sinking down. "
    O. K. Now, the reason I mentioned all of that was be-
cause the question asked "Have difficulties with performance
practice been a significant problem in having your works
performed to your own satisfaction?" Obviously, in the
performance of this piece, it may, at some time in the
future. If another group wanted to do this piece, and if
this group was not a black group and wanted to be involved
in the procession, I could see that there would be some difficulties with performance practice--inflection, phrasing,
and so forth. There are certain pieces which people who
have had limited experience with jazz (or no experience with
jazz) would have difficulty performing, although that hasn't
been a major problem yet. Let me give as an example
Piece for Four. If the trumpet player had never played any
jazz and didn't understand much about the idiom, he would
tend to have difficulty with some of the phrasing and so forth.
In several of my orchestral works there are individual parts
in which the phrasing called for is phrasing associated with
jazz.

7. Q: What major works are currently in progress? Please

describe and discuss.

A: At this point, I am between works. I plan to start on a
work for tenor and electronic sound in the near future.
The last piece I finished was a piece for clarinet and electronic sound called <u>Echoes</u>. One of the things I'm involved
in with this piece is to let the clarinet and the electronic
sound source, which is a prerecorded tape, interact with
one another as closely as possible. One of the ways I do
this is by amplifying the clarinet; then the prerecorded tape
is played back through the same mixer that also accepts
the input from the clarinet. The tape is designed in such
a way that at times it is difficult to determine what is the
tape and what is the clarinet.

8. Q: Given unlimited time and finances (and no restrictions whatsoever), what would you write?

A: Well, I don't know--I really don't know. The last few commissions I've had gave me pretty much a carte blanche as
to what I could write, like the Oakland piece which involved
large orchestra and two choruses. [20] That's quite a rare
opportunity. Also, there wasn't a big rush on it; I had almost two years to do it, so that's almost like unlimited
time.

Q: Since we're on the subject of finances, what are the special
financial considerations involved in writing in the electronic
medium?

A: There are two kinds of expenses. First there are the expenses for the composer to create the work. Second there
are the expenses of putting on the performance. Let's address ourselves first to the expense of the composer. For-
tunately, since I have been associated with universities that
had electronic studios--frequently electronic studios which
I either originated or developed or of which I was one of the
co-directors--I was in the position of having the university
support the studio in terms of buying equipment and making
some of the money needed for expendable supplies and
equipment available. Had I not been in that situation--had
I not been a professor at Oberlin Conservatory where I developed the tape studio, or had I not been a professor at
Berkeley where I am one of the co-directors of the studio--
I would have not had access to that equipment and would
have had to pay out of my own pocket for the equipment or
for rental time in someone else's studio. That would have
been very expensive, and in some instances, prohibitive.
Now to the problem of the expenses of putting on the
production of music which involves the electronic media.
If a piece uses the electronics in the form of a prerecorded
tape, there is some additional expense because one has to
have a good quality tape recorder, playback system, and
speakers. At least in the early years--and by the early
years I mean up to the late 1960s, in this country anyway--
since most producers of musical performances weren't

accustomed to doing this, they considered it above and beyond their obligations to provide this equipment; it then
involved the added expense of going to some recording company and renting special speakers and a good quality tape
recorder and amplification system. Now electronic music
is so much a standard part of contemporary music that almost every institution that produces contemporary music has
at least adequate playback facilities. [21] For example, if I
were having a performance at Indiana University or at any
other major university in the country, I could count on the
fact that they have good quality playback facilities. It would
be no more expensive than having a good piano available on
the stage.

In essence, what I'm saying is that at one time it was
more expensive; at this time it's usually not that expensive.
Now, if the electronics are live electronics, that is, if they
are designed to be produced at the same time the performer
is performing them, that's very expensive and most institutions are not equipped to handle that at this point. You'd
have to hire somebody with special equipment to come in
and do that; this is generally viewed as an additional burden
and that's a problem. I haven't faced that problem because
I haven't done any pieces to this point that call for live
electronics. My work is usually prepared on prerecorded
tapes.

9. Q: If given the opportunity would you choose to devote yourself
to composition on a full-time basis? Why or why not?
   A: Well, I really don't know because I enjoy teaching. I'm
fulfilled by teaching and I find that it complements what I
do. Basically I'm a gregarious person and composition is
a solitary activity, you know; I enjoy it, but I also enjoy
interacting with people. Teaching gives me an opportunity
to meet a lot of different people, exchange ideas, and so
forth. I like to do that. On the other hand, one can do
that as a composer on a full-time basis because when one
goes around and lectures about his music (or about other
music) one still comes into contact with people. If I had
the resources I don't know whether I would teach full-time
in a university or whether I would teach occasionally and
lecture occasionally; I'd probably work out some kind of
arrangement like that.

10. Q: How would you describe your compositional style?
    A: I don't know how I can answer that. I think I've talked
about it in general already. [22]

11. Q: What have been the influences of other composers, styles,
and other types of music on your compositional style?
    A: I've talked about that already, both in the article and in
answering previous questions. [23]

12. Q: Has your style changed across your career? If so, what

influenced these changes or developments?

A: Well, I sort of answered that a few minutes ago when we talked about specific techniques that I'd used--first, sort of a pan-tonal style, then serialism, then the intervallic cell technique, and then the importance of timbre, texture, and density.[24] The only thing I would add is that it's difficult to pinpoint changes that have affected your style. I think that over the years I've become much more involved in Afro-American music from an analytical point of view. I've been involved in Afro-American music my whole life--playing it and participating in it--but in the last ten years I've been much more systematic about studying the history and structure of this music and I think that these studies may have unconsciously affected my music. As I said in the article,[25] that's not usually at the foreground level; it's usually at the background level and affects certain kinds of decisions about the role of timbre, about pacing and intensity and so forth, as opposed to having something in the music which is as clearly discernible as a blues. I think it's been that kind of thing. For example, one of the things that interests me about much of the music of Africa is that the music tends to be stratified; that is, it tends to consist of a number of relatively independent layers going on simultaneously. Each of these layers is characterized by a distinct timbre, so that the sound ideal is a heterogeneous one; one can hear each of the distinct layers independently of each other. For example, in a typical West African ensemble, one will have a bell, a rattle, handclaps, and a drum or drums (most often a series of at least three or four different drums). Now, each one of those levels--the bell, the rattle, the handclapping, the drums, and perhaps the song--is clearly distinct, that is, they don't blend in terms of color; the aesthetic ideal is one in which there is not this homogenous blend. I think that has affected my approach to composition just because I'm influenced by African and Afro-American music. I think that forms the basis for my essential approach, but I'm also influenced by a number of other things; it's my personal reinterpretation of all those things that makes it somewhat different.

Q: Were there any conscious influences that moved you from pan-tonality to serialism to working in cells, then to working with other kinds of materials?

A: I don't think so. It had to do with a certain amount of growth and widening my perspective in terms of what was possible. The earliest "formal" music I wrote was music that I wrote as a result of my studies in school. Therefore, it tended to be based on the kind of music I was listening to and studying then. For example, Prelude and Line Study (1959) for woodwind quartet is a piece in which the line study is essentially a little fugue, a quasi-serial fugue as a matter of fact. It was influenced by some twentieth-century fugues I had been studying. The next

piece I wrote was <u>Trio for Flute, Cello, and Piano</u>. I still
like that piece very much. It was sort of a breakthrough
in that I was able to get a flow, a rhythmic drive which
showed other influences that I can't pinpoint. Harmonically
it tended to be related to the kind of music I was excited
about then; however, it's a combination of characteristics--
on the one hand it has the rhythmic drive and flow of music
which I attribute to my Afro-American heritage, and on the
other hand the harmony tends to be based a great deal on
the quartal harmonies of Hindemith. Yet another part of it
had to do with my fascination at that time with Bartok's
music. Those examples show influences at one level, but
a general answer to your question is that my style changed
through growth and broadening my perspectives.

13. Q: When you are listening to music for your own enjoyment,
what are your preferences?

A: Well, it depends on the mood that I'm in. I like certain of
the music of Stravinsky. I like much of the later music of
Miles Davis. I like to dance, and I like a lot of soul music.
I like the music of Coltrane. As I said, I guess the major
influence in jazz--through the spiritual quality and the in-
geniousness of his approach--has been Charlie Parker. But
then how one translates that into what I do, or how one translates Stravinsky, in some instances, into what I do is another story. My style in general tends to be somewhat
eclectic, and it draws from a number of different sources;
I hope it comes out reflecting a single view, or certainly
a single conception. But I listen to a number of different
kinds of music. I'm interested in African music; I've done
studies of African music[26] and I listen to African music.
To a certain extent, I'm interested in certain kinds of
Javanese music. I'll listen to <u>any</u> music and to <u>all</u> kinds
of music. I'm a big Beethoven fan, and I get very excited
about Beethoven symphonies. So it depends on how I feel
at that particular moment.

Notes to Chapter XV

1. Olly Wilson, "The Black-American Composer," <u>The Black Perspective in Music</u> 1 (Spring 1973): 34-35.

2. For additional remarks by Dr. Wilson on the problems of defining black music see DeLerma, <u>Black Music in Our Culture</u>, pp. 71-
76. The material cited is a portion of a panel discussion in which
T. J. Anderson, Hale Smith, and Olly Wilson were the primary
participants.

3. Olly Wilson, "The Black-American Composer," <u>The Black Perspective in Music</u> 1 (Spring 1973): 33-36.

4. The factors to which Dr. Wilson refers are discussed in the

previous paragraph: "In the work of many black composers, for example, the elements easily identified with the black experience are features of the foreground of their music. That is, they are clearly distinguishable since they form the external as well as internal aspects of the musical events shaped by the composer. "

5. Olly Wilson, "Wendell Logan: Proportions, " Perspectives of New Music 9 (Fall-Winter 1970): 135-142.

6. See also the discussion of his use of timbre in II-5.

7. Olly Wilson, "The Black-American Composer, " The Black Perspective in Music 1 (Spring 1973): 36.

8. Olly Wilson, "The Black American Composer, " The Black Perspective in Music 1 (Spring 1973): 36.

9. Dr. Wilson can be contacted at the following address: Dr. Olly Wilson, University of California, Department of Music, Berkeley, California 94720.

10. The title of this composition is listed on the Desto recording as Piano Piece for Piano and Electronic Sound.

11. Piano Piece

12. Sextet (1963)

13. Olly Wilson, "The Black American Composer, " The Black Perspective in Music 1 (Spring 1973): 33.

14. Eileen Southern, The Music of Black Americans (New York: W. W. Norton and Company, Inc., 1971). The section dealing specifically with Dr. Wilson appears on pp. 476-478.

15. The work was commissioned by the Oakland Symphony to be performed at the opening of their new hall, the renovated Paramount Theater. Dr. Wilson discusses his utilization of the structural aspects of the hall in his response to II-6.

16. In his performance notes for Piano Piece, Dr. Wilson indicates where keys are to be struck or played in clusters, where strings are to be plucked inside the piano with the fingernail, and how the piano is to be prepared with the following items placed inside: a lightweight wooden ruler with a metal edge, three 3"-diameter metal rings (notebook type), and three metal protractors approximately 3-3/4" in length.

17. The title of this composition is Echoes. A description of this work can be found in Dr. Wilson's response to II-7.

18. Wendell Logan, "Olly Wilson: Piece for Four, " Perspectives of New Music 9 (Fall-Winter 1970): 126-134.

19. This is also relevant to I-3.

20. Spirit Song

21. When asked about the financial considerations for small institutions and private individuals (in terms of purchasing equipment) Dr. Wilson responded: "Most universities, and even small junior colleges nowdays, have moogs or synthesizers of some kind around so that a person can at least be introduced to the electronic medium. Another development relevant to this problem of finances is the production of a number of inexpensive synthesizers whose cost is not prohibitive. A young composer who is isolated could invest $1000 or $1500 to get some basic equipment to get started, and when you figure the cost of pianos and the cost of musical instruments in general, that's a reasonable amount."

22. See his responses to II-5 and II-12.

23. Olly Wilson, "The Black-American Composer," The Black Perspective in Music 1 (Spring 1973): 34-35. See also his responses to I-1, II-5, II-12, and II-13.

24. Dr. Wilson's discussion of his use of these techniques appears in II-5.

25. Olly Wilson, "The Black-American Composer," The Black Perspective in Music 1 (Spring 1973): 34-35.

26. During the 1971-1972 academic year Dr. Wilson was in Ghana, studying and doing research on West African music.

LIST OF COMPOSITIONS

AKWAN (1972)
Piano/electronic piano and orchestra. 16 min. 25 sec. Recorded by Richard Bunger, pianist, and the Baltimore Symphony Orchestra, Paul Freeman, conductor (Columbia M-33434: Vol. 8, Black Composers Series). Commissioned by Richard Bunger with a grant from the Martha Baird Rockefeller Foundation. First performance (1973) by the University of California (Berkeley) Orchestra, Michael Senturia, conductor; Richard Bunger, piano.

AND DEATH SHALL HAVE NO DOMINION (1963)
Tenor and percussion. Three movements separated by two percussion interludes. Text by Dylan Thomas. App. 20 min. First performance (1963) at the University of Iowa (Iowa City) by William Abbott, tenor, and the University of Iowa Percussion Ensemble.

BIOGRAPHY (1966)
    Soprano, flute, harp, and percussion. Text by LeRoi Jones.
    6 min. First performance (1967) at the University of Missouri
    (St. Louis) by Rosalyn Wykes, soprano, and the St. Louis Group
    for New Music.

BLACK MARTYRS (1972)
    Electronic sound. 20 min. In commemoration of Martin Luther
    King, Jr., Malcolm X, and Medger Evers. Commissioned by
    Pitzer College (Claremont, Calif.) and designed especially for
    the Salathe Tower and the Pitzer College Quadrangle. First
    performance (1973) at Pitzer College.

BLACK MASS
    Electronic music for the Berkeley (Calif.) Black Cultural Center
    production of the LeRoi Jones play Black Mass. First perform-
    ance (1971) at the University of California (Berkeley).

CETUS (1967)
    Electronic sound. 9 min. 15 sec. Recorded on Turnabout TV-
    34301 (Electronic Music, Vol. IV). First performance (1968)
    at the Symposium for Contemporary Music, Illinois Wesleyan
    University, Bloomington, Illinois. Received the 1968 Dartmouth
    Arts Council Prize, awarded in the first international competi-
    tion for electronic compositions.

CHANSON INNOCENTE (1965)
    Contralto and two bassoons. Text by e. e. cummings. 4 min.
    Commissioned by Stephen Bassoon. First performance (1966)
    at the Wisconsin College Conservatory (Milwaukee). Marlee
    Sabo, soprano; Stephen Bassoon and Lawrence D'Attlio, bassoons.

DANCE MUSIC I (1963)
    Wind ensemble. 3 movements. 10 min. First performance
    (1963) at the University of Iowa (Iowa City) by the University
    of Iowa Wind Ensemble.

DANCE MUSIC II (1965)
    Wind ensemble. 15 min. First performance (1965) at Florida
    A & M University by the Florida A & M University Wind Ensem-
    ble; danced by the Florida A & M University Dance Ensemble.

DANCE SUITE (1962)
    Wind ensemble. 15 min. First performance (1962) by the
    Florida A & M University Wind Ensemble.

ECHOES (1974-1975)
    Clarinet and electronic sound. 11 min. First performance
    (1975) at the University of Redlands (Calif.). Phil Rehfeldt,
    clarinet.

THE EIGHTEEN HANDS OF JEROME HARRIS (1971)
    Electronic ballet.

GLORIA (1961)
Chorus (SATB) unaccompanied. 3 min.

IN MEMORIAM, MARTIN LUTHER KING JR. (1969)
Chorus (SATB) and electronic sound. Text by Olly Wilson, after Martin Luther King, Jr. 25 min. Recorded by the Oberlin College Choir, Robert Fountain, conductor (Oberlin College Choir Recordings, series 1, volume 19: The Oberlin College Choir). First performance (1969) at Oberlin College by the Oberlin College Choir, Robert Fountain, conductor.

INTERVENTION (1960)
See TWO DUTCH POEMS.

MARC GREETS THINGS IN THE MORNING (1960)
See TWO DUTCH POEMS.

PIANO PIECE (1969)
Piano and electronic sound. App. $10\frac{1}{2}$ min. Recorded by Natalie Hinderas (Desto DC-7102/7103: Natalie Hinderas Plays Music by Black Composers). First performance (1970) at Oberlin College; Richard Bunger, piano.

PIECE FOR FOUR (1966)
Flute, trumpet, contrabass, and piano. Three movements. 15 min. 15 sec. Recorded by Robert Willoughby, flute; Gene Young, trumpet; Bertram Turetzky, contrabass; and Joseph Schwartz, piano (Composers Recordings Inc. CRI SD-264). First performance (1967) at the Contemporary Music Festival, Oberlin, Ohio. Robert Willoughby, flute; Gene Young, trumpet; Olly Wilson, contrabass; Renay Landsman, piano.

PRELUDE AND LINE STUDY (1959)
Flute, clarinet, bass clarinet, and bassoon. Two movements. 7 min. First performance (1959) at the University of Iowa (Iowa City) by the Washington University (St. Louis) Woodwind Quartet.

SEXTET (1963)
Flute, clarinet, bassoon, horn, trumpet, and trombone. Five movements. 18 min. First performance (1963) at the University of Iowa (Iowa City) by the University of Iowa Sextet.

SOLILOQUY (1962)
Solo contrabass. 4 min. First performance (1962) at Florida A & M University; Olly Wilson, contrabass.

SOMETIMES (in progress)
Tenor and electronic sound. This is a work for electronic tape and tenor voice based on the spiritual "Sometimes I Feel Like a Motherless Child." To be premiered in 1976 by William Brown, tenor.

SPIRIT SONG (1973)
Soprano, double chorus, and orchestra. Two movements. Text adapted by the composer from traditional spirituals. 22 min. Commissioned by the Oakland Symphony Orchestra. First performance (1974) by the Oakland Symphony Orchestra, the Castlemont High School Choir, and the women's voices of the Oakland Symphony Chorus. Harold Farberman, conductor; Gwendolyn Lytle, soprano.

STRING QUARTET (1960)
Three movements. 20 min. First performance (1960) by the Graduate String Quartet of the University of Illinois.

STRUCTURE FOR ORCHESTRA (1960)
One movement.

THREE MOVEMENTS FOR ORCHESTRA (1964)
22 min. First performance (1964) at the University of Iowa (Iowa City) by the University of Iowa Orchestra, James Dixon, conductor.

TRIO FOR FLUTE, CELLO, AND PIANO (1959)
8 min. First performance (1959) at the University of Iowa (Iowa City) by the Washington University (St. Louis) Trio.

TWO DUTCH POEMS (1960)
Contralto and piano. Intervention (text by Roland Holst); Marc Greets Things in the Morning (text by Paul Van Ostaiijen). 4 min. First performance (1960) at the University of Illinois; Nina Steffel, contralto.

VIOLIN SONATA (1961)
Violin and piano. One movement. 5 min. First performance (1961) at the Contemporary Music Festival, Central State University, Wilberforce, Ohio. Elwin Adams, violin.

VOICES (1970)
Orchestra. 12 min. Commissioned by the Boston Symphony Orchestra and the Fromm Foundation. First performance (1970) by the Tanglewood Festival Orchestra, Gunther Schuller, conductor.

WRY FRAGMENTS (1961)
Tenor and percussion. Four movements. Text by James Cunningham. 2 min. First performance (1961) by Robert Hansberry, tenor, and the Florida A & M University Percussion Ensemble.

BIBLIOGRAPHY

Part I: Works about the composer

"Black Composers. " Newsweek, 15 April 1974.

Brooks, Tilford. "A Historical Study of Black Music and Selected Twentieth Century Black Composers and Their Role in American Society. " Ed. D. dissertation, Washington University, 1972.

Claghorn, Charles E. Biographical Dictionary of American Music. West Nyack, N. Y.: Parker Publishing Company, 1973.

De Lerma, Dominique-René, ed. Black Music in Our Culture: Curricular Ideas on the Subjects, Materials, and Problems. Kent, Ohio: Kent State University Press, 1970.

Logan, Wendell. "Olly Wilson: Piece for Four. " Perspectives of New Music 9 (Fall-Winter 1970): 126-134.

Roach, Hildred. Black American Music: Past and Present. Boston: Crescendo Publishing Company, 1973.

Southern, Eileen. "America's Black Composers of Classical Music. " Music Educators Journal 62 (November 1975): 46-59.

_____. The Music of Black Americans. New York: W. W. Norton, 1971.

Who's Who Among Black Americans, 1st ed. (1975-76), s. v. "Wilson, Olly W. "

Part II: Works by the composer

Wilson, Olly W. "The Black American Composer. " The Black Perspective in Music 1 (Spring 1973): 33-36.

_____. "The Compositions of Arnold Schoenberg. " Fine Arts 13 (February 1967).

_____. "The Significance of the Relationship between Afro-American Music and African Music. " The Black Perspective in Music 2 (Spring 1974): 3-22.

_____. "Wendell Logan: Proportions. " Perspectives of New Music 9 (Fall-Winter 1970): 135-142.

APPENDICES

Appendix A

ADDRESSES OF PUBLISHERS APPEARING IN THE TEXT

AAMOA PRESS
Afro-American Music Opportunities Association, Inc.
2909 Wayzata Boulevard
Minneapolis, Minnesota 55405

ABC DUNHILL MUSIC
11538 San Vincent Boulevard
Los Angeles, California 90049

ALAMEDA MUSIC
c/o Belwin Mills
25 Deshon Drive
Melville, New York 11746

AMERICAN COMPOSERS ALLIANCE
170 West 74th Street
New York, New York 10023

AMERICAN COMPOSERS EDITIONS
170 West 74th Street
New York, New York 10023

ASSOCIATED MUSIC
866 Third Avenue
New York, New York 10022

ATSOC MUSIC
P. O. Box 270
Radio City Station
New York, New York 10019

BACK DOOR MUSIC
Current address unknown

BECABIVERIP
c/o William Harris
269 West 72nd Street
New York, New York 10023

BEECHWOOD MUSIC CORPORATION
1750 North Vine Street
Hollywood, California 90028

BELWIN MILLS
25 Deshon Drive
Melville, New York 11746

BOTE & BOCK
c/o Associated Music
866 Third Avenue
New York, New York 10022

CANYON PRESS
P. O. Box 1235
Cincinnati, Ohio 45201

FRANCO COLUMBO
c/o Belwin Mills
25 Deshon Drive
Melville, New York 11746

COMPOSERS FACSIMILE EDITION
1815 North Kenmore Avenue
Los Angeles, California 90027

Subsidiary of American Composers Alliance
170 West 74th Street
New York, New York 10023

CREATIVE JAZZ COMPOSERS, INC.
P. O. Box 467
Bowie, Maryland 20715

CROSSROADS MUSIC
56 Ferry Street
Newark, New Jersey 07105

DAWN OF FREEDOM PUBLISHERS
176 Flat Hills Road
Amherst, Massachusetts 01002

DUCHESS MUSIC
c/o MCA
445 Park Avenue
New York, New York 10022

EMBASSY MUSIC
c/o Abington Press
201 Eighth Avenue South
Nashville, Tennessee 37302

FEMA MUSIC PUBLICATIONS
P. O. Box 395
Naperville, Illinois 60540

EDWARD FISHER MUSIC
c/o Gopam Enk. Inc.
8467 Beverly Boulevard
Suite 200
Los Angeles, California 90048

FRANK MUSIC
119 West 57th Street
New York, New York 10019

GALAXY MUSIC
2121 Broadway
New York, New York 10023

GENERAL MUSIC
c/o Boston Music Company
116 Boylston Street
Boston, Massachusetts 02116

H. W. GRAY
159 East 48th Street
New York, New York 10017

HANCOCK MUSIC
827 Folsom Street
San Francisco, California 94107

HIGHGATE PRESS
c/o Galaxy Music
2121 Broadway
New York, New York 10023

HUFFMAN PUBLISHING
c/o Interpub Inc.
Box 1929
Melbourne, Florida 32901

THE INTERNATIONAL LIBRARY
OF PIANO MUSIC
432 Park Avenue South
New York, New York 10016

KILYNN MUSIC
c/o Mietus Copyright Management
527 Madison Avenue
Suite 317
New York, New York 10022

KINGS CROWN MUSIC PRESS
c/o Galaxy Music
2121 Broadway
New York, New York 10023

LEEDS MUSIC
c/o MCA Music
455 Park Avenue
New York, New York 10022

E. B. MARKS
c/o Belwin Mills
25 Deshon Drive
Melville, New York 11746

MCA MUSIC
455 Park Avenue
New York, New York 10022

MENTION MUSIC
157 West 57th Street
Suite 200
New York, New York 10019

MERPINE MUSIC
c/o Publishers Licensing Corporation
40 West 55th Street
New York, New York 10019

MODERN AGE MUSIC
P. O. Box 8305
Universal City, California 91608

MODERN MUSIC
5810 South Normandie Avenue
Los Angeles, California 90044

MONTREAL BRASS QUARTET
SERIES
c/o Montreal Symphony Orchestra
Quebec, Canada

NEW VALLEY MUSIC PRESS
Sage Hall 21
Smith College
Northampton, Massachusetts
01060

NOLSEN MUSIC
Current address unknown

NOSNIBOR MUSIC
Current address unknown

PAB MUSIC
c/o ABC Dunhill Music
11538 San Vincent Boulevard
Los Angeles, California 90049

PEER/SOUTHERN MUSIC
1740 Broadway
New York, New York 10019

PEMBROKE/CARL FISCHER
c/o Fischer Inc.
62 Cooper Square
New York, New York 10003

J. C. PENNEY
The Soul of '76 is available from
the J. C. Penney Company and
can be ordered through any of its
retail outlets.

C. F. PETERS
373 Park Avenue South
New York, New York 10016

PINE KNOB MUSIC
P. O. Box 569
Englewood, New Jersey 07631

PRESTIGE MUSIC
c/o Parker Music
10th and Parker Street
Berkeley, California 94710

ROBBINS MUSIC
7165 Sunset Boulevard
Los Angeles, California 90046

RUSS-HIX MUSIC
12 East 41st Street
Suite 1104
New York, New York 10017

SAM FOX MUSIC PUBLISHERS
62 Cooper Square
New York, New York 10003

SELMA MUSIC
c/o Morty Craft
345 West 58th Street
Apartment 15-W
New York, New York 10019

STARFLOWER PRODUCTIONS INC.
Current address unknown

STUDIO PR
224 South Lebanon Street
Lebanon, Indiana 46052

THREE FIFTEEN WEST FIFTY-
THIRD STREET CORPORATION
315 West 53rd Street
New York, New York 10019

TOSCI MUSIC
c/o Belwin Mills
25 Deshon Drive
Melville, New York 11746

UNART MUSIC
Attn: M. Dave
6920 Sunset Boulevard
Los Angeles, California 90028

UNICHAPPELL MUSIC
810 7th Avenue
32nd Floor
New York, New York 10019

UNITED CHURCH PRESS
1505 Race Street
Philadelphia, Pennsylvania 19102

WAHWATSON MUSIC
Current address unknown

WARNER BROTHERS
75 Rockefeller Plaza
New York, New York 10019

WEINTRAUB MUSIC
c/o Music Sales Corporation
33 West 60th Street
New York, New York 10023

M. WITMARK & SONS
c/o Music Publishers Holding
   Corporation
619 West 54th Street
New York, New York 10019

ADDRESSES OF RECORDING COMPANIES APPEARING IN THE TEXT

AAMOA RECORDS
Afro-American Music Opportunities Association, Inc.
2909 Wayzata Boulevard
Minneapolis, Minnesota 55405

AMERICAN RECORDING SOCIETY
Current address unknown

AMPEX RECORDS
Current address unknown

ARGO RECORDS
c/o Argo Sight & Sound, Ltd.
539 West 25th Street
New York, New York 10001

ARISTA/FREEDOM RECORDS
1776 Broadway
New York, New York 10019

ATLANTIC RECORDS
75 Rockefeller Plaza
New York, New York 10019

BLUE NOTE RECORDS
c/o United Artists Records
6920 Sunset Boulevard
Hollywood, California 90028

BYG RECORDS
Current address unknown

CADET RECORDS
c/o Platinum Recording Company, Inc.
96 West Street
Englewood, New Jersey 07631

CAMBRIDGE RECORDS
473 Washington Street
Wellesley, Massachusetts 02181

CANTERBURY RECORDS
Larry Powell
House of Sounds
c/o WIMS Radio
Michigan City, Indiana

CAPITOL RECORDS
1750 North Vine Street
Hollywood, California 90028

CBS RECORDS
51 West 52nd Street
New York, New York 10019

CENTURY RECORDS
Saugus, California

CHESS/JANUS RECORDS
8776 Sunset Boulevard
Los Angeles, California 90069

COLUMBIA RECORDS
c/o CBS Records
51 West 52nd Street
New York, New York 10019

COMMAND RECORDS
c/o ABC Records, Inc.
8255 Beverly Boulevard
Los Angeles, California 90048

COMPOSERS RECORDINGS INC.
170 West 74th Street
New York, New York 10023

CONCEPT RECORDS
c/o New Music Distribution
Service
6 West 95th Street
New York, New York 10025

CONTEMPORARY RECORDS
8481 Melrose Place
Los Angeles, California 90069

CTI RECORDS
c/o Creed Taylor Inc.
1 Rockefeller Plaza
New York, New York 10020

DECCA RECORDS
c/o MCA Records
100 Universal City Plaza
Universal City, California 91608

DELMARK RECORDS
7 West Grand Avenue
Chicago, Illinois 60610

DESTO RECORDS
CMS-Desto
14 Warren Street
New York, New York 10007

EASTERN RECORDINGS
Eastern ERS-513: Contempo-
rary Black Images in Music
for the Flute
Available from
T&T Associates
Suite 502
Alexander Building
P. O. Box 292
Raleigh, North Carolina
27601
Eastern ERS-542: St. Steph-
en's Church Choir Sings
Address inquiries to
Dr. Clarence Whiteman
3413 Foster Avenue
Ettrick, Virginia 23803
Eastern ERS-549: Lord, We
Give Thanks To Thee
Address inquiries to the
Music Department
Virginia State College
Petersburg, Virginia 23803

EDUCATIONAL RECORD REFER-
ENCE LIBRARY
Franco Columbo, Inc.
c/o Belwin Mills
25 Deshon Drive
Melville, New York 11746

EMPIRICAL RECORDS
Current address unknown

ESP RECORDS
ESP-Disk Records
290 West End Avenue
New York, New York 10023

FANTASY RECORDS
Tenth and Parker Street
Berkeley, California 94710

FERMATA RECORDS
Current address unknown

FIRST EDITION RECORDS
333 West Broadway
Louisville, Kentucky 40202

FISK UNIVERSITY RECORDS
Music Department
Fisk University
Nashville, Tennessee 37203

FLYING DUTCHMAN RECORDS
c/o RCA Victor
1133 Avenue of the Americas
New York, New York 10036

FOLKWAYS RECORDS
Folkways/Scholastic Records
701 7th Avenue
New York, New York 10036

GOLDEN CREST RECORDS
220 Broadway
Huntington Station, New York
11746

GRT OF CANADA
Current address unknown

IMPULSE RECORDS
c/o ABC Records, Inc.
8255 Beverly Boulevard
Los Angeles, California 90048

ISIS RECORDS
Address inquiries to
Jamey Aebersold
1211 Aebersold Drive
New Albany, Indiana 47150

KAPP RECORDS
c/o MCA Records
100 Universal City Plaza
Universal City, California 91608

LOUISVILLE RECORDS
c/o First Edition Records
333 West Broadway
Louisville, Kentucky 40202

MAINSTREAM RECORDS
1700 Broadway
New York, New York 10019

MARK RECORDS
Current address unknown

MCA RECORDS
100 Universal City Plaza
Universal City, California 91608

MERCURY RECORDS
c/o Phonogram, Inc.
One IBM Plaza
Chicago, Illinois 60611

MGM RECORDS
c/o Polydor Inc.
810 Seventh Avenue
New York, New York 10019

MILESTONE RECORDS
10th and Parker Street
Berkeley, California 94710

MOODVILLE RECORDS
Current address unknown

MPS RECORDS
BASF Systems, Inc.
Bedford, Massachusetts 01730

NOLC RECORDS
Current address unknown

NONESUCH RECORDS
c/o Elektra/Asylum
962 North La Cienega
Los Angeles, California 90069

OBERLIN COLLEGE CHOIR RE-
CORDINGS
Dean's Office
Oberlin Conservatory of Music
Oberlin, Ohio 44074

OVATION RECORDS
1249 Waukegan Road
Glenview, Illinois 60025

PABLO RECORDS
c/o RCA Victor
1133 Avenue of the Americas
New York, New York 10036

PEOPLE RECORDS
c/o Polydor Inc.
810 Seventh Avenue
New York, New York 10019

PHILIPS RECORDS
c/o Phonogram Inc.
One IBM Plaza
Chicago, Illinois 60611

PICKWICK RECORDS
Pickwick Building
8-16
43rd Avenue
Long Island, New York 11101

POLYDOR RECORDS
810 Seventh Avenue
New York, New York 10019

PRESTIGE RECORDS
10th and Parker Street
Berkeley, California 94710

QUALITY (CANADA) RECORDS
Current address unknown

RCA VICTOR RECORDS
1133 Avenue of the Americas
New York, New York 10036

RICHSOUND RECORDS
Richsound 4112N10: The Undine
Smith Moore Song Book
Address inquiries to the
Music Department
Virginia State College
Petersburg, Virginia 23803

RIVERSIDE RECORDS
c/o ABC Records, Inc.
1330 Avenue of the Americas
New York, New York 10019

SABA RECORDS
c/o MPS Records
BASF Systems, Inc.
Bedford, Massachusetts 01730

SAM FOX
62 Cooper Square
New York, New York 10023

SAVOY RECORDS
625 Pennsylvania Avenue
Elizabeth, New Jersey 07201

SILHOUETTES IN COURAGE
22 East 40th Street
New York, New York 10016

SILVER CREST RECORDS
220 Broadway
Huntington Station, New York
11746

SOCIETY OF PARTICIPATING
ARTISTS
404 Broadway
Saratoga Springs, New York
12866

SONET RECORDS
Address inquiries to
J & F Record Sales
44 North Lake Avenue
Pasadena, California 91101
or

Rounder Records
186 Willow Avenue
Somerville, Massachusetts
  02144

TRIP RECORDS
Springboard International Records, Inc.
947 U.S. Highway No. 1
Rahway, New Jersey 07065

TURNABOUT RECORDS
c/o Vox Records
211 East 43rd Street
New York, New York 10017

UNITED ARTISTS RECORDS
6920 Sunset Boulevard
Hollywood, California 90028

UNIVERSITY OF ARIZONA
  RECORDS
Address inquiries to the
Music Department
University of Arizona
Tucson, Arizona
      or
Elsie A. Phillips
Librarian, Music Collection
University of Arizona
Tucson, Arizona

UNIVERSITY OF ILLINOIS PRESS
Urbana, Illinois 61801

VERVE RECORDS
c/o Polydor Inc.
812 Seventh Avenue
New York, New York 10019

VOX RECORDS
211 East 43rd Street
New York, New York 10017

WARNER BROTHERS RECORDS
3300 Warner Boulevard
Burbank, California 91505

WARWICK RECORDS
Current address unknown

WORD RECORDS
P.O. Box 1790
Waco, Texas 76703

Appendix C

COMPOSITIONS CLASSIFIED BY MEDIUM

ALTO FLUTE (SOLO)

Three Short Pieces for Alto Flute. Noel Da Costa

ALTO FLUTE IN COMBINATION WITH MULTIPLE ENSEMBLES
AND/OR SOLOISTS

Concerto for Flute and Jazz Band. For flute/alto flute, jazz
ensemble, and string quartet. David N. Baker

BALLET MUSIC

Dangerous Games. Archie Shepp
The Eighteen Hands of Jerome Harris. Olly Wilson
Forces of Rhythm. Coleridge-Taylor Perkinson
Ode to Otis. Coleridge-Taylor Perkinson
Othello. George Russell
The Peloponnesian War. Archie Shepp
The Rope. For solo dancer and piano. Ulysses Kay
Sangre Negro. David N. Baker

BAND

Afro-Cuban Suite. David N. Baker
Concert Sketches. Ulysses Kay
Expansions. Hale Smith
Forever Free. Ulysses Kay
Four Silhouettes. Ulysses Kay
In Memoriam Zach Walker. T. J. Anderson
Majorca. Oliver Nelson
Rotations. T. J. Anderson
Short Suite. Ulysses Kay
Solemn Prelude. Ulysses Kay
Somersault: A Twelve-Tone Adventure for Band. Hale Smith
Take a Chance: An Aleatoric Episode for Band. Hale Smith
Trinal Dance. Hale Smith

BARITONE AND CHAMBER ENSEMBLE

Four Glimpses of Night. For baritone, flute, clarinet, bass clarinet, tenor saxophone, trumpet, piano, and percussion. Noel Da Costa

BARITONE AND PIANO

Prayer of Steel. Noel Da Costa

BARITONE IN COMBINATION WITH MULTIPLE ENSEMBLES AND/OR SOLOISTS

Song of Jeremiah. For baritone, chorus (SATB), and orchestra. Ulysses Kay

BASS AND CHORUS (SATB)

A Lincoln Letter. Ulysses Kay

BASS IN COMBINATION WITH MULTIPLE ENSEMBLES AND/OR SOLOISTS

Listen to the Silence. For chorus (SATB), bass soloist, and jazz ensemble. George Russell
Phoebus, Arise. For soprano, bass, chorus (SATB), and orchestra. Ulysses Kay

BASS-BARITONE AND CHAMBER ENSEMBLE

Quote-Unquote. For bass-baritone, oboe, trumpet, and percussion. Talib Hakim

BASS-BARITONE IN COMBINATION WITH MULTIPLE ENSEMBLES AND/OR SOLOISTS

Comes Tomorrow. For chorus (SATB), soloists (soprano, contralto, tenor, and bass-baritone), & jazz ensemble. Hale Smith

BRASS ENSEMBLE

Three Jazz Moods. David N. Baker

BRASS OCTET

Heralds. Ulysses Kay

BRASS QUARTET

Brass Quartet. Ulysses Kay

BRASS QUINTET

Music for Brass. George Walker
Passions. David N. Baker
Psalm Tune Variations. Noel Da Costa
Sketches. Talib Hakim
Soundpiece for Brass Quintet. Howard Swanson

BRASS QUINTET AND ORCHESTRA

Quintet Concerto. Ulysses Kay

BRASS QUINTET AND PIANO

Sonata for Brass Quintet and Piano. David N. Baker

CHAMBER MUSIC--BRASS

Brass Quartet. Ulysses Kay
Heralds. For brass octet. Ulysses Kay
Heralds II. For three trumpets. Ulysses Kay
Music for Brass. For brass quintet. George Walker
Passions. For brass quintet. David N. Baker
Psalm Tune Variations. For brass quintet. Noel Da Costa
Romanza and March. For three trombones. David N. Baker
Serenade No. 2. For four horns. Ulysses Kay
Sketches. For brass quintet. Talib Hakim
Soundpiece for Brass Quintet. Howard Swanson
Three Fanfares for Four Trumpets. Ulysses Kay
Three Jazz Moods. For brass ensemble. David N. Baker

CHAMBER MUSIC--STRINGS

Connections: A Fantasy for String Quintet. T. J. Anderson
Currents. For string quartet. Talib Hakim
Fugue in F. For String trio. Undine S. Moore
Pastorale. For string quartet. David N. Baker
Sonata for Viola, Guitar, and Contrabass. David N. Baker
Sonata for Violin and Cello. David N. Baker
String Quartet. Olly Wilson
String Quartet No. 1. T. J. Anderson
String Quartet No. 1. David N. Baker
String Quartet No. 1. Coleridge-Taylor Perkinson
String Quartet No. 1. George Walker

String Quartet No. 2.   Ulysses Kay
String Quartet No. 2.   George Walker
String Quartet No. 3.   Ulysses Kay
Vista No. II.   For string octet.   Howard Swanson

CHAMBER MUSIC--WOODWINDS

Divertimento in Three Movements for Eleven Woodwind Instru-
  ments.   Oliver Nelson
Duo.   For flute and clarinet.   Talib Hakim
Fantasy for Woodwind Quintet.   David N. Baker
Five Etudes and a Fancy.   For woodwind quintet.   T. J. Ander-
  son
Peace-Mobile.   For woodwind quintet.   Talib Hakim
Prelude and Line Study.   For flute, clarinet, bass clarinet,
  and bassoon.   Olly Wilson
Soundpiece for Woodwind Quintet.   Noel Da Costa
Theme and Variations.   For woodwind quintet.   David N. Baker
Titles.   For flute, oboe, clarinet, and bassoon.   Talib Hakim
Woodwind Quintet.   Oliver Nelson
Woodwind Quintet from The Black Frontier.   David N. Baker

CHAMBER MUSIC--MIXED

Afro-American Suite.   For flute/alto flute, violoncello, and
  piano.   Undine S. Moore
Ballade.   For horn, alto saxophone, and violoncello.   David N.
  Baker
Chime Tones.   For horn, vibraphone, and chimes.   Noel Da
  Costa
Contours.   For oboe, bassoon, horn, trumpet, violoncello,
  and contrabass.   Talib Hakim
Contrasts.   For violin, violoncello, and piano.   David N. Baker
Elements.   For flute/alto flute, clarinet/bass clarinet, violin/
  viola, violoncello, piano, and glass and bamboo wind and hand
  chimes.   Talib Hakim
Encounter.   For flute, oboe, clarinet, bassoon, horn, trumpet,
  and trombone.   Talib Hakim
Facets.   For woodwind quintet and piano.   Ulysses Kay
Fanfare Rhythms.   For four trumpets and percussion.   Noel
  Da Costa
Fanfare Rhythms.   For trumpet choir and percussion.   Noel
  Da Costa
Five Bagatelles for Oboe, Violin, and Harpsichord.   T. J.
  Anderson
Five Easy Pieces for Violin, Piano, and Jews Harp.   T. J.
  Anderson
Four.   For clarinet, trumpet, trombone, and piano.   Talib
  Hakim
Grass: A Poem for Piano, Strings, and Percussion.   Cole-
  ridge-Taylor Perkinson

In the Circle. For four electric guitars, Fender bass, and percussion. Noel Da Costa

Inner-Sections. For flute, clarinet, trombone, piano, and percussion. Talib Hakim

Introduction, Cadenzas, and Interludes for Eight Players. For flute/alto flute, oboe, clarinet, harp, piano, violin, viola, and violoncello. Hale Smith

Moments. For alto saxophone, bassoon, and horn. Talib Hakim

Music for Three. For violin, violoncello, and piano. George Walker

Mutations. For bass clarinet, horn, trumpet, viola, and violoncello. Talib Hakim

Occurrence for Six. For flute, clarinet, bass clarinet, tenor saxophone, trumpet, and contrabass. Noel Da Costa

Piece for Four. For flute, trumpet, contrabass, and piano. Olly Wilson

Portraits. For alto flute, bass clarinet, percussion, and piano. Talib Hakim

Riff Time. For violin, violoncello, piano, and percussion. Noel Da Costa

Roots. For violin, violoncello, and piano. David N. Baker

Roots and Other Things. For flute/alto flute, oboe/English horn, clarinet/bass clarinet, trumpet, horn, trombone, viola, violoncello, and contrabass. Talib Hakim

Sextet. For flute, clarinet, bassoon, horn, trumpet, and trombone. Olly Wilson

Sonata for Brass Quintet and Piano. David N. Baker

Sonata for Piano and String Quintet. David N. Baker

Sonata for Tuba and String Quartet. David N. Baker

Spaces. For contrabass and trumpet. Noel Da Costa

Statement and Responses. For flute, oboe, bass clarinet, trumpet, trombone, tuba, viola, violoncello, and contrabass. Noel Da Costa

Suite for Flute and Oboe. Ulysses Kay

Three Play Short Five. For bass clarinet, percussion, and contrabass. Talib Hakim

Time...On and On. For violin, tenor saxophone, and prerecorded electronic sounds. Noel Da Costa

Timelessness. For flugelhorn, horn, trombone, tuba, percussion, contrabass, and piano. Talib Hakim

Transitions: A Fantasy for Ten Instruments. For flute, clarinet, bassoon, horn, trumpet, trombone, violin, viola, violoncello, and piano. T. J. Anderson

Trio for Flute, Cello, and Piano. Olly Wilson

Trio for Flute, Oboe, and Piano. Howard Swanson

Variations for Six Players. For woodwind quintet and piano. Hale Smith

CHAMBER OPERA
Blood Wedding. Hale Smith

CHAMBER ORCHESTRA

Antiphonys for Chamber Orchestra. George Walker
Dirge for Chamber Orchestra. Oliver Nelson
Night Music. Howard Swanson
Reflections on the 5th Ray. For chamber orchestra and narra-
tor. Talib Hakim
Scherzi Musicali. Ulysses Kay
Shapes. Talib Hakim

CHORUS (CHILDREN'S VOICES) AND INSTRUMENTAL ENSEMBLE

Tambourines. For children's chorus, piano, and Fender bass.
Noel Da Costa

CHORUS (CHILDREN'S VOICES) AND ORGAN

Two Prayers of Kierkegaard. Noel Da Costa

CHORUS (CHILDREN'S VOICES) AND PIANO
I See the Moon. Noel Da Costa

CHORUS (DOUBLE CHORUS) IN COMBINATION WITH MULTIPLE
ENSEMBLES AND/OR SOLOISTS

Counterpoint. For double chorus, solo quintet (SSATB), and
organ or two pianos. Noel Da Costa
Spirit Song. For orchestra, double chorus, and soprano. Olly
Wilson

CHORUS (SAB) AND ORGAN

To Light That Shines. Ulysses Kay

CHORUS (SAB) AND PIANO

I Would Be True. Undine S. Moore

CHORUS (SATB)

Alleluia. Undine S. Moore
As Joseph Was A-Walking. Ulysses Kay
Benediction. Undine S. Moore
The Blind Man Stood on the Way and Cried. Undine S. Moore

Bound for Canaan's Land. Undine S. Moore
Choral Prayers in Folk Style. Undine S. Moore
Daniel, Daniel Servant of the Lord. (SSAATTBB) Undine S. Moore
Fare You Well. Undine S. Moore
Five Songs to the Survival of Black Children. David N. Baker
Flowers in the Valley. Ulysses Kay
Gloria. Olly Wilson
Hail! Warrior! Undine S. Moore
How I Got Over. Undine S. Moore
How Stands the Glass Around? (SSATB) Ulysses Kay
I Just Come from the Fountain. Undine S. Moore
I'm Coming Home. Hale Smith
I'm Going Home. Undine S. Moore
I'm So Glad Trouble Don't Last Alway. (SAATBB) Noel Da Costa
Into My Heart's Treasury. Undine S. Moore
Let Down the Bars O Death. (SSATB) Noel Da Costa
Let Us Make Man in Our Image. Undine S. Moore
Little Lamb. Noel Da Costa
Long Fare You Well. Undine S. Moore
Lord, We Give Thanks to Thee. Undine S. Moore
Mother to Son. (SSAATTBB) Undine S. Moore
A New Song. Ulysses Kay
Psalm 23. (SSATB) Coleridge-Taylor Perkinson
Psalm 96. George Walker
Rise Up Shepherd. Noel Da Costa
Sinner, You Can't Walk My Path. Undine S. Moore
Stars. George Walker
Striving After God. Undine S. Moore
Tambourines to Glory. Undine S. Moore
Thou Dost Lay Me in the Dust of Death. David N. Baker
Thou Hast Made Us for Thyself. Undine S. Moore
... Through the Valley... Noel Da Costa
Two Dunbar Lyrics. Ulysses Kay
Two Kids. Hale Smith
Two Shaker Songs. Noel Da Costa
Walk Thro' the Streets of the City. Undine S. Moore
We Are Climbing Jacob's Ladder. (SSATTB) Noel Da Costa
What's in a Name? (SSATB) Ulysses Kay
When Susannah Jones Wears Red. Undine S. Moore
With This Small Key. George Walker
A Wreath for Waits. Ulysses Kay

CHORUS (SATB) AND BASS SOLOIST

A Lincoln Letter. Ulysses Kay

CHORUS (SATB) AND CHAMBER ENSEMBLE

Fredome-Freedom. For chorus (SATB), two pianos, electric

bass, and percussion. Coleridge-Taylor Perkinson
I'm Coming Home. For chorus (SATB) with optional piano and/
or rhythm section accompaniment. Hale Smith
Tone-Prayers. For chorus (SATB), percussion, and piano.
Talib Hakim

CHORUS (SATB) AND CHAMBER ORCHESTRA

In Memoriam--Beryl Rubenstein. Hale Smith
Parables. Ulysses Kay

CHORUS (SATB) AND ELECTRONIC SOUND

In Memoriam, Martin Luther King Jr. Olly Wilson

CHORUS (SATB) AND JAZZ ENSEMBLE

Catholic Mass for Peace. David N. Baker

CHORUS (SATB) AND JAZZ SEPTET

Lutheran Mass. David N. Baker

CHORUS (SATB) AND LARGE INSTRUMENTAL ENSEMBLE

Stephen Crane Set. For chorus (SATB), flute, oboe, English
horn, clarinet, bass clarinet, bassoon, two horns, two trumpets, trombone, bass trombone, and percussion. Ulysses Kay

CHORUS (SATB) AND ORCHESTRA

Inscriptions from Within. Ulysses Kay

CHORUS (SATB) AND ORGAN

Alleluia. Undine S. Moore
Choral Triptych. Ulysses Kay
Epigrams and Hymn. Ulysses Kay
Four Hymn-Anthems. Ulysses Kay
Grace to You, and Peace. Ulysses Kay
Hymn-Anthem on the Tune "Hanover." Ulysses Kay
I Have a Dream. Noel Da Costa
O God of Light and Love. Noel Da Costa
Psalm 23. David N. Baker
Psalm 84. George Walker
Psalm 117. George Walker

Psalm 148. George Walker
Who Shall Separate Us from the Love of Christ? Undine S.
Moore

CHORUS (SATB) AND PIANO

Any Human to Another. David N. Baker
Choral Triptych. Ulysses Kay
The Epicure. Ulysses Kay
Fredome-Freedom. Coleridge-Taylor Perkinson
Hymn-Anthem on the Tune "Hanover." Ulysses Kay
I Dream a World. Noel Da Costa
I'm Coming Home. Hale Smith
In Memoriam--Beryl Rubenstein. Hale Smith
Three Lyrics for Chorus. George Walker
A Time for Remembering. Undine S. Moore
Who Shall Separate Us from the Love of Christ? Undine S.
Moore

CHORUS (SATB) AND RHYTHM SECTION

I'm Coming Home. Hale Smith

CHORUS (SATB) AND STRING ORCHESTRA

Choral Triptych. Ulysses Kay

CHORUS (SATB) IN COMBINATION WITH MULTIPLE ENSEMBLES AND/OR SOLOISTS

The Beatitudes. For chorus (SATB), soloists, narrator, jazz
ensemble, string orchestra, and dancers. David N. Baker
Black America: To the Memory of Martin Luther King, Jr.
For jazz ensemble, narrators, chorus (SATB), soloists, and
string orchestra. David N. Baker
Comes Tomorrow. For chorus (SATB), soloists (soprano, con-
tralto, tenor, and bass-baritone), and jazz ensemble. Hale
Smith
Listen to the Silence. For jazz ensemble, chorus (SATB), and
bass soloist. George Russell
Once There Was a Man. For narrator, chorus (SATB), and
orchestra. Ulysses Kay
Personals. For narrator, mixed chorus, and brass ensemble.
T. J. Anderson
Phoebus, Arise. For soprano, bass, chorus (SATB), and or-
chestra. Ulysses Kay
Prepare Me One Body. For soprano or tenor, chorus (SATB),
and organ. Noel Da Costa
Psalm 22. For chorus (SATB), narrators, jazz ensemble,

string orchestra, and dancers. David N. Baker
Song of Jeremiah. For baritone, chorus (SATB), and orchestra.
Ulysses Kay
A Song of Mankind. For chorus (SATB), orchestra, jazz ensemble,
rock band, vocal soloists, lights, and sound effects. David N.
Baker

CHORUS (SSA)

A Christmas Alleluia. Undine S. Moore
Christmas Carol. Ulysses Kay
Is There Anybody Here? Undine S. Moore

CHORUS (SSA) AND LARGE INSTRUMENTAL ENSEMBLE

Hundredth Psalm. For chorus (SSA), brass, and strings. Coleridge-Taylor Perkinson
Sound Images. For female chorus, brass ensemble, strings, and
percussion. Talib Hakim

CHORUS (SSA) AND ORGAN

Five/Seven. Noel Da Costa
Gloria (In Memoriam). George Walker
Psalm 105. George Walker

CHORUS (SSA) AND PIANO

The Birds. Ulysses Kay
Emily Dickinson Set. Ulysses Kay
Sir Olaf and the Erl King's Daughter. Undine S. Moore
Tears, Flow No More. Ulysses Kay

CHORUS (SSA) IN COMBINATION WITH MULTIPLE ENSEMBLES
AND/OR SOLOISTS

The Last Judgment. For chorus (SSA), speaker, piano, and
percussion. Noel Da Costa

CHORUS (TREBLE VOICES)

The Lamb. Undine S. Moore
Teach Me to Hear Mermaids Singing. Undine S. Moore

CHORUS (TREBLE VOICES) AND PIANO

Pentagraph. Ulysses Kay

CHORUS (TTBB)

Come Away, Come Away Death. Ulysses Kay
Nightingales. Howard Swanson
No Condemnation. Undine S. Moore
Rise Up Shepherd and Follow. Undine S. Moore
Triple Set. Ulysses Kay
Triumvirate. Ulysses Kay

CHORUS (TTBB) AND INSTRUMENTAL ENSEMBLE

This House. For male chorus and four chromatic pitch pipes.
T. J. Anderson

CHORUS (TTBB) IN COMBINATION WITH MULTIPLE ENSEMBLES
AND/OR SOLOISTS

Glory to God. For chorus (TTBB), narrator, flute, organ,
and piano with optional brass and percussion. Undine S.
Moore

CHORUS (TWO-PART) AND PIANO

Lord, Make Us More Holy. Undine S. Moore

CHORUS (UNISON) AND ORGAN

O Spirit Who Dost Prefer Before All Temples. Undine S.
Moore

CHORUS (UNISON) AND PIANO

O Spirit Who Dost Prefer Before All Temples. Undine S.
Moore

CHORUS (UNSPECIFIED) IN COMBINATION WITH MULTIPLE
ENSEMBLES AND/OR SOLOISTS

A Ceremony of Spirituals. For soprano, soprano/tenor saxo-
phone, orchestra, and chorus. Noel Da Costa
Dunbar. For solo voice, chorus, and orchestra. Coleridge-
Taylor Perkinson

CLARINET AND CHAMBER ORCHESTRA

Six Pieces for Clarinet and Chamber Orchestra. T. J. Anderson

CLARINET AND ELECTRONIC SOUND

    Echoes. Olly Wilson

CLARINET AND FLUTE

    Duo. Talib Hakim

CLARINET AND PIANO

    Introduction and Allegro. Undine S. Moore
    Introduction, March, and Allegro. Undine S. Moore
    Perimeters for Clarinet and Piano. George Walker
    Swing Set. T. J. Anderson

CLARINET AND PIANO (FOUR HANDS)

    Five Fancys for Clarinet and Piano (Four Hands). George
    Walker

CLARINET IN COMBINATION WITH MULTIPLE ENSEMBLES AND /
OR SOLOISTS

    Trio Concertante. For clarinet, trumpet, trombone, and band.
    T. J. Anderson

CONTRABASS (SOLO)

    In Space. Noel Da Costa
    Soliloquy. Olly Wilson

CONTRABASS AND CHAMBER ENSEMBLE

    Blue Mix: A Composition in the Form of a Chart. For contra-
    bass/Fender bass, violoncello, contrabass, and percussion.
    Noel Da Costa

CONTRABASS AND TRUMPET

    Spaces. Noel Da Costa

CONTRABASS IN COMBINATION WITH MULTIPLE ENSEMBLES
AND /OR SOLOISTS

    Concerto for Bass Viol and Jazz Band. For bass viol, jazz
    ensemble, string quartet, and solo violin. David N. Baker

Levels: A Concerto for Solo Contrabass, Jazz Band, Flute Quartet, Horn Quartet, and String Quartet. David N. Baker
Piece for Orchestra. For orchestra and jazz soloists (alto saxophone and bass). Oliver Nelson

CONTRALTO AND CHAMBER ENSEMBLE

Chanson Innocente. For contralto and two bassoons. Olly Wilson

CONTRALTO AND PIANO

I Want to Die While You Love Me. Undine S. Moore
Songs for Contralto and Piano. Oliver Nelson
Two Dutch Poems. Olly Wilson

CONTRALTO IN COMBINATION WITH MULTIPLE ENSEMBLES AND/OR SOLOISTS

Comes Tomorrow. For chorus (SATB), soloists (soprano, contralto, tenor, and bass-baritone), and jazz ensemble. Hale Smith
Soundpiece for Contralto, String Quartet, and Piano. Oliver Nelson

DANCE OPERA

The Confession Stone. Noel Da Costa

ELECTRONIC SOUND

Black Martyrs. Olly Wilson
Cetus. Olly Wilson

ENGLISH HORN AND STRING ORCHESTRA

Pietá. Ulysses Kay

FILM SCORES

Alpha Caper. Oliver Nelson
Amazing Grace. Coleridge-Taylor Perkinson
Blow-Up. Herbie Hancock
Bold New Approach. Hale Smith
Crossroads Africa. Coleridge-Taylor Perkinson
Death of a Gunfighter. Oliver Nelson

Death Wish. Herbie Hancock
The Education of Sonny Carson. Coleridge-Taylor Perkinson
Encounter and Response. Oliver Nelson
Going Home. Ulysses Kay
Happy Birthday Mrs. Craig. Coleridge-Taylor Perkinson
Istanbul Express. Oliver Nelson
The Lion, the Griffin, and the Kangaroo. Ulysses Kay
The MacMasters. Coleridge-Taylor Perkinson
Memphis to Mobile. Coleridge-Taylor Perkinson
Money to Burn. Oliver Nelson
New York, City of Magic. Ulysses Kay
Nosotros. Ulysses Kay
The Quiet One. Ulysses Kay
Skullduggery. Oliver Nelson
The Spook Who Sat by the Door. Herbie Hancock
A Thing of Beauty. Ulysses Kay
Thomasine and Bushrod. Coleridge-Taylor Perkinson
Together for Days. Coleridge-Taylor Perkinson
Trans Europa Express. Oliver Nelson
A Warm December. Coleridge-Taylor Perkinson
Zig Zag. Oliver Nelson

FLUTE (SOLO)

Prelude. Ulysses Kay
Silver Blue. Noel Da Costa
Three Brevities. Hale Smith

FLUTE AND CLARINET

Duo. Talib Hakim

FLUTE AND LARGE INSTRUMENTAL ENSEMBLE

Aulos. For flute, two horns, string orchestra, and percussion.
Ulysses Kay

FLUTE AND OBOE

Suite for Flute and Oboe. Ulysses Kay

FLUTE AND PIANO

Aulos. Ulysses Kay
Six Poemes Noir pour Flute et Piano. David N. Baker
Three Pieces for Flute and Piano. Undine S. Moore

FLUTE IN COMBINATION WITH MULTIPLE ENSEMBLES AND/OR SOLOISTS

Concerto for Flute and Jazz Band. For flute/alto flute, jazz ensemble, and string quartet. David N. Baker

GUITAR

Concerto for Self-Accompanied Guitar. George Russell
Guitarra. Ulysses Kay

HARP AND CHAMBER ORCHESTRA

Music for Harp and Orchestra. Hale Smith

HIGH VOICE (SOLO)

Vocalise. Noel Da Costa

HIGH VOICE AND CHAMBER ENSEMBLE

Biography. For soprano, flute, harp, and percussion. Olly Wilson

Block Songs. For soprano and children's toys. T. J. Anderson

Fantasy. For soprano, brass ensemble, and harp. David N. Baker

Five Epitaphs. For soprano and string quartet. Noel Da Costa

Give and Take. For soprano, flute/alto flute, oboe/English horn, viola, violoncello, and percussion. David N. Baker

In the Landscape of Spring. For soprano, flute, clarinet, percussion, and piano. Noel Da Costa

November Song. A concert scene for soprano, violin, saxophone, and piano. Noel Da Costa

Numbers. For soprano, percussion, and contrabass. Talib Hakim

Set-Three. For soprano, violoncello, and piano. Talib Hakim

Six Players and a Voice. For soprano, clarinet, trumpet, violoncello, percussion, and piano. Talib Hakim

Song-Short. For soprano, alto flute, English horn, bass clarinet, horn, and trombone. Talib Hakim

Songs of the Night. For soprano, string quartet, and piano. David N. Baker

Tone-Poem. For soprano, percussion, and piano. Talib Hakim

Triptych on Texts of Blake. For soprano, violin, violoncello, and piano. Ulysses Kay

Two Love Songs of John Donne. For soprano, string quartet, and woodwind quintet. Hale Smith

Variations on a Theme by M. B. Tolson. For soprano, alto saxophone, trumpet, trombone, piano, violin, and violoncello. T. J. Anderson

HIGH VOICE AND ORCHESTRA

Horizon '76. T. J. Anderson
In Memoriam Malcolm X. T. J. Anderson
Three Pieces after Blake. Ulysses Kay

HIGH VOICE AND ORGAN

Beyond the Years. Noel Da Costa
Love, Let the Wind Cry How I Adore Thee. Undine S. Moore

HIGH VOICE AND PIANO

Abyss. David N. Baker
Beyond the Rim of Day. Hale Smith
Five Settings for Soprano and Piano. David N. Baker
Four Haiku Settings. Noel Da Costa
Heart, Have You Heard the News? Undine S. Moore
I Am in Doubt. Undine S. Moore
Love, Let the Wind Cry How I Adore Thee. Undine S. Moore
Lyric for True Love. Undine S. Moore
Men Shall Tell of the Lord. David N. Baker
Ode to Silence. Talib Hakim
Set Down! Undine S. Moore
To Be Baptized. Undine S. Moore
Two Songs. Noel Da Costa
Two Songs for Julie-Ju. Noel Da Costa
Uphill. Undine S. Moore
Watch and Pray. Undine S. Moore

HIGH VOICE IN COMBINATION WITH MULTIPLE ENSEMBLES AND/OR SOLOISTS

A Ceremony of Spirituals. For soprano, soprano/tenor saxo-
phone, orchestra, and chorus. Noel Da Costa
Le Chat Qui Pêche. For soprano, orchestra, and jazz quartet
(alto/tenor saxophone, piano, bass, and drums). David N.
Baker
Comes Tomorrow. For chorus (SATB), soloists (soprano, con-
tralto, tenor, and bass-baritone), and jazz ensemble. Hale
Smith
The Confession Stone. For soprano, trio (SSA), and instru-
mental ensemble. Noel Da Costa
Phoebus, Arise. For soprano, bass, chorus (SATB), and
orchestra. Ulysses Kay
Prepare Me One Body. For soprano or tenor, chorus (SATB),
and organ. Noel Da Costa
Spirit Song. For double chorus, orchestra, and soprano. Olly
Wilson

HORN QUARTET

    Serenade No. 2. Ulysses Kay

JAZZ ENSEMBLE

    Abstract. Archie Shepp
    Actual Proof. Herbie Hancock
    Adumbratio. David N. Baker
    African Sunrise. Oliver Nelson
    Afrique. Oliver Nelson
    Afro-American Sketches. Oliver Nelson
    Aftermath. Oliver Nelson
    Al-Ki-Hol. David N. Baker
    All About Rosie. George Russell
    Almost. David N. Baker
    Alone and I. Herbie Hancock
    Altoitis. Oliver Nelson
    Anacruses. Oliver Nelson
    And What If I Don't? Herbie Hancock
    Anjisa. David N. Baker
    Apocalypse. David N. Baker
    April B. David N. Baker
    Attica Blues. Archie Shepp
    Aucon. David N. Baker
    Au Demain. David N. Baker
    Auev. David N. Baker
    Aujour d'Hui. David N. Baker
    Aulil. David N. Baker
    Back Back. Archie Shepp
    Baja Bossa. Oliver Nelson
    Ballad for a Child. Archie Shepp
    The Ballad of Hix Blewitt. George Russell
    Bash. David N. Baker
    Basheer. Archie Shepp
    Bebop Revisited. David N. Baker
    La Belle Fleur. David N. Baker
    Berlin Dialogue for Orchestra. Oliver Nelson
    Big City Blues. George Russell
    Bily. David N. Baker
    Bird (To the Memory of Charlie Parker). David N. Baker
    A Bird in Igor's Yard. George Russell
    Birdhouse. Herbie Hancock
    Black, Brown, and Beautiful. Oliver Nelson
    Black Man, Black Woman. David N. Baker
    Black Thursday. David N. Baker
    Blase. Archie Shepp
    Blind Man, Blind Man. Herbie Hancock
    Blues and the Abstract Truth. Oliver Nelson
    Blues at the Five Spot. Oliver Nelson
    Blues for Bird. David N. Baker
    Blues for Brother George Jackson. Archie Shepp
    Blues for M.F. Oliver Nelson

Blues in Orbit. George Russell
Bob's Blues. Oliver Nelson
De Boogie Man. David N. Baker
Booze Blues. Oliver Nelson
Bopol. Oliver Nelson
Bossa Belle. David N. Baker
Bougaloo. David N. Baker
Brother. David N. Baker
Brushstrokes. David N. Baker
Bubbles. Herbie Hancock
Buck. David N. Baker
Bus Ride. David N. Baker
Butch and Butch. Oliver Nelson
Butterfly. Herbie Hancock
Call Me By My Rightful Name. Archie Shepp
Calypso-Nova No. 1. David N. Baker
Calypso-Nova No. 2. David N. Baker
Cantaloupe Island. Herbie Hancock
Cascades. Oliver Nelson
Cat in a Tree. Oliver Nelson
Catalyst. David N. Baker
Cattin'. David N. Baker
CFB. David N. Baker
Chameleon. Herbie Hancock
Chariots. David N. Baker
The Chased. Archie Shepp
Le Chat Qui Pêche. David N. Baker
Ché. David N. Baker
Check It Out. David N. Baker
Chromatic Universe: Parts 1, 2, and 3. George Russell
Cinquatre. David N. Baker
Clegre. David N. Baker
Coltrane in Memoriam. David N. Baker
Concerto for Billy the Kid. George Russell
Consequences. Archie Shepp
The Creeper. Oliver Nelson
The Critic's Choice. Oliver Nelson
Un Croque Monsieur (Poem: For Losers). Archie Shepp
Crossings. Herbie Hancock
Cubana Be Cubana Bop. George Russell
Cuzin' Ducky. David N. Baker
Cuzin' Larry--The Champ. David N. Baker
Cuzin' Lee. David N. Baker
DABD. David N. Baker
Dakiap. David N. Baker
Dave's Waltz. David N. Baker
The Day John Brown Was Hanged. George Russell
D. C. Divertimento. George Russell
Delicado. Archie Shepp
Digits. David N. Baker
Dimensions. George Russell
Disc-o-mite. Oliver Nelson
Do De Mi. David N. Baker
Do You See What I See? Oliver Nelson

Doin' It. Herbie Hancock
A Dollar Short and a Day Late. David N. Baker
Dolphin Dance. Herbie Hancock
Don't Stand Up. Oliver Nelson
Driftin'. Herbie Hancock
The Drive. Oliver Nelson
Dumpy Mama. Oliver Nelson
Early Morning. Oliver Nelson
The Egg. Herbie Hancock
Elegy for a Duck. Oliver Nelson
Empty Pockets. Herbie Hancock
Eros and Agape. David N. Baker
Etc. David N. Baker
An Evening Thought. David N. Baker
The Eye of the Hurricane. Herbie Hancock
Ezz-thetic. George Russell
Fat Albert Rotunda. Herbie Hancock
Fat Mama. Herbie Hancock
The Felix Walk. David N. Baker
Fellow Delegates. George Russell
Fiesta. Archie Shepp
Firewater. Herbie Hancock
First Day of Spring. David N. Baker
Flight for Freedom. Oliver Nelson
Flute Salad. Oliver Nelson
Folklike. David N. Baker
For Mods Only. Archie Shepp
Freein' Up. George Russell
The Funeral. Archie Shepp
Funky But Blues. Oliver Nelson
Fuup Blues. David N. Baker
Gentle Thoughts. Herbie Hancock
Geo Rus. David N. Baker
The Georgia Peach. David N. Baker
Gingerbread, Gingerbread Boy. Archie Shepp
Golgatha. David N. Baker
Goodbye to Childhood. Herbie Hancock
Green Minus Yellow. David N. Baker
A Groove. Oliver Nelson
Guitar Blues. Oliver Nelson
Hambone. Archie Shepp
Hang Up Your Hang Ups. Herbie Hancock
Happenings. Oliver Nelson
Harlem Pipes. David N. Baker
He Who Lives in Fear. Herbie Hancock
Heartbeat. Herbie Hancock
Hello World. David N. Baker
A Helluva Town. George Russell
Herman's Theme. David N. Baker
Hey Ho. Herbie Hancock
HHHCCC. David N. Baker
Hidden Shadows. Herbie Hancock
Ho! Oliver Nelson

Hobo Flats. Oliver Nelson
Hoe Down. Oliver Nelson
Honesty. David N. Baker
Hornets. Herbie Hancock
Hoy Hoy. David N. Baker
I Have a Dream. Herbie Hancock
I Hope in Time a Change Will Come. Oliver Nelson
I Saw Pinetop Spit Blood. Oliver Nelson
The I. U. Swing Machine. David N. Baker
Images. Oliver Nelson
Impressions of Berlin Suite. Oliver Nelson
In a Japanese Garden. Oliver Nelson
In Passing. Oliver Nelson
In Time. Oliver Nelson
Infinity. David N. Baker
Invocation to Mr. Parker. Archie Shepp
It Is the Year of the Rabbit. Archie Shepp
J & B. Oliver Nelson
J Is for Loveliness. David N. Baker
Jack Rabbit. Herbie Hancock
Jack's Blues. George Russell
Jams and Jellies. Oliver Nelson
Jazz Bug. Oliver Nelson
Jazzhattan Suite. Oliver Nelson
Jessica. Herbie Hancock
A Jump Ahead. Herbie Hancock
Just Before September. David N. Baker
K. C. C. David N. Baker
The Kennedy Dream Suite. Oliver Nelson
Kentucky Oysters. David N. Baker
Kilimanjaro. Oliver Nelson
King Cobra. Herbie Hancock
Knights of the Steamtable. George Russell
Lacypso. David N. Baker
The Lady from Girl Talk. Oliver Nelson
Lamb of God. Oliver Nelson
Latino. Oliver Nelson
Lazie Kate. Oliver Nelson
Le Roi. David N. Baker
Lem and Aide. Oliver Nelson
Let's Get It On. David N. Baker
Light Blue, Dark Blue. David N. Baker
Like a Blessed Baby Lamb. Archie Shepp
Li'l Brother. Herbie Hancock
Little One. Herbie Hancock
The Little Princess. David N. Baker
A Little Waltz. David N. Baker
Living Time: Events I-VIII. George Russell
Livingstone I Presume. George Russell
The Lone Ranger and the Great Horace Silver. David N. Baker
A Lonely Place. George Russell
Louis Armstrong in Memoriam. David N. Baker
Lou's Good Dues Blues. Oliver Nelson

Lumo. David N. Baker
Lunacy. David N. Baker
Lydia and Her Friends. George Russell
Lydian April. David N. Baker
Lydian Lullaby. George Russell
Lydian M-1. George Russell
The Lydiot. George Russell
MA 279 Bougaloo. David N. Baker
Maba Tila. David N. Baker
The Mac Man. Archie Shepp
Madness. Herbie Hancock
The Magic of Ju-Ju. Archie Shepp
Maiden Voyage. Herbie Hancock
Majorca. Oliver Nelson
Make a Joyful Noise. David N. Baker
Malcolm, Malcolm--Semper Malcolm. Archie Shepp
M'am. David N. Baker
Mama Lou. Oliver Nelson
Mama Rose. Archie Shepp
Mama Too Tight. Archie Shepp
Mama Tu. David N. Baker
Manhattan-Rico. George Russell
Martin Was a Man, a Real Man. Oliver Nelson
Le Matin des Noire. Archie Shepp
Mauma. David N. Baker
May in December. George Russell
The Maze. Herbie Hancock
The Meetin'. Oliver Nelson
Mid-Evil. David N. Baker
Mimosa. Herbie Hancock
Le Miroir Noir. David N. Baker
Miss Clara. George Russell
Miss Fine. Oliver Nelson
Mon. David N. Baker
Money Blues. Archie Shepp
Monkin' Around. David N. Baker
A Morning Thought. David N. Baker
New Donna. George Russell
Night Sound. George Russell
Nina, Ever New. David N. Baker
Nita. George Russell
Nocturne. Oliver Nelson
None a Place Me Be. David N. Baker
Now and Then. George Russell
Odjenar. George Russell
Oh Jazz, Po' Jazz. George Russell
Oh! Oh! Here He Comes. Herbie Hancock
Oliloqui Valley. Herbie Hancock
Los Olvidados. Archie Shepp
On This Night (If That Great Day Would Come). Archie Shepp
111-44. Oliver Nelson
One Finger Snap. Herbie Hancock
One for a Dime. Archie Shepp

One for Bob. Oliver Nelson
One for J.S. David N. Baker
One for the Trane. Archie Shepp
121 Bank. David N. Baker
The Original Mr. Sonny Boy Williamson. Archie Shepp
Ostinato. Oliver Nelson
Ostinato (Suite for Angela). Herbie Hancock
Othello Ballet Suite. George Russell
The Outer View. George Russell
Palm Grease. Herbie Hancock
Pan-Daddy. George Russell
Passion. David N. Baker
Patterns. Oliver Nelson
Peace, My Brother. David N. Baker
Penick. David N. Baker
People Music. Herbie Hancock
Peter Plays Some Blues. Oliver Nelson
The Pickaninny (Picked Clean--No More--Or Can You Back
  Back Doodlebug). Archie Shepp
The Pleasure Is Mine. Herbie Hancock
Po' Ned. David N. Baker
Poem for Malcolm. Archie Shepp
A Portrait of Robert Thompson as a Young Man. Archie Shepp
Post No Bills. Oliver Nelson
Prelude. David N. Baker
The Prisoner. Herbie Hancock
The Professor. David N. Baker
Promise of the Sun. Herbie Hancock
Rain Dance. Herbie Hancock
Rain Forest. Archie Shepp
Ramu. David N. Baker
Refractions. Oliver Nelson
Requiem. Herbie Hancock
Requiem. Oliver Nelson
Requiem--Afterthoughts. Oliver Nelson
Rex. David N. Baker
Riot. Herbie Hancock
Roly Poly. David N. Baker
Round Johnny Rondo. George Russell
Ruben's Rondo. Oliver Nelson
Rufus (Swung His Face at Last to the Wind, Then His Neck
  Snapped). Archie Shepp
The Sad Sergeant. George Russell
Samba da Rua. Archie Shepp
Sangre Negro. David N. Baker
Scag. Archie Shepp
Screamin' the Blues. Oliver Nelson
The Screamin' Meemies. David N. Baker
Self-Help Is Needed. Oliver Nelson
Shadows. David N. Baker
Shazam. Archie Shepp
Shima 13. David N. Baker
Shufflin'. Oliver Nelson

The Silver Chalice. David N. Baker
Simplicity. David N. Baker
Six and Four. Oliver Nelson
Sketchy Blue-Bop. Talib Hakim
Skull Session. Oliver Nelson
Sleeping Giant. Herbie Hancock
Slow Drag. Archie Shepp
Sly. Herbie Hancock
Soft Summer Rain. David N. Baker
Soleil d'Altamira. David N. Baker
Son-Mar. David N. Baker
The Sorcerer. Herbie Hancock
Sorry 'bout Dat. Archie Shepp
Soul of a Summer's Day. David N. Baker
The Soul of '76. David N. Baker
Soul Six. David N. Baker
Spank-a-Lee. Herbie Hancock
Speak Like a Child. Herbie Hancock
Spepai. David N. Baker
Spider. Herbie Hancock
Splooch. David N. Baker
Spoo Pee Doo. Archie Shepp
Spooks. Archie Shepp
Steam. Archie Shepp
Step Right Up. Oliver Nelson
Steppin' in It. Herbie Hancock
Stereophrenic. David N. Baker
Stick 'em Up. Archie Shepp
Stickin'. David N. Baker
Stolen Moments. Oliver Nelson
Straight Ahead. Oliver Nelson
The Stratus Seekers. George Russell
Stratusphunk. George Russell
Succotash. Herbie Hancock
Suite from Black America. David N. Baker
Sun Touch. Herbie Hancock
Survival of the Fittest. Herbie Hancock
Swamp Rat. Herbie Hancock
Swingdom Come. George Russell
Swiss Suite. Oliver Nelson
Take Me With You. Oliver Nelson
Takin' Lydia Home. George Russell
Teenie's Blues. Oliver Nelson
Tell Me a Bedtime Story. Herbie Hancock
Terrible T. David N. Baker
That's the Way, Lord Nelson. David N. Baker
Theme. George Russell
There's a Yearnin'. Oliver Nelson
Thing. David N. Baker
Things New. George Russell
Thoughts. George Russell
Three Bags Full. Herbie Hancock
Three for a Quarter. Archie Shepp

Three for Malcolm. David N. Baker
Three Plus One. Oliver Nelson
Three Seconds. Oliver Nelson
3, 2, 1, 0. Oliver Nelson
Three Vignettes. David N. Baker
Tipsy. Oliver Nelson
Top Stuff. Oliver Nelson
Touareg. Archie Shepp
Toys. Herbie Hancock
The Traitor. Herbie Hancock
Triangle. Herbie Hancock
A Tribute to Someone. Herbie Hancock
A Tribute to Wes. David N. Baker
Tuffy. David N. Baker
Twenty-Fifth and Martindale. David N. Baker
Two Faces of the Black Frontier. David N. Baker
U-Jamaa. Archie Shepp
Uncla. David N. Baker
Unclee. David N. Baker
Vein Melter. Herbie Hancock
Verism. David N. Baker
Vibrations. David N. Baker
Volupte. George Russell
Vortex. David N. Baker
W830007K. David N. Baker
Walpurgisnacht. David N. Baker
Walt's Barbershop. David N. Baker
The Waltz. David N. Baker
Waltz from Outer Space. George Russell
War Gewesen. David N. Baker
Watermelon Man. Herbie Hancock
The Wedding. Archie Shepp
West India. Archie Shepp
West of Benchazi. George Russell
Western Song. David N. Baker
When? David N. Baker
Where Poppies Bloom. Archie Shepp
Wherever June Bugs Go. Archie Shepp
Whew!! David N. Baker
Whole Nelson. Oliver Nelson
Wiggle-Waggle. Herbie Hancock
A Wind in Summer. David N. Baker
Witch Hunt. George Russell
Yasmina. Archie Shepp
Ye Hypocrite, Ye Beelzebub. George Russell
Yearnin'. Oliver Nelson
You'll Know When You Get There. Herbie Hancock
You're What This Day Is All About. Archie Shepp

JAZZ ENSEMBLE AND ORCHESTRA

Reflections. David N. Baker

JAZZ ENSEMBLE AND TAPE

> Electronic Sonata for Souls Loved by Nature.   George Russell
> A Summer's Day in 1945.   David N. Baker

JAZZ ENSEMBLE IN COMBINATION WITH MULTIPLE ENSEMBLES
AND/OR SOLOISTS

> The Beatitudes.   For chorus (SATB), soloists, narrator, jazz
> ensemble, string orchestra, and dancers.   David N. Baker
> Black America: To the Memory of Martin Luther King, Jr.
> For jazz ensemble, narrators, chorus (SATB), soloists, and
> string orchestra.   David N. Baker
> Comes Tomorrow.   For chorus (SATB), soloists (soprano, con-
> tralto, tenor, and bass-baritone), and jazz ensemble.   Hale
> Smith
> Concerto for Bass Viol and Jazz Band.   For bass viol, jazz
> ensemble, string quartet, and solo violin.   David N. Baker
> Concerto for Flute and Jazz Band.   For flute/alto flute, jazz
> ensemble, and string quartet.   David N. Baker
> Concerto for Trombone, Jazz Band, and Chamber Orchestra.
> David N. Baker
> Concerto for Trumpet, Jazz Band, and Chamber Orchestra.
> David N. Baker
> Concerto for Tuba, Jazz Band, Percussion, Choir, Dancers,
> Slides, and Tape Recorders.   David N. Baker
> Concerto for Two Pianos, Jazz Band, Chamber Orchestra, and
> Percussion.   David N. Baker
> Levels: A Concerto for Solo Contrabass, Jazz Band, Flute
> Quartet, Horn Quartet, and String Quartet.   David N. Baker
> Listen to the Silence.   For jazz ensemble, chorus (SATB), and
> bass soloist.   George Russell
> Psalm 22.   For chorus (SATB), narrators, jazz ensemble,
> string orchestra, and dancers.   David N. Baker
> A Salute to Beethoven.   For piccolo, flute, oboe, clarinet,
> bassoon, horn, backstage flute choir, jazz ensemble, and
> pre-recorded tape.   David N. Baker
> A Song of Mankind.   For chorus (SATB), orchestra, jazz en-
> semble, rock band, vocal soloists, lights, and sound effects.
> David N. Baker

JAZZ NONET (TRUMPET, ALTO SAXOPHONE, TENOR SAXO-
PHONE, TROMBONE, BARITONE SAXOPHONE, GUITAR, PIANO,
ELECTRIC BASS, AND DRUMS)

> Adumbratio.   David N. Baker
> April B.   David N. Baker
> Black Thursday.   David N. Baker
> Calypso-Nova No. 1.   David N. Baker
> Check It Out.   David N. Baker
> Le Chat Qui Pêche.   David N. Baker
> The Dude.   David N. Baker

Honesty. David N. Baker
Kentucky Oysters. David N. Baker
Let's Get It On. David N. Baker
Lunacy. David N. Baker
MA 279 Bougaloo. David N. Baker
One for J.S. David N. Baker
125th Street. David N. Baker
Penick. David N. Baker
Prelude. David N. Baker
The Professor. David N. Baker
Roly Poly. David N. Baker
The Seven League Boots. David N. Baker
Son-Mar. David N. Baker
Terrible T. David N. Baker

JAZZ ORCHESTRA

Soundpiece for Jazz Orchestra. Oliver Nelson

JAZZ ORCHESTRA IN COMBINATION WITH MULTIPLE ENSEMBLES
AND/OR SOLOISTS

A Black Suite for Narrator, String Quartet, and Jazz Orchestra.
Oliver Nelson

JAZZ QUARTET

That's the Way, Lord Nelson. For trumpet, tenor saxophone,
bass, and percussion. David N. Baker

JAZZ QUARTET IN COMBINATION WITH MULTIPLE ENSEMBLES
AND/OR SOLOISTS

Le Chat Qui Pêche. For soprano, orchestra, and jazz quartet
(alto/tenor saxophone, piano, bass, and drums). David N.
Baker

JAZZ SEPTET (TRUMPET, ALTO SAXOPHONE, TENOR SAXO-
PHONE, TROMBONE, PIANO, BASS, AND DRUMS)

Aulil. David N. Baker
Folklike. David N. Baker
Herman's Theme. David N. Baker
Maba Tila. David N. Baker
Le Miroir Noir. David N. Baker
Satch. David N. Baker
Set. David N. Baker
Shima 13. David N. Baker

Twenty-Fifth and Martindale. David N. Baker
W830007K. David N. Baker

JAZZ SEXTET

Jazz Suite for Sextet in Memory of Bob Thompson. For trumpet, tenor saxophone, trombone, piano, bass, and drums.
David N. Baker

JAZZ TRIO AND ORCHESTRA

Two Improvisations for Orchestra and Jazz Combo. For
orchestra and jazz trio (piano, bass, and drums). David N.
Baker

MARIMBA AND WIND ORCHESTRA

Concerto for Xylophone, Marimba, and Vibraphone. For wind
orchestra and soloist (xylophone, marimba, and vibraphone).
Oliver Nelson

MEDIUM VOICE AND PIANO

The Bereaved Maid. George Walker
Fugitive Songs. Ulysses Kay
I Went to Heaven. George Walker
Lament. George Walker
A Red, Red Rose. George Walker
Response. George Walker
So We'll Go No More A-Roving. George Walker
Sweet, Let Me Go. George Walker
Three Spirituals for Voice and Piano. George Walker
The Valley Wind. Hale Smith
With Rue My Heart Is Laden. George Walker

MEZZO-SOPRANO AND CHAMBER ENSEMBLE

In the Landscape of Spring. For mezzo-soprano, flute, oboe,
clarinet, bass clarinet, horn, trumpet, viola, violoncello,
contrabass, and percussion. Noel Da Costa

NARRATOR AND CHAMBER ORCHESTRA

Reflections on the 5th Ray. Talib Hakim

NARRATOR AND ORCHESTRA

The Western Paradise. Ulysses Kay

NARRATOR(S) IN COMBINATION WITH MULTIPLE ENSEMBLES AND/OR SOLOISTS

The Beatitudes. For chorus (SATB), soloists, narrator, jazz ensemble, string orchestra, and dancers. David N. Baker

Black America: To the Memory of Martin Luther King, Jr. For jazz ensemble, narrators, chorus (SATB), soloists, and string orchestra. David N. Baker

A Black Suite for Narrator, String Quartet, and Jazz Orchestra. Oliver Nelson

Glory to God. For chorus (TTBB), narrator, flute, organ, and piano with optional brass and percussion. Undine S. Moore

The Last Judgment. For chorus (SSA), speaker, piano, and percussion. Noel Da Costa

Once There Was a Man. For narrator, chorus (SATB), and orchestra. Ulysses Kay

Personals. For narrator, mixed chorus, and brass ensemble. T. J. Anderson

Psalm 22. For chorus (SATB), narrators, jazz ensemble, string orchestra, and dancers. David N. Baker

OBOE AND PIANO

Brief Elegy. Ulysses Kay
Suite in B. Ulysses Kay

OBOE AND STRING ORCHESTRA

Brief Elegy. Ulysses Kay

OPERAS

Blood Wedding. Chamber opera. Hale Smith
The Boor. Ulysses Kay
The Capitoline Venus. Ulysses Kay
The Cocktail Sip. Noel Da Costa
Jubilee. Ulysses Kay
The Juggler of Our Lady. Ulysses Kay
Malcolm. David N. Baker
The Passion of Justice According to Judicial Documentation. Coleridge-Taylor Perkinson

ORCHESTRA

Address for Orchestra. George Walker
Chamber Symphony. T. J. Anderson
Classical Symphony. T. J. Anderson
Complex City for Orchestra. Oliver Nelson
Concepts. Talib Hakim
Concerto for Orchestra. Ulysses Kay
Concerto for Orchestra. Howard Swanson
Contours. Hale Smith
Danse Calinda Suite. Ulysses Kay
Fantasy Variations. Ulysses Kay
Harlem Children's Suite. For elementary orchestra. Ulysses
  Kay
Intervals. T. J. Anderson
Introduction and Allegro. T. J. Anderson
Kosbro. David N. Baker
Markings. Ulysses Kay
New Dances. T. J. Anderson
Of New Horizons. Ulysses Kay
Orchestral Set. Hale Smith
Portrait Suite. Ulysses Kay
Presidential Suite. Ulysses Kay
Pyknon Overture. T. J. Anderson
The Quiet One Suite. Ulysses Kay
Quietly... Vamp It and Tag It. Noel Da Costa
Re/Currences. Talib Hakim
Reverie and Rondo. Ulysses Kay
Ritual and Incantations. Hale Smith
Serenade for Orchestra. Ulysses Kay
A Short Overture. Ulysses Kay
Short Symphony. Howard Swanson
Sinfonia in E. Ulysses Kay
Southern Harmony. Ulysses Kay
Spirituals for Orchestra. George Walker
Squares: An Essay for Orchestra. T. J. Anderson
Structure for Orchestra. Olly Wilson
Suite for Orchestra. Ulysses Kay
Symphony. Ulysses Kay
Symphony for Orchestra. George Walker
Symphony in Three Movements. T. J. Anderson
Symphony No. 1. Howard Swanson
Symphony No. 2. Howard Swanson
Symphony No. 3. Howard Swanson
Theater Set. Ulysses Kay
Three Movements for Orchestra. Olly Wilson
Umbrian Scene. Ulysses Kay
Variations for Orchestra. George Walker
Visions of Ishwara. Talib Hakim
Voices. Olly Wilson

ORCHESTRA AND JAZZ ENSEMBLE

    Reflections. David N. Baker

ORCHESTRA AND JAZZ TRIO

    Two Improvisations for Orchestra and Jazz Combo. For orchestra and jazz trio (piano, bass, and drums). David N. Baker

ORCHESTRA IN COMBINATION WITH MULTIPLE ENSEMBLES AND/OR SOLOISTS

    A Ceremony of Spirituals. For soprano, soprano/tenor saxophone, orchestra, and chorus. Noel Da Costa
Le Chat Qui Pêche. For soprano, orchestra, and jazz quartet (alto/tenor saxophone, piano, bass, and drums). David N. Baker
Dunbar. For solo voice, chorus, and orchestra. Coleridge-Taylor Perkinson
Once There Was a Man. For narrator, chorus (SATB), and orchestra. Ulysses Kay
Phoebus, Arise. For soprano, bass, chorus (SATB), and orchestra. Ulysses Kay
Piece for Orchestra. For orchestra and jazz soloists (alto saxophone and bass). Oliver Nelson
Song of Jeremiah. For baritone, chorus (SATB), and orchestra. Ulysses Kay
A Song of Mankind. For chorus (SATB), orchestra, jazz ensemble, rock band, vocal soloists, lights, and sound effects. David N. Baker
Spirit Song. For soprano, double chorus, and orchestra. Olly Wilson

ORGAN

    Chielo. Noel Da Costa
Electronic Organ Sonata No. 1. George Russell
Maryton (Hymn Tune Variations). Noel Da Costa
Organ Suite No. 1. Ulysses Kay
Organ Variations on "Nettleton." Undine S. Moore
Spiritual Set for Organ. Noel Da Costa
Triptich for Organ: Prelude, Processional, Postlude. Noel Da Costa
Two Meditations. Ulysses Kay

PERCUSSION ENSEMBLE

    Sonatina for Percussion. Coleridge-Taylor Perkinson

Suite (Sweet) Louis: A Tribute to Louis Armstrong.   David N.
Baker

PERCUSSION ENSEMBLE AND PIANO

Placements.   Talib Hakim

PIANO

Anticipations, Introspections, and Reflections.   Hale Smith
The Cuckoo.   Howard Swanson
Evocation.   Hale Smith
Extempore Blue.   Noel Da Costa
Faces of Jazz.   Hale Smith
First Nocturne.   Ulysses Kay
Five Short Pieces for Piano.   David N. Baker
For One Called Billy.   Hale Smith
Four Inventions.   Ulysses Kay
In Time.   Oliver Nelson
Lem and Aide.   Oliver Nelson
Majorca.   Oliver Nelson
The Meetin'.   Oliver Nelson
Nocturne.   Oliver Nelson
One for Brucie.   Oliver Nelson
A Piano Piece.   Talib Hakim
Piano Sonata No. 1.   Coleridge-Taylor Perkinson
Piano Sonata No. 2.   Coleridge-Taylor Perkinson
Prelude and Caprice.   George Walker
Romantic Young Clown.   Undine S. Moore
Scherzo.   Coleridge-Taylor Perkinson
Scherzo for Piano.   Undine S. Moore
Second Nocturne.   Ulysses Kay
Shufflin'.   Oliver Nelson
Six and Four.   Oliver Nelson
Sonata for Piano.   David N. Baker
Sonata No. 1.   Howard Swanson
Sonata No. 1 for Piano.   George Walker
Sonata No. 2.   Howard Swanson
Sonata No. 2 for Piano.   George Walker
Sonata No. 3.   Howard Swanson
Sonata No. 3 for Piano.   George Walker
Sound-Gone.   Talib Hakim
Spatials.   George Walker
Spektra.   George Walker
Stolen Moments.   Oliver Nelson
Ten Short Essays.   Ulysses Kay
There's a Yearnin'.   Oliver Nelson
Three Seconds.   Oliver Nelson
Toccata.   Coleridge-Taylor Perkinson
Two Nocturnes.   Howard Swanson
Two Pieces for Piano.   Noel Da Costa

Valse Caprice. Undine S. Moore
Visions. Ulysses Kay
Watermelon. T. J. Anderson

PIANO AND BRASS QUINTET

Sonata for Brass Quintet and Piano. David N. Baker

PIANO AND ELECTRONIC SOUND

Piano Piece. Olly Wilson

PIANO AND ORCHESTRA

Akwan. For piano/electric piano and orchestra. Olly Wilson
Concert Music for Piano and Orchestra. Hale Smith
Piano Concerto. George Walker

PIANO AND ORGAN

Reflections for Piano and Organ. Undine S. Moore

PIANO AND STRING ORCHESTRA

Ancient Saga. Ulysses Kay

PIANO AND STRING QUINTET

Sonata for Piano and String Quintet. David N. Baker

PIANO AND WOODWIND QUINTET

Facets. Ulysses Kay
Variations for Six Players. Hale Smith

PIANO (FOUR HANDS)

Five Portraitures of Two People. T. J. Anderson
Two Short Pieces. Ulysses Kay

PIANO (FOUR HANDS) AND CLARINET

Five Fancys for Clarinet and Piano (Four Hands). George
Walker

PIANO (TWO PIANOS)

Romance for Two Pianos. Undine S. Moore
Sonata for Two Pianos. David N. Baker
Sonata for Two Pianos. George Walker

PIANO (TWO PIANOS) IN COMBINATION WITH MULTIPLE ENSEMBLES AND/OR SOLOISTS

Concerto for Two Pianos, Jazz Band, Chamber Orchestra, and Percussion. David N. Baker

SAXOPHONE

Saxophone Sonata. Oliver Nelson

SAXOPHONE AND JAZZ ENSEMBLE

Modality, Tonality, and Freedom. David N. Baker

SAXOPHONE AND STRINGS

Fantasy Piece for Soprano Saxophone and Strings. Howard Swanson

SAXOPHONE AND STUDIO ORCHESTRA

Concert Piece for Saxophone and Studio Orchestra. Oliver Nelson

SAXOPHONE IN COMBINATION WITH MULTIPLE ENSEMBLES AND/OR SOLOISTS

A Ceremony of Spirituals. For soprano, soprano/tenor saxophone, orchestra, and chorus. Noel Da Costa
Le Chat Qui Pêche. For soprano, orchestra, and jazz quartet (alto/tenor saxophone, piano, bass, and drums). David N. Baker
Piece for Orchestra. For orchestra and jazz soloists (alto saxophone and bass). Oliver Nelson

STRING OCTET

Vista No. II. Howard Swanson

STRING ORCHESTRA

Antiphonys for String Orchestra. George Walker
Baker's Shuffle. David N. Baker
Black-Eyed Peas and Cornbread. David N. Baker
Blue Strings. David N. Baker
Blues. David N. Baker
By Yearning and by Beautiful. Hale Smith
Calypso-Nova No. 1. David N. Baker
Calypso-Nova No. 2. David N. Baker
Evening Song. David N. Baker
First Day of Spring. David N. Baker
The Jamaican Strut. David N. Baker
Little Princess Waltz. David N. Baker
Lyric for Strings. George Walker
Mod Waltz. David N. Baker
Music for Strings. Howard Swanson
Sinfonietta No. 1 for Strings. Coleridge-Taylor Perkinson
Six Dances for String Orchestra. Ulysses Kay
Slow Groove. David N. Baker
Somber Time. David N. Baker
Suite for Strings. Ulysses Kay
The Sunshine Bougaloo. David N. Baker
Triplet Blues. David N. Baker

STRING QUARTET

Currents. Talib Hakim
Pastorale. David N. Baker
String Quartet. Olly Wilson
String Quartet No. 1. T. J. Anderson
String Quartet No. 1. David N. Baker
String Quartet No. 1. Coleridge-Taylor Perkinson
String Quartet No. 1. George Walker
String Quartet No. 2. Ulysses Kay
String Quartet No. 2. George Walker
String Quartet No. 3. Ulysses Kay

STRING QUARTET AND TUBA

Sonata for Tuba and String Quartet. David N. Baker

STRING QUINTET

Connections: A Fantasy for String Quintet. T. J. Anderson

STRING QUINTET AND PIANO

Sonata for String Quintet and Piano. David N. Baker

STRING TRIO

Fugue in F. Undine S. Moore

TELEVISION

Admiral Byrd. Ulysses Kay
The Barbara McNair Show. Coleridge-Taylor Perkinson
The Black Frontier. David N. Baker
Brushstrokes. David N. Baker
Ceremonies in Dark Old Men. Coleridge-Taylor Perkinson
Chase. Oliver Nelson
Essay on Death. Ulysses Kay
F.D.R.: From Third Term to Pearl Harbor. Ulysses Kay
The Fall of China. Ulysses Kay
Girl Talk. Oliver Nelson
Ironside. Oliver Nelson
It Takes a Thief. Oliver Nelson
J. T. Coleridge-Taylor Perkinson
The Land. Ulysses Kay
Longstreet. Oliver Nelson
The Lou Rawls Special. Coleridge-Taylor Perkinson
Matt Lincoln. Oliver Nelson
Meet the Artist. David N. Baker
The Name of the Game. Oliver Nelson
Nightside. Coleridge-Taylor Perkinson
Nuances of Hale Smith. TV and radio background music. Hale
  Smith
Room 222. Coleridge-Taylor Perkinson
The Shape of Things. Ulysses Kay
Six Million-Dollar Man. Oliver Nelson
Submarine! Ulysses Kay
The Three Musketeers. Ulysses Kay
The Trial of Captain Henry Flipper. David N. Baker

TENOR AND CHAMBER ENSEMBLE

Attitudes. For tenor, violin, violoncello, and piano. Coleridge-
  Taylor Perkinson
Beyond Silence. For tenor, clarinet, trombone, viola, violon-
  cello, and piano. T. J. Anderson

TENOR AND ELECTRONIC SOUND

Sometimes. Olly Wilson

TENOR AND PERCUSSION

And Death Shall Have No Dominion. Olly Wilson

Wry Fragments. Olly Wilson

TENOR AND PIANO

The Black Experience. David N. Baker

TENOR IN COMBINATION WITH MULTIPLE ENSEMBLES AND/OR SOLOISTS

Comes Tomorrow. For chorus (SATB), soloists (soprano, contralto, tenor, and bass-baritone), and jazz ensemble. Hale Smith
Prepare Me One Body. For soprano or tenor, chorus (SATB), and organ. Noel Da Costa

THEATER

Babu's Juju. Noel Da Costa
Black Mass. Olly Wilson
Blue Soap. Archie Shepp
Fun House. Noel Da Costa
God Is a (Guess What)? Coleridge-Taylor Perkinson
The Great MacDaddy. Coleridge-Taylor Perkinson
I Heard My Woman Call. David N. Baker
The Knee-High Man. Noel Da Costa
Lady Day: A Musical Tragedy. Archie Shepp
Lysistrata. Hale Smith
Malcochon. Coleridge-Taylor Perkinson
Man Better Man. Coleridge-Taylor Perkinson
The Passion of Justice According to Judicial Documentation. Coleridge-Taylor Perkinson
Promise and Performance. David N. Baker
The Shell Fairy. T. J. Anderson
The Singing Tortoise. Noel Da Costa
Slave Ship. Archie Shepp
Song of the Lusitanian Bogey. Coleridge-Taylor Perkinson
To Damascus. Coleridge-Taylor Perkinson
A Trio for the Living. Noel Da Costa
Yerma. Hale Smith

TREBLE INSTRUMENT AND PIANO

A Short Movement for Treble Instrument and Piano. Coleridge-Taylor Perkinson

TROMBONE (SOLO)

Street Calls. Noel Da Costa

TROMBONE AND ORCHESTRA

Concerto for Trombone and Orchestra. George Walker

TROMBONE AND PIANO

Concerto for Trombone and Orchestra. George Walker
Four Preludes for Trombone and Piano. Noel Da Costa

TROMBONE IN COMBINATION WITH MULTIPLE ENSEMBLES AND / OR SOLOISTS

Concerto for Trombone, Jazz Band, and Chamber Orchestra.
David N. Baker
Trio Concertante. For clarinet, trumpet, trombone, and band.
T. J. Anderson

TROMBONE TRIO

Romanza and March. David N. Baker

TRUMPET (SOLO)

Gabriel's Tune for the Last Judgment. Noel Da Costa
Passages. Noel Da Costa

TRUMPET AND BAND

Exchanges. Hale Smith

TRUMPET AND CHAMBER ORCHESTRA

Blue/s Forms II. Coleridge-Taylor Perkinson

TRUMPET AND CONTRABASS

Spaces. Noel Da Costa

TRUMPET AND ORCHESTRA

Blue/s Forms II. Coleridge-Taylor Perkinson

TRUMPET AND PIANO

Exchanges. Hale Smith

TRUMPET IN COMBINATION WITH MULTIPLE ENSEMBLES AND/OR SOLOISTS

Concerto for Trumpet, Jazz Band, and Chamber Orchestra.
David N. Baker
Trio Concertante. For clarinet, trumpet, trombone, and band.
T. J. Anderson

TRUMPET CHOIR AND PERCUSSION

Fanfare Rhythms. Noel Da Costa

TRUMPET QUARTET

Three Fanfares for Four Trumpets. Ulysses Kay

TRUMPET QUARTET AND PERCUSSION

Fanfare Rhythms. Noel Da Costa

TRUMPET TRIO

Heralds II. Ulysses Kay

TUBA AND STRING QUARTET

Sonata for Tuba and String Quartet. David N. Baker

TUBA IN COMBINATION WITH MULTIPLE ENSEMBLES AND/OR SOLOISTS

Concerto for Tuba, Jazz Band, Percussion, Choir, Dancers, Slides, and Tape Recorders. David N. Baker

VIBRAPHONE AND WIND ORCHESTRA

Concerto for Xylophone, Marimba, and Vibraphone. For wind orchestra and soloist (xylophone, marimba, and vibraphone). Oliver Nelson

VIOLA AND CHAMBER ENSEMBLE

Epigrams. For viola, flute, clarinet, bass clarinet, bassoon, vibraphone, and piano. Noel Da Costa

VIOLA AND ORCHESTRA

Concerto for Viola and Orchestra. Coleridge-Taylor Perkinson

VIOLA AND PIANO

Sonata for Viola and Piano. David N. Baker

VIOLIN (SOLO)

Blue Forms. Coleridge-Taylor Perkinson
Improvisation #1 for Unaccompanied Violin. David N. Baker
Improvisation #2 for Unaccompanied Violin. David N. Baker
Suite for Unaccompanied Violin. David N. Baker

VIOLIN AND ELECTRIC PIANO

Jes' Grew #1: Chant Variations for Violin. Noel Da Costa

VIOLIN AND JAZZ ENSEMBLE

Concerto for Violin and Jazz Band. David N. Baker

VIOLIN AND PIANO

Deliver My Soul. David N. Baker
Duo for Violin and Piano. Hale Smith
Epicedal Variations. Hale Smith
Ethnic Variations on a Theme of Paganini. David N. Baker
Five Portraits. Ulysses Kay
Magnolia Blue. Noel Da Costa
Nocturne. Howard Swanson
Partita in A. Ulysses Kay
Sonata for Violin and Piano. David N. Baker
Sonata for Violin and Piano. George Walker
Variations and Fugue on "The Ash Grove." Coleridge-Taylor
 Perkinson
Violin Sonata. Olly Wilson

VIOLIN AND VIOLONCELLO

Sonata for Violin and Cello. David N. Baker

VIOLIN (TWO VIOLINS)

"Still Music" No. 1. Noel Da Costa

VIOLONCELLO (SOLO)

Lamentations: A Black/Folk Song Suite for Unaccompanied Cello. Coleridge-Taylor Perkinson
Two Pieces for Unaccompanied Cello. Noel Da Costa

VIOLONCELLO AND CHAMBER ORCHESTRA

Concerto for Cello and Chamber Orchestra. David N. Baker

VIOLONCELLO AND ELECTRONIC INSTRUMENTS

Electric Stere-Opticon. David N. Baker

VIOLONCELLO AND ORCHESTRA

Commentary. Coleridge-Taylor Perkinson
Dialogus for Cello and Orchestra. George Walker

VIOLONCELLO AND PIANO

The Dude. David N. Baker
Five Verses With Vamps. Noel Da Costa
Piece for Violoncello and Piano. David N. Baker
Sonata for Cello and Piano. George Walker
Sonata for Violoncello and Piano. David N. Baker
Sonata for Violoncello and Piano. Hale Smith
Sonata for Violoncello and Piano. Howard Swanson
Suite for Violoncello and Piano. Howard Swanson

VIOLONCELLO AND VIOLIN

Sonata for Violin and Cello. David N. Baker

VOCAL QUINTET (SSATB) IN COMBINATION WITH MULTIPLE ENSEMBLES AND/OR SOLOISTS

Counterpoint. For double chorus, solo quintet (SSATB), and organ or two pianos. Noel Da Costa

VOCAL SOLOIST(S) (UNSPECIFIED) IN COMBINATION WITH MULTIPLE ENSEMBLES AND/OR SOLOISTS

The Beatitudes. For chorus (SATB), soloists, narrator, jazz ensemble, string orchestra, and dancers. David N. Baker

Black America: To the Memory of Martin Luther King, Jr.
For jazz ensemble, narrators, chorus (SATB), soloists, and
string orchestra. David N. Baker
Dunbar. For solo voice, chorus, and orchestra. Coleridge-
Taylor Perkinson
A Song of Mankind. For chorus (SATB), orchestra, jazz
ensemble, rock band, vocal soloists, lights, and sound effects.
David N. Baker

VOCAL TRIO (SSA) IN COMBINATION WITH MULTIPLE ENSEMBLES AND/OR SOLOISTS

The Confession Stone. For soprano, trio (SSA), and instrumental ensemble. Noel Da Costa

VOICE AND GUITAR

A Walk With a Child. David N. Baker

VOICE AND PIANO

Cahoots. Howard Swanson
A Death Song. Howard Swanson
Four Preludes. Howard Swanson
Ghosts in Love. Howard Swanson
I Will Lie Down in Autumn. Howard Swanson
In Time of Silver Rain. Howard Swanson
Joy. Howard Swanson
The Junk Man. Howard Swanson
The Negro Speaks of Rivers. Howard Swanson
Night Song. Howard Swanson
Nine Elizabethan Love Lyrics. Coleridge-Taylor Perkinson
Pierrot. Howard Swanson
Saw a Grave Upon a Hill. Howard Swanson
Snowdunes. Howard Swanson
Songs for Patricia. Howard Swanson
Songs to Spring. Coleridge-Taylor Perkinson
Still Life. Howard Swanson
Thirteen Love Songs in Jazz Settings. Coleridge-Taylor Perkin-
son
Three Songs of Robert Hillyer. Coleridge-Taylor Perkinson
To Be or Not To Be. Howard Swanson
Two Songs for Children. Ulysses Kay
The Valley. Howard Swanson

VOICE AND STRING ORCHESTRA

Songs for Patricia. Howard Swanson

WIND ENSEMBLE

Dance Music I. Olly Wilson
Dance Music II. Olly Wilson
Dance Suite. Olly Wilson

WIND ORCHESTRA

Fugue and Bossa. Oliver Nelson
Septet for Winds. Oliver Nelson
Trigon. Ulysses Kay

WOODWIND QUINTET

Fantasy for Woodwind Quintet. David N. Baker
Five Etudes and a Fancy. T. J. Anderson
Peace-Mobile. Talib Hakim
Soundpiece for Woodwind Quintet. Noel Da Costa
Theme and Variations. David N. Baker
Woodwind Quintet. Oliver Nelson
Woodwind Quintet from The Black Frontier. David N. Baker

WOODWIND QUINTET AND PIANO

Facets. Ulysses Kay
Variations for Six Players. Hale Smith

XYLOPHONE AND WIND ORCHESTRA

Concerto for Xylophone, Marimba, and Vibraphone. For wind
  orchestra and soloist (xylophone, marimba, and vibraphone).
  Oliver Nelson

-A-

Griffin, Paul 88
Grinnell College 108
Grip, The (Baker) 44
Groove, A (Nelson) 226
Grout, Donald 362
Guadeloupe-Calypso (Baker;
    jazz ensemble) see Walt's
    Barbershop
Guadeloupe-Calypso (Baker;
    orchestra, soprano, and jazz
    quartet) see Le Chat Qui
    Pêche
Guernica (Picasso) 179
Guevera, Ché 38
Guggenheim Fellowship 139,
    278, 337, 357, 379
Guggenheim Foundation 294,
    295, 301
Guigi, E. 372
Guillén, Nicholas 334
Guitar Blues (Nelson) 226
Guitarra (Kay) 153
Gunzenhauser, Stephen 105
Gurdjieff, Georges Ivanovitch
    17, 282
Gustafsson, Rune 283
Guy, Buddy 136

-H-

Had I a Heart (Kay) see
    Triple Set
Haerle, Dan 38, 62
Hagedorn, Hermann 153
Hagen, Earle 121
Hail! Warrior! (Moore) 195
Hakim, Talib Rasul 29, 105,
    106; bibliography 107;
    biography 93; interview 93-
    103; list of compositions
    104-107; photograph 94
Hal McKusick Octet 285
Hal McKusick Quartet 283,
    285
Hal McKusick Sextet 287
Hambone (Shepp) 290, 305
Hamer, Martin J. 90
Hamilton, Chico 305, 317
Hammerskjold, Dag 156
Hampton, Slide 17
Hampton Institute 70, 72, 183,
    185

Hampton Institute Choir 85,
    87, 88
Hancock, Eugene 91
Hancock, Herbie 127, 128,
    129, 130, 131, 132, 133,
    134, 135, 136; bibliography
    137-138; biography 108;
    interview 109-126; list of
    compositions 127-137;
    photograph 109
Handel, George Frederick
    23, 255, 265, 346
Handy, D. Antoinette 70,
    75, 90, 91, 159, 193, 334
Hang Up Your Hang Ups (Han-
    cock) 130-131
Hans Kindler Foundation 358,
    373
Hansberry, Robert 400
Hansen Company (publisher)
    117
Hanson, Howard 139, 161,
    372
Hanson, Pauline 2, 8
Happenings (Nelson) 226
Happy Birthday Mrs. Craig
    (Perkinson) 271
Happy Song (Redding) 246,
    272
Harlem Air Shaft (Ellington)
    293
Harlem Children's Suite (Kay)
    154
Harlem Chorale 91
Harlem Pipes (Baker; jazz
    ensemble) 44
Harlem Pipes (Baker; melody
    and chord symbols) 45
Harlem Pipes (Baker; orches-
    tra and jazz trio) see
    Two Improvisations for Or-
    chestra and Jazz Trio
Harlem School of the Arts
    139, 154
Harpham, Dale (Capt.) 152
Harris, Carl 185, 194, 195,
    196, 197, 198, 199
Harris, Hilda 313, 334
Harris, William G. (Beaver)
    295, 303, 306
Harrison, Guy Fraser 2, 10,
    11, 12
Harrison, Paul Carter 271

John Hay Whitney Fellowship
357
Johnny (Nelson) 228
Johns, Altona Trent 174,
184, 197, 330
Johnson, David 241
Johnson, Georgia Douglas
188, 196
Johnson, Hall 241, 332
Johnson, Harry A. 184
Johnson, Hattie 330
Johnson, J. J. 17, 29, 234,
287
Johnson, James Weldon 88,
244
Johnson, Louis E. 136
Johnson, Samuel 165
Johnson, Thor 1, 2, 8, 157
Johnston, Leroy 374
Jolly Rompers, The 292
Jones, A. M. 17
Jones, Elvin 48
Jones, Hank 226, 229
Jones, Harold 348, 353
Jones, Howell 183
Jones, LeRoi 308, 398; see
also Baraka, Imamu
Jones, Philly Joe 48
Jones, Quincy 29, 108, 203,
226
Jones, Robert 11
Jones, T. Marshall 183
Jonson, Ben 272
Joplin, Scott 1, 4, 77, 208,
382
Jordan, Clifford 126
Josea, Joe 128
Joy (Swanson) 351
Joyce, James 215
Joyner, John 34
Joys and Fears (Kay) see
The Quiet One Suite
Jubilee (Kay) 155
Juggler of Our Lady, The (Kay)
155
Juilliard School of Music 86,
139, 160, 166, 173, 174,
374, 376; Orchestra 145;
Repertory Project 166
Jump (DaCosta) see Sound-
piece for Woodwind Quintet
Jump Ahead, A (Hancock) 131-
32

June Bug Graduates Tonight
(Shepp) 296
Jungleaire (Nelson) see Afro-
American Sketches
Junior League of Atlanta 164
Junk Man, The (Swanson) 351
Just Before September (Baker)
47
Just Blue/s (Perkinson) see
Blue Forms

-K-

K. C. C. (Baker) 47
Kaleidoscope (Baker; jazz en-
semble, chorus, et al) see
Black America
Kaleidoscope (Baker; violin,
violoncello, and piano) see
Contrasts
Kansas State University Chamber
Orchestra 158
Kansas State University Con-
cert Chorale 158
Kapp, Paul 360
Kapralik, Dave 295
Karamu House 334
Karamu Theater (Cleveland,
Ohio) 313, 329, 330, 332,
334, 335
Karr, Gary 39
Katahn, Enid 10
Kay, Ulysses Simpson 29,
148, 158, 159, 160, 163;
bibliography 168-171; biog-
raphy 139-141; interview
141-147; list of composi-
tions 147-168; photograph
140
Keager, Dr. 200
Keble, John 152
Keeling, Kenneth 184
Keeney, Susan D. 376
Kelley, Robert 379
Kemble, Fanny 186
Kennedy, John Fitzgerald 12,
151
Kennedy, Joseph Jr. 329
Kennedy, Matthew 197
Kennedy Center see John F.
Kennedy Center for the
Performing Arts

152, 166
Longfellow, Samuel 151
Longstreet (Nelson) 205, 229
Longstreet, Stephen 297
Lopez, Trini 136
Lorca, Garcia 329, 335
Lord, Make Us More Holy
  (Moore) 197
Lord, We Give Thanks to Thee
  (Moore) 173, 189, 193, 197
Lord Have Mercy (Moore)
  see Choral Prayers in
  Folk Style
Lord's Prayer, The 92
Los Angeles Philharmonic 207
Lou Rawls Special, The (Per-
  kinson) 272
Louis Armstrong In Memoriam
  (Baker) 49
Lou's Good Blues (Nelson)
  see Lou's Good Dues Blues
Lou's Good Dues Blues (Nelson)
  229
Louisville Philharmonic Society
  161
Louisville Symphony Orchestra
  21, 38, 62, 139, 141, 161,
  166, 313, 330, 350
Love, Let the Wind Cry How
  I Adore Thee (Moore) 197
Love Divine (Kay) see Four
  Hymn-Anthems
Lovelace, A. 330
Lowell, James Russell 256, 271
Loyola University Bicentennial
  Choral Festival 200
Luening, Otto 72, 139
Lullaby (Kay) see Bleeker
  Street Suite
Lullaby (Perkinson) see
  Three Songs of Robert Hill-
  yer
Lully, Lullay (Kay) see A
  Wreath for Waits
Lumo (Baker) 49
Lunacy (Baker) 49
Lund University (Sweden) 277
Lurie, B. 375
Lutheran Church of America
  225
Lutheran Mass (Baker) 49
Lydia and Her Friends (Russell)
  285

Lydian April (Baker) 49
Lydian Chromatic Concept of
  Tonal Organization, The
  (Russell) 277, 281, 282,
  286, 287
Lydian Lullaby (Russell) 285
Lydian M-1 (Russell) 285
Lydiot, The (Russell) 278,
  285
Lynne, Gloria 136
Lyric (Kay) see Short Suite
Lyric for M.K. (Walker) see
  Lyric for Strings
Lyric for String Orchestra
  (Walker) see Lyric for
  Strings
Lyric for Strings (Walker)
  358, 361, 370, 373
Lyric for True Love (Moore)
  197-198
Lysistrata (Smith) 332
Lytle, Gwendolyn 400

-M-

MA 279 Bougaloo (Baker) 49
M'am (Baker) 50
Maba Tila (Baker) 49
Mac Man, The (Shepp) 305
Macallister, Scott 8
McArthur, Herbert 185
MacCawthall, James 135
McDaniel, Lorna 84, 85, 91
McDonald, Boyd 372, 373
MacDonald, Brian 304
McDonald, Sylvia 372, 373
MacDowell Colony Fellowship
  1, 357, 358
McElroy, Beverly 34
McIver, Ray 271
McKay, Claude 34, 43, 244
McKim Fund of the Library of
  Congress 152
McKusick, Hal 283, 285;
  see also Hal McKusick
  Octet; Hal McKusick Quar-
  tet; Hal McKusick Sextet
McLain, Lyn 105
MacMasters, The (Perkinson)
  272
McNair, Barbara 239, 270
McPartland, Marian 44

Moravian Church   153
More, Helen F.   167
More Blues and the Abstract
   Truth (Nelson)   230
More Soul (Nelson)   230
Morehouse College   1; Glee
   Club   12
Morgan, Lee   291, 292
Morgan State College Choir
   374
Morman, Wilson   105
Morning Comes to Conscious-
   ness, The (Swanson) see
   Four Preludes
Morning Thought, A (Baker)
   51
Morrison, Toni   175
Morton, Jelly Roll   77
Moses, Don   55
Moses, Gilbert   308
Mosque Auditorium (Richmond,
   Va.)   179, 200
Mother Goose Suite (Ravel)
   205
Mother to Son (Hughes)   182
Mother to Son (Moore)   189,
   198
Motley, John L.   179, 197,
   199, 271
Motown   206
Mozart, Wolfgang Amadeus
   94, 108, 192, 211, 240,
   247, 250, 265, 266, 267,
   315, 327
Mozart Society (Fisk Univer-
   sity)   174
Mozarteum   239
Mulligan, Gerry   282
Murasaki shikibu (writer)   315
Murdock, Douglas   43
Murphy, Howard   174, 181
Murray, John (Rev.)   151
Murray, Pauli   34
Museum of Modern Art   149,
   157
Music (Kay) see Triumvirate
Music, Dr.   135
Music for Brass (Sacred and
   Profane) (Walker)   373
Music for Harp and Orchestra
   (Smith)   332
Music for Strings (Swanson)
   351

Music for Strings, Percussion,
   and Celeste (Bartok)   267
Music for Three (Walker)
   373-374
Music in Our Time series
   97, 104, 106
Music Minus One series   239
Musical Offering (Bach)   263
Musikk Konservatoriet of Oslo
   (Norway) Chorus of   284
Mussorgsky, Modest   214
Mutations (Hakim)   104
Muzak   29
Mwandishi (album)   108, 123,
   126
My Angel (Shepp)   306
My God, My God (Baker) see
   Psalm 22
My Indianapolis (Baker) see
   Reflections
My People (DaCosta)   88-89
My Scarf Is Yellow (Smith)
   see Faces of Jazz
Mystic, The (Kay) see
   Fugitive Songs
Mystic Shadow (Kay) see
   Stephen Crane Set

-N-

Nagel, Robert   331
Nagrin, Daniel   307
Naked Camera, The (Hancock)
   see Blow-Up
Name of the Game, The (Nel-
   son)   205, 231
NANM Young Pianists Award
   183
Narrative of Frederick Doug-
   lass, The   175
Nashville Little Symphony   8
Nashville Symphony Orchestra
   11
NASM   183
Nassau Community College
   93
Nassau County Office of Cul-
   tural Development   332
National Academy of Record-
   ing Arts and Sciences award
   203
National Association of Negro

Musicians 239, 245, 270
National Black Theater 239
National Catholic Music Educators Association 37
National Endowment for the Arts 1, 4, 10, 15, 22, 93, 278, 295, 301, 330, 357, 374
National Endowment for the Humanities 184, 185, 295
National Gallery of Art 374, 375
National Gallery Orchestra 148
National Institute of Arts and Letters 379
National Lutheran Campus Ministry 49
National Music Award 278
National Orchestra Association 150
National Symphony 139, 146, 167
Native Son (Wright) 292
Negro American: A Documentary History, The (Quarles) 175
Negro Ensemble Company 239, 258, 270, 271, 272, 274
Negro History Week 207, 248, 252; see also Black History Week
Negro Speaks of Rivers, The (Hughes) 101
Negro Speaks of Rivers, The (Swanson) 337, 351
Nelson, Jim 61
Nelson, Lucille 205
Nelson, Oliver Edward 221, 222, 223, 224, 225, 226, 227, 228, 229, 230, 231, 232, 233, 234, 235; bibliography 236-237; biography 203-205; interview 205-221; list of compositions 221-236; photograph 204
Net, The (Russell) see Othello
Netherlands Radio Hilversum 239
New Americans, The (Baker) see The Black Frontier
New Concerto (Hancock) 132
New Dances (Anderson) 11

New Donna (Russell) 278, 285
New England Chamber Festival 372
New England Conservatory of Music 277
New England Festival Chamber Orchestra 372
New Jersey Oratorio Society Male Chorus (Atlantic City) 154
New Jersey Symphony Orchestra 154
New Music Ensemble (University of North Carolina) 104
New Orleans Philharmonic 167
New Philharmonia Orchestra 377
New School for Social Research 93, 290, 357
New Song, A (Kay) 157
New Symphony Orchestra of London 162
New World Symphony (Dvorak) 176
New World Trio 337, 348, 353
New York All-City High School Chorus 256, 271
New York Chamber Players 93
New York City College of Music 93
New York, City of Magic (Kay) 157
New York City Opera Company 183
New York City Symphony 161
New York Critics Circle Award 337, 345, 352
New York Cultural Center 91
New York Ensemble of the Philharmonic Scholarship Winners 351
New York Historical Society 273
New York Little Symphony 160
New York, N.Y. (album) 278
New York Philharmonic 179, 183, 221, 240, 242, 341, 349, 352